Architectural Materialisms

New Materialisms
Series editors: Iris van der Tuin and Rosi Braidotti

New Materialisms asks how materiality permits representation, actualises ethical subjectivities and innovates the political. The series will provide a discursive hub and an institutional home to this vibrant emerging field and open it up to a wider readership.

Titles available
What if Culture was Nature all Along?
Edited by Vicki Kirby
Critical and Clinical Cartographies: Architecture, Robotics, Medicine, Philosophy
Edited by Andrej Radman and Heidi Sohn
Architectural Materialisms: Nonhuman Creativity
Edited by Maria Voyatzaki

Forthcoming titles
Queer Defamiliarisation and New Materialism: Writing Feminist Matter(s)
By Helen Palmer
Place-making: Art, Practice, Pedagogy
By Tara Page

Architectural Materialisms

Nonhuman Creativity

Edited by Maria Voyatzaki

EDINBURGH
University Press

Edinburgh University Press is one of the leading university presses in the UK. We publish academic books and journals in our selected subject areas across the humanities and social sciences, combining cutting-edge scholarship with high editorial and production values to produce academic works of lasting importance. For more information visit our website: edinburghuniversitypress.com

First published in hardback by Edinburgh University Press 2018

Edinburgh University Press Ltd
The Tun – Holyrood Road
12(2f) Jackson's Entry
Edinburgh EH8 8PJ

Typeset in 11/13 Adobe Sabon by
IDSUK (DataConnection) Ltd

A CIP record for this book is available from the British Library

ISBN 978 1 4744 2057 0 (hardback)
ISBN 978 1 4744 7454 2 (paperback)
ISBN 978 1 4744 2058 7 (webready PDF)
ISBN 978 1 4744 2059 4 (epub)

Contents

Part III

Acknowledgements

I sincerely hope that this collection will prove to be a landmark and that its landscapes of thought can reboot the debate on architectural materialisms in times when nonhuman creativity can reorient the discipline and its cognitive mapping. It has been a pleasure working with the important thinkers who have made invaluable contributions to this book. I am deeply indebted for their encouragement and patience in making it happen. Furthermore, I am thankful for the friendships that this collaboration has strengthened or yielded. Thanks to Lars, Manuel, Kas, Mark, Marcos, Jussi, Luciana, Pia, Julieanna, Jen, Fernando, Levi and Vera. The support of the series editors and the publishing team and advisors has been tremendous and, for this, I wish to express my thanks, especially to Rosi Braidotti, Iris van der Tuin, Carol Macdonald, Esrev Ersoy, Kirsty Woods, Andrew Kirk and James Dale. I would also like to thank my local team, Lina Di Ciocco-Kiryttopoulou and Dimitris Apostolidis, for contributing to the proofreading, suggestions and formatting of the book. Last but not least, I owe gratitude to Constantin Spiridonidis and Emmanouil Zaroukas who have been my life's spiritual companions, in a reciprocal, affective and sympathetic teacher–student–teacher perpetual intellectual feedback loop, often cross-fertilising the missing parts of each other's past, present, and times yet to come.

Architectural Materialisms: Nonhuman Creativity

Maria Voyatzaki

This volume gathers more than a dozen voices from a diverse group of architects, designers, performing artists, film-makers, media theorists, philosophers, mathematicians, programmers, researchers and educators. While originating from Austria, Colombia, Finland, Mexico, New Zealand, Germany, Great Britain, Greece, Italy, Portugal, Switzerland, the Netherlands and the USA, they are all intellectual migrants – scholarly nomads – scattered around three continents, speaking eight different native languages. Diversity in this book is also a function of a convergence of well-established authors who pioneered the discussion on architectural materialisms and the emerging figures of the younger generation who are currently researching the subject. With the exception of the recently published *Critical and Clinical Cartographies: Architecture, Robotics, Medicine and Philosophy*,[1] and after a long period of silence and apathy in the literature on architecture and creativity, due to a preoccupation with hands-on experimentation and tooling as well as with isolating domain-biased research, it is now high time to reflect on this matter critically and globally as such contemplation is not just timely, but essential.

The Vitality of Matter

The belief that humans were driven out of their natural habitat or environment immediately after their creation is deep-rooted and has been cultivated since the ancient myths of human origin depicted in Greek cosmogony and other religious discourses. This belief was based on the notion that humans differed in relation to all other beings, thus justifying the human imperative stance towards all other beings around them. Their further development and evolution were not only dictated by their distinctive natural characteristics, but were primarily defined by the consequences of sin committed either by divine forces, as in the Epimethean and Promethean narratives, or by the humans themselves, as in the case of the Judeo-Christian-Islamic religious testaments. To cope with the consequences of this sin, according to Bernard Stiegler,[2] humans had to act upon matter, developing techniques which, although regarded as the horizon of all possibilities to come, were, nevertheless, repressed as an object of thought throughout the anthropocentric tradition.

Life and matter were conceived as separate entities, parsing the sensible world as vibrant life – beings – and dull matter – things. In this division, matter was thought as passive, raw, brute or inert, moving or being transformed only on encountering an external force or agent, following a linear logic of cause and effect. It was uniform, discrete, measurable, quantifiable and suitable for exploration by Newtonian physics and Euclidean geometry. The constructed, the artificial, the artefact and all cultural manifestations had to follow the predominant features of the alive 'into an idea of teleologically ordained, rational progress' as Rosi Braidotti points out.[3] This was the reason why the movement and behaviour of matter were considered as predictable, replicable, hence controllable, as obeying the laws of motion introduced by physics. Matter was approached as the permanent subject of the action of beings, the life of which was defined by philosophers such as Henri Bergson 'as a tendency to act on inert matter'.[4]

Abstract preconceptions about the human-alive developed in the context of this widespread and well-established assumption of the binary opposition between self-regulating life and matter, between the given and the constructed, the natural and the artificial, the soul and the body. They were based upon what was commonly taken as distinctive and unique about humans, the 'gifts of the gods', such as language, consciousness, intelligence, rationality, intentionality, subjectivity, but also their derivatives, such as values, meaning, morality and beauty. All these appeared more significant as they were directly used to affirm human dominance over nature and the material world.

The polarisation between life and matter led humans to believe that the only source of vitality was the soul or the spirit, thus stifling their opportunity to discover and explore other living powers, those of material formations, not only edibles, commodities, artefacts or machines, but also physical phenomena and materials. This limitation inhibited the appreciation of their strong impact on human wills, behaviours, designs, decisions, mental and bodily structures and identities, their lives, social structures, institutions and politics, and, ultimately, delayed their project to develop sustainable, symbiotic relations with them.

Engaged with their anthropocentric understandings, humans considered themselves as the only actants or agents in the project of inhabiting earth, and elided or excluded from their projects all nonhuman actants and the material powers surrounding or even inhabiting the human body; powers with the capacity to assist, damage, improve, ennoble, humiliate and impede the body or inhibit its will to eventually drive its own designs and decisions. By conceiving matter as passive-opaque and of inert plenitude, humans underestimated or, even more, neglected matter's own modes of self-transformation, self-organisation and directedness that render it recognisable as indeterminate, constantly forming, transforming and reforming in contingent and, eventually, unpredictable ways. Humans would not come to terms with the notion that 'matter becomes' rather than 'matter is'.

Scientific research clearly disclosed the self-transformational and self-organisational capacities of matter that questioned the substantialist Cartesian conception of matter as passive, massive and opaque, of a measurable plenitude that occupied space, as well as that of matter as a mass in motion, producing and consuming energy under the attraction and repulsion acting upon it, as introduced by the Newtonian origin of classical mechanical physics. In the twentieth century, Einstein's theory of relativity revealed that there was no distinction between mass and energy because the two supposedly opposing poles were interchangeable and convertible into one another; therefore, they were in a sense equivalent. Evidence of the existence of atoms, the energy of the charged nucleus and spinning electrons, the exploration of the relation between the mass of nucleus and electrons and the atoms' volume, the study of protons and neutrons, particles, quarks and gluons divulged a new ontology of matter based upon complexity, instability, fragility, unpredictability and interactivity. Matter has since been conceived as vibrant, recalcitrant, animated and living, exhibiting self-organising properties which, in the complexity of their environments, could cause unpredictable effects and produce novel configurations. Matter is no longer about being, but about becoming. As Jane Bennett states, vital materiality runs through and across bodies, human and nonhuman.[5] Matter is embodied in the alive, creating assemblages, that is, ad hoc groupings of divergent elements, of materials of all sorts, articulated through flows of information and interpenetrating them.

This understanding further questions the postmodern orthodoxy that materiality is always secondary to the logical or semiotic structures it encodes, and that the body is primarily a linguistic and discursive construction, a 'play of discourse systems', as Michel Foucault declared in his *Archaeology of Knowledge*. This disembodiment of meaning is inscribed in the pervasive Western philosophical tradition, which is founded upon a conception of a mind/body split, reflected in the drastic separation between the humanities and the sciences. According to this division, terms clearly framed by the concept of mind, such as ideas, concepts, reason and judgement, were always at the epicentre of the disciplinary preoccupations of the humanities, marginalising or even totally excluding considerations of the body. Similarly, notions about the mechanics of the body, its biological, physical, chemical and structural characteristics, marginalised or even totally excluded considerations of the mind. Katherine Hayles points out how information, conceived as an inseparable part of meaning in a postmodernist context, was progressively conceptualised as an autonomous entity, separate from all kinds of material forms, organic or abiotic, cultural or technological, introducing new forms of synergy between the sciences and the humanities, the body and the mind, the material and the immaterial.[6]

The detachment of information from its body, the meaning, initiated by Alan Turing and elaborated by cyberneticists and information theorists, immaterialised information by stripping it of its body, the message. The binary form of one/zero enabled it to cross all forms of materiality: from hardware and software that merge telecommunications with computer technologies, to flexible accumulation as the mode of production of late capitalism and the geopolitical understandings of global growth and sustainable development; from the physical habits related to or supported by digital devices, such as eye focus, sound tuning, hand and finger motions, body posture and neural connections, to the patterns of living that emerge from and depend on access to big data and the instantaneous global transmission of messages; from the investigation and reinterpretation of the deep structures of the natural world based upon the coexistence of matter with information and the revelation of other forms of sensing, cognition and thinking beyond those of the human, to the enactment of self-organisational principles to create artificial, evolutionary mechanisms or cyborgs.

The ontological dualism or the dialectical reconciliation of the polarities of anthropocentrism is replaced by a 'monological account of emergent, generative material being'[7] framed by a monistic world view that stresses the self-organising, auto-poietic force of living matter, the distant origin of which contemporary thinkers find in Spinoza's philosophy.[8] Spinoza spoke of the tendency of matter to conglomerate or form heterogeneous groupings.

The idea of the vitality of matter is not at all recent. Contemporary scholars such as Bennett and Braidotti detect different versions of the questioning of the ontological dualism of life–matter in the philosophical concepts and claims of thinkers such as Epicurus, Spinoza, Nietzsche, Thoreau, Darwin, Bergson, Driesch, Adorno, Foucault, Serres and Deleuze. Diana Coole and Samantha Frost define, as a common ground for the emerging new materialism, the antipathy towards oppositional ways of thinking under which a new ontology is defined. New materialism dissipates onto-theological dualisms such as life/matter, human/animal, will/determination, organic/inorganic as well as the dialectical reconciliations between these polarities by accepting the 'monological account' mentioned by Coole and Frost.[9]

Even though no variety of new materialism has yet created a dominant orthodoxy, its primary theoretical and philosophical hypotheses are defended by scientific research, either on the matter embodied in the alive conducted by all branches of biology, or on the characteristics of the vitality of matter carried out by all branches of the natural sciences. This research direction invites scientific investigation to develop through trans- and cross-disciplinary encapsulations, hence, through transverse approaches, innovative modes of analysis and ways of conceptualising and investigating material reality. It also invites a better appreciation of the urgent contemporary challenges related to the environmental, demographic, geopolitical and economic changes and challenges that the contemporary world is encountering. Through the support of theoretical discourses about complexity and chaos, materialism advocates the instability, fragility and interactivity of our multifaceted environments, but also, and above all, the inextricability of all sociocultural formations and the materiality of these environments.

The rejection of anthropocentric dualisms and the foundation of a new materialist ontology was extensively reinforced and strengthened by the technological acceleration towards the end of the twentieth century, and the omnipresence of planetary computation in more recent times. Underpinned by the development of cybernetics and information theories, the most basic level of this universe is composed of units that have a simple on–off function and, from there on, everything else is built. As the state of each unit depends upon the state of its adjacent units, the properties of each emerge as the result of their interactions with their environment. However, there is another order of emergence developed by second-order cybernetics that grants special privilege to those properties that give the system the capacity to process information. This condition creates the ground for the development of artificial intelligence, and perhaps artificial life, self-organising systems and other forms of cognition, as this second emergence evokes the capacity of the system to evolve.[10]

The fast development of computation systems accelerates research towards quick and flexible responses of these systems to random stimuli from the environment. Instead of implementing predefined patterns, computing machines can now use this randomness as the creative ground from which new patterns can emerge. In this context and taking into account the tremendous development of the capacities of computation in robotics, artificial intelligence and artificial life, it is no longer clear whether the sophisticated judgements, new forms of creative abstraction and organisational patterns put forward by contemporary machines are not, in some instances, more unpredictable, hence, more innovative in comparison to those made by humans.[11] This machinic vitality is not about determinism, inbuilt purpose or finality but rather about becoming and transforming.[12] Humans and intelligent machines can no longer be considered as two different bodies, with one enacting and the other representing, but as both comprising an inseparable and embodied assemblage, entwined with the production of identities and new forms of subjectivity, rendering their division meaningless.

We are encountering the emergence of a new context for which the establishment of an overall orthodoxy is impossible, and the quest for its appreciation is addressed by multiple domains, subject areas and practices. What kind of architecture can be expected to surface, following the dynamics and questionings of the contemplation, in this neomaterialist context? Isn't architecture a material practice in the way it labours on, exploits and interacts with nature?[13] Isn't architecture's power present in any of its attempts to represent material reality? We define architectural materialisms as the contemplation that places contemporary speculations on the vitality of matter and materiality at the epicentre of their questioning, ethos and praxis. In this neomaterialist context, the new dialectic relationship between technology and society can bring about technosocial transformations and, with them, meaningful changes in architecture. These speculations are open to re-conceptualisations of architecture infected by concepts and ideas about vital materiality coming from other disciplines. By transversally crossing the disciplinary boundaries of philosophy, biology, material sciences, humanities and media theory, new and profound insights into contemporary thinking and creating architecture emerge. The main target is to creatively merge the dynamism of materiality and the capacities of nonhuman machines towards prototyping spatiotemporal designs and constructs that suggest and promote alternative conceptions of the human, of ethics, aesthetics and politics.

The Nonhuman Embodiment

Architecture in anthropocentrism was always motivated by an abstract, intellectual or fictionally composed conception of the human and its body. This was the driving force for its assumptions, theorisations and design practices. It was the origin, the inspirational framework of design creativity and the reference for the legitimisation of design proposals. The history of architecture in anthropocentrism is nothing more than the history of the impact that the non-linear changes in the conception of the human body made on humanity's spatial manifestations. Architecture in this context was nourished, framed and conducted by a different ontological understanding of what the human was, or what it should become. The building and the city were thought, conceived and designed to mirror the human body.

The human-centred world view initiated one of the most – if not *the* most – important revolutions in the history of building and in the process of space production; namely, the separation of manual labour from intellectual. With few exceptions, the way we widely appreciate, practise and teach architecture nowadays is the outcome of a division of labour in the domain of constructing habitable spaces that took place in the Renaissance, which developed and defined the thinking and praxis of architecture in anthropocentrism over the subsequent five centuries. That was the result of a shift that occurred in the fifteenth and, predominantly, the sixteenth century; a world view once founded on the immaterial relation to divine supremacy and focused on glorifying its godly origin then shifted to a human-centred world view focused on human experience, observation, discovery and action. This shift, initially fostered by a new social structure dominated by the commerce-based bourgeoisie, relativised the religious order and promoted the culture of the human spirit as its proper power, beyond its given affluence. In this new context, knowledge was no longer of an exclusively religious order, but was laicised to become the sign of the aristocratic and monarchic power.

According to this view the parts of the whole are progressively dissociated, obtaining an identity based not only on their usage, that is, their role in the whole, but also on their exchange value as defined and controlled by the emerging and progressively established powerful trading nobility. The universe is now conceived as a collection or assemblage of 'things', which as commodities obtain a quantitative relationship and become individualised or rather conceivable beyond their proper use and the everyday practices linked to them.[14] What is important is not so much the knowledge of the proper quality of each object, but the appreciation of the relations between objects through which the place and the milieu of human experience are defined.

The repercussions of the shift from the ideal of the submissive believer to the cultured thinker and from the religious power to the human thinking power on spatial manifestations at the time were vast. Building and space turned into a new mechanism for manifesting the emerging power of human culture. This explains why the medieval 'master builder', the architect[15] who had responsibility for the technical and formal aspects of a building, abandoned the building site as a workplace and chose the workshop to operate remotely from the building site. The architect was the noble figure who conceived and elaborated the form and the organisation of spaces before their materialisation.

Architecture was to become the work of a thinker, distinct from the work of a maker, sustained by a premise profoundly grounded as true in the human-centred model of reality, prevalent over the last five centuries. This premise suggested that the distinction between 'subject' and 'object' was not a result of historically situated human perception but, on the contrary, a question of ontology. This bifurcated ontology was 'natural' since humans and nonhumans were inherently distinct before and after their mutual encounter, as the former was the active subject and the latter the passive object; the former was the alive and the latter was the inanimate, material thing. It was the virtual and the abstract that dictated the materialisation of the actual and the concrete. Following Alberti, it was quite possible to project whole forms in the mind without resorting to the material. The idea governed the making; and the 'creating mind' became the meaningful and symbolic epicentre of the human-centred understanding of the world, reconsidering Aristotle's 'understanding mind'[16] of antiquity and replacing the 'believing mind' of medieval theocentric times.

The creating mind ideal introduced a new ethics with respect to the creative act according to which authorship was exclusively attributed to the idea. In differentiating the creator-designer from the creator-maker, the former was granted the exclusive authorship and maternity of the creative outcome conceived as a process of genesis.[17] Architecture in the anthropocentric era was conceived as an autographic art according to Goodman's taxonomy.[18] The constructor, as allographer-author who dealt with the materiality of the building, was reduced to a simple craftsman of, in most cases, inferior social status. The constructor would not impose but would primarily tease a form[19] out of an active material, collaborate with it, fight with it, reconcile and attune with it, in a perpetually dynamic relationship. This subject–object relationship, extensively developed in all theocentric pre-capitalistic societies, was no longer part of the creative process after the Renaissance. Ideas were definitely superseding materiality in the process of the creation of spatial forms that were conceived as objects created through an object-based process.

In anthropocentrism, the emphasis on materiality was dictated by an abstract image of the human body. The body was the continual reference point for architecture, deployed not only to legitimise architectural creations, but implicitly to assure through these creations the proper construction of the human as such. Driven by the powers of mind, architecture wished to conceive and construct, through the building, its preconceptions about the human body, which were neither, necessarily, an ideal standard nor an objective statistical average or middle ground. Its overall project was to disclose a systematised standard of recognisability and sameness by which 'everything else could be assessed, regulated and allotted to a designated social location.'[20] The figure thus conceived constituted a highly regulatory, normative and ethical convention with a strong instrumental impact on all social and cultural practices in all its political extensions. The social project of architecture was to design a human by constructing and materialising spaces to host its particular life. Architecture undertook to create a body with material substance to embody its thinking. Architecture, in general, and design, in particular, became important for this very reason.

Even though building materials, in this context, were inseparable from and integrated with architectural forms, they were always conceived as the assistants of the ideas dictating the form and as the allies of structure,[21] thus maintaining an inferior position as compared to design ideas. Style, explicitly or implicitly, was a central issue in architecture, and the so-called *parti* of the Beaux Arts tradition or the concept of the modern and, particularly, postmodern vocabulary had a deterministic role in the design process. Building materiality has stood on the fence of the overall design process and has engaged the architect less in designing the form of a building, because the aesthetic codes were relatively limited, since they were defined by the dominant tendencies and, at times, manifestos while the available palette of materials was relatively restricted.

The Renaissance resurrected from antiquity the binary opposition between soul and body, but progressively replaced the soul with the mind in its de-theocentralisation project. The body was the glorification of natural beauty, as it incorporated in its form and dimensions the aesthetics of symmetry and proportions dictated by Euclidean geometry. In becoming the main subject of observation, the human body was analysed through geometry for the purpose of scrutiny in an effort to establish the laws of natural beauty that would drive architectural creation. The so-called '*homo Vitruviano*' of Da Vinci was not only a proposed proportional system defining natural beauty but also a description of the formal, mechanical and functional structure of the human form. The mind was invited to build this natural beauty by designing the body before its construction. The building, in turn, as material artefact and as body, would embody this mental outcome as the glorification of human thinking.

The Enlightenment initiated a conception of the human, focusing on its reason and rationality, and defined its body as the supreme functional organism, operating under reasonable causes that aimed at consistent effects. This appreciation prevailed throughout modernism. The concern for the functionality of architectural creations and their materiality was inspired and guided by this conception of the human. Modernism progressively introduced a new role for materiality in architectural design. For the values of rationality, functionality and clarity to be expressed, modernism distinguished form and its materiality by distinguishing form from structure, the load-bearing and the non-load-bearing. Notions inspired by the human body, such as the skeleton, constituted a particular way of understanding building materiality as frame and brickwork, which led construction towards those materials that could, through their properties, better respond to the expressive demands of the concept.

This typological classification of materials as bearing and non-bearing formed a distinct compositional/design ethos and style expressing a new relationship between form and materiality. The use of a limited palette of building materials, such as metal, glass and concrete, all moulded with known properties and structural behaviour, would indicate the positioning of standardised and mass-produced, repetitive components. The building material, as a prefabricated product coming directly from the industry, was forced to take certain positions in the construction system, influencing the formal aspects of architectural creation. Materiality appeared to be progressively involved in the design process as an agent of the engineering of architectural creation.

The so-called linguistic turn of the 1960s and 1970s introduced a totally new conception of the human body. The postmodern, social constructivist approach was aligned with the same binary opposition (self-regulating life versus matter, given versus constructed, natural versus artificial, mind versus body) and focused on the social analysis and critique of social mechanisms, considered as 'man-made', historically contingent structures. For the postmodern orthodoxy the body is, primarily if not entirely, a linguistic construction. Discursive analysis and the humanities disembodied discourses and meaning, and saw the human body as a play of discourse systems, a discursive construction, in the same way that cybernetics stripped information of its body. The materiality of the body was an important vehicle of meaning, but was always secondary to the logical and semiotic structures it would encode. As Manuel DeLanda would argue, the linguisticality of these structures was exclusively addressed to the human experience. Hayles detects a new kind of subjectivity emerging from this new condition 'constructed by the crossing of the materiality of informatics with the immateriality of information'.[22]

With meaning as its focal point, postmodern architecture, in the 1970s and 1980s, attributed to materials a new role in the design process, that of the agent of meaning. Materiality became one of the possible signifiers with which the architect 'syntaxed' the meaning of a building. The act of creation was no longer defined as composition, but as syntax. Form and materiality were both meaningful and designed in order to contribute to the expressivity of architectural creation. This perspective opened up the production of building materials to a new spectrum of choices and possibilities that would broaden the expressive vocabulary of architects, contributing to the generation of increasingly genuine architectural forms.

This new condition offered the elevation of the building a new identity. It was a distinctive building element and, on a number of occasions, detached from the rest of the building, gave the façade a new substance and appreciation. The body became skin, a meaningful material cladding the modernist body. As building skin or as artefact cladding, the building façade gradually overcame its exclusive expressive or communicative aspect in order to acquire other roles, such as the protection of the body of the building from the environment, climate, noise and other internal or external elements. The façade was an intelligent skin, to use the term more consistently, which interacted dynamically with stimuli – that is what it is designed to do.[23] The intelligent skin was often designed and made from materials which could also be intelligent. Building materiality appeared to be involved in the design process as the agent of intelligence of architectural creation.

Materiality as engineering, materiality as sense and materiality as intelligence are just three of materiality's most prevalent manifestations in the design process. Materiality is approached, viewed and conceived, each time, through the lens of the dominant conception of the human and its body from which the values, principles and priorities dominating architectural creation at a certain period emerge. If the main project of architecture in anthropocentrism has always been to create and impose a human figure, will that still be valid in the so-called posthuman times? How is the conception of the human developing in the contemporary, new-materialist context, and how is that affecting architectural logos and praxis? And if these are all valid questions, then what is the new human that will emerge from contemporary architectural theorisations and experimentations?

The fundamental assumption motivating this current shift in the conception of the human of nature and of artefacts is that between nature and culture, between the human and the artefact, there is a continuum. The binary opposition between the given and the constructed, already discussed, is being profoundly reconsidered and replaced by a non-dualistic understanding of the natural and the artificial, of the human and architecture. The boundaries between the natural and the artificial cannot be clearly defined and have become increasingly blurred as a result of recent technological and scientific advances.

According to this new world view, broadly illuminated by these advances, humans lose their presumed uniqueness in possessing cognitive abilities that direct their intentions, and the freedom to make decisions and actions in exercising their exclusive right to master nature through their artefacts. Consequently, they are being displaced from their position as the dominant agent and controller of natural elements and artificial things, to be relocated within the natural and artificial environments, where unintended and unanticipated effects are bound to play a significant and predominant role.

As we shift from energy to linguistics and information-based conceptions of the human, as well as from human-centred to geocentric perspectives, as Braidotti would state, an investigation of the crucial agents that form and transform the earth indicates that these are no longer humans. Those who have always considered themselves as the most developed are no longer conceived as autonomous and capable of acting alone. Donna Haraway reaffirms this through her statement that 'the greatest planetary terraformers and reformers are bacteria and all other relative organisms'.[24] They are always present in all kinds and forms of life, affecting and controlling the development, the transformations and the adaptation mechanisms of the alive. This explains how all species, including humans, are conceived as dynamic assemblages of organic life and of abiotic actors that permanently interact with their multiple and complex environments. These environments exist at different scales, which, following Isabelle Stengers,[25] are at micro (matter, atoms and molecules), meso (materials and embodiment) or macro scales (macrophysics) and interact through flows of information interpenetrating them, from the DNA code to the global reach of the World-Wide Web.

All these changes in the conception of the human affect architecture profoundly. The design of the building is emancipated from its references to the human body in order to experiment on a new conception of the building as a living artefact. The new conception of matter has affected the dominant conception of architectural materiality as a passive, mute, stable and unchangeable substance imposed and manipulated exclusively by the designer. Based upon the new understandings of the vitality of matter, the materiality of the building becomes the focal point of architectural contemplation understood as a non-linear dynamic system, in other words, a system with emergent capacities and tendencies resulting from the dynamic behaviour of the components responsible for its performance or, rather, for its performativity. These capacities and tendencies are now considered as fundamental agents of architectural creation that, in their dynamic interaction with their environments, bear changes that can reorganise material into new, contingent structures and forms that can have significant effects on the generation of architectural form. It is a conception of an agile materiality.

Based upon this new appreciation of the vitality of matter, the materiality of the building has become the focal point for the majority of contemporary design experiments. These experiments are directed by a new understanding of design, defined as a (morpho)genetic process that is able to offer the artefact different capacities of self-organisation and self-adaptation to multiple and ever-changing environments. They are directed towards speculation about new forms of enaction or embodied action, that is, forms of active engagement of the building/organism with its environments. By rethinking itself as a dynamic, insightful living system, architecture has to reconfigure itself as a living organism, engineered to be a new, artificial species that never existed before and to orchestrate new relationships with its multiple environments. The main design issue is no longer to create an artefact to imitate or represent outstanding human traits, but to embody in the materiality of the building new forms of perception, cognition and intelligence for the purpose of self-organisation and for generating the artificial life of a building.

These experiments have been shaped through the powerful support of the ubiquitous presence of computability and information technologies. Recent developments of digital technologies in contemporary design and fabrication revive and revisit the morphogenetic power of matter. Digital technologies and contemporary scripting have fostered the investigation of complexity through the appropriation of an increased resolution of matter captured by big data. Materiality has been reconsidered extensively with the appearance of computational models that allow material to be encoded and hardware that allows even for the real time and simultaneous manipulation and malleability of matter. The shift that this perception has generated radically is that, in computational terms, the creation of any form is understood as yet another natural and systemic process which, through the computation power of search and retrieve, can be modelled and tested. Any artefact and, consequently, any architectural creation is now conceived as a material entity generated as part of a broader, natural, social and cultural ecosystem.

Nonhuman Creativity

Architecture, as a unique 'instrument' to transform the human milieu, has always been about the new. Its profound project is to create the 'other', the unexpected, the alternative, the better, the innovative. Its fundamental *raison d'être* is to do old things in new ways and to offer unprecedented alternatives. To accomplish this project, ideas that are transient, borderless and evasive about the 'other' have to be fused with the solidity of material means towards fixing and stabilising this transience and evasiveness, rendering them the cognitive currency of human communities.

Novelty in architecture is the outcome of an innovative enfolding of intelligence and matter – be it of a human, animal, vegetable or mineral nature – based on a new way of abstracting the perceived reality. The capacity to invent specific abstractions that tend to challenge the boundaries of the established is what we call creativity. A radically innovative, formal elaboration is the one which introduces a new abstraction. Fusions of the elements of existing abstractions are potentially innovative but not radical. As all attempts at innovation are mediated through tools, techniques and media, their role in innovation is imperative.

The distinction between designer and master-builder, established in anthropocentrism, has produced as a direct consequence the emergence of tools and techniques (drawing, modelling, scripting, testing) capable of assisting the work of architects in a reliable, virtual space, with different media simulating and visualising the real one. All these tools and techniques have been designed as extensions of human cognitive capacities and, as such, impose on the outcome of their use the logics of their construction and, consequently, generally control architectural thinking. The architect is made to imagine or invent only those forms and spatial arrangements that can be properly considered by the tools and techniques deployed. This condition also defines the limitations of creativity and innovation. The project of creativity is to bring about an innovative abstraction of our cognition and sensing. This project involves the creation of new axioms. This regression from the abstract to the axiomatic and vice versa is always regulated and constrained by the performativity of the representation tools, techniques and media deployed. This may explain how novelty in architecture is accompanied by the introduction of new tools, techniques and media that can allow for this novelty to come forth. Hacking these tools, techniques and media can radicalise novelty.

For architecture to create there needs to be abstraction as well as tools, techniques and media that can simplify or 're-read' the complexity of reality. Abstraction, tools and techniques are all juggled according to the values of a dominant world view. In anthropocentrism, this abstraction aimed at defining a certain way of organising a rational appreciation of reality. This specific appreciation was accomplished through geometry, initially Euclidean and later projective geometry, which introduced a conception of spaces and objects structured by configurations of points, lines, planes and volumes. Design thinking and creative practice developed in line with these elements. The use of geometry in the construction and implementation of representation tools and techniques rationalised human appreciation and offered the possibility of presentations in two dimensions of the real position of the represented objects, that is, their real metric relationships. This way a new conception of the universe was put forth, emerging from the human-centred world view, engendering nature as a universe of things, conceived as a rational and objective appreciation based on a subjective visual experience. Geometrical drawing was not only the means through which architectural ideas were elaborated, but also an order revealing the hegemony of the architect in materialising these forms by commanding materials to be arranged (composed) in a preconceived manner. The distinction between designer and master-builder, thinker and maker,[26] royal and nomadic scientist, noble scientist and metallurgist,[27] discursive and affective, sapient and sentient,[28] top down and bottom up, epistemology and ontology are progressively and definitely established through the tools and techniques used in the deep structures of architectural creation.

By replacing the Euclidean visual cone of the Albertian perspective with the geometric beam of the multilateral, parallel rays of Durand and modernism, a total abstraction of human experience was established. This was a significant and meaningful shift that introduced an abstract definition of the human milieu that no longer made reference to what the immobile Renaissance eye could see as an individual experience of the real, but as a rational, abstract, mental construction of the Kantian human; a move from a subject observing the infinite to a subject located in the infinite. This depersonalisation of the drawing through geometrical/mathematical abstraction and projection of a conceived form on the drawing board sustained the absolute rationalisation of the visualisation of both space and object. The focal point of this abstracted visualisation was not to present what would be seen, but mainly to reveal how things would be arranged. It was not only about understanding but also about demonstrating this arrangement. This explains why the design process after the Enlightenment would no longer depart from the external view of the façade, focusing on what the eye could see, as was the case of the Albertian perspective, but from the plan, which divulged the internal – functional – order of the designed space and demonstrated its functional rationality, not directly perceived by the human senses.

It has been almost half a century since information technology produced tools to assist architectural design, establishing different forms and contents in its relationship with architectural creation. Attempts to incorporate machines in the design process have been inspired by the posthuman context; however, they are anchored to their anthropocentric premises. Even though contemporary experiments place materiality at the epicentre of architectural logos and praxis, they are rather remote from the construction of a conceptual armoury, capable of re(in)forming our conceptions regarding reasoning, ethics, aesthetics and politics, enriched by new forms of cognition and abstractions formulated by intelligent machines. Furthermore, although architectural research is focused on reconnecting sensing and making and, therefore, thinking on a material base, it has not yet broken away from the strict limits of the human sensorial domain.

The impact of anthropocentrism on architecture and the different myths, abstractions, axioms or protocols that architecture has been affiliated with have shaped its history as a discipline in a perpetual effort to construct social narratives of various world views in time. Architecture has always been engaged, inspired and directed by its own mythologies, which organise and concretise arguments for its own social and cultural project. It is now challenged to get away from the commitment to represent its pre-existing mythologies and to move towards the construction of new ones yet to come; this is an expression emerging from new speculations on the ontology of the material beyond the human as a cognitive and sensing entity. Architecture is looking towards updating its axiomatics in a materiality through which it should be considered as an ethico-aesthetic praxis. It is looking for the creative abilities of the new conceptions of matter. How can materiality's mental and abstract pole affect its course, which will be further folded and become abstract thinking and reason, without losing its close affinity to trouble and complexity?[29] Should we not be delaying decisions on linearity or the so-called affective turn, even the question of what is that we are discussing: the materiality of construction or the construction of materiality?[30]

The new project of architecture is to allow the sensing of the world differently through machine-mediated experimentation in order to generate new temporary and circumstantial axioms and updated abstractions that operate as speculative spatio-temporal organisations. Contemporary architectural experiments taking place in different research and educational environments and practices follow two different directions. There are experiments either with materiality or within materiality. In the first case, experiments focus on new materials, new fabrication methods and new techniques, thus predicating the emergence of new design methods and processes. In this way they tend to reduce architecture to a technical process, strongly related to engineering and implicitly allied and aligned with the positivist myth that technological development can save the world and can resolve problems and contemporary questions related to the built environment. In the second case, experiments within materiality start from the critique of the top-down logic of the previous case and are oriented towards the creation of possibilities for emergent spatio-temporal material constructs. This approach, a panacea, is very close to being trapped in a misleading optimism that everything that emerges from the bottom up is efficient and for this reason appropriate.

For any experimentation on the materiality of architecture to be valid and relevant to the new project of architecture, it might have to combine top-down and bottom-up trajectories, that is to say 'an abductive inference that synthetically manipulates parameters'.[31] This experimentation is about materials, but also about speculation. It is about the ways in which qualities can be embedded in this experimentation, but also about the ways in which new qualities of crafting can be discovered by working with machines. Furthermore, it is about the exploitation of the granularity (dustism) that large data sets can provide. Inhuman affects revise reasoning and reposition culture as a speculative force that moves away from the banality of presentism.[32]

Architecture might have to cross-infect human and nonhuman for a symbiotic creativity that would yield new materials whose potential to self-organise would create flows of heterogeneous spatio-temporalities and variations. This heterogeneity, a pursued abstraction related to the 'other', could be achieved by fading in and out of material trajectories. New materials, or what Robin Mackay (following Lyotard) would call *les immatériaux*, 'have nothing to do with the dematerialisation or the disappearance of materials into the spiritual or the virtual',[33] but with materials whose properties we can get to know even if they do not exist. Mackay continues to offer speculations on anonymous materials, employing throughput high computation to embed desired properties at the quantum level. However, to embed certain characteristics and qualities of matter to computation we need a passage through the abstract. With this statement he forces an update and advocates a bridge between the affective (empirical) and the rational (abstract).

Materiality could be thought of at a micro-scale, such as dust that can 'powder' and granulate geometries, producing random otherness thereafter. Algorithms are like managing and manipulating matter in its dust existence. Dust geometries are cognitive constructs; they are abstractions. The big data idea and its relationship with materiality allow us to consider thousands of particles at the same moment, in a way that ordinary, limited and small data sets could not achieve. Particles not only change under observation (particle waves) but also in the way they observe and interact with other entities. In a sense 'intra-action' is prior to interaction.[34] Think of intra-action as the analogue, the event, the matter prior to the digital, the objects and their relations, the material. By moving down scales we start to observe an unprecedented reality of matter that redistributes and reconstructs materiality, a new aesthetic vocabulary as Jussi Parikka[35] suggests and, hence, a new architecture altogether. An architecture released from the tyranny of the grand geometers. Ontological indeterminacy is coupling with our epistemological uncertainty, and this forces us to invent new orientations in construction and fabrication.

Computation and fabrication were long associated with the aesthetics of the continuum. Philosophical virtual continuity was represented in artefacts, as actual curvilinear constructions of a continuously deposited paste. As a consequence, actual entities lost their discreteness and buildings became landscapes. Conversely, a discrete approach to the actual never betrays its virtual continuity. Discrete fabrication, in this sense, can yield individual or separate unit production in either low volumes with very high complexity, or in high volumes of low complexity that require extremely flexible manufacturing systems that can improve quality and time-to-market speed while cutting costs and limiting waste. Fabrication is discrete either in its printed voxels or in its aggregates of modular elements. Agent-based, cellular and 3D-printed voxels are cases of a discrete conception of design that suggests sympathy as a mode of continuity.

Robotics could acquire added value in the exploration of unprecedented fabrication techniques and unimaginable scales of construction. A world can be constructed and approached at a scale radically different from the human scale. A domain for the construction of new conceptual resources is now wide open. It would be a fatal error to use and apply the same concepts interscalarly. Reza Negarestani is right about the inadequacy of both top-down and bottom-up models, precisely because they descend or ascend scales with the same conceptual armature.[36] By pulverising, we aim to revise our concepts, in other words to re-cut the world and to allow for the constitution of new events, new materials, new construction methods, new scales. Machines provide us with a new sensibility.[37] As Benjamin Bratton states, 'new technologies do not allow for new forms but new technologies allow for new models about what is to be made'.[38]

New speculative, but not dogmatic, axioms and mythologies are expressed with the machinic parrhesia; the world, and therefore architecture, becomes a challenging project. Digitising the analogue, once again, but this time with aspirations towards a new earth, the returning Gaia, by experimenting with its dust we can construct new perspectives on matter. It is experimentation with the 'other', the 'xenon' that aims at proposing a new way of forming an innovative view of earth by redefining its geopolitics and territorial disputes, from polluted waters that travel through nations to micro particles in the air. Architecture is working on 'xenomateriality' to define new polities, new spatio-temporal assemblages with specific demands.

What if architecture, always considered as driven exclusively by human cognition and perception, could amplify its everlasting explorations for novelty by escaping from its human-centred entanglements and opening itself up to creative symbioses and dependencies with other, nonhuman forms of cognition and sensing?

What if architecture, for centuries conceived as a sophisticated, artefact-making act and shaped by human uniqueness, could be conceived as a dynamic interface, an agent in the process of shaping the human by contributing together with all other artefacts surrounding its existence to the modification, development and formation of its abilities, attitudes, thinking and affect?

What if architecture were no longer about hosting, accommodating, managing, spatialising, expressing, manifesting and signifying human needs, but about designing the human itself? What if humans came to terms with the fact that they are artefacts of the nonhuman, the dynamic outcome of the nonhuman designer?

What if architecture, always dedicated to protecting humans from precarious nature, could outline its mission to resourcefully integrate human activities on the planet into the dynamics of the alive?

What if architecture, having already accepted the extended embodiment of digital means in different phases of its creative process, ceased to consider them simply as tools and machines, and identified them as organs of thinking creatively and innovatively, orchestrating human and nonhuman cognition, perception and action?

What if architecture, always seeking transcendent and eternal aesthetics, could reinvent what the ancient Greeks called beautiful, *ωραίον* (*hóraion*), and encompass in architectural logos and praxis the dynamics of time and of becoming, dictated by its reciprocal engagement with all interfaces surrounding it?

What if architecture, always thought and practised through geometrically based representations, could be liberated from their rigorous constraints and boundaries and opened up in its formal explorations to material computation at all scales and away from standardisation, sameness and repetition?

What materiality can we attribute to such an architecture that would enable us to think, ask new questions, change our abilities, challenge our certitudes, form or transform our fears, anxieties and dreams, abandon our given truths and allow for unknown worlds and perspectives to come? What materiality can become the means for a project without an end, an objective or a clear target, but geared to affect and reconstruct the subject that created it? The reconstructed nonhuman, as a creator of the human, introduces new materialism as a new condition, the posthuman condition, which is characterised by a distinct symbiosis of human and nonhuman, developed under the philosophical predicament that both share a common ground that consists of matter and cognition. This capacity of the materiality to generate forms and possibilities driven by its own inherent and natural self-assembling capacities and cognition renders the question of nonhuman creativity absolutely pertinent and imperative.

This book supports such scrutiny by offering a spectrum of ideas concerning this relationship and by mapping the contemporary contemplation of its forms and characteristics as they are currently documented. Through its contributions, the book examines how contemporary speculations on matter shift materiality to the epicentre of architectural contemplation and affect its ethos and praxis. As we encounter the emergence of a new paradigm for which the establishment of an overall orthodoxy is still impossible, this book, following the contemporary quest for a better understanding of this model of reality, allows architecture, philosophy, material sciences, humanities and media theory to cross their disciplinary boundaries and to offer a profound insight into contemporary thinking and the creation of architecture in this new framework defined as posthuman.

The depth of the research contained in the book is, therefore, conceived horizontally. Matter and materiality are debated, nowadays, among transdisciplinary groups of social scientists, economists, anthropologists, geographers, media theorists, sociologists, philosophers and others. Transdisciplinary research is increasing awareness, fostering knowledge exchange and promoting ways of thinking differently. The role of materialism in social discourse is reconsidered and associated with large-scale and energy-intensive projects.

Architectural Materialisms: Nonhuman Creativity brings together voices from various disciplines to expose aspects of matter in contemporary architecture. The chapters are at the forefront of the current contemplation of matter, how to approach it, and its significance for and within architecture. The authors resonate with the editor's own premise that matter in contemporary posthuman times has to be rethought in the rich and multifaceted context of contemporary computational architecture, and in the systemic and ecological contexts of pervasive computer simulations. This means a return to fundamental questions of how to construct a new world yet to come. Moreover, the reader, through the various approaches presented by the authors' perspectives, will appreciate that creativity can come from allowing matter to take the lead in the feedback loop of the creative process towards a relevant outcome evaluated as such by a matter of concern actualised within the ecological milieu of design.

The book revolves around a discourse that rests on a transdisciplinary model and wishes to map the distribution of hypotheses, concepts and diagrams from one discipline to another. What becomes the focus of the book is the authors' speculative dimension on their multifaceted role of discussing materiality by recognising that a transdisciplinary mode is first and foremost a speculative praxis in our effort to trace materiality and its effects on creativity. What the book is not interested in is discussing technicalities and unidirectional approaches to materiality. Moreover, the book retreats from a historical linear timeline of inquiry and establishes a sectional mapping of materiality's importance in the emergent posthuman future of architecture.

Overview of the Chapters

The contributors occupy a middle ground with capacities that allow them to wear more than one hat. The first part of the collection opens with Manuel DeLanda's chapter 'Causality and Meaning in the New Materialism'. Though at first glance antithetical, these two concepts can be brought together by making changes to their traditional usage. Causality must cease to be thought of as linear, so that the same cause always produces the same effect, and instead be conceived as nonlinear and catalytic, hence, able to bring about novelty. This involves considering not only the capacity to affect the entity acting as a cause, but also the capacity to be affected by the one in which the effect is produced. Meaning also requires reconceptualisation. Specifically, two different senses of the word must be distinguished: semantic content or signification, and relevance or significance. Once these distinctions are made, the two concepts are connected using the ecological theory of perception: animals and humans perceive the opportunities and risks afforded by the environment, that is, the capacities to affect and be affected that are significant to them.

The next chapter, 'Tangible versus Intangible Materiality: Interpreting Gaudí and the Colliding Forces of Traditional and Innovative Construction' by Mark Burry, is about stone. For architects, stone is the most enduring of all materials available to construct their dreams. The chapter draws on critical aspects of the Catalan architect Antoni Gaudí's personal development and life on the construction site for the Sagrada Família basilica during and after his death. Insights into the paradox of tangible versus intangible materiality are explored: interpreting Gaudí's position with regard to the colliding forces of traditional and innovative construction at a time of rapidly increasing industrialisation and material invention. The chapter does so by building a matrix to explicate aspects of the continuation 'framework' developed by Gaudí, which was posthumously handed down to his successors.

Kas Oosterhuis follows up with his chapter 'Internalising Continuous Variation', in which he sees nonhuman creativity fostering a new architecture based on continuous variation both in its theoretical and its technical and material dimensions. The chapter depicts the trajectory of ONL, his practice, and how with this mission it has moved to the third industrial revolution that has revolutionised architecture as a whole. In this chapter Oosterhuis redefines the fundamentals in three phases; phase A: mass production, phase B: mass customisation – in which phase ONL's built projects are positioned – and moving into the upbeat of phase C: distributed robotic design, production, assembly and operation, in which phase the achievements of Hyperbody's interactive architecture are positioned. He concludes by challenging the traditional role of the architect that has shifted, nowadays, to that of an expert.

Marcos Cruz, in his chapter 'Paramateriality: Novel Biodigital Manifolds', suggests a new way of biointegrated design which explores non-building, unthinkable novel materials that are products of *in vivo* research on living organisms and forms that are physically built and yield new aesthetics, resulting from novel hybrid techniques of production. Nonhuman creativity comes from this new aesthetics and from the *in vitro* mathematical systems and material computation that run parallel.

In 'A Vital, Architectural Materialism: A House-person's Escape from the Anthropocentric', Pia Ednie-Brown takes a vitally materialist approach to discussing the nonhuman creativity that comes from a house, which, like any creative project, is a living creature whose personality changes in time and whose vitality of matter is wild. Architecture as assemblages of forces, humans as forces that become part of a tangled ecology, and the house, acting like any personality, perpetually evolving and being discovered while in relation to us humans, it is yet another responsibility of which we are never utterly in control.

Julieanna Preston and Jen Archer-Martin's 'Performing Bitumen, Materialising Desiré' attempts to reveal the agential voices of the assemblages, human and nonhuman agents, such as human embodiment in the form of performance as yet another self-organising pile, an assemblage of events operating across scales of temporality, materiality and affectivity, and of bitumen, a vital and vibrant surface of our living.

The second part of the collection consists of two chapters. In 'Machine-oriented Architecture: Oikos and Ecology', following his ontology which focuses on what it means to give an account of something, Levi R. Bryant not only defines building as a machine, but building as a void and an enclosure which architecture operates in, through and on. He goes on to sketch the outlines of a machine-oriented architecture and the ways in which distributions of space operate on bodies, create subjectivities and form communities. He concludes by asking what a revolutionary enclosure would be to connect it with our ability to create enclosures that act upon us and potentially enhance our becomings and movements.

In his rich and elaborate piece, 'The Compass of Beauty: A Search for the Middle', Lars Spuybroek criticises the doctrine of emergence for hindering the beauty of the reversal that allows wholes to connect to parts of other wholes; a beauty that is inherent in things. Things can neither exist nor can they make a claim on their environment without being beautiful. The chapter tries to deal with the question of how beauty constructs this intersection between the two states. He calls this intersection the middle and goes on to sketch its historical transformations and its subsequent variations, combining the two main agents of variability, smoothness and roughness. Things and feelings are both constructed in the same system. That forces subjectivism out of the scene, and materialism prevailing as matter is simply what matters. For Whitehead, beauty is about both mutual adaptation and patterned contrasts, about massiveness and intensity, about smoothness and roughness. These things have a consciousness of their own, a nonhuman thought. The essay develops a biaxial structure into a genuine fourfold, and from there into a circular system where aesthetic feelings are equated with material objects.

The third part of the collection starts with Jussi Parikka's contribution, 'Architectures of Air: Media Ecologies of Smart Cities and Pollution', in which he discusses air pollution and waste as media, data and environmental art created in the contemporary smart city. The way these otherwise unwanted elements are sensed and perceived unveils political subjectivity in an urban context and as data feedback from various readings, understandings and governance approaches to the city. This sort of a materiality is one that is about folds between architecture, data and the chemistry of the air, a media ecology of multiple materialities. The creative power of smog intertwines old computational infrastructures of urban pollution and new infrastructures such as monitors, programming and data storage.

Luciana Parisi, in her chapter 'The Intelligence of Computational Design', goes on to discuss the creative act towards novelty that comes from the nonhuman computational synthesis of logics and the granular calculation of variations away from human cognition and perception based on given premises. The chapter proposes an instrumental approach to design as a technology or a cognitive activity able to transform the environment by inducing new correlations of vast amounts of varied data flows. This chapter addresses the emergence of this neomaterialist approach as a symptom of a new conceptualisation of nature that no longer corresponds to the cybernetic view of an artificial system of feedback relations. It further points out some important inconsistencies between the computational conception of nature and the new rationality of the natural.

Fernando Zalamea's 'Grothendieck Topoi: Architectural and Plastic Imagination beyond Material Number and Space' begins with an emphatic argument that, from mathematics to its plastic influence, Grothendieck topoi can be used to understand human and nonhuman creativity in three variously relevant and yet different disciplines; that of cinema through the work of Andrei Tarkovsky, architecture through the work of Frank Gehry and art through the work of Anselm Kiefer. The chapter starts by introducing the work of Alexandre Grothendieck from a conceptual standpoint, focusing on his topos theory (1962), a general setting which encompasses both arithmetic (number) and geometry (space) under a common abstract perspective (sheaves: a far-reaching tool that helps to glue the local and the global). Grothendieck's revolution, wider than Einstein's interlacing of space and time, has radically changed mathematics, but its plastic influence beyond the specialty has yet to be developed.

Vera Bühlmann, in 'Vicarious Architectonics, Strange Objects, Chance-bound: Michel Serres's Exodus from Methodical Reason', explores Serres's position on philosophy for architecture, suggesting that chance and necessity are not in conflict, as necessity originates in chance and chance comprehends necessity. Matter in its quantum physical character is controlled by computational and chance-bound calculation, but how can knowledge be new if it is rule-based? Serres's exodic knowledge is capitalised in the case of this chapter as a way of looking at elements as coded, discretised and distributed while unaccountable and inaccessible, allowing building as an autonomous entity to be a function of rarity, that is, having compatibility with the totality of economic and political power without being dominated or harnessed by them.

Maria Voyatzaki, in her 'Transmythologies', begins by dwelling on the question: if technical, material objects are inorganic, organised beings, possessing their own dynamics that give to matter the hallmark of vital activity with a strong claim on human experience, behaviour and perception, then what is happening with architecture? As architecture throughout its history has always been defined on the basis of a certain world view and in reference to a certain conception of the human, what will architecture become in the posthuman turn or even more in the nonhuman? How is its broad spectrum of established ideas, values and practices problematised by this new philosophical debate on architectural thinking and practice in our globalised and technologically mediated world? This final chapter examines these questions in terms of three main issues: the new conceptions of architecture that could emerge from contemporary materialisms, the new understandings of the material outcome of creative architectural work, and the influences of the above conceptions and understandings on the development of the creative process.

Notes

1. A. Radman and H. Sohn (eds), *Critical and Clinical Cartographies: Architecture, Robotics, Medicine and Philosophy* (Edinburgh: Edinburgh University Press, 2017).
2. Bernard Stiegler, *Technics and Time, 1: The Fault of Epimetheus*, trans. Richard Beardsworth and George Collins (Stanford: Stanford University Press, 1998).
3. Rosi Braidotti, *The Posthuman* (Cambridge: Polity, 2013), p. 13.
4. Henri Bergson, *Creative Evolution* (Mineola, NY: Dover Publications, 1998 [1911]), p. 96.
5. Jane Bennett, *Vibrant Matter: A Political Ecology of Things* (Durham, NC: Duke University Press, 2010).
6. N. Katherine Hayles, *How We Became Posthuman* (Chicago: University of Chicago Press, 1999).
7. Cf. D. Coole and S. Frost (eds), *New Materialisms. Ontology, Agency and Politics* (Durham, NC: Duke University Press, 2010), p. 8.
8. Braidotti, *The Posthuman*.
9. Coole and Frost (eds), *New Materialisms*, p. 8.
10. Cf. Hayles, *How We Became Posthuman*, p. 243.
11. Radman and Sohn (eds), *Critical and Clinical Cartographies*, attribute to robotics the same potential to create and innovate.
12. Braidotti, *The Posthuman*, p. 91.
13. The same question is central in Radman and Sohn (eds), *Critical and Clinical Cartographies*.

14. J.-M. Savignat finds in the Gothic cathedral the symbolic representation of this assemblage of formal and autonomous objects. J.-M. Savignat, *Dessin et architecture du moyen age au XVIIIe siècle* (Paris: École nationale supérieure des beaux-arts, Ministère de la culture et de la communication, 1981).
15. According to the etymology of the Greek (-origin) word 'architect', as it is described by Daniel Payot in his book *Le Philosophe et l'architecte: Sur quelques déterminations philosophiques de l'idée d'architecture* (Paris: Aubier Montaigne, 1982).
16. Aristotle suggested that man's brain and culture enable him to understand the world while training and the work of his hands enables him to make a contribution to it.
17. Filarete carries the verisimilitude of his organic conception so far as later to designate the client as father and the architect as mother of a building. The architect should develop his design in his own mind, 'ponder upon it, and give free rein to his imagination for seven to nine months over it'. Hanno-Walter Kruft, *A History of Architectural Theory from Vitruvius to the Present* (New York: Princeton Architectural Press, 1994), p. 54.
18. Nelson Goodman distinguishes the arts into autographic (in connection to their authors) and allographic (scripted), attributing authenticity to the former as an auto-feedback process that qualifies the author as the one who has the original conception of the idea. Nelson Goodman, *Language of Art: An Approach to a Theory of Symbols* (Indianapolis: Bobbs-Merrill, 2nd edn, 1976).
19. Cf. also Manuel DeLanda, 'Material Complexity', in N. Leach, D. Turnbull and C. Williams (eds), *Digital Tectonics* (London: Wiley Academy Editions, 2004), p. 19.
20. Cf. Braidotti, *The Posthuman*, p. 26.
21. Catherine Slessor, 'Material Witnesses', *The Architectural Review*, 207 (2000), p. 43.
22. N. Katherine Hayles follows Donna Haraway in defining informatics as the technologies of information as well as the biological, social, linguistic and cultural changes that initiate, accompany and complicate their development. Hayles, *How We Became Posthuman*, pp. 29, 192.
23. Christian Schittich (ed.), *Building Skins: Concepts, Layers, Materials* (Munich: Birkhäuser, 2001), pp. 86–7.
24. Donna Haraway, 'Staying with the Trouble: Anthropocene, Capitalocene, Chthulucene', in Jason W. Moore (ed.), *Anthropocene or Capitalocene? Nature, History and the Crisis of Capitalism* (Oakland, CA: Kairos PM Publishers, 2016).
25. Isabelle Stengers, 'History through the Middle: Between Macro and Mesopolitics', interview with Isabelle Stengers by Brian Massumi and Erin Manning, 25 November 2008, http://www.inflexions.org/n3_History-through-the-Middle-Between-Macro-and-Mesopolitics-1.pdf (last accessed 15 March 2017).

26. Mario Carpo, *The Alphabet and the Algorithm* (Cambridge, MA: MIT Press, 2011).
27. Gilles Deleuze and Félix Guattari, *A Thousand Plateaus: Capitalism and Schizophrenia*, trans. Brian Massumi (Minneapolis: University of Minnesota Press, 1987).
28. Reza Negarestani, 'The Labor of the Inhuman', in R. Mackay and A. Avanessian (eds), *Accelerate: The Accelerationist Reader* (London: Urbanomic, 2014).
29. Haraway, 'Staying with the Trouble'.
30. Emmanouil Zaroukas, 'The Myths of the Human: The Human as Political Being; The Political Substance of Architecture', lecture given at Aristotle University of Thessaloniki, 23 March 2016.
31. Negarestani, 'The Labor of the Inhuman', p. 436. The crucial part is that this discourse takes place within the abstract mode of thinking, that is, logic. We can find here both Whitehead and Peirce arguing for the abductive premises of logic. Whitehead argues for the ingress of eternal objects within the actual occasion, which forces that occasion to be speculative about its future.
32. Emmanouil Zaroukas, 'Architecture at the Age of Ant(i(que))-humanism', lecture given at Aristotle University of Thessaloniki, 21 December 2015.
33. *Les immatériaux* is a term borrowed by Robin Mackay from the exhibition 'Les Immatériaux', organised by Jean-François Lyotard and Thierry Chaput, director of the Centre de Création Industrielle de Paris, at Centre Pompidou, March 1985, thirty-five years after its inauguration.
34. Karen Barad, 'Intra-actions', *Mousse Magazine 34*, ed. Adam Kleinman, summer 2012, http://moussemagazine.it (last accessed 15 March 2017).
35. Jussi Parikka, 'Earth Forces, Contemporary Land Arts, Technology and New Materialist Aesthetics', *Cultural Studies Review*, 21.2 (2015), pp. 47–75, http://epress.lib.uts.edu.au/journals/index.php/csrj/index (last accessed 15 March 2017).
36. Negarestani, 'The Labor of the Inhuman'.
37. Emmanouil Zaroukas, 'From Hacking to the Incomputable', lecture given at Aristotle University of Thessaloniki, 23 December 2015.
38. Benjamin Bratton, 'On Speculative Design', *Dis Magazine*, February 2016, http://dismagazine.com/discussion/81971/on-speculative-design-benjamin-h-bratton/ (last accessed 15 March 2017).

PART I

CHAPTER 1

Causality and Meaning in the New Materialism

Manuel DeLanda

At first sight the concepts of causality and meaning seem quite alien to each other, at least in the context of materialist philosophies in which causal relations are thought to exist between mind-independent entities, while meanings are taken to belong exclusively to human minds and human societies. This sharp divide is not characteristic of other philosophies, idealist or empiricist. In an idealist philosophy, such as that of Kant and his followers, causality is conceived as a conceptual condition of human experience, together with other concepts such as space and time. Hence, causality and meaning can go together. In an empiricist philosophy, such as that of Hume and his followers, causality is defined as the observed constant conjunction of two events, like the collision of two billiard balls and the changes in the state of motion of the two colliding balls. Here meaning is also linked to causality via the mediating role of the observer. But for a materialist philosopher, causality is an objective relation in which *one event produces another event*, whether there is a human being witnessing this production or not.[1] Hence, if meanings are conceived as something inherently conceptual or linguistic, their relation with causes becomes problematic.

In this chapter I want to argue that the disconnection between causality and meaning is only apparent. These two concepts, on the other hand, need to be re-analysed in order for their relation to become intelligible to a materialist. Let us begin by enriching the concept of causality to get rid of its ancient connotations of linearity. The formula for linear causality is 'Same Cause, Same Effect, Always'. Different forms of nonlinear causality can be derived by challenging the different assumptions built into this formula. The word 'same' can be challenged in two ways because it may be interpreted as referring both to the *intensity* of the cause ('same intensity of cause, same intensity of effect') as well as to the very *identity* of the cause. Let us begin with the simplest departure from linear causality, the one challenging sameness of intensity. As an example, we can use Hooke's Law capturing a regularity in the way solid bodies respond to loads, such as a metal spring on which a given weight is attached. In this case the event 'changing the amount of weight supported by the spring' is the cause, while the event 'becoming deformed' – stretching if pulled or shrinking if pushed – is the effect. Hooke's Law may be presented in graphic form as a plot of load versus deformation, a plot that has the form of a straight line (explaining one source of the meaning of the term 'linear'). This linear pattern captures the fact that if we double the amount of weight supported by the spring, its deformation will also double, or more generally, that a material under a given load will stretch or contract by a given amount which is always proportional to the load.

While some materials such as mild steel and other industrially homogenised metals do indeed exhibit this kind of proportional effect, many others do not. Organic tissue, for example, displays a J-shaped curve when load is plotted against deformation. A gentle pull on one's lip, for example, produces considerable extension, but after that a much stronger tug results in relatively little additional extension.[2] In other words, a cause of low intensity produces a relatively high-intensity effect up to a point, after which increasing the intensity of the cause produces only a low-intensity effect. Other materials, such as the rubber in a balloon, display an S-shaped curve representing a more complex relation between intensities: at first increasing the intensity of the cause produces almost no effect at all, as when one begins to inflate a balloon and the latter refuses to bulge; as the intensity increases, however, a point is reached at which the rubber balloon suddenly yields to the pressure of the air rapidly increasing in size, but only up to a second point at which it again stops responding to the load. The J-shaped and S-shaped curves are only two of several possible departures from strict proportionality, and this implies that the terms 'linear' and 'nonlinear' are not a dichotomy: nonlinear patterns represent a variety of possibilities of which the linear pattern is but a limiting case.

A stronger form of nonlinear causality is exemplified by cases that challenge the very identity of causes and effects in the formula 'Same Cause, Same Effect, Always'. When an external stimulus acts on an organism, even on a very simple bacterium, the stimulus acts in many cases as a mere trigger for a response by the organism. A biological creature is defined internally by many complex series of events, some of which close on themselves, forming a causal loop (like a metabolic cycle) exhibiting its own internal states of stability as a whole. A switch from one stable state to another, the effect, can in this case be triggered by a variety of stimuli. That is, in such a system *different causes can lead to the same effect*. For similar reasons two different components of a biological entity, each with a different set of internal states, may react completely differently to external stimulation. That is, *the same cause can lead to different effects* depending on the part of the organism it acts upon. An often-quoted example is the vegetable hormone auxine, which applied to the tips of a plant stimulates growth but applied to the roots inhibits growth.[3] This type of nonlinear causality is referred to as 'catalysis' and it is not a monopoly of biological creatures. Though enzymes are indeed the most precise and powerful catalysts on Earth, metallic substances can also play this role in both nature and industry.

Philosophically, what matters about nonlinear causal relations is that they force us to take into account not only an entity's *capacity to affect*, but also its *capacity to be affected*. The latter is not just the passive side of the active capacity to affect but equally active on its own, although depending on activity at another level of organisation, that of the components' parts. In the case of organic tissue or rubber, for example, their nonlinear response curves are explained by facts about the microstructure of the materials determining their capacity to be affected by a load. And by the time we consider cases such as a bacterium, its capacity to be affected (depending on the metabolic state it happens to be in at the moment) dominates its response to external causes, the latter having been reduced to mere triggers. Thus, the crucial change in our conception of causality is contained in the concept of *affect*: the capacities to affect and be affected that characterise objective entities.[4] The name of the concept is somewhat unfortunate because it connotes something emotional, and there is, to be sure, such a thing as the capacity of humans (and other animals) to be affected emotionally, as well as their capacity to affect others emotionally. But emotions do not have a monopoly on affects, the latter being a characteristic of all things, organic and inorganic, human and nonhuman.

Let me elaborate this important point. When a philosopher believes in the existence of a mind-independent world, as most materialists do (with the exception of many contemporary Marxists), he or she needs to specify just what defines the autonomous identity of its contents. This identity is partly explained by a material entity's properties: its mass and weight; its location in space and time; its shape, and so on. Thus, an object such as a knife is characterised by its length and weight, and by its being sharp or dull, a geometrical property of the cross-section of its blade. Roughly, if this cross-section has a triangular shape (that is, if it is pointy) then the knife is sharp, or else it is dull. Now, a sharp knife has, in addition, the capacity to cut things, but this characteristic of its identity is different from its properties. The latter are both real and actual: the knife is either sharp or dull right now. The former, on the other hand, are real but not necessarily actual: the knife may never have been used and its capacity to cut may never have been actually exercised, but that does not make it less real. The technical term for a characteristic that is real but not actual is *virtual*. When the knife is used, on the other hand, its capacity to cut becomes actual but, unlike properties that characterise an enduring state, this actualisation is always in the form of an event: to cut. And, moreover, the event is always double, to cut/ to be cut, because a capacity to affect must be coupled to a capacity to be affected in order to become actual: a knife can cut bread and cheese but not a solid block of titanium. The former, but not the latter, have the capacity to be cut. Finally, an implication of the relational status of affects is that one and the same thing may possess different capacities depending on the kind of entity with which it interacts. A knife has the capacity to cut when interacting with bread; the capacity to kill when interacting with a living animal; and the capacity to murder when interacting with a human being.

The relational character of affects implies that the mind-independent world that the New Materialists believe in is not closed and finished. Unlike the properties of things, which can be listed more or less exhaustively, capacities form an open-ended set, since we can never know what a thing may be capable of when interacting with a million other things. Moreover, the set of properties itself is open ended, although in a different way. Most properties of medium-sized objects, that is, the kinds of objects we can perceive with unaided senses, are what is called *emergent*. That is, these properties are the result of an object's components interacting in specific ways, but they themselves are not possessed by the components. The concept of an emergent property was born in the field of chemistry in the late eighteenth century. Chemists perform analytical operations on substances, such as analysing water into its component substances, oxygen and hydrogen. But they also perform synthetic operations, such as placing oxygen and hydrogen gases in the right proportions and using an electric spark to force them to combine into water. Hence, chemists routinely witness that the properties of a substance disappear when broken down into components but reappear, or emerge, when these are combined again. And since properties are partly responsible for capacities (a knife must be sharp to be capable of cutting), this applies to the latter as well: both oxygen and hydrogen are fuels, that is, if added to a fire they will stimulate combustion; but water has the opposite capacity, it puts out fires. Because the relation part-to-whole that yields emergent properties is recursive – a given whole with emergent characteristics can become one of the components of a more complex whole with different and novel characteristics – the list of emergent properties is also open ended. Chemists have been producing novel substances through synthesis at an increasingly higher rate, to the point where their domain increases every year by hundreds of thousands of new substances. In other words, there are every year more substances than the entire chemical community can study, and this has the consequence that an honest chemist cannot believe in the final truth: that goal, the complete description and explanation of all substances and chemical reactions, recedes ever further into the horizon.

The importance for materialism of the concept of an emergent property, and that of the emergent capacities that these properties sustain, cannot be exaggerated. But the history of these concepts contains episodes of mystification that have made philosophers sceptical of them. As just mentioned, it was chemists who introduced the concept, but it remained confined in this field until John Stuart Mill gave us a definition: an emergent property is a property of a whole that is more than the sum of its parts.[5] Mill did not use the word 'emergent', a word that was introduced in 1875 by another philosopher, George Henry Lewes, in the context of a discussion of joint causes and their effects. When two separate causes simply add or mix themselves in their joint effect, so that we can see their agency in action in that effect, the result is a mere 'resultant', but if there is novelty or heterogeneity in the effect, then we may speak of an 'emergent'.[6] Both authors viewed the difference between physics and chemistry as pivoting on *the possibility of explanation*: while in physics, to explain an effect is to deduce it from a general law, in chemistry deduction is not possible because of the existence of novelty in the effect. To know what effect the combination of two causes will have, what substance will be synthesised from the interaction of two different substances, for example, one needs actually to carry out an experiment. Mill did not think that this was a reason for despair: in due time, chemical laws could be discovered that made the properties of water, for instance, deducible from those of oxygen and hydrogen. But to Lewes this possibility implied that water would cease to be an emergent and would become a resultant. In other words, something is an emergent only to the extent that we cannot deduce it from a law and it ceases to be so the moment a law becomes available. This is an unfortunate conclusion, one that involves a serious misunderstanding of the nature of explanation in general and of causal explanation in particular.

The philosopher Samuel Alexander went so far as to urge his followers to accept emergent properties with 'natural piety', that is, accepting them as brute fact, in a way that admits of no explanation.[7] Despite some mystical overtones in the work of Alexander – such as his arrangement of emergent levels of ascending grade into the sequence space-time, life, mind, deity – neither he nor the other emergentists accepted the existence of entities such as a 'life force', 'vital energy', or 'entelechy'. In fact, the notion of emergence was for them a way of getting rid of those suspect notions.[8] The real problem with their position, what caused the concept of emergence to be suspected of mysticism, was their rejection of explanation. Contemporary realist philosophers, on the other hand, have embraced the concept of 'emergent property' precisely because they do not see any problem in accounting for irreducible properties through some mechanism. As the philosopher Mario Bunge puts it, the 'possibility of analysis does not entail reduction, and explanation of the mechanisms of emergence does not explain emergence away'.[9] The rehabilitation of causal explanations in recent decades is partly due to the work of philosophers such as Bunge who have rid the concept of causality of its connotations of linearity and homogeneity.

Before moving to the question of meaning and its place in materialist philosophy, let us give a more detailed account of the concept of explanation. As just argued, an emergent property must be accounted for by giving mechanisms of emergence, that is, by showing how the *causal interactions between the components of a whole* result in the creation of novel properties. But in addition to a concrete mechanism there is sometimes the need to add some factors that are *mechanism-independent*. As an example, let us take the periodic circulatory patterns that characterise certain wind currents (such as the trade winds or the monsoon) and the underground lava flows that drive plate tectonics. These circulation patterns, known as 'convection cells', are emergent phenomena enjoying a large degree of stability: the trade winds brought Columbus to America, and continue to display emergent order to this day, while the convection cells of lava underlying plate tectonics have been circulating for millennia. More importantly, the same stable periodicity can be observed in phenomena that are entirely different in detail, such as certain chemical reactions that, rather than ending in a final steady-state of their final products, approach a state in which one chemical substance is exclusively produced and then a different substance is produced, alternating to a perfect beat. The causal mechanism behind these so-called 'chemical clocks' (a mechanism based on autocatalysis) is entirely different from the mechanism behind convection cells (based on differences in temperature and density). Hence, the explanation of emergent rhythmic patterns needs something in addition to causal interactions. This something else is *the objective structure of a space of possibilities*, a structure given in many cases by a *distribution of singularities*.

The simplest singularities (maxima and minima) were discovered in the eighteenth century by the mathematician Leonard Euler using his invention, the calculus of variations. By the mid-nineteenth century all the different processes studied by classical physics (optical, gravitational, mechanical, electrostatic) had been given a variational form and were, therefore, unified under a single least principle: the tendency to minimise the difference between kinetic and potential energy. In other words, it was discovered that a simple singularity structured the space of possibilities of all classical processes. The unification of all known fields of physics under a single equation from which effects could be derived deductively led in some philosophical circles to doubting of the very usefulness of the notion of a causal mechanism: if we can predict the outcome of a process using variational methods then what is the point of giving a causal explanation? But as Euler himself argued, explanations in terms of singularities and causes (or final and effective causes) are not mutually exclusive but complementary. Thus, we said above that a living cell may have several available stable states and that different external causes may act as triggers or catalysts that force the cell to adopt one of these states. In this case, in order to fully explain the phenomenon, we need both the singularities defining these stable states (for example a minimum in the concentration of a metabolic product) as well as the triggers.

In the late nineteenth century, singularities began to appear in other branches of mathematics such as the study of topological spaces, abstract spaces where the familiar notions of length, area and volume are meaningless. The mathematician Henri Poincaré, for example, explored the relations between the maxima and minima of the variational calculus and the newly discovered topological singularities. More specifically, he used topology to investigate the structure of the space of possible solutions to specific mathematical models. Since these models are used to predict the future states of a particular physical process, each solution to the equation representing one state, the space of all solutions is known as *state space* (or 'phase space'). The structure of state space,

Poincaré found, is defined by different types of singularities. Some have the topological form of a point, much like the maxima and minima of the variational calculus. The existence of a point singularity in the state space of a process defines a tendency to be in a steady state, that is, either a state of no change or one in which change takes place uniformly (as in the steady flow of a liquid). Singularities with the topological shape of a closed loop (limit cycles) define stable oscillations, that is, the tendency of a process to have a precise rhythm and to return to this very rhythm when disturbed by external shocks.[10] Poincaré even got a glimpse of the more exotic singularities that today are referred to as 'strange' or 'chaotic' attractors.[11] Explaining a given emergent effect such as a convection cell or a chemical clock involves describing not only a concrete mechanism but also the singularities – limit cycles, in this case – that structure their associated possibility space.

In the case of mechanisms, it was important to distinguish linear from nonlinear causality to counteract the criticism that the homogeneous effects of the former made causal explanation of emergence impossible. In the case of mechanism-independent structures, a similar distinction must be made to counteract the idea that explanation is deduction from a general law, and that emergence implies the absence of such a law. The state space of linear differential equations is structured by a single point singularity while that of nonlinear equations can have many singularities of different types. Given that the tendency to approach a singularity is entirely deterministic, knowing the structure of a linear state space is sufficient to deduce what the final state of a process will be. But with multiple singularities, each with its own sphere of influence or 'basin of attraction', that knowledge is not enough. There are several possible tendencies and several possible outcomes, so the one currently actualised is largely a product of the *history* of the process. In other words, the current state cannot be deduced from the equation alone because it depends on the historical path that the process followed.

Let us move on to trace the link between causality and meaning. As was remarked above, to an idealist for whom causality is a concept that organises experience, the link is direct: to be able to perceive two events as having a causal connection, we must understand the meaning of the concept. But when causality is defined as the objective production of one event by another event, with no connection whatsoever to human experience, meanings would seem to be entirely irrelevant. This impression is wrong. The seeming absence of a connection is due to two grave mistakes: a semiotics that privileges symbols at the expense of other signs, and a confusion between two senses of the word 'meaning', one referring to the *signification* of linguistic signs, the other to the *significance* of actions. Let us begin with the first problem: an impoverished semiotics. At the end of the nineteenth century, Charles Sanders Peirce introduced a classification of signs that included three categories: symbols, signs that stand for what they represent by a conventional relation; icons (for example drawings, diagrams, maps) that stand for what they represent by a relation of similarity (or isomorphism); and finally, *indices or traces*, signs that indicate what they stand for by having a causal relation to it.[12] The classic example of an index is the relation between fire and smoke (the presence of smoke indicates that of fire), but other examples include fingerprints and footprints, tree rings, symptoms of disease, facial expressions and, I would argue, most of the information that reaches our senses from the world. The semiotics that grew around the linguistics of Saussure, privileging as it did conventional symbols (the famous arbitrariness of the signifier), not only neglected all pictorial or graphic signs, but it entirely forgot that there are signs that point to what they stand for by having a causal relationship with it. Had these 'natural signs' become part of our current semiotic theory, the link between meaning and causality would not seem as tenuous as it does today.

But the main source of confusion in this regard is that the word 'meaning' is used in multiple ways and that philosophers and social scientists do not keep the different senses apart. When someone asks, in the midst of a conversation, 'What do you mean?', this is normally a request for the dictionary definition of a word, or in the case of a sentence containing an ambiguous term, a request for disambiguation. In both cases the word 'meaning' is used to denote the semantic content of a word or sentence, that is, its signification. But if a distraught friend comes to us for advice and utters the sentence 'My life has no meaning', it would be foolish to take that as a request for semantic content. Rather, what our troubled friend is trying to say is 'My life feels unimportant, irrelevant, it feels like I do not make a difference to anyone.' In this case, the word 'meaning' is used to denote significance. That the two words are entirely different can be seen from the fact that something without signification is termed 'nonsensical', whereas something without significance is termed 'trivial'. If the word 'meaning', in the expressions 'this word has a meaning' and 'this life has meaning', are two entirely different words, then using them as if they were the same word can lead to erroneous conclusions. In particular, it may lead to the mistake of thinking that everything around us, everything that makes us feel relevant and capable of making a difference, is a linguistic matter, and therefore that our activities are nothing but an enacted text.

The connection between causality and meaning can now be stated: it is a link with the notion of significance, not of signification. The connection can be easily grasped if we think of the practices in which these two terms are involved: interpretation and explanation. To interpret a text, in the way in which priests of different religions hermeneutically analyse sacred texts, is to answer questions about semantic content. To explain an event, on the other hand, is to single out the factors that made a difference in the outcome, the factors that were important and relevant, and to push to the background those factors that are insignificant. Much as social scientists routinely confuse signification and significance, they use the term 'interpretation' when the correct one is 'explanation'. Thus, when a sociologist observes two chemists arguing after a laboratory experiment in which the outcome is not clear, they tend to characterise the situation as one in which each chemist has a different interpretation of what happened. This allows them to think of the situation as involving something linguistic, and hence as being ultimately determined by social conventions. But in reality, the two chemists are arguing because they have different explanations of the outcome of the experiment, and even though they are using language in their argument, what they are arguing about is what causal factors explain the surprising or unexpected outcome: is it that the two substances invoked in the chemical reaction were not adequately purified and the impurities influenced the result? Or is it that the temperature or pressure affecting the reaction caused it to yield a different product? Or was it something else that they do not know how to control for? In other words, the argument is not about the signification of words or sentences, but about the significance, importance or relevance of the different causal factors.

At this point we must extend the concept of explanation to apply it to social problems. So far, giving an explanation has been characterised as supplying a causal mechanism, and in some cases, a mechanism-independent factor, such as the singularities structuring a possibility space. Explanations can be conceived as answers to 'Why' questions, but 'Why' questions about human behaviour and social events often demand answers that are not causal. To return to our example, when two chemists argue about the outcome of an experiment, in addition to having an honest disagreement about how different causal factors make a difference to the outcome, the two scientists' behaviour needs to be explained by giving *reasons* (such as the shared values of different sub-communities of chemists) and *motives* (such as advancing their respective careers).[13] Let me illustrate this with another example. In 2005 the city of New Orleans was flooded in one of the worst urban catastrophes of recent times. Now, if we ask the question 'Why was New Orleans flooded?' the answer is a causal one: because Hurricane Katrina crashed against the coast, pushing large amounts of water into the Mississippi river, causing it to overflow and overwhelm the levee system. But if we ask instead 'Why were poor neighbourhoods in New Orleans disproportionally affected?', we need to give not causes but reasons. Specifically, we need to explain that because water seeks the lowest level, property on high land tends to be in more demand than that in lower-lying areas. As a consequence, prices in the latter will be lower, and poor people will tend to concentrate there. Prices, as collectively set by demand and supply, provide reasons to buy or sell. Finally, if while watching our television screens we see a person from a rich neighbourhood trapped on a roof of a poor section of town and ask: 'What is that person doing in that neighbourhood?', the answer could be: 'He is a doctor, tending to poorer patients, and he was trying to rescue some of them when he was overwhelmed by the waters.' In this case, we must give a motive as the explanation. In what follows I will concentrate on causes, but it is important to keep in mind that significant factors may also include reasons and motives.

One philosophical problem that depends, for its formulation, on the distinctions just drawn is the problem of subjective experience. On the one hand, there are philosophers who believe in the linguisticality of experience: the way we make sense of visual perception, for example, is by assigning each percept to a linguistic (or conceptual) category. Some philosophers (Kant) believe that some of these categories are inborn, while others believe that we cut out the world using socially transmitted categories (social constructivists). This not only implies that human experience is drastically different from that of other mammals (since they do not possess language) but that the experience of human beings from distant cultures is also radically different: since symbols are arbitrary and conventional, and since each culture has its own symbols, then each culture literally lives in a different world. Now, it is certainly true that perceptual experience must be *meaningful* to the subject, but this refers to significance, not signification. How we make sense of what the world presents us depends on being able to sort the contents of experience into that which is important and relevant, and that which does not make a difference to us now. The former becomes figure, the rest of the insignificant stuff is thrown together into an undifferentiated background. This sorting out of the contents of experience into that which makes a difference and that which does not can be performed by nonhuman animals, and this implies that there is some continuity between their visual experiences and ours. To connect this point with the ideas that started this chapter, what is significant in the surroundings is that which has the capacity to affect (and be affected by) an animal. In one model of animal visual perception, for example, what animals see, the part of their visual experience that affects their behaviour, is the opportunities and risks that their environment affords them. These are referred to by the term affordances.[14]

Let me give some examples of affordances. A solid piece of ground affords or supplies a walking animal with the opportunity to move on it, but the surface of a lake does not, at least if the animal is too large. But because affordances are relational (much like affects are), that same water surface can provide a small insect with the opportunity to walk. A piece of ground before an avalanche affords an animal movement in all directions, while after the avalanche it may be so cluttered that opportunities for passage are limited and have to be negotiated. A cliff, on the other hand, affords a walking animal the risk of falling and injuring itself, a risk that is not afforded to a flying animal. A hole on the side of the mountain affords a rabbit a place to hide from a pursuing fox, but only if it is of the right size: large enough to fit the rabbit but not so large that the fox can also fit. The concept of affordance is very important because it brings together causality (capacities to affect and be affected) and meaning (significance). It is also an interesting concept for architects because in the original model, information about opportunities and risks is transmitted in nature by *surface layouts*. With the exception of transparent or translucent objects, most opaque ones present us only with their outer surfaces. An animal can study these surface layouts to perceive the difference between a cluttered piece of ground and an uncluttered one; it can also perceive the sudden discontinuity between the ground and the vertical wall of a cliff; as well as the difference between a hole (illuminated as a concave surface would be) and a protuberance of the same shape (illuminated as a convex surface would be). Similarly, architects depend on surface layouts not only to functionally and aesthetically organise space, but also to communicate this functionality to the users of architectural structures: enclosing walls afford an obstacle to those outside the space, but for the same reason afford privacy to those inside; doors afford passage from one enclosed space to another; hallways afford passage from one area to another; staircases afford passage from one floor to another. Thus, an architectural structure can be conceived as being meaningful to its users without reducing it to a text, a manoeuvre that flattens the analysis and deprives the structure of its materiality. Surface layouts, in natural as well as in humanly built environments, can be conceived as indices, as natural signs that indicate the capacities to affect and be affected of the objects bound by those surfaces.

Let us conclude this chapter with some general remarks. Bringing together causality and meaning forces us to distinguish two forms of human culture: symbolic and material. The former is the familiar one involving narratives of different kinds (foundational legends, stories of survival, fiction); a host of rhetorical figures and the practices of persuasion in which they figure; conventional units of measure; rules constituting the identity of games such as chess, and so on. Clearly, symbolic culture is important and shapes a large part of our daily lives. But in addition, there is the culture of blacksmiths, carpenters, potters, cooks, tailors, and the thousand other crafts practised around the world. Although the practitioners of these crafts may approach their materials (metal, wood, clay, food, cloth) using some symbols (such as the link between different metals and different planets), they spend most of the time performing *causal interventions* into the materials: melting and hammering metals; cutting and joining wood; moulding and baking clay; preparing sauces; sewing and fitting clothes. Because of the overlaps (and even, sometimes, the mutual interpenetration) between the two forms of culture, it is hard to give absolute criteria to distinguish them, but with some care some defining characteristics can be glimpsed. First, as forms of culture the content of the different practices must be transmitted across generations. There are two ways in which this can be done. One is to transmit cultural content through lectures or books, the other is to teach it by example and learn it by doing. This distinction is connected to the two forms of knowledge distinguished by the philosopher Gilbert Ryle: *knowing that and knowing how*.[15] The former is about linguistically coded knowledge, such as that expressed by declarative sentences: knowing that Columbus discovered America, or knowing that the hydrogen atom has only one proton in its nucleus. The latter is about embodied knowledge, the skills and abilities that a master craftsman helps to develop in an apprentice by first showing him or her how an operation on materiality is performed, then by supervising the day-to-day exercise of that operation. This is how knowing how to solder two metals, or how to join two pieces of wood, is taught and learned.

These two forms of knowledge are not mutually exclusive. We use language to theorise about know-how, and words may be used in the teaching of skills to direct the attention of the learner to subtle differences in performance, or even just to encourage learning. And conversely, some of the basic infrastructure of symbolic culture in literate societies is constituted by skills, such as knowing how to read or knowing how to write. Nevertheless, the two are separate forms and one may exist without the other. The teaching of skills by example need not involve a single word, hence does not depend on signification, but it does involve assessments of significance. Thus, a master blacksmith must inculcate in his disciples a sense of what makes and what does not make a difference in their practice: does letting a metal object cool down slowly (annealing) as opposed to forcing it to cool down faster (quenching) make a difference in the final product? Yes, the first operation yields a ductile metal with the capacity to yield without breaking, the second a rigid metal with the capacity to hold on to a shape. The first is needed for the body of a sword, the second for its edge. Although this assessment, as just now expressed, used words, we can imagine a blacksmith teaching these distinctions to someone from a different linguistic background entirely by applying the operations to an actual piece of metal, and then showing the disciple the different results: see, rigid metal is brittle, it chips easily; ductile metal dents easily but it won't break. Significant differences in process that lead to significant differences in product can be taught by example and learned by doing.

Architects, whose practice exists at the intersection of these two forms of culture, must never yield to the pressure of making everything around us a linguistic matter. And in order to do so, they must operate with an enriched concept of causality that includes all capacities to affect and be affected, as well as with a better-analysed concept of meaning in which the distinctions between signification and significance have not been elided. Only then will the discourse of architectural theory be able to leave the wasteland of the late twentieth century.

Notes

1. Mario Bunge, *Causality and Modern Science* (New York: Dover, 1979), p. 47.
2. James E. Gordon, *The Science of Structures and Materials* (New York: Scientific American Books, 1988), p. 20.
3. Bunge, *Causality*, p. 156.
4. Manuel DeLanda, *Philosophy and Simulation* (London: Bloomsbury, 2011), pp. 3–4.
5. John Stuart Mill, *A System of Logic. Ratiocinative and Inductive* (London: Longmans, 1889).

6. George Henry Lewes, *Problems of Life and Mind*, vol. II (London: Trübner & Co., 1875), p. 412.
7. Samuel Alexander, *Space, Time, and Deity*, vol. II (London: MacMillan, 1920), pp. 46–7.
8. C. Lloyd Morgan, *Emergent Evolution* (New York: Henry Holt, 1931), p. 8.
9. Bunge, *Causality*, p. 156.
10. June Barrow-Green, *Poincaré and the Three Body Problem* (Providence, RI: American Mathematical Society, 1997), pp. 32–3.
11. Ian Stewart, *Does God Play Dice: The Mathematics of Chaos* (Oxford: Basil Blackwell, 1989), pp. 70–1.
12. Charles Sanders Peirce, 'Of Reasoning in General', in *The Essential Peirce: Selected Philosophical Writings* (Bloomington: Indiana University Press, 1998), pp. 13–17.
13. Max Weber, *The Theory of Social and Economic Organization* (New York: Free Press of Glencoe, 1964), p. 99.
14. James J. Gibson, *The Ecological Approach to Visual Perception* (Boston: Houghton Mifflin, 1979), pp. 15–16.
15. Gilbert Ryle, *The Concept of Mind* (New York: Barnes and Noble, 1949), ch. 2.

CHAPTER 2

Tangible versus Intangible Materiality: Interpreting Gaudí and the Colliding Forces of Traditional and Innovative Construction

Mark Burry

The twenty-first-century architect is confronted by a bewildering choice of innovative materials compared with any previous era. Many have emerged with claims of durability which, while backed up by guarantees, offer none of the tried-and-tested confidence that can only be gained through prior use and experience, for there is none. Just as architects start to adapt to the ultralight world of carbon fibres that can take on some of the tensile tasks conventionally undertaken by high-strength metals, along comes graphene for them to absorb into their palette of possibilities. There is also an emerging range of technologies for them to grapple with, not least robotics and digital fabrication. While we would have difficulty in finding many architects who spanned the pre- and post-industrial eras, we can review aspects of a singular building in this regard – the extraordinary Sagrada Família basilica (1882–ongoing), the *magnum opus* of Catalan architect Antoni Gaudí (1852–1926). An internationally prominent building, it can take us on a construction technology journey across time.

On Stone

This chapter is built around stone. For architects, stone is the most enduring of all the materials available with which to construct their dreams. As a premium building material, it is manifestly tangible in all respects, whether cliff face, at the quarry or fully worked and incorporated within the built structure: stone is stone.

Looking at a brief history of this one material, its evolving use at the Sagrada Família basilica exemplifies the tensions that will remain with designers for many years to come, regardless of the increasing mechanisation of building material production and construction procedures, namely the role of materials and their specific use within the creative process. To what extent do emerging materials and techniques speak for themselves in design? Whereas the stonemason, for instance, assesses the grain of a particular stone, and determines where to cut it optimally and how to orient it in the construction as part of the creative process, are there equivalent nonhuman creative processes at work today when using a robot stone-cutter? This chapter reveals how using a traditional material such as stone, and absorbing it into a world of advanced technology in an exceptional project, affords an evolution that can enrich building craft rather than threaten it, and sponsor a human–nonhuman creative dialogue in so doing (Figure 2.1).

The great monuments that survive in such relative abundance do so because stone is enduring. The very durability of masonry existentially means that a building may no longer serve its original purpose, yet the stonework remains. If not repurposed, the masonry structure can survive as a stranded cultural artefact far longer than buildings made from other construction materials: a stone ruin has a very different presence than, say, a brickwork ruin. Stonehenge in Wiltshire, England, is one such survivor with an uncontested majesty that transcends the simple and inconvenient fact that nobody knows how it minutely functioned, nor can they put it to any alternative use today. Scholars might speculate on what its general function might have been – whether it was simply ceremonial or was, in fact, an immense and improbable structure imbued with practical purpose such as an astronomical instrument. No matter – the rings of great sarsens and lintels located in the middle of nowhere are in no one's way. Stonehenge survives millennia beyond the date of its creation, and will no doubt continue to do so, a silent voice for the anonymous human effort that yielded the structure, which has been rewarded ultimately through its monumental material permanence.

While dismantling masonry does not require the same level of effort compared with creating the original edifice, unnecessary demolition nevertheless represents a significant expenditure with no benefit; hence the survival of ruined castles centuries after their last use as community fortifications. Other than the relatively – and fortunately – rare circumstance of cultural vandalism ideologically undertaken for the purposes of iconoclastic erasure, or the more prosaically inspired pillaging of

Figure 2.1 Until 1989 nearly all the stone was dressed on site using saws where possible, and manual techniques to complete the task: highly skilled work, tough on the muscles as well as the ears and lungs.

material from a redundant structure towards the creation of another, it is rather expensive to demolish a stone edifice simply for the sake of its removal, so they survive.

Trainee architects enter their learning academies already knowing that stone has been the stuff of architecture worldwide, simply through their own familiarity with the built environment, even in places where local buildings are predominantly made of lighter materials. In such situations, at least some of the major civic buildings that they routinely encounter within their community will have been made from stone, and in the New World as much as in the Old, they will have been enculturated with the idea that stone implies status. They will come across books such as Ruskin's *Stones of Venice* in their libraries, and they will have had their instinctive knowledge coloured by both philosophical arguments as well as practical craft considerations, before being honed through higher education. In anticipation of a life of drawing not stone-cutting, Ruskin exhorts his readers to blur the division between thinking and making:

> And yet more, in each several profession, no master should be too proud to do its hardest work. The painter should grind his own colours; the architect work in the mason's yard with his men; the master-manufacturer be himself a more skilful operative than any man in his mills; and the distinction between one man and another be only in experience and skill, and the authority and wealth which these must naturally and justly obtain.[1]

Ayn Rand (1905–82) further harmonised the relationship between architect, quarry and artifice when Howard Roark, principal protagonist and architect star of her novel *The Fountainhead*, sustains his commitment to architecture during a period of profound professional disappointment by resorting to working at a quarry with herculean zeal, heroically toiling until such time as he can resume his seat at the drawing board.[2]

Until the beginning of the twentieth century architects typically devoted a sixth of their education as students to 'descriptive geometry' classes. No strangers to the term 'stereotomy' (the science and art of cutting stone), they learned the vital projective geometry that allowed them to represent the intersection of geometries as a framework for architectural composition, with strategies for how best to resolve the overall masonry composition into its requisite stone components.

Ruskin encouraged architects to engage physically with the building crafts in the belief that only through experiencing what the master craftsperson physically confronts with the materials of choice might

Figure 2.2 Honest toil – master stonemason at work on site. Contrast this with the situation in Figure 2.12, where all stone-cutting is undertaken off site.

the designer truly value those materials' intrinsic attributes, and the qualities they relied upon and therefore specified for the building's making (Figure 2.2). This brings us to Gaudí, and a potential paradox between his material philosophy and his working practice, with all materials, but especially stone, as exemplified in his forty-three years as architect for Barcelona's Sagrada Família basilica.

On the one hand, Gaudí grew steadily aware of the impossibility of being able to complete the design for this, his *magnum opus*, within his lifetime, still less the actual building, and so furnished an elaborate strategy to enable its *posthumous* completion using a geometrically based schema. In fact, rather than bequeathing 'plans' to his successors, the arrangements that he passed on could be more accurately described as a 'framework'.[3] This chapter draws on aspects of Gaudí's personal development and life on the site of the building construction after his death, offering insights into the paradox of tangible versus intangible materiality, interpreting Gaudí's position with regard to the colliding forces of traditional and innovative construction. It will do so by building a matrix to explicate aspects of the role of the continuation 'framework' developed and handed on by Gaudí to his successors.

1. Traditional materials / traditional techniques	2. New materials / traditional techniques
3. Traditional materials / contemporary techniques	4. New materials / contemporary techniques

Traditional Materials / Traditional Techniques

Irrefutably, the whole of Gaudí's oeuvre has to be interpreted by means other than through reading his thoughts on paper: with the exception of a few personal letters, and a document written with his friend Eduard Toda in his teenage years, Gaudí wrote not a word about architecture, neither his approach to design nor his practice.[4] The Sagrada Família basilica has therefore become an essential source of understanding for one of the world's most enigmatic and original architects.

Gaudí began life as the son of a coppersmith in the Tarragona province town of Reus, south of Barcelona. We can presume that watching his father at work transforming a sheet of copper into a vessel such as a kettle would have given material substantiation to an intuitive spatial ability. As a creative act the transformation of a plane into a volume is implied in much of his later work, where he consciously adopted doubly ruled surfaces as the *lingua franca* for all the formal design decisions he made during his last twelve years. Curiously for such a vital creative force, Gaudí was reactionary in his attitude to construction, although at first glance the sheer expressionism of his work suggests the opposite. His 'disciples' – the young architects who came to listen to him on site in his later years – went there to be lectured on Gaudí's latest discoveries in exchange for proselytising the project to the broader community, and thereby helping to raise funds. As they became more familiar with the theoretical and philosophical foundations, they were made more aware of his innate conservatism. They came to appreciate that Gaudí accepted that design, by its very nature, is innovative, but why risk novel construction materials and methods when traditional approaches had stood the test of time?

Ineffable proof of this position is revealed through his reluctance to take up Portland cement and contemporary concrete despite his close friend and patron, Count Eusabi Güell, being the first to manufacture Portland cement in Spain, establishing his factory in rural Catalunya (Castellar de N'Hug, Berguedà) in 1904, twenty-two years before Gaudí died.[5] In fact, it was not confirmed definitively that Gaudí had ever used concrete until the early years of the twenty-first century, when a core sample extracted from the pinnacle of the Nativity façade was analysed as being concrete. It is hard to imagine how he himself envisaged that the construction of such fantastic sculptural finials, the equivalent of several storeys in height, could be achieved using any other material, so it must be assumed that he would have conceded the adoption of concrete as a last resort.

In 1923, just a few years before Gaudí's death, his principal assistant on site, Domènech Sugranyes i Gras, had published a paper through the Col.legi d'Arqitectes de Catalunya prognosticating that the vaults to the basilica would need to be built using concrete to some extent.[6] Given Sugranyes's key role as amanuensis it is impossible to imagine that he would have been reporting to Catalonia's most learned architectural community anything that did not have Gaudí's blessing.

In the Sagrada Família museum in the crypt below the nave, there are four 1:50 scale models of the four distinct evolutions of the nave design, including the one that has now been completed (Figure 2.3). Three are by

Figure 2.3 The four iterations of the design development for the nave are grouped together in the museum as 1:50 scale 3D printed models (models by Dr David Puig).

Gaudí, but the first, the original design for the Temple Sagrada Família (as it was originally proposed), is by the architect Francisco de Paula del Villar y Lozano (1828–1901), who resigned from the project in 1883, after the first year of construction, as the result of a disagreement with the building's commissioners: the architect was asked to make savings by specifying cheaper materials and techniques, and was not prepared to make such a concession. Gaudí, who qualified as an architect in 1878, had therefore been practising for just five years when he was commissioned to be the executive architect working on del Villar's project. With little prior architectural achievement through which we can comprehend his appointment to complete what was effectively a parish church, we might assume that this impoverished young architect from humble origins in the provinces seemed a safe choice.

Although the project was starved of resources in the 1880s, during the following decade it received an important single donation that allowed Gaudí to spread his wings somewhat and make a bolder proposition. He added an extra aisle on each side of the nave, greatly boosting the area and therefore the volume of the building. With a certain amount of strategic foresight he decided to focus on completing one conspicuous element of the building first – the Nativity façade – rather than ploddingly building the entire perimeter stone by stone. The building was and still is funded solely through donations, and Gaudí surmised that donors would be encouraged to continue donating if part of the building was reaching for the heavens, thereby pulling the rest with it over an inevitably extended timeframe.

While an unfortunate pace of development from the client's viewpoint, this nevertheless gave Gaudí the luxury of time to reflect on del Villar's original proposal's lack of ambition. Given his predecessor's employment of the Gothic Revival language for the project, it stimulated Gaudí to make a radical reappraisal of Gothic itself, and what he regarded as its deficiencies. Principal among these are flying buttresses. While regarded as a medieval technical triumph in load dispersal by architectural historians, Gaudí described them as crutches. He observed that the interiors of the great cathedrals were more dimly lit than ideal, and correctly evaluated the cause as the lateral piers that buttress the nave walls, acting as vertical louvres occluding direct sunlight reaching the interior during much of the day.

The first of the series of 1:50 scale models referred to above is the original proposal by del Villar, and the second faithfully reconstructs Gaudí's first of three iterations: the 'neo-Gothic' version, where he first attempts to 'rectify' traditional Gothic, but through tactics around space and statics, not new materials. The third 'parabolic' iteration dates from 1914, and substantially deploys the parabola as the most structurally efficient curve. The fourth and final version, the so-called 'hyperbolic' version, was completed during his final years (1921–26). It is characterised by a substantial deployment of doubly ruled surfaces – a combination of hyperbolic paraboloids and hyperboloids of revolution, with helicoids. We can deduce from both versions 3 and 4 that he would have been translating the lessons he learned from the funicular ('hanging') model he built for the Colònia Güell chapel, approximately between the years 1898 and 1906. He was already looking at reducing the need for lateral wall buttressing by building a horizontal diaphragm 15 metres above floor level to accommodate the choir in his first (neo-Gothic) version and, in so doing, bracing against lateral loads halfway up the wall.

To an extent Gaudí must have felt straitjacketed through not being able to translate the funicular model directly to the evolving design for the Sagrada Família basilica. It was an appropriate paradigm structurally except for the Gothic bays not being able to accommodate the whims of gravity which would surely have distorted the seriality, the distinctive hallmark of all Gothic cathedrals. By this time, Gaudí had clarified his conception of the basilica interior as being a forest. Indeed, on entering the completed basilica today it is the first impression the visitor receives, regardless of which side or end of the building they enter by. At least he was able to distil the relevant components of the theory of statics that he gleaned from the Colònia Güell chapel to the basilica, using an inverted force diagram to translate the forces down from the roof vaults via the branching columns to the supporting columns below. At once we have the singular spatial and metaphorical power of the forest of stone tree trunks, branches and vaulted canopy, as well as the structural authority of an effectively equilibrated structure, optimised to the performance of the various stones he had selected for the hierarchy of columns that populate the interior (Figure 2.4).

Gaudí built his own testing apparatus which assayed the compressive strengths of a selection of stones, ultimately settling on porphyry for the four massive central columns undertaking most of the work of supporting the 172.5 metre high central tower. Around this group is a ring of eight basalt columns. The central nave is supported by granite columns, and the side aisles by sandstone.

Once the nave reached the design phase, commencing in the mid-1970s, Gaudí's structural regime had to be reconsidered with fresh eyes.

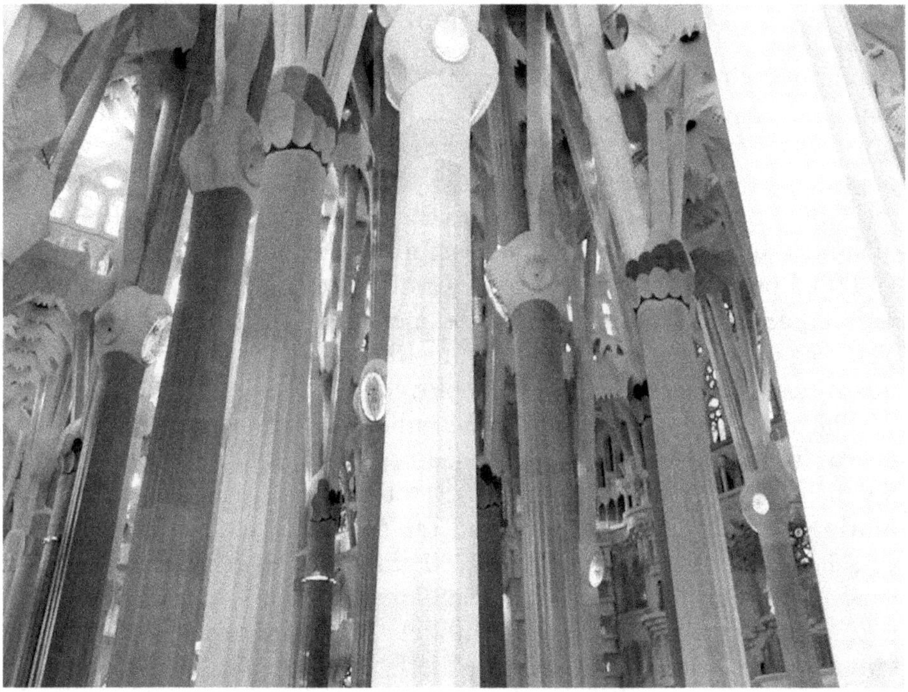

Figure 2.4 Nave columns built as the trunks of trees that form a great forest.

In the 1990s it was recalculated using FEA methods with no dimensional adjustments required. All the columns lean on their central axis, giving them axial alignment to the majority of the horizontal and vertical loading. Around that time it became necessary to calculate the structure for a potential seismic event of Richter scale 7.5, hence the introduction of reinforced concrete, whereas Gaudí had originally proposed ashlar masonry alone.

When we compare the third 'parabolic' version with his fourth and final, the 'hyperbolic' version, we see the complete application of Gaudí's innovative call on doubly ruled surfaces to refine his project in at least two fundamental new directions. First, there is a natural conclusion to all his various investigations into a holistic architecture with a foundation on the fundamental (as opposed to stylistic) lessons of nature, through to a coherent and highly original synthesis. Secondly, in so doing, he passed on an approach to design that was eminently translatable by others without the personal oversight all his work had required up to this point.

New Materials / Traditional Techniques

We do not know exactly when concrete first entered any architectural dialogue between Gaudí and his collaborators. The first public revelation of its inevitable entrance into the range of advanced constructional possibilities was through the learned paper that Sugranyes delivered to the College of Architects in 1923 referred to above. With the luxury of hindsight, all of the highly controlled plasticity of Gaudí's fourth and final proposal for the Sagrada Família seems to demand a material rethink, and this is what took place once the design for completing the nave began in earnest during the late 1970s, by which time substantial quantities of concrete had been deployed.

The challenge of continuing the building in the years after Gaudí's death included ongoing financial insecurity and the catastrophic Spanish Civil War that ran from 1936 to 1939. During that time revolutionaries attacked the site and set fire to Gaudí's studio, having smashed his elaborate 1:25 and 1:10 scale models for the nave. In the years of disarray following the war, surviving 'Gaudí disciples' painstakingly sought to recover the model fragments, and plan the construction of the second transept, the Passion façade. Although quite different in certain characteristics, such as the elliptical plan for the towers (the Nativity towers are circular) and the four towers being on an arc rather than a straight line, essentially this second group is a version of Gaudí's prototype.

With the substantial completion of the second transept in the 1970s, thoughts turned towards the great challenge of converting Gaudí's third and final version of the nave into a constructed reality. This involved a combination of the model fragments, photographs of the models prior to their destruction, and the input of two surviving disciples, Architect Directors Lluís Bonet i Gari and Isidre Puig i Boada who, as they approached their nineties, brought their familiarity with Gaudí's intentions to the drawing board.

During Gaudí's last fourteen years he designed first the 'parabolic' version of the nave referred to above, and subsequently the 'hyperbolic' version, the definitive version. What makes it definitive? The general supposition is that a series of disasters beset Gaudí around 1914, including the loss of his private client base, several important projects being abandoned semi-completed, and a debilitating illness that required a long convalescence. During this time he no doubt reflected on his situation, and the need to strategise the completion of the Sagrada Família basilica after his death, which he clearly anticipated as likely to occur well before any possible completion date. He did this brilliantly through the introduction of doubly ruled surfaces, a set that comprises only three members including the plane, hyperbolic paraboloid and hyperboloid of revolution. This back story is explained in more detail in other publications.[7] The important point to convey here is that Gaudí implemented a parametric geometrical codex that allowed his successors to proceed to restore the 1:25 and 1:10 models with confidence, and complete the interior, inaugurated on 7 November 2010.

While Gaudí left the pathway to representation through geometry, he never had the chance to put any of his scaled model prototyping into practice. This was left to others, who ironically married the fundamental plasticity of concrete at building scale to the same material characteristics of Gaudí's preferred scale-modelling medium: plaster of Paris. Specifically, his successors scaled-up Gaudí's modelling technique, deftly moving from plaster to concrete, except that the new medium was referred to as 'artificial stone', not concrete. This was not a branding move but, rather, a genuinely philosophical take. From the Romans onwards much of Barcelona has been constructed from the highly durable Montjüic sandstone, the durability of which is attested by the surviving fragments of the city being more than two millennia old. The source of the stone is the Montjüic promontory that adjoins the city, and which can no longer provide what has turned out to be a globally unique stone through its status as a protected national park. A combination of the supply of Montjüic stone being reduced to that rescued from local demolitions and the continually unfavourable financial circumstances made a rethinking of real to artificial stone justifiable. The recently applied seismic restrictions also combined with the logical alignment of the reinforcement bars to the rulings of the doubly ruled surfaces to help affirm the practical decision-making of that time.

Naturally, there has been significant comment about this decision, and the question of whether the Master would have adopted the material himself continues to be debated, despite the evidence cited earlier about Gaudí's intentions in having opposed the use of concrete for almost two decades. He had designed himself into a corner, and had created a situation that, simply for structural reasons, let alone the more favourable financial aspects, required reinforced concrete. In such a context, the reason for concrete being treated conceptually as artificial stone is that the chemistry of the several types of cement and types and sizes of aggregate used replicates the natural production of sedimentary stone such as Montjüic.

Does this really matter? Consider the following quote:

> Bonet and his predecessors may have captured the geometries of Gaudí's design, but the fervid textures of his overworked surfaces, and his vital fusion of structural logic, formal serendipity and an original sense for materials and craft (early-twentieth-century craft at that) are completely lost. Take in the mad profusion of sculpture and fussy surfaces of the lower parts of the Nativity Portal, for example, which are liquid, lumpy and dark like a poured sandcastle (and quite scatological as Catalan art tends to be, from Joan Miró to Antoni Tàpies, revelling in the plastic richness of mud). And now turn to the raw concrete porch of the Passion Facade on the opposite side, with its awkwardly angled piers and architraves.[8]

The author David Cohn titled the piece quoted above 'Gaudi's Sacred Monster: Sagrada Familia, Barcelona, Catalonia', in one of the world's leading architectural journals. The 'raw concrete porch' referred to is, in fact, made of stone, but facts often do not intrude on what can come across as emotional responses to the fact that Gaudí's posthumous collaborators are adding to his material and technical lexicon. The ability of the real and artificial stone to dissemble in both directions, even when the identifier is standing close to the object in question, is consistent throughout the building, but is not enough to narrow criticism to a less viscerally charged negative reaction. If such sentimental reaction is provoked by concrete mimicking stone, the next section will trouble the purist still further: the entry of robotic stone-cutting to the project.

Traditional Materials / Contemporary Techniques

There have been three phases to the robotisation of stone production at the Sagrada Família basilica. The first was a computer-controlled saw, and the second, a robot-mounted saw with seven axes of movement used to cut ruled surfaces. The most recent phase is the entire construction now being undertaken off site outside Barcelona using digital fabrication, with operations on site now effectively reduced to assembly only.

In 1990 the Sagrada Família Basilica Foundation teamed up with a local stonemason, Marbres Juyol (L'Hospitalet de Llobregat, Barcelona), to commence working with a robot saw to cut the daunting number of stonework elements that comprise the drums for the nave columns (Figure 2.5). These pieces are used as permanent formwork for the columns, all of which are inclined to some degree, as noted previously. Surprisingly, the computer numerical controlled (CNC)

Figure 2.5 Robot saw cutting (eight-sided central nave column).

technology entered the project a year or two before the architects had found a design software equal to the challenge that Gaudí had set out through his geometrical codex and constructional schema. Eventually a parametric design software from the aeronautical, rather than architectural, stable was selected, and this has remained as the mainstay for much of the design through to the completion of the design for the Glory façade, the principal façade for the building. This was the last part to be designed, and will most likely be the last part of the building to be constructed, being scheduled for completion in 2026.

All the main columns were designed by Gaudí to have base profiles composed of cotangential convex and concave parabolas. Any horizontal section through these columns is a combination of the same parabolas, self-intersecting to varying degrees as the columns rise in height (Figure 2.6). The significance of this is that a robot saw can follow the profile using two axes of movement with great simplicity; on completion it can shift by the 2.5 mm blade width in the third axis, and repeat the parabolas, but displaced slightly around

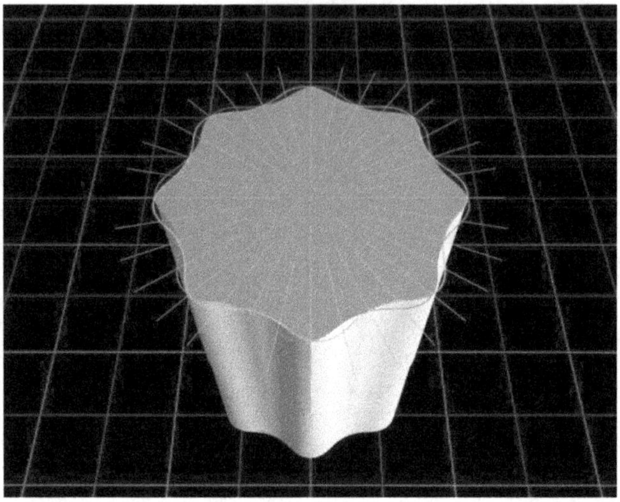

Figure 2.6 Nave columns: geometrical description of the derivation of their uniquely morphing sectional profile.

the axis of the column. The eight-sided column made from granite, the second smallest in the series of four, is fourteen drums high, and each drum is a metre deep. Each of the elements of the drum took 36 hours to produce. To produce the eight elements for each drum therefore required 12 complete days, and hence each column took 168 days to complete. Hence, producing the stone elements with Gaudí's simplexified complexity was made much quicker with this level of technical innovation and support than working by hand, though it was still not a fast operation.

Jordi Barbany i Triadú, proprietor of Granits Barbany (Llinars del Vallès, Barcelona), a highly accomplished stonemason and sculptor, made significant advances towards mechanically assisted production through the introduction of a 5-axis robot arm from the car industry coupled with a 2-axis turntable – seven degrees of movement in total. The pinnacle of achievement to date has been the production of the stone components for the narthex above the porch to the Passion façade. The elements of Gaudí's original design have been derived from a highly detailed glass plate negative reproduction of a drawing of the façade portico that he laboured over for an extended period. It is a 2½ dimensional depiction of the spatial qualities of the façade entrance with intense shadowing giving a sense of the relative depths.

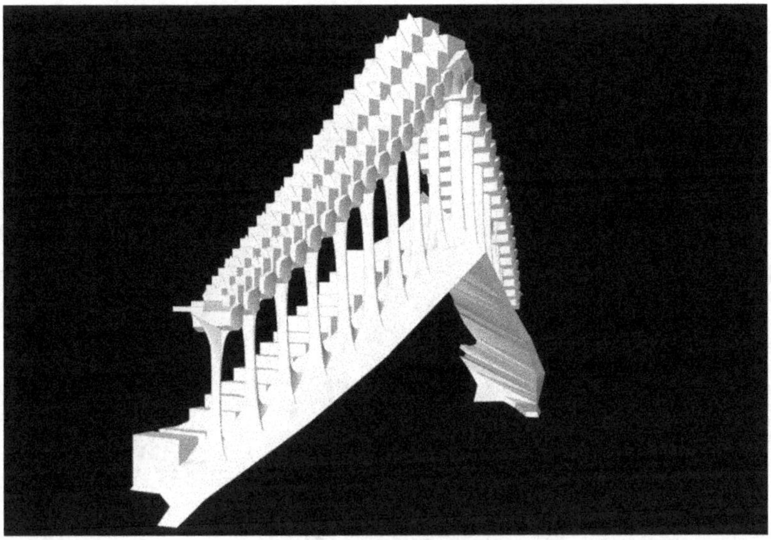

Figure 2.7 Passion façade narthex parametric design model. Every dimension is interlinked such that a change in any dimension will ripple through the whole composition (parametric 4D model by Jane Burry).

The project had been through several iterations prior to the digital era when, for the first time, a computational zeroing-in on the potential of Gaudí's choice of geometry could be undertaken far more profoundly than Gaudí would have been able to achieve had he had the chance to take the project forward to construction himself. Not only could the composition be treated algorithmically in an appropriately holistic strategy, but the entire façade was modelled parametrically such that major or minor changes could be proposed with the consequential knock-on effects rippling through the whole composition (Figure 2.7); all the elements are geometrically implicated with each other, and conform to an underlying mathematical and proportional rigour. The resulting parametric 4D model could also be used to produce files that could go directly to the stonemason's robots (Figure 2.8).

All the stonework for the narthex was produced by Jordi Barbany at his yard based 40 km to the north of Barcelona (Figures 2.9, 2.10). He was present for every major decision from the commencement of the final design for the project in 2002. This is to say that not a single architectural decision was made without reference to the stonemason. While file-to-factory appears to risk the complete disassociation

Figure 2.8 Robot-cut full-scale prototypes of three of the proposed narthex columns for the Passion façade narthex made from painted polystyrene, testing both the visual effect and veracity as well as possible routes to semi-automated production of granite columns.

Figure 2.9 In order to give the robot the least amount of work to do, a diamond-encrusted wire cuts the smallest possible blank for the robot to work on.

Figure 2.10 A combination of seven axes of movement allows the robot-borne cutter to produce columns over 6 metres in length from a single piece of granite.

of the designer from the maker – at odds with the sentiments that Ruskin expressed in the quote at the beginning of this chapter – the workflow for this challenge placed the architect in a context where engagement with the makers had never been more intense (Figures 2.11, 2.12).[9]

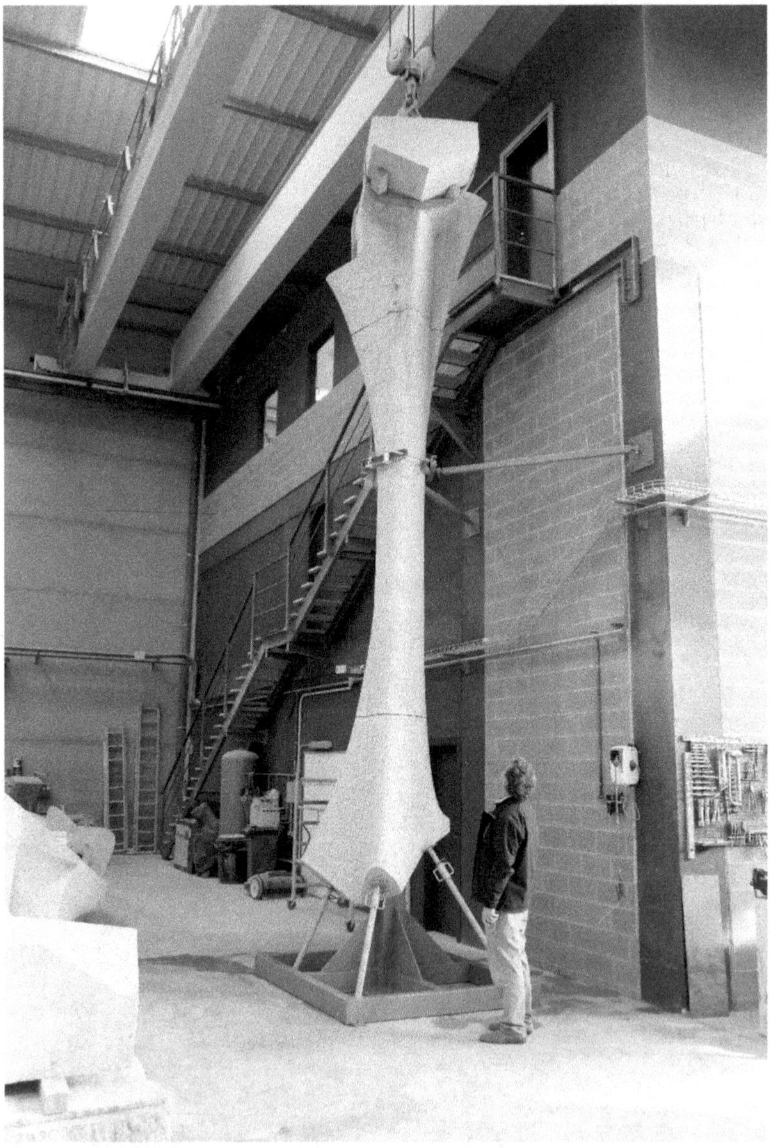

Figure 2.11 A completed column, cut entirely by robot-borne saws, over 9 metres in height.

Figure 2.12 Columns for the Sagrada Família basilica Passion façade awaiting delivery to site, ready to incorporate into the narthex. No additional work is required on site in the twenty-first century, whereas in a previous generation the construction site was also the masons' yard.

New Materials / Contemporary Techniques

In this section of the matrix shown on page 51 we draw the account to a close. At the time of writing, 2017, nine years away from the projected 2026 completion date, extraordinary technological advances are being executed on a palette of traditional materials augmented by concrete and steel. The Glory façade has been designed from a minimum of surviving material from Gaudí's own studies for this, the principal entry point to the building. Detailed design of the façade has not yet commenced, but when it does the designers are going to face challenges that may not be solvable with current materials and technologies. Just as Gaudí himself had to come to terms with the same conundrum in his later years, so too are the Sagrada Família designers of tomorrow.

Conclusion

This chapter has advanced the proposition that when using a traditional material such as stone, and absorbing a world of advanced technology into design and traditional production processes, such 'modernisation' affords an evolution that can enrich the craft of building rather than threaten it. The migration from the stonemason working with traditional tools to the world's most technologically sophisticated robot-assisted stonecutting has taken less than twenty years, and its story has been necessarily compressed here into a few paragraphs. Counter-intuitively, the greater the technological sophistication employed with time-honoured materials, the greater the opportunity there is for non-human creativity to exert a positive influence on all that the human mind brings to the design and crafting of buildings.

Acknowledgements

Much of the design research reported here was significantly funded by the Australian Research Council. This support has been within the framework of a long-standing commitment by the Sagrada Família Basilica Foundation to commission university design research teams to assist investigations on site into their needs for innovative design, design representation and digital fabrication.

Credits for Stone Production: Sagrada Família Basilica

Marbres Juyol: Sr Alfons Juyol i Arenas (L'Hospitalet de Llobregat, Barcelona), stonemasons, produced the granite columns for the central nave, transepts and apse. They also produced the basalt columns and many of the other major stone elements in the interior such as the principal altar.

Granits Barbany: Sr Jordi Barbany i Triadú (Llinars del Vallès, Barcelona), stonemasons, produced the columns for the Passion façade and many other major external elements for the emerging towers in the centre of the building.

Notes

1. John Ruskin, *The Stones of Venice (The Nature of Gothic)* (1853), Book II.VI.XXI.
2. Ayn Rand, *The Fountainhead* (New York: Plume, 2005 [1943]).
3. M. C. Burry, *The Expiatory Church of the Sagrada Família* (London: Phaidon, 1993).
4. A. Gaudí and E. Toda, 'Poblet, datos y apuntes', 26 July 1870, unpublished manuscript.
5. See http://patrimoni.gencat.cat/en/collection/asland-cement-museum (last accessed 27 August 2017).

6. F. Sugranyes, *Disposició Estàtica del Temple de la Sagrada Família* (Barcelona: Anuari de l'Associació d'Arquitectes de Catalunya, 1923).
7. Burry, *The Expiatory Church*.
8. D. Cohn, 'Gaudi's Sacred Monster: Sagrada Familia, Barcelona, Catalonia', *Architectural Review*, 25 July 2012, https://www.architectural-review.com/buildings/gaudis-sacred-monster-sagrada-familia-barcelona-catalonia/8633438.article (last accessed 27 August 2017).
9. M. C. Burry, 'Robots at the Sagrada Família Basilica: A Brief History of Robotised Stone-Cutting', in D. Reinhardt, R. Saunders and J. Burry (eds), *Robotic Fabrication in Architecture, Art and Design* (Cham: Springer International Publishing, 2016), pp. 2–15.

CHAPTER 3

Internalising Continuous Variation

Kas Oosterhuis

Internalising tools and techniques for multiplicity, for the swarm, for interactivity, for interoperability, for my signature style, for data exchange, for collaborative design and engineering, for mass customisation, for quantum behaviour and ultimately for the alien. These are some of the challenges that the paradigm shift to an architecture based on continuous variation will eventually have to deal with. A consistent application of the principles of continuous variation in all aspects of design and building will revolutionise the profession. In 2014 we found ourselves in a decisive decade of transition to the new economy of the third industrial revolution, of which theory, practice and education have been proactively implemented by ONL and Hyperbody in the past twenty to thirty years. Many theoretical writings, interactive prototypes and built works on the grand scale of architecture are living proof of their having internalised the principles of continuous variation. The portfolio of ONL builds upon the fundamentals of the great period of industrial prefabrication of the decades following the Second World War. Industrial prefabrication back then was aimed at maximising the sameness of building components. Now, in the second decade of the twenty-first century, industrial made-to-measure techniques and procedures are developing to maximise the similarities between constitutive building components – similar but not the same – allowing for continuous variation in their dimensions and their detailing. The very fundamentals of architectural production have been completely redefined with respect to the retroactive fundamentals as proposed by Koolhaas for the Architecture Biennale 2014 in Venice. Future prospects call for a continuous variation in the materials as well, thus leading to a greater freedom of architectural expression. This chapter describes the redefinition of fundamentals in three stages – phase A: mass production; phase B: mass customisation – in which phase ONL's built projects are positioned; and moving into the upbeat of phase C: distributed robotic design, production, assembly and operation, in which phase the achievements of Hyperbody's interactive architecture shall be positioned. We find ourselves now living inside this challenging transitional decade from Phase B into Phase C, leaving the traditionalists and modernists trapped in Phase A. While acting in this transition phase from B to C we will have to redefine our role into 'experts formerly known as architects'.

In the context of this chapter I will confine the notion of continuous variation to verifiable and quantifiable features of the transformative nature of a series of unique elements that are similar but not the same. Such elements may be unique in size, dimensions, shape and time, elements that are just that; that appear just there and then, unique like birds in a swarm, cars on the highway, galaxies in a universe, quanta in an intraverse, unique bodies of entangled information. From the viewpoint of the maker, one internalises continuous variation so as to be the bird, to be the car, to be the galaxy, to be the informed body.

Drip Paintings

In the late 1940s Jackson Pollock, high on jazz, suddenly changed from abstraction of reality into creating a new reality of its own, not metaphorically related to nature or the built environment, hence no longer picturesque or abstract. He was already used to taking an overdose of paint on his brush, and eventually started to like the actual dripping itself, without any desire to relate it to recognisable imprints on his retina. Thus, Pollock started to appreciate images for what they were, not for what they looked like and made one think of. Drips are drips, and that's it; no longer a depiction of nature, no deeper meanings or metaphors. Drips of paint were produced by brush movements swinging above a canvas spread out on the floor of his barn. Pollock indeed was internalising the principles of continuous variation.

Powerlines Paintings

Now let's have a closer look at the work of the contemporary artist Ilona Lénárd, Hungarian by birth and educated as an actress in Budapest. Born around the time Pollock made his last paintings, she grew up in the context of a socialist country, as a teenager stuffed with forward-looking ideals for a better society, which unfortunately, eventually, closed into itself by demonising a critical societal discourse. Once living in the Netherlands, however, Lénard could never fully accept the decadence of neoliberalism and remained faithful to the transparent premises of concrete art: what you see is what you get. Lénárd's recent

POWERLINES series represents the renaissance of *Art concrète*,[1] but she takes a necessary further step. No longer does the image have to be simple and visually controllable; rather, it is visual complexity based on simple rules that are the true generators of the work of art, as mediated by her arm/hand movements. Lénárd spreads out the canvases on the ground of the studio like Pollock did, builds up intense kinetic energy in her body, and then in sudden outbursts intuitively draws calligraphic lines with fierce and powerful gestures, which she labels as Powerlines. In her recent TANGLE series, FLOW series and TWIG series Lénárd creates her personal universe (Figure 3.1), pulling the viewer into the depth of the painting. As is stated in the first bullet point of the *Art*

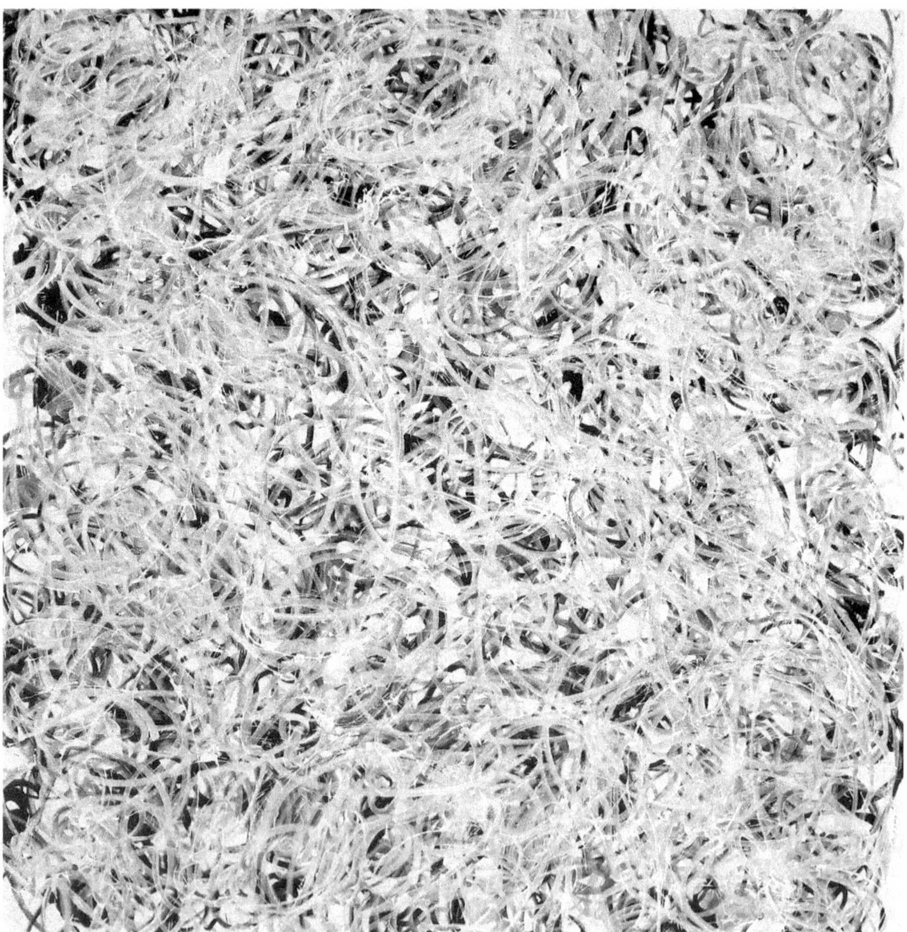

Figure 3.1 Ilona Lénárd. Omniverse 01. Acrylic marker on canvas. Dimensions 190 x 180 cm (2015).

concrète manifesto: art is universal. The arm/hand movements follow the logic of continuous variation. Each movement is different, yet based on the same intention. The visual complexity comes from the entanglement of many such interlacing procedural gestures.

DAF Variomatic

My first encounter with the principles of continuous variation was rooted in my early childhood years, in the understanding of the continuous variable transmission (CVT) of the Dutch DAF cars. A revolutionary invention was achieved by the Dutch engineer Hubert Van Doorne[2] in the late 1950s, inspired by an idea of Leonardo da Vinci. Van Doorne developed a seamless gear system, allowing a rubber band to rotate over two variable axes, one connected to the motor, the other connected to the drive shafts. The conical axes change diameter so as to switch continuously from gear to gear. No longer were there a mere four or five gears, but an endless number of gears. One of the hilarious features of the CVT was that the DAF Variomatic could drive just as fast backwards as forwards. In relation to our current understanding of continuous variation in engineering architecture this is significant, since our open design systems and our peer-to-peer data-exchange systems are bidirectional in nature as well.

Variomatic House

Back in 2000 we, at ONL,[3] were looking at applying the principles of continuous variation to housing, defining the contours of a truly mass-customised home, which we called the Variomatic. I designed a set of variable positions of vertexes driving the geometry of the house; variable positions of the top of the pitched roof, variable positions for the width and depth of the house, variable grip points for the slope of the front and the back of the roof. Playing with the variables, one could design a bungalow or a two-storey house. In order to manipulate the vertexes, we designed an app *avant la lettre*, a PC-based interactive tool programmed on the French Nemo game design platform[4] to change the values, either by pulling the points so as to change the geometry, or by typing in values for the parameters. The app visualises the 3D model and also generates the plans and the area of the rooms. We were designing the design tools, just as we did earlier in the Attractor Game, which is the urban design tool for generating the landscaping, planting and water system for the neighbourhood of Reitdiep in Groningen in 1998. It does not need a lot of explanation to show in retrospect that we were decades ahead of our digitally illiterate colleagues, since for the first time in this decade parametric design systems are becoming popular and fashionable, thanks to the release of the Grasshopper plug-in for Rhino in 2007–08.

Robotic Painting

In 1994 Ilona Lénard, Menno Rubbens and I, together forming the management team of the Attila Foundation, invited Portuguese artist Leonel Moura to join the Sculpture City Workshop, which was one of the constituent components of the Sculpture City event at the RAM Gallery in Rotterdam. Among the other invited people were Marcos Novak, Stephen Perrella (1956–2008), Lars Spuybroek and Maurice Nio, who back then was interested in literature in relation to architecture. After the millennium shift he became interested in the idea of having small robots execute the procedural acts of putting ink on the canvas. Mechanical drawing machines had been designed long before; in the 1950s Jean Tinguely fabricated his *machines à dessiner*, but nothing like this had been done before: a swarm of small robots crawling on the canvas following simple rules. Leonel Moura Henrique Garcia Pereira created a self-proclaimed new kind of art called Symbiotic Art using ingenious little swarming organisms executing simple algorithms (Figure 3.2).

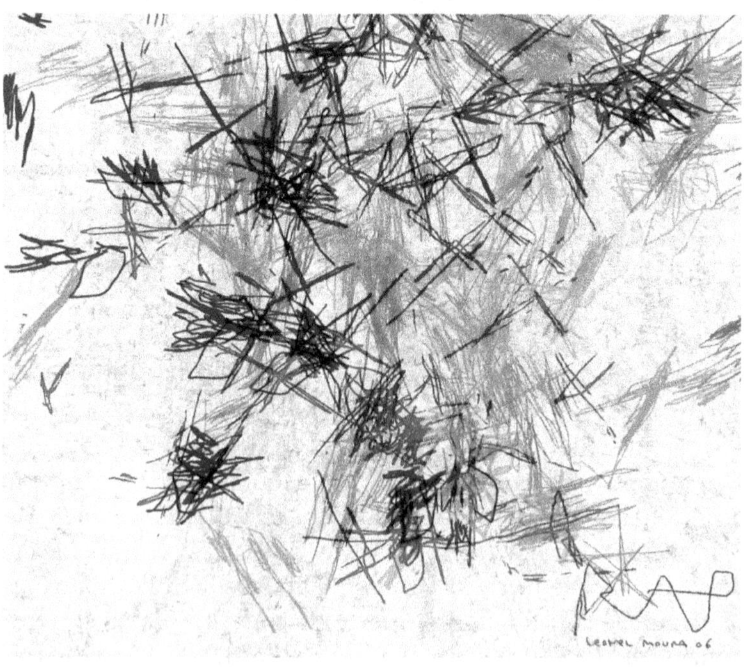

Figure 3.2 Leonel Moura. Robotic painting. Ink marker on canvas (2006).

BMW GINA

In 2002 Chris Bangle initiated a top-secret research project at the BMW design studio in Munich, where he had just become the head of design. Bangle imagined a car body that would be programmable, a car body that could change its character, and built a working prototype, GINA. The seamlessly changing configurations were achieved by embedding industrial muscles into the body of the car, fixed to the exterior curved feature lines. Between these curves, an elastic fabric was stretched so as to adapt to the changing tensile forces caused by the inward/outward bending curves driven by the muscles. In 2009 a video that presented GINA was released, after Bangle had left BMW and stepped away (temporarily?) from the car industry, disappointed by the irrational power games forced upon him by the not so innovative BMW bosses. Later he wrote the hilarious essay Peter Teuffel, sharing his vision of the future of car design while criticising the flawed power structures inside the car industry. The GINA prototype was nothing less than a revolution in thinking in the car industry. Bangle imagined a car that would respond to individual profiles as set by the driver. From a smartphone, the driver would set his or her preference for a more or less muscular car; the driver could customise the car to become truly unique, and even manipulate its uniqueness over time. Eventually the GINA prototype formed the basis for a new BMW aesthetic of muscular feature lines with hollow surfaces stretched between the lines, a stylistic approach that has been called 'flame surfacing', thus feeding back the principles of dynamic, adaptive systems into the appearance of otherwise static objects.

Trans-Ports v.1.0

In 1999, hanging out in a Philippe Starck designed bar on Sunset Boulevard, Marcos Novak, Ilona Lénárd and I were imagining a transarchitectures project that we eventually called Trans-Ports. Novak had coined the word transarchitectures around 1997 as the title of a series of exhibitions, curated by Odile Fillion and Michel Vienne. We developed the concept of two harbour-based, physically built, adaptive pavilions that would interact with each other over a long distance. Basically, the design concept meant that moving around in one of the pavilions would cause turbulence to the other at the other side of the world. No further details were discussed at that time, but we agreed to identify the concrete local potential for building such long-distance interacting structures. Back in the Netherlands, I modelled a proactive structure and showed it at

Figure 3.3 Kas Oosterhuis / ONL. Trans-ports version 1 (1999).

the first Archilab Conference in Orléans, curated by Frédéric Migayrou and Marie-Ange Brayer. There I showed a short animation of a mouldable, blue, bread-like form that was changing shape and content in real time (Figure 3.3). In fact, the Hyperbody concept was born there and then, in 1999. The idea was as simple as it was irresistibly logical: why would we use animation software but stop the animation when it comes to building? I argued that the motion should continue in the existence of the building; the building should be a programmable structure that receives, processes and produces information in a new disguise in real time. I baptised my initiative Trans-Ports, a portal to the new paradigm of programmable buildings. We designed the Trans-Ports building to pump up and move down, to swing sideways, by embedding actuators as structural parts of the construct, maximising the stroke of a series of large pneumatic pistons that were pumping the pavilion into undefinable shapes. Both Chris Bangle and my ONL team were independently experimenting with exactly the same continuously variable Festo actuators, in the early 2000s, without being aware of the other doing so.

Trans-Ports v.3.0 at the Venice Biennale 2000

After an invitation by Massimiliano Fuksas, the curator of the Venice Architecture Biennale in 2000, I was given the chance to build with my team of young nerdy information architects[5] the interactive installation

Figure 3.4 Kas Oosterhuis / ONL. Trans-ports self-explaining mode (2000).

Trans-Ports 2000 in the central 15 x 15 m space of the Italian Pavilion. We designed Trans-Ports so as to behave in real time in three distinct modes of operation: 1) Handdrawspace mode, an art installation designed by Ilona Lénárd; 2) Floriade mode, which featured an interactive 300 m long *route architecturale* through the first iteration of the WEB of North Holland; and 3) Self-explaining mode (Figure 3.4), using the geometry of the Waterpavilion (Neeltje Jans, 1997) as the vehicle to actually change the shape and content of the structure in real time. Three large screens demarcated the circular interactive arena, and proximity sensors hung from the ceiling identified people's movements and patterns and sent information to the customised game software. The arena itself acted as the game controller; people would move inward and outward, and rotate along the three concentric circles in order to steer the interactive painting Handdrawspace, to navigate the Floriade and to move the body of the Waterpavilion. Immersed in the sound and vision, one could really feel the interaction. Trans-Ports 2000 was one of the first ground-breaking projects for the new field of continuously variable interactive architecture, shown for the first time at the Biennale, in the pleasant company of the equally ground-breaking Hyposurface installation by Mark Goulthorpe of DeCoi. In the same year 2000, I was invited to take the Digital Architecture chair at the TU Delft, which gave me the opportunity to unfold the new paradigm of a continuously variable interactive architecture in the academic context. I immediately renamed it Hyperbody, soon to become an internationally acknowledged research centre for interactive architecture based on complex geometries.

Adaptive Façade

The principles of continuous variation find their way in both static and dynamic architectural systems. Parallel to several prototypical hypotheses, either in the form of interactive installations or as design games, I naturally set myself to think about possible practical applications. In the end, one must find a business model that works and brings in the money. It was my expectation that within five years after the launch of Trans-Ports v.1.0 we would actually build a programmable building on 1:1 scale, to start with as a pavilion, with larger built structures expected to follow soon. It is now fifteen years since the first public presentation of Trans-Ports v.1.0, and almost twenty years since the design for the interactive behaviour of the Waterpavilion (Figure 3.5), and it has not happened yet. Have we been naive, or was the concept of buildings that

Figure 3.5 Kas Oosterhuis, Ilona Lénárd / ONL. Waterpavilion sensorium (1997).

change shape and content in real time not so urgent after all? The costs involved is not the issue, since back in 2000 we made careful calculations that concluded that a fully programmable structure would cost, proportionally, twice as much as a regular building at most. The Waterpavilion with its interactive behaviour was built for approximately €1500/sq m, while we estimated the costs of Trans-Ports (double-checked by established Dutch engineers) to be in the order of magnitude of €3000/sq m. As a rule of thumb, dynamic structures would double the cost, yet they would perform more efficiently, and earn back their investment over a period of less than ten years when it comes to pure functional applications. As an example of a purely functional application, ONL designed an interactive façade that could be attached to almost any regular building, using the combination of pneumatic cushions driven into varying configurations by pneumatic muscles or electronic pistons, connected in a diagrid system to the edges of the cushions. The adaptive façade would work through an interplay between shortening/stretching the muscles and inflating/deflating the cushions. The muscles act as the tensile components, the cushions as the compressive components. The adaptive façade features continuous variation, from completely open to completely closed, according to changing circumstances either as a result of reset user preferences from within or changed weather conditions outside. Smartphone-based applications and sensor data would inform the individual constituent components of the adaptive façade to act, either to close more or to open more. Other applications that were perhaps more likely to touch solid ground are the design of intense, experience-rich commercial environments, where the consumer actually is tempted to pay for the thrill of the interaction.

NSA Muscle/Muscle Body

In full accordance with our original expectations, we received an invitation to exhibit at the Centre Pompidou in the 'Non-standard Architectures' show, curated by Frédéric Migayrou. We proposed a programmable body 6 m in length and 3 m in width and height. The design concept was to have this body behave in real time by actuating 72 muscles wrapped around the inflated body. The body was kept under constant pressure, while the muscles would vary their pressure individually so as to cause rotational movements, hopping movements and potentially even slow walking movements. The initial Trans-Ports v.3.0 image appeared on the front page of the French daily newspaper *La Libération*. Sensor discs were attached to the nodal points of the enveloping muscular diamond grid to seduce the public to interact with the movement of the body and the sounds. The discs were installed with proximity sensors, infrared sensors and touch sensors, designed and actuated by Bert Bongers. The central organ of the NSA Muscle is its brain, positioned inside the inflated body. Being inside the NSA Muscle felt like participating in a North Pole expedition, not least because of the pumping sounds of the valves. From the inside one could see all 72 light blue tubes running from the valves to the 72 muscles. The NSA Muscle was the first 1:1 built prototype, with many to follow at Hyperbody at the TU Delft, of bodies and spatial environments displaying interactive behaviour in real time. With our team, we proved in practice that programmable buildings did indeed have a future; we realised the paradigm shift towards an interactive architecture because we wanted it to work. Architecture would never be the same – at least that was what we had in mind – but daily practice turned out to be a harsher environment, and clients to build the prototypes on the grand scale of architecture have not shown up until now. The Muscle project showed that by its real-time behaviour the architectural body passes through a billion possible configurations, continuously variable with never a dull moment.

SpaceGraph

Since 2002 Hyperbody has attracted a dozen PhD candidates and established a fruitful relationship between research and education. On a few occasions, I asked my PhD candidates to build prototypes of open collaborative design systems in game development software. One example is relevant here. The SpaceGraph interactive application[6] shows a system of 3D reference points and their 3D voronoi constructs to be manipulated in real time. The reference points may be dragged into any position and the 3D voronoi cells will build up immediately, serving as an example of the challenging paradigm of Immediate Architecture. What I wanted to visualise with the application is that taking complexity as the default condition is inclusive with respect to regular spatial arrangements. On the other hand, when a regular and square design system is taken as the default condition, then this system locks out a possible description of a complex geometry. Therefore, such traditional drawing systems are xenophobes by nature, while non-standard spatial definitions are effortlessly inclusive of historic architectural paradigms in their systemic set-up. The simple platonic shape can be easily described in a system that supports complexity, just by arranging the reference points on a set of straight lines. Continuous variation may be stretched all the way from standard to non-standard when taking non-standard as the default condition.

Interactive Wall

More important than any theory or any animation is the actual building of prototypes to test the continuous variation of interactive building components. In the end, each building is built up from a series of components, either prefabricated or moulded on site. While the NSA Muscle project can still be seen as an art installation, and is definitely regarded by traditional architects as such, it is necessary to link the new paradigm of real-time continuous variation to the very building blocks that buildings are made of. This needs a complete redefinition of the building block. No longer can these be seen as static and straight components, but each one must be considered as a fully mouldable and programmable unit. Hyperbody took a first step in this direction with the realisation of the Interactive Wall project in 2009 (Figure 3.6) in collaboration with Festo. On my initiative, in my function as chair of Hyperbody, we designed a linear series of seven wall components, each of them able to move individually and each having two embedded actuators and a proximity sensor in the base so as to respond to the passing crowd. The sensor sends its signal to the brain, which processes the incoming data and translates it into a signal to the embedded actuators, which in turn push the Fin Ray® shape[7] from standing straight up into a curve. The principle of the Fin Ray® structure is that the top of

Figure 3.6 Hyperbody / Festo. Interactive Wall (2009).

the stretched triangular shape remains always exactly vertically above the centre of its base. This prototype convinced us that we could start to think of applying interactive building components at the grand scale of architecture, leading to an architecture that lives in a state of continuous variation. But a lot of practical research has to be executed before we can think of the structure of, say, high-rise buildings to incorporate actuating building components. We have seen the dancing Dubai Towers design concept for the Lagoon in Dubai at the Cityscape Real Estate Fair in 2010, but that dance is limited to the metaphor; they do not move in real time. The first actuators embedded in high-rise buildings are intended to counteract strong winds; they act as muscles making the tower stand upright against the wind, just as a body balances itself all the time as to avoid falling. The best definition of walking and standing up is preventing oneself from falling down. Maintaining balance is an internalised form of continuous variation.

Emotive Sound Barrier

When architects use a description like dancing towers, they typically use it as a metaphor, not to describe its real existing behaviour. Towers do not dance. But could they? Dancing means displaying behaviour that is not purely functional. Although dance may be derived from socially meaningful rituals, and still is a socially relevant ritual, there is a good portion of emotion that comes from deep within the body. Each body moves differently; each body, albeit a member of the same family or the same social group, moves in a fusion of top-down dictated ritual movements and spontaneous gestures from within. Dance is a lucky marriage between dry reasoning and wet emotion.

Now what if buildings could dance? This was one of the questions that we, at ONL, asked ourselves when conceiving the design and behaviour of the Emotive Sound Barrier in 2012. The other question was: why would there be a barrier if there is no sound? Put otherwise, if there is no train to generate noise, the sound barrier has no function and should not be there. Such compelling logic led us to design the Emotive Sound Barrier in the form of a series of interacting components that could each individually curl up so as to wrap around the train and muffle the sound it produces only at that particular moment when the train passes. Following our in-house guidelines for interactivity of 'just then, just there, just that', 'there is only a barrier when you need one' is one of the one-liners I often use in this context. So much for the functional part based on rational thinking. We wanted the barrier to behave emotionally as well; therefore, we programmed the Emotive Sound Barrier to dance away after the train has passed, for its own sake, just to express the pure joy of movement; it is said to enjoy its own dance, and people love to watch it. There is a continuous variation in time from functional to emotional behaviour, based on a continuous variation in the degree of curvature of the constituent components.

ProtoSPACE 4.0

To fully take advantage of the potential of programmable architecture I have felt the need to develop a deeper understanding of the parametric nature of the constituent building. With my Hyperbody team of 2010[8] we parametrically designed and engineered, CNC-produced and dry-assembled twenty, large, unique building blocks to form a 10 per cent section of the protoSPACE 4.0 pavilion. The physical structure consists of a thick package of CNC milled polystyrene foam of varying depth, with a 2 mm exterior coating of sprayed polyurea, reinforced with recessed wooden strips to provide sufficient grip for the connectors. The pure innovation of this parametric building block is that it combines structure, skin and climatic performance in one component. Furthermore, it hosts a range of possible performative subcomponents such as windows to provide natural light, openings for ventilation, lockers for small heat pumps for heating and/or cooling, and storage space for interactive furniture that would pop up from the floor, wall or ceiling. There is continuous variation from floor to wall to roof on all faces of the building. There is continuous variation in physical depth according to the structural calculations and performative requirements. There is continuous variation from one component to another with respect to the function that the components have adopted, in other words, to which family of components in the interacting swarm of components it belongs. Every component owns a parametric relationship with its neighbours, and with other members of the component family. Every component can be addressed in real time in the design process and, when containing performative subcomponents, it can be addressed in real time to talk to its peers. The climatic performance is achieved by a distributed swarm of interacting smaller devices that talk to each other, as mediators between the weather conditions outside, the requested climatic conditions inside and individual user preferences. Two or three components on pneumatic hinges would cluster together to form a door component, in the same manner that the iWEB doors were conceived. The design of

Figure 3.7 Hyperbody / ONL / Kas Oosterhuis. Protospace 4.0 (2010).

protoSPACE 4.0 (Figure 3.7) followed the earlier developed design principle of 'One Building, One Detail',[9] which was applied in 2002 so uncompromisingly for the WEB of North Holland, the original pavilion for the Floriade World Flower Expo in 2002 which took place in Haarlemmermeer in The Netherlands, after which it was disassembled and in 2006 re-assembled at the TU Delft and renamed the iWEB, where all the details are similar but not the same.

Climbing Wall

In the practice of ONL we further developed the design-to-production method of mass-customised unique series of parametric building components for the Amsterdam Climbing Wall project. Faithful to ONL's principle of 'One Building, One Detail', we conceived one single triangular component (Figure 3.8), which allows us to build complex, doubly curved surfaces of relatively low resolution. The resolution is defined by the size of the triangular panels, which have a flat surface in themselves. A population of hundreds of such flat panels in Spaceland constitute the doubly curved Climbing Wall (Figure 3.9), comparable in resolution to the number of pixels in a thumbnail jpg in Flatland. Needless to say, there is continuous variation from one panel to another to achieve the impression of doubly curved walls and arches. To achieve the structural innovation, we scripted in Grasshopper the continuous variation of the supporting beams and of the edges of the plywood panels as well. The

Figure 3.8 ONL. Climbing Wall component (2012).

Figure 3.9 ONL. Climbing Wall Amsterdam (2012).

structural invention is the open node; the gravity forces and the forces caused by the climbers are transferred from beam to skin to beam. In that way, bypassing the node, a structure–skin continuum is established. The skin has thus become a structural component, exactly as in the case of shipbuilding technology, where the steel skin connects the steel frames so as to jointly bear the load.

The other innovation that we brought to life was to open up the design game for non-expert designers, yet expert climbers. Via an application, climbers were invited to tweak the vertexes of the parametric model themselves in order to build the challenges for climbing the walls and clinging to the arches. Having set the structural constraints in the script with respect to the angles between two adjacent panels, the climbers did actually produce a rough model of the climbing wall themselves, later to be streamlined by us, imposing our aesthetic opinion on the supple curves of that model. ONL sets the design rules, the users play by the design rules. This I consider the future of architecture – to set the design rules for any building, but leave ports open to other experts to play the design game according to their own will and skill. The exciting paradigm shift is towards open participatory design systems, not compromising the aesthetic principles of the designer of the game, nor the functional or even arbitrary choices made by the users. The power of continuous variation is extended to a group of players, rather than limited to the exclusive role of the architect-player. The making of architecture becomes a collaborative act of co-creation, and leads to a new set of agreements for co-authorship. Some players will be really good, producing excellent designs, while other players of the same design game might be lousy, producing more average designs, yet never truly bad designs since that is prohibited by the constraints that are inherent in the game.

Bálna Budapest

The principles of continuous variation are applied in the works of ONL on various scale levels and in different categories. One category I wish to present is the variomatic transformation from old to new, via roof to body, continuously varying in pitch and in character, as if it were a musical score. The mixed-use Bálna Budapest project (Figure 3.10) features a step-by-step transformation from renovated old warehouses towards a new body. On the city side of the Bálna the pitch of the roof matches the pitched roofs of the existing warehouses. From there the spinal cord and its wings rise up towards the upper ridge of the roofs and then suddenly leave the scene so as to become the signature fold line of the forward leaning body. The sharp fold gradually fades out so as to join

Figure 3.10 Kas Oosterhuis, Ilona Lénárd / ONL. Bálna Budapest (2014).

the surfaces at either side of this feature line, only to come down to the plaza level at one single point, which forms the singularity point of the whole complex. Note that the design scheme is based on the global symmetry of the body along the long axis, while local contextual conditions are responsible for local asymmetries in the façades of the old warehouses. Towards the forward cantilevering front part of the building the constituent components are stretched to their maximum size, which communicates the feeling that the head is accelerating so much that it stretches – in a process of continuous variation – the front parts much more than the components that are fixed at the other end. The design concept is that the now is so strongly moving forward that it stretches and rewrites history in one bold stroke of continuous variation.

LIWA Tower

There is one more aspect of continuous variation by parametric design that needs to be discussed before arriving at a conclusion on the importance of the programmability of the building body as the prerequisite for designing buildings, either as static end-products or as real-time living entities. That aspect is the relation between global parameters and local parameters. As an eloquent example, I use the design for the LIWA

Tower in Abu Dhabi which ONL recently completed. The master plan by RMJM for the Capital Centre district in Abu Dhabi allowed for a maximum of 21,604 sq m gross floor area (GFA) development on the plot. This includes the podium levels that the tower was supposedly placed upon. First of all, I wanted a tower that stood with its feet on the ground, not hovering helplessly above a podium. The reason: I wanted to touch the very material the tower is made of, still faithful to the 'One Building, One Detail' approach, which entails that the design system used in the air must be the same as that which comes to the ground. I wanted freedom of expression combined with maximum profit for the developer, which means that I wanted to realise exactly 21,604 sq m GFA, which we eventually did. The area is introduced in our parametric design system as a fixed global parameter. All building components are related to each other in the parametric concept. The drivers for playing with the parameters are the eight vertically rising curves. Tweaking the vertexes that define the trajectories of the curves means changing the local parameters that establish the GFA. Fixing the global parameter of the GFA means that tweaking one curve has an inclusive effect on the other curves so as to compensate the total GFA, by either building further outward or folding more inward. We designed the system such that we balanced the fixed global parameter with the continuously variable local parameters. Thus, we not only pleased the client but also created the maximum freedom of autonomous architectural expression for ourselves.

Programmability

The programmability of building bodies is a prerequisite for implementing continuous variation of building components in the design-to-production process. In the design process, each component needs to be able to be addressed in real time. Basically, within each executable computation process – say in the 3D design software – each command is executed in (almost) real time. But most programmes are closed systems, not open to external information. With the application of the Climbing Wall we opened the design system to external experts producing data that changed the configuration of the design. In a well-defined parametric design system there are billions of possible configurations, and they are all fine, as long as they do not infringe the rules of the design game. As we have seen in the interactive projects Trans-Ports, NSA Muscle, SpaceGraph, Interactive Wall and Emotive Sound Barrier, the external data are imported into the parametric design system in real time. Information keeps flowing in, in well-defined packages of data, and informs the reconfiguration of the now open design system.

Internalising Continuous Variation

From the point of view of the designer, working with the principles of continuous variation means that the designer has to feel as if he or she is a component acting in a dynamic relationship with the immediately neighbouring components. The parametric designer feels and acts like a bird in a flock, playing by the simple rules that he or she has set for himself or herself. The designer internalises continuous variation. The designer develops empathy with the smallest constituent components, yet switches to chopper mode so as to become empathic with the swarm. The scalable empathy of the designer switches with the position of the constituent components in its ecology; the designer's empathy switches from houses to the city, from cars to the highway, from cells to the body, from local to global parameters. The components listen to their neighbours, the swarm listens to its environments. Both the smallest components and their host bodies process incoming data in real time, and convey to their partners in their ecology fresh information to feed upon. Buildings and building components act in their continuously variable actor networks.

Notes

1. Theo van Doesberg, *Manifesto Art Concret*, Paris, 1930.
2. DAF stands for van Doorne's Automobiel Fabriek.
3. Design studio ONL (Oosterhuis–Lénárd) in Rotterdam, founded in 1989, dedicated to the fusion of art and architecture on a digital platform.
4. Nemo later became Virtools, now absorbed by Dassault under the name 3DVia.
5. Ole Bouman (adviser), Bert Bongers, André Houdart, Nathan Lavertue and Richard Porcher.
6. SpaceGraph, PhD research Immediate Architecture, Hyperbody, Christian Friedrich, 2006.
7. Fin Ray® is a registered invention of Festo AG.
8. protoSPACE 4.0 team Hyperbody: Kas Oosterhuis, Gijs Joosen, Chris Kievid, Owen Slootweg, Jelle Feringa in collaboration with master students and Komplot Mechanics, 2010.
9. Kas Oosterhuis, *Towards an Emotive Architecture* (Basel: Birkhäuser, (2002).

CHAPTER 4

Paramateriality: Novel Biodigital Manifolds

Marcos Cruz

Form Follows Material

This chapter is focused on the emergence of a new sense of materiality in which biointegrated design is promoting a technological and aesthetic shift in architecture. It follows on from past research focused on an increasing interdisciplinarity traded between designers, engineers, biologists and artists that has given rise to novel materials, hybrid techniques of production and radically new living forms.[1] In this process, computation is playing a critical role in allowing us to increase the formal precision of design and manufacturing and the customised replication of components, while also making us reconsider the ontological value of 'material' as a central subject area of architecture. As a result of our post-digital condition, we can talk about a novel material-led computation in which the employed fabrication procedures are hybrid, including analogue and digital, conceptual and physical, chemical and biological, as well as natural and synthetic processes. We are today developing a heightened awareness of the physical expression and performance of artefacts, in which form and tectonics do not follow function or programme; instead, form follows material or, in other words, the morphology of components and buildings is essentially the result of the chosen materials and the associated digital design and manufacturing protocols of construction.[2] These allow us to invent forms that have a far higher level of geometric complexity than before and that are potentially infused with biological growth. The use of innovative tools is prompting us to rethink our past with its traditional products and techniques, enabling us to utilise them in an entirely new way. Common materials, such as timber, clay or concrete, are being developed into sophisticated compounds.[3] 3D printing and discrete and non-discrete assembly procedures are also extending the possibilities of current construction. While computation in the twentieth century was primarily explored via surface modelling with rather limited options for realisation, current work is programmed and then physically tested. Multi-material simulations are helping to conceive designs with a control and predictive rigour that is time-based and iterative. We are therefore achieving an unprecedented level of resolution that can be potentially understood as ornamental. Design is becoming more material-deep, and data-heavy computational models are leading directly to the construction of multifunctional prototypes. My argument in this chapter is that new material conditions are challenging established norms and creating what could be argued as the advent of a new paramateriality in architecture.

The prefix 'para' implies here a sense of being alongside, parallel to or beyond the normal repertoire of what we are used to in conventional design. In literature, paramateriality describes a state that is somewhere between the material and the immaterial. It is used in contexts where our imagination is defined via our external senses through quasi-material stimuli.[4] But in architecture the notion of being paramaterial is inherently physical. It refers to materials that are parameter driven and thus infinitely flexible in mixture and form. Paramaterials create a counterpart to parametric methods, the latter being more focused on mathematical systems that are expressed through drawings or animations, while the former centre on chemical and biological systems that are physically built. Paramateriality is ultimately what underlies the advent of biointegrated design (Figure 4.1).

Material Touch

Our society is evolving an increasingly material consciousness that is reflected in how we engage with objects and spaces all around us. We are experiencing a shift from being exclusively driven by vision to being more sensitive to touch.[5] It is now common sense that we are decoding and communicating with our context more and more via haptic interfaces. What is so important about touch is that it is the sense that from our childhood most fundamentally supports us in shaping our memories. It enables us to produce a portfolio of emotions through which we relate to the materiality of nature, people and objects; it produces in us our inner material cognition and intuition. While vision relates more to a sense of distance, touch promotes a sense of proximity and, in some cases, also of intimacy. Our vision is more prone to control or scrutinise our surrounding, whereas touch gets us close to things. If the eye has a seminal role in classifying and hierarchising whatever surrounds us

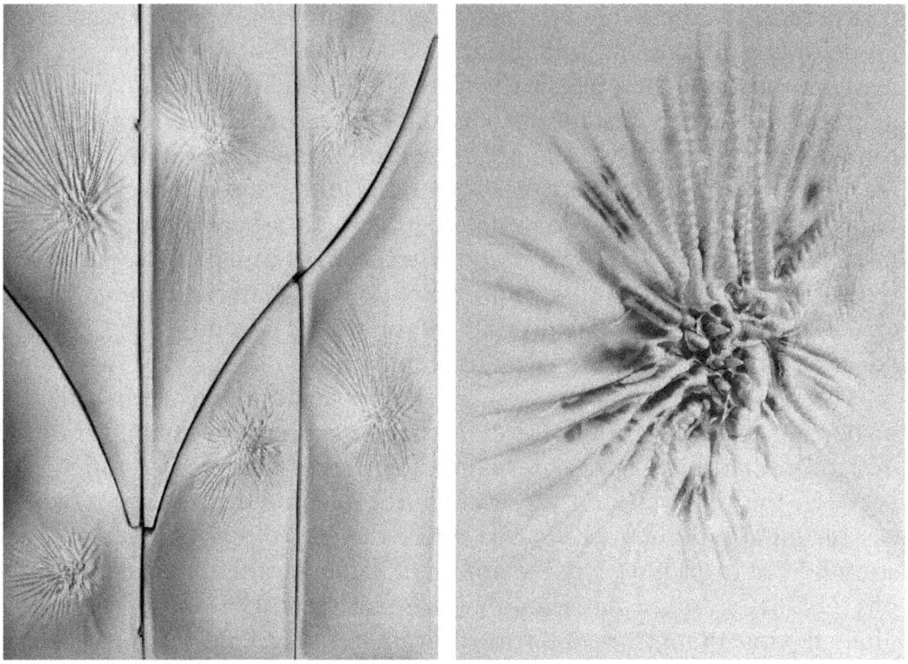

Figure 4.1 C-Biom.A group / Institute of Advanced Architecture of Catalonia (IAAC), responsive manifolds – clay casts able to sense the environment through their microbiome, 2016.
Project: Nina Jotanovic; Supervision: Professor Marcos Cruz; Manufacturing: Ceramica Cumella; Synthetic biology: Núria Conde Pueyo
Photo: Nina Jotanovic

from a distance, touch allows us to experience it close up.[6] This is why new tactile experiences are central to our involvement with the touch-intense environment we nowadays live in.

We are, on the other hand, overcoming aesthetic and moral values that have for a long time classified intellectual, theoretical and spiritual dimensions as being higher than physical and corporeal ones, which were mostly assigned to a lower rank. Matter is here conceptually understood as a culturally constructed phenomenon that changes over time and in different contexts. It is also to some extent existential as it is the result of how we relate ourselves to our own body. For architects, the role of matter is essential and has been interpreted in distinct ways. When associated with traditional materials with clear and orthogonal geometrical forms, it has led to a common and established sense of material order. On the contrary, the use of non-standard substances and textures has often been expressed with an extreme organicity or pliability. This has conveyed a sense of being too 'bodily' and lacking structural vigour and geometric control, reflecting what we have for long repressed – that is, the visceral side of our human anatomy. In our Western history, this ambiguous relationship with the body helps explain why society has had difficulties with accepting what is in essence formless and amorphous. This is particularly meaningful today when the biologicalisation of our world is shifting our attention from the visual attractiveness of outer 'skin' to the tactile and performative complexity of inner 'flesh'.[7] In architecture, new modes of production and advanced computation are defining a renewed sense of expression that goes beyond these past preconceptions. We are enriching the role of concepts (intellectual) with added material values (bodily), and extending our visual perception with haptic experiences, while, at the same time, exploring an unconventional materiality that can eventually be hybridised with nature.[8]

Soft, Porous and Viscous Materials

Our intensified interaction with the built environment is happening via a plethora of gadgets and spaces. From computer touchscreens and scanning devices to novel textiles and composites, we are expanding and diversifying our material cognition as we interface and communicate with our surroundings. In design, a new grammar is being explored and applied in toys, appliances and furniture that is shifting our interest from a hard-edged to a softer-edged materiality. Physical properties that enhance a sense of cuddliness, comfort or pleasure, yet also allow for a more volumetric depth that is lightweight, are qualities that we are privileging. We are also interested in more viscous and liquid conditions through the utilisation of gels, while giving ever more attention to health and environmentally friendly solutions. Looking at Young's Modulus diagrams helps in understanding how our attention has moved from stiffer and less absorbent materials – metals and alloys, a variety of stones and bricks – to explore pliable and/or more porous materials – including polymers, elastomers and cork. Foam composites, in particular, although well known for insulation purposes, are being reconsidered for potential new applications, facilitating constructions that can be easily shaped, as seen in the Algae-Cellunoi by marcosandmarjan. When compared with traditional wood, steel and glass, foams and sponges belong to a completely different genre of substances where mechanical or biological stress (force per unit area) can substantially alter the strain and form of the compound (Figure 4.2).

Figure 4.2 marcosandmarjan, Algae-Cellunoi – wall installation for 9th ARCHILAB 2013 – Naturalizing Architecture, FRAC Centre, Orleans France.
Project: Professor Marcos Cruz, Professor Marjan Colletti with Guan Lee and Richard Beckett; Collaboration: Olivia Pearson, Emu Masuyama, Jessie Lee, Keith McDonald, Jonas Brazys, Cullum Perry; Fabrication: Grymsdyke Farm; DMC London; Algae technology: Marin Sawa with Nixon Group and Hellgardt Group (Imperial College); Richard Beckett (UCL); Sponsors: Bartlett School of Architecture; Grymsdyke Farm; Innsbruck University
Photo: François Lauginie

Performative Materials

Architects nowadays are undoubtedly more reliant on having a higher understanding of materials than before, as this allows them to take full advantage while digitally fabricating them. At a time when in theory any substance can be engineered, the ability to characterise it in more detail potentiates the relationship between form and matter, and, in this way, enhances efficiency and aesthetics in new ways. Like chemists, contemporary designers need high-end knowledge in material science to explore the ultra-high performativity of compounds and their resistance to compression, their ductility and their longevity. In addition the identification of pH level, pore size and/or choice of aggregates determines the hydrophilic level of components, which will in turn regulate the level of biocolonisation that is to be avoided or encouraged on buildings. Moreover, the combination of different properties can then lead to a multifunctional materiality that is particularly important in bioreceptive design, where water is selectively concentrated in areas via capillary action within the same volumetric entity.

Beyond traditional applications, materials are also being considered as able to become living entities in their own right, capable of breathing and sweating. Designers are aiming to fully programme them so that they can transform and be truly responsive to the environment. Such conditions need to be manipulated on nano- and microscopic scales. But recently we have also gained more awareness about the role of controlling surface morphologies on larger scales as they affect overall building performance. In bioreceptive façades, for example, it is vital to consider how their geometric variation can augment or diminish the irrigation, absorption and retention of moisture, and consequently inhibit or enhance biological growth. However, this intermediate scale is not only functional; it is where materiality can be experienced on a 1:1 scale. The three-dimensional patterns of the surface and the textural language can acquire great ornamental expression. When zooming out further, the overall contour then starts to delineate the form and dimension of the entire construct; the broader architectural and climatic contextualisation defines parameters that influence the definition of materials on smaller scales.

We are facing here a multiscalar approach in which both top-down and bottom-up processes are complementary, and designs are being tested on a scale where one affects the other and vice versa.[9] This methodological reciprocity is vital for what Neri Oxman describes as 'functionally graded materials' where composites are determined via chemical and morphological manipulations. With advanced robotics, different areas of the same mass can be simultaneously extruded with distinct mixtures creating an anisotropic materiality (Figure 4.3).[10]

Composite Materials

Companies and research institutes are testing and design-engineering a range of innovative solutions. In architecture schools, research platforms such as the BiotA Lab at the Bartlett in London and the C-Biom.A group at the IAAC in Barcelona, as well as the Mediated Matter Research Group at the MIT, are exploring new material designs through prototyping and applied construction. These experiments are leading to what one could define as a new composite materiality with variable gradients of matter and structure. Not surprisingly, a growing trend is focused on

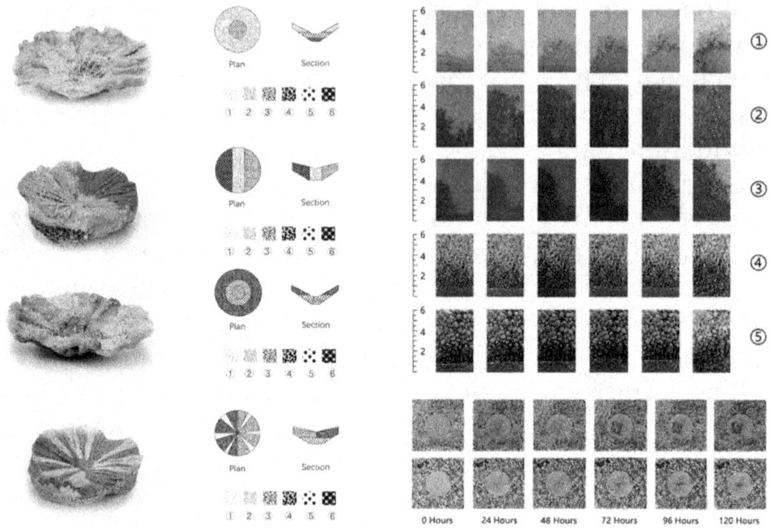

Figure 4.3 BiotA Lab / Bartlett School of Architecture UCL, selective evaporative studies of magnesium phosphate concrete, 2016
Project team: Yuxin Jiang, Xinhe Lin, Zhili Wang, Qungyue Zeng; Supervision: Professor Marcos Cruz, Richard Beckett, Dr Chris Leung, Javier Ruiz; Technical supervision: Dr Sandra Manso
Photo: Qungyue Zeng

exploring natural materials that are widely available, in order to preserve those of which sources are scarce. Ceramics and terracottas, for example, are very accessible, easy to mould and can be recycled. Corn-based fusions, along with cellulose and biopolymer mixtures, are also being created and applied through 3D printing. Moreover, a variety of hydrogels are being studied to allow for more ecological solutions where algae and other microorganisms can proliferate according to the level of humidity in the air. On the other hand, cementitious materials are of huge importance as they include different types of cements, Portland concrete being the most widely used construction material on earth. But concrete is unsustainable, and so there is a need for alternative solutions. Coconut fibre, as a waste product, is being proposed to reinforce the structural integrity of concrete. Cactus mucilage mortar reinterprets traditional construction techniques in places such as Mexico, while new forms of claycrete mixes for lightweight components offer more earth-bound, affordable yet hardy solutions. There is research being done on sulphur-based cement that is seen as a possible substitute for concrete due to its structural efficiency, yet establishes an unusually acidic environment that in turn offers the conditions for specific plants to grow.

Most important is the renewed interest in magnesium phosphate concrete (MPC), which is currently being tested to create bioreceptive conditions that stimulate algae, mosses and lichens to thrive on façades without the need for additional irrigation or maintenance.[11] This material is also being tested in combination with cork aggregates with the aim of developing thermal and acoustic features that are simultaneously lighter and more sustainable.[12] Even though the pathway from academic experimentation to commercial production can be slow and difficult, some experimental products have found their way on to the market. Myco-boards and foams are being produced with mycelium as a new organic binder that creates very effective insulation.[13] Furthermore, a new type of biologically grown bricks is being developed. Instead of having to be fired, these bricks use biocement in which bacteria are induced to grow sand aggregates together through microbial-induced calcite precipitation (Figure 4.4).[14]

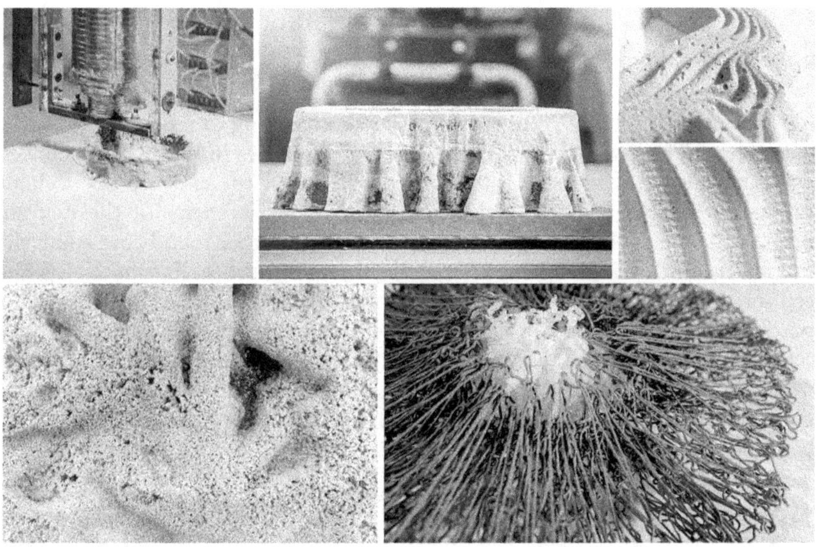

Figure 4.4 C-Biom.A group/IAAC – BiotA Lab/Bartlett UCL, material research, 2015–16. Upper row (left): In:Sand:Out – robotic printing with sulphur concrete. Project: Kunaljit Singh Chadha; Supervision: Professor Marcos Cruz
Upper row (right): Design for ageing building – cactus mucilage mortar casts. Project: Yessica Mendez; Supervision: Prof Marcos Cruz
Lower row (left): Pervious branching – moss seeding on bioreceptive brick. Project: Chang Lui, Zhixiong Yang, Chae Ah Ahn; Supervision: Professor Marcos Cruz, Richard Beckett, Javier Ruiz
Lower row (right): Filatures – prototype of façade screen with mycelium growth. Project: You Han Hu, Cheng-Hsiang Lew, Yuan Jiang, Xia Chen Wei; Supervision: Professor Marcos Cruz, Richard Beckett, Javier Ruiz

Bioreceptive Design

Currently perhaps the most fundamental change we are witnessing is the emergence of materials that are conceived as hosts for nature to grow on. Research projects in the BiotA Lab are showing that the fabricated matter of building components performs as mini-scaffolds for microorganisms and cryptogams to proliferate on. Scaffolding, originally an architectural term understood in the construction industry, has been integrated into the medical sciences, where work has focused on creating biological substitutes that restore, replace or regenerate damaged tissue on small-scale structures. The concept of these bioscaffolds has now been reintroduced in design and architecture, where the use of CNC and robotic technologies has allowed for an extreme filigree to stimulate organisms to intermingle with the building surface. The use of such bioscaffolds is creating a bioreceptivity that is self-regulated, dynamic and ever changing according to the vicissitudes of speciation, climate and scale. Like the performativity of materials, scaffolds also need to be discussed at different scales. As stated in bioreceptive design:

> for architecture, bioscaffolds can be designed according to the notion of scalar hierarchies. The lower level is defined by the properties of the material chosen, which should have a degree of porosity but not at the expense of mechanical strength. The medium level describes how the geometry of the material property space of the larger level volume is filled. Rather than being solid, this internal geometry is designed as spatial lattices as such to facilitate tissue or cell integration upon seeding. Typically this means that a level of cellular or porous structure exists that allows for the movement of water, nutrients, and cells throughout the volume. The larger level defines the overall geometry of the object in its final form. Providing a structural framework on which cells can grow, this allows a predetermined geometry to be achieved which may or may not be typical in nature.[15]

Today we know that all external surfaces will be biocolonised at some point in time, and that they will consequently go through a process of ageing that does not imply decay or ruin. It is merely a stage in which materials become 'naturalised' due to their inherent micro-capacity to serve as scaffolds for vegetative growth. It is therefore vital to handle materials as templates in a permanent ageing process.[16] This is not only a process focused on measuring physical fatigue, but one in which nature and the built environment evolve into a unified whole. One could argue that this is architecture's path towards becoming a built ecology.[17] Designing for ageing buildings implies a change from architecture being exclusively centred on structure and space (both physical and social) to embrace an entirely new biological and environmental agenda. For that, bioscaffolding provides an essential infrastructure that allows bioreceptivity to be an accepted part of buildings. This defines what one could call a new bioreceptive materiality that integrates an ever-changing biota that flourishes in, on and around buildings. The common purpose of making objects and spaces appear eternally new and clean doesn't make sense any more, and is shifting in favour of an impure and evolving growth aesthetic[18] in which bioreceptivity is seen as a protective rather than a destructive process for architecture.[19]

To help understand bioreceptive design, it is worth pointing out that our traditional understanding of skin as flat and superficial is limiting and in fact does not apply. As one of architecture's most fundamental metaphors, we have for long considered the building skin as an epidermal condition that reflects our own skin, which has prompted us to pursue the ideal of pure and uniform geometry.[20] For bioreceptive design, however, the concept of a bark is more appropriate.[21] Skin is an envelope that stands for an idea of defence and control of a climatically controlled interior whose privacy is vulnerable to external threats. In contrast, the architectural bark implies a more three-dimensional substratum that is geometrically varied. It is associated with the plant world and represents the roughness of an exfoliating crust. The bark works as a protection, but also as a receptacle that attracts and hosts an ever-changing ecology of bacteria, plants and fauna that constantly adjust to climatic changes, in itself creating an additional protective layer. The variability of vertical to horizontal patterns, for instance, influences the speed of water drained off or retained on the surface to eventually be absorbed into the material. The bark is a thicker and more complex skin-flesh. It is a biointegrated condition where the external inhabitability develops in the immediacy of interior dwelling (Figure 4.5).

Fabricated and Grown Materiality

Bioreceptive design entails a highly elaborated fabrication process that results from progressive high-definition simulations being directly translated into physical prototypes. This increases their environmental performativity and allows for complex geometries to be manufactured.

Figure 4.5 BiotA Lab / Bartlett School of Architecture UCL, bioreceptive façade panels, 2016. Funded project: Robotic seeding of bioreceptive materials; Project team: Professor Marcos Cruz, Richard Beckett, Dr Sandra Manso, Dr Chris Leung, Bill Watts; Sponsor: Engineering and Physical Sciences Research Council UK; Industrial Partner: Laing O'Rourke

Photo: Paul Smoothy

But there is no specific preference as to which type of computational technique or procedure to use and apply. In fact, many fabricated components rely on a combination of systems that are both additive and subtractive; they follow the protocols of cutting and milling, extrusion and infusion, in an often-recursive way in order to acquire full precision of components. This new fabricated materiality for architecture not only describes a finished, physical state; it is rather a 'medium' that is process-driven and in flux, and the product of endless testing.[22] There is simply no predefined design that can dictate in totality the materiality of the objects and components a priori. Bioreceptivity requires a work methodology in which design and fabrication are fundamentally entangled with the ontology of place and climate, and is therefore critical for the expression and performance of architectural construction from the bottom-up. While CNC cutting techniques – laser and plasma cutting, for example – can break through any stiffness, the use of CNC milling privileges softer conditions where shapes are subtracted from the overall tectonic mass. 3D printing, robotic extrusions and voxel jetting, on the other hand, work as additive systems, implying materials that are viscous and/or liquid in their state of being shaped into their final form. With water, glues, nylons or other polymer binders, these projections or extrusions can only be achieved with mixtures that develop from being initially soft to gradually stiffen over adjustable time exposures.

While natural materials are restricted by what can be extracted from nature, and traditional human-made compounds are engineered to become mostly uniform and reproducible products, bioreceptive paramaterials are defined by processes in which hybrid fabrication techniques allow for chemical, mechanical and morphological variability. Key questions in the construction industry that drive their development are: How can solids be solidified in new ways? How sustainable is their production? What multifunctional properties can these new solids have? One aim is certainly to offer a gradient for seamless transitions between what is naturally grown and artificially made. An important attempt has been made in the Algae-Cellunoi wall by marcosandmarjan, where the surface morphology created an intensified geometric progression from components to algae receptors. Another aim is to produce novel compounds that are internally and externally imbued with cellular tissue. In this context, it is interesting to explore biomineralisation processes that occur in nature, where living organisms produce minerals that gradually stiffen existing tissue or geological aggregates. While today our main construction materials – concrete, bricks, metal and glass – are unsustainable due to the high emissions of carbon during their production – through firing, melting, blowing and burning – biomineralised aggregates are grown and compacted over time. These bio-geological sedimentations, being corals, pearls or other more earth-bound formations, offer a great alternative to conventional, heat-dependent production techniques.

However, notwithstanding the advanced state of contemporary techniques, we still have a long way to go until we achieve a full biomineralisation that is cost effective and structurally controllable. On the other hand, innovations in medicine are worth looking at, most specifically in surgery where cutting-edge systems are implemented when operating on living matter. The incorporation of technologically sophisticated equipment and the use of bioelectronics in the human body are taking our understanding of materiality to a radically new level. Rather than a medium, our body is becoming an interface between hard and soft, natural and artificial, and the inner and outer world of the human anatomy. Robotic operation procedures, as well as the insertion of an increasingly sophisticated apparatus into our bodies, establishes a mutually supportive system between our genetically constructed tissue and human-made devices that are becoming ever more seamless and grown into a whole. In architecture, such an advanced state of minimally invasive operations and the use of biomaterials are challenging us to imagine the future state of our practice. As argued in the context of neoplasmatic design, certain architects will become 'designer surgeons' who will have the knowledge and skills to conceive a new type of grown materiality. Beyond current fabrication and construction methods, such multidisciplinary practitioners will be able to operate and grow the new architectural flesh of our buildings.[23]

Inlucent Materiality

The aesthetic consequences of such processes result from the depth of perception and embedded tissue that occurs within the same body mass. It suggests a very different concept when compared with traditional materials where the state of opacity and transparency, so important for the modernists, describes a sense of uniformity and light that is able to pass through it. Even when translucent – a term more associated with postmodern culture – the prefix 'trans' still denotes a state of transience of light through a material that tends to be only skin-deep and made of a single substance. The incorporated matter in the body involves cellular tissue that is thick, viscid and gooey; hence the notion of traditional layered construction in architecture does not apply. In our human body, biological tissue is more of an embedded amalgam of cellular growth. Light does not transit through but gets trapped, creating what the cultural historian Steve Connor described as a 'transubstance',[24] or what could be described as the 'inlucent' materiality of embedded or incorporated matter.[25] This aesthetic is already having its effects in emerging algae-impregnated hydrogel prints produced in the BiotA Lab, and will certainly be important for work that is considered biointegrated and living architecture (Figure 4.6).

Figure 4.6 BiotA Lab / Bartlett School of Architecture UCL, inlucent hydrogel 3D prints with embedded algae, 2016. Project team: Julie Hagopian, Sanika Mohite, HQ Qian Huang, Valery Xinyi Zhou; Supervision: Profesor Marcos Cruz, Richard Beckett, Dr Chris Leung, Javier Ruiz; Technical supervision: Dr Brenda Parker, Dr Chris Leung

Photo: Julie Hagopian

From the Representation of Nature to Nature as a Model

Before exploring the hypothesis of a grown architecture further, it is worth making a historic detour to explore the relationship between biology and design, which has in the past been very different from today. Since early times, nature motifs have been illustrated on building façades, for example. These have included plants, animals and humans that were represented as part of complex narratives. Different eras idealised nature in distinct manners, the strongest manifestation being reached in the late Baroque and Rococo periods, when an unprecedented juxtaposition and repetition of figural ornaments and biological patterns clad entire walls. It is perhaps in late nineteenth-century European Art Nouveau that buildings articulated the most exuberant side of nature, with highly curvilinear, warped, convoluted and entangled geometries, as seen in Victor Horta's and Antoni Gaudí's architecture. Simultaneously in America, Louis Sullivan expressed the splendour of a quasi proto-parametric logic of biological motifs with three-dimensional and highly tectonic ornamentations. In all these cases nature was fetishised following symbolic, allegorical and pictorial motivations.

A few decades later a different understanding emerged that looked at nature as a model. The legacy of D'Arcy Thompson's *On Growth and Form* and the use of concrete and steel structures laid the basis for unprecedented spatial complexity.[26] Following a nature-inspired approach, architects and engineers such as Eero Saarinen, Frei Otto, Pier Luigi Nervi, Felix Candella, Eduardo Torroja and Eladio Dieste, among many others, analysed highly curvilinear forms, extrapolating the physics of animal and plant anatomy to that of buildings and infrastructures. This defined a structural biomimesis that, although still present, has gradually shifted today to a more environmentally led biomimicry in design.

Integrated Nature and Nature as Programmable Matter

What explains this shift is the way in which we gradually got used to understanding nature differently from before. With ornamentation extensively erased from architecture, and urban contexts becoming increasingly overcrowded in the early twentieth century, nature stopped being illustrated as a model, but was perceived as an ecological counterpoint to our polluted urban life. A gradual awareness of nature's fundamental role as environmental regulator took place. Early planners acknowledged this role by enlarging nature's presence in newly conceived garden cities. Modernist architects followed these examples and proposed a zoning strategy in which the height and density of buildings as free-standing objects were increased in order to free horizontal green space on the ground. As shown in Le Corbusier's famous *Plan voisin* and the view from one of the high-rise tower balconies, nature was rather like a painting to be contemplated from a distance. The landscape was to be looked at through the framed 'eyes' of the architecture. But driven by the aesthetics of cleanliness and purity, with empty space and air considered a sterile medium, the modernists somehow continued to idealise nature. Although their aim was to create a sense of harmony, they, nonetheless, considered architecture and biology two entirely separate fields.

Not everybody applied this separation and detachment strictly though. Perhaps driven by the beauty and lushness of sub-tropical and tropical vegetation, which was indeed less controllable, modernists in South America thought differently. As seen in the paradigmatic case of Niemeyer's house in Rio de Janeiro, they let nature be integrated into buildings. Also in North America, Bruce Goff and later John Lautner followed this trend by transgressing rocks and vegetation from the outside to the inside of their houses. By integrating the surrounding gardens, they proposed a biological and geological transgression that created a seamless transition between hard exteriors and soft interiors, exploring a sense of 'wildlife' within the 'ordered' geometry of domestic life. These projects became precursors of more recent projects where the biocolonisation of façades and roofs turned nature into an integral part of buildings. Interesting examples include the Town Hall in Fukuoka by Emilio Ambasz and the Sportplaza Mercator in Amsterdam by Venhoeven CS, as well as the marcosandmarjan Chong Qing Nan Lu towers in Taipei. Green walls have also been applied in interior spaces all over; however, they have proven to be expensive and unsustainable. Additionally, aquatic algae has been integrated in façades, such as the BIQ algae-house in Hamburg, with the aim of producing biomass, yet still with limited results in terms of profitability and the need for complex maintenance. More experimentally, the Alga(e)zebo pavilion of marcosandmarjan has integrated nature on three different scales, while the Silk Pavilion by Neri Oxman has attempted to incorporate nature as an active constructor.

William Katavolos put forward a more radical vision in the post-war period when he illustrated in *Organics and Evolutionary Architecture* how a chair, an edifice and even a whole city could be grown from a genetically engineered seed. Along the same lines, John Johansen created the idea of *Nanoarchitecture*, in which the molecular engineered house was conceived as a pre-programmed structure that felt like an inhabitable tree. For him, the molecular building process was mechanical rather than biological. With synthetic materials, living cells were scripted to replicate and be assembled by nanobots, without employing any hard structures and construction techniques. Peter Cook followed a similar line with his Veg-House project, exploring the idea of a hybridisation between architecture and nature through time. His project suggested a series of new domestic appliances and spaces that became

Figure 4.7 marcosandmarjan, Alga(e)zebo – Wonder Installation for the London Olympics, 2012. Design team: Professor Marcos Cruz, Professor Marjan Colletti; Manufacturing: Formstaal / CSI, Stralsund Germany; Engineering: Bollinger, Grohmann und Schneider, Vienna Austria; Photobioreactors: Richard Beckett / DMC London with UCL Algae (Dr Saul Purton, Marco Lizzul, Lamya A Haj, Laura Stoffels, Joanna Szaub; Joanne Field at the Culture Collection of Algae and Protozoa, Scottish Marine Institute)
Photo: Virgilio Ferreira

part-object and part-vegetation. The programmable materiality implicit in these projects and the overtly organic aesthetic of the work, different from nature-applied or nature-inspired, entailed a total hybridisation of nature and design that is ultimately neoplasmatic (Figure 4.7).

Biointegrated Materiality: Biology as Design Medium

In this context, *Neoplasmatic Design*[27] and *BioDesign*[28] were two key publications that catalogued numerous art and architecture projects that employed biological matter as a new design medium. The selection of work demonstrated how material experiments, installations and prototypes required new work settings that go beyond traditional studios, implying new modes of production. Such projects outline a new methodological and aesthetic dimension in which today's *avant-garde* is being developed within the confines of medical and biotechnological laboratories. Advances in synthetic biology and biochemical engineering are enabling designers to create work with an entirely new definition. They are putting forward a biointegration of bacteria and plants in surfaces, creating what one could define as a new biological materiality of the built environment. But rather than what Oron Catts and Ionat Zurr once termed as semi-living, these projects are in fact biointegrated living composites.[29] They are synthetically made and infused with biological matter, creating an alternative understanding to what we have been traditionally used to. The ever-dynamic dimension of vegetative growth means that such materiality is in constant change without necessarily becoming stable. Echoing the complexion of a tree bark, biointegrated materials are intermingled with nature, defining a slow-motion activity that is in continual adjustment and adaptation to the environment.

Extreme Environments

So far, I have argued that the production of innovative materials and manufacturing techniques has triggered the emergence of a new sense of materiality that is computationally driven. A new emphasis has been given to novel composites that are soft, porous and viscous, while having multi-performance features that are aimed at being environmentally friendly and sustainable. I have stated that new compounds are being fabricated with enhanced bioreceptive features, triggering a paradigm shift in design that is becoming more permeated with nature, aesthetically inlucent and geometrically complex. These changes are creating biodigital manifolds with a new biointegrated materiality.

Probably the most significant factor to consider is the impact of the context in which any project is located. With climatic changes happening in an increasingly unpredictable way, nature and architecture have to find ways to adjust to the radical settings that are unfolding. In fact nature has for long adapted to extreme environments, with species developing extraordinary characteristics when living in highly acidic or alkaline, or extreme thermal, saline, aerobic or anaerobic conditions, or when exposed to light or hydric stress, as well as pollution and radioactivity, just to mention a few. We can find in these extreme surroundings vital information about how mesophiles have developed into extremophiles over millennia, and have found alternative mechanisms to live and reproduce and thus proliferate in milieus that are removed from more moderate environments. These observations were key for Henk Jonkers's bio-concrete, in which extremophiles were inserted in the material with the capacity to thrive in such an alkaline medium in order to self-heal cracks.[30] In the future more and more of such radical forms of life will give us clues and solutions for new designs.

Paramaterial Topologies: Perpendicular Surface Morphologies

When compared with traditional materials that are conceived to be uniform and usually flat in their surface morphology, new paramaterial composites are sophisticated agglomerates that are digitally driven and engineered with multiple capabilities. They are drawn to have a geometric depth, scale and topological variance. But topology does not mean here what early digital thinkers defined as a surface modulation that was highly curvilinear, but conceptually flat and in fact little three-dimensional. Paramaterial topologies suggest a different type of geometry, one that goes beyond the Euclidean logic of points, lines and planes. The topologies of biointegrated designs are closer to infinitely dense point clouds. They are scripted through the coding of agent-based systems that generate a correlation of dots, paths and nodes that outline different behavioural rules. Paramaterial topologies are developed from inside out and follow a bottom-up approach that is stigmergic and evolutionary. New digital simulations are able to calculate and delineate ever-shifting flows and networks of particles that create complex matrices that in their liminal-edge condition define a highly articulate sense of surface. When considering that any material, being flat or texturised, is three-dimensional when analysed and viewed from a micro perspective, this is even more significant. Biointegrated designs are changing our notion of topology from being a curvilinear unity to becoming an infinite array of perpendicularly aligned branched or cellular surface morphologies. The intensity of particles or terminals describes the level of permeability of the surface; highly dense systems create a visual continuum, while scattered arrangements demarcate voids that are perceived as openings in the surface (Figure 4.8).

Towards a Paramateriality

In this chapter I have tried to demonstrate that beyond our common means there is a new sense of materiality emerging that is driven by engineered composites that use advanced computational tools to define both design and fabrication. Perhaps more than being new and a replacement of what we are used to in common buildings, this is creating a parallel line of physical expression that supplements and extends our material cognition. Derived from the concept of 'lateral thinking' as an alternative method to find creative solutions, one could argue that there is a lateral materiality emerging here that is highly inventive and

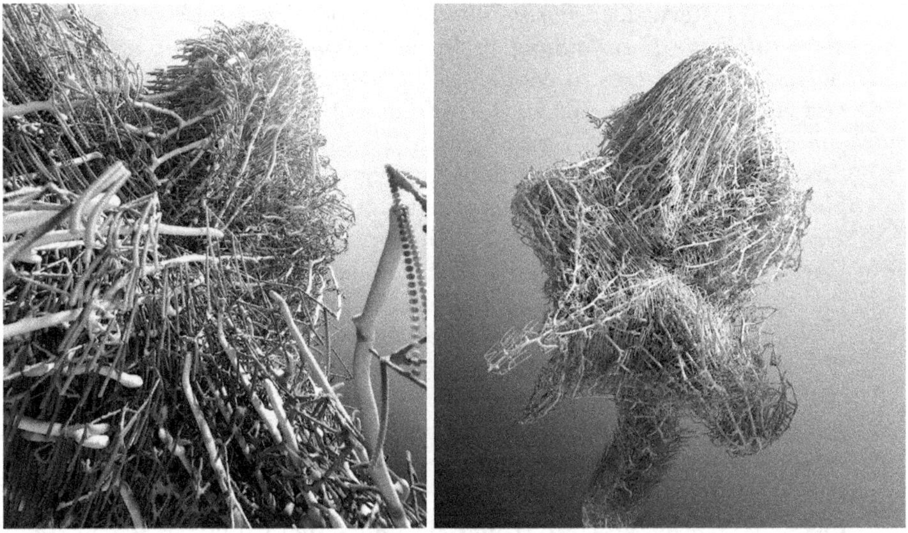

Figure 4.8 Unit 20 / Bartlett School of Architecture UCL, growth simulations with Houdini, 2016. Project: Chris Falla; Supervision: Professor Marcos Cruz, Professor Marjan Colletti

that is opening innovative paths towards a more hybrid, ecological and biointegrated future.[31] Novel biodigital manifolds perform beyond and above the conventional. They create a growing synthesis between the natural and the artificial and outline architecture's path towards a new paramateriality in design.

Notes

1. Marcos Cruz, *The Inhabitable Flesh of Architecture*, Part I (Farnham: Ashgate, 2013), p. 7.
2. 'Form follows material' creates a counterpoint to other similar expressions, including the famous modernist statement 'form follows function' (Louis H. Sullivan, 'The Tall Office Building Artistically Considered', *Lippincott's Magazine*, March 1896, p. 407); 'form follows libido' (Sylvia Lavin, *Form Follows Libido – Architecture and Richard Neutra in a Psychoanalytic Culture*, Cambridge, MA: MIT Press, 2007); 'form follows form' (Matt Bohm, Robert Stone and Robert Nagel, 'Form Follows Form: Is a New Paradigm Needed?', *Digital Collection – The American Society of Mechanical Engineers*, November 2009); 'form follows fun' (Bruce Peter, *Form Follows Fun: Modernism and Modernity in British Pleasure Architecture 1925–1940*, Kindle Edition, 2013); 'form follows nature'

(Rudolf Finsterwalder, *Form Follows Nature: Eine Geschichte der Natur als Modell für Formfindung in Ingenieurbau, Architektur und Kunst / A History of Nature as Model for Design in Engineering, Architecture and Art*, Birkhäuser, 2015); 'form follows flow' (Laia Mogas Soldevila, Jorge Duro Roya and Neri Oxman, 'Form Follows Flow: A Material-driven Computational Workflow for Digital Fabrication of Large-Scale Hierarchically Structured Objects', *ACADIA – Computational Ecologies: Design in the Anthropocene*, 2015); 'form follows feeling' (Terrence M. Curry, 'Form Follows Feeling – The Acquisition of Design Expertise and the Function of Aesthetics in the Design Process', *Architecture and the Built Environment*, June 2017); 'form follows technology' (Ian Adamson, 'Form Follows Technology', *Payette* website (online), June 2016).

3. Note that the term 'compound' is different from composite, the latter referring to engineered materials produced from multiple constituents with clearly differentiated physical or chemical characteristics that stay distinct when merged together. Compounds, on the contrary, are bonded together, creating an entirely new substance that cannot be disintegrated or decomposed.
4. See Zachary Fisher, '"Such shaping fantasies": Shakespeare's Paramaterial Phantasy Literature', http://senseshaper.com (last accessed 17 May 2017).
5. Numerous writings have focused on the contemporary importance of touch, including Constance Classen (ed.), *The Book of Touch* (Oxford: Berg, 2005); Steven Connor, *The Book of Skin* (London: Reaktion, 2004); Claudia Benthien, *Skin. On the Cultural Border between Self and the World* (New York: Columbia University Press, 2002); Juhani Pallasmaa, *The Eyes of the Skin. Architecture and the Senses* (London: Academy Editions, 1996).
6. For more, see Cruz, *The Inhabitable Flesh of Architecture*, p. 27.
7. The term 'biologicalisation of our world' was originally used in Marcos Cruz and Steve Pike, 'Neoplasmatic Design: Design Experimentation with Bio-architectural Composites – Introduction', *Architectural Design – Neoplasmatic Design*, 78.6 (2008), p. 8.
8. Ibid., pp. 4–5.
9. This multi-scalar approach reflects the micro-meso-macro scale relationship discussed in Marcos Cruz and Richard Beckett, 'Bioreceptive Design: A Novel Approach Towards Biodigital Materiality', *Architectural Research Quarterly*, 20.1 (2016), pp. 51–64.
10. See Neri Oxman's definition of functionally graded materials, and her differentiation regarding functionally gradient geometrical, structural and material anisotropy. N. Oxman, 'Programming Matter', *Architectural Design – Material Computation: Higher Integration in Morphogenetic Design*, 82.2 (2012), pp. 93–4.
11. 'Computational Seeding of Bioreceptive Materials' is an EPSRC-funded project developed by the BiotA Lab multidisciplinary team (Marcos Cruz

(PI), Richard Beckett, Sandra Manso, Chris Leung, Bill Watts and Javier Ruiz, with Industrial Partner Laing O'Rourke) at the Bartlett UCL.

12. This research is being developed by Marcos Cruz and Amorim Cork Composites, Portugal.
13. See http://www.ecovativedesign.com (last accessed 20 October 2016).
14. See http://biomason.com (last accessed 20 October 2016).
15. Cruz and Beckett, 'Bioreceptive Design', p. 58.
16. The idea of 'material as template' is derived from the article by Neri Oxman, 'Templating Design for Biology and Biology for Design', *Architectural Design – Material Synthesis: Fusing the Physical and the Computational*, 85.5 (2015), p. 102.
17. This concept was first explored by the author in a TEDx talk entitled 'Architecture's Path Towards Ecology' given at University College London on 3 June 2012.
18. The idea of an impure aesthetic goes back to the author's investigations into the abject and disgust in design. For more, see Cruz, *The Inhabitable Flesh of Architecture*, pp. 41–66. The concept of impurity was also used in relation to the emergence of bioreceptive design. See Cruz and Beckett, 'Bioreceptive Design', pp. 52–3.
19. There are numerous studies that investigate the protective role of plant growth on building facades. Two key articles are Nick A. Cutler, Heather A. Viles, Samin Ahmad, Stephen McCabe and Bernard J. Smith, 'Algal "Greening" and the Conservation of Stone Heritage Structures', *Science of the Total Environment*, 442 (2013), pp. 152–64; Heather Viles, 'Greening Stone Conservation: Exploring the Protective Role of Plants and Microbes', in *12th International Congress on the Deterioration and Conservation of Stone* (New York: Columbia University Press, 2012).
20. The notion of skin described here is a bourgeois understanding that still prevails today. For more on the bourgeois body and skin, see the introduction and 'Part I – Disgusting Flesh' in Cruz, *The Inhabitable Flesh of Architecture*.
21. The idea of an architectural bark has been described in Cruz and Beckett, 'Bioreceptive Design', pp. 51–2.
22. This expression is extrapolated from Adrian Forty's description of 'concrete as medium' when he argues that 'concrete can be more accurately described as a process than as a material'. See Adrian Forty, *Concrete and Culture* (London: Reaktion, 2012), pp. 10, 44.
23. For more, see Marcos Cruz, 'Designer Surgeons', *Architectural Design – Neoplasmatic Design*, 78.6 (2008), pp. 46–51.
24. Connor, *The Book of Skin*, p. 226.
25. See 'Part III – Synthetic Neoplasms', in Cruz, *The Inhabitable Flesh of Architecture*.
26. D'Arcy Wentworth Thompson, *On Growth and Form* (Cambridge: Cambridge University Press, 1992 [1917]).

27. See *Architectural Design – Neoplasmatic Design*, 78.6 (2008), special issue.
28. William Myers, *BioDesign: Nature, Science, Creativity* (London: Thames and Hudson, 2012).
29. See Oron Catts and Ionat Zurr, 'Growing Semi-Living Structures: Concepts and Practices for the Use of Tissue Technologies for Non-Medical Purposes', *Architectural Design – Neoplasmatic Design*, 78.6 (2008), pp. 30–5.
30. http://www.citg.tudelft.nl/en/research/projects/self-healing-concrete/ (last accessed 20 October 2016).
31. I am here following my previous argument about lateral design and extrapolating to that of a new lateral materiality. For more, see Marcos Cruz, 'Lateral Design', in *Archithese – Universitäre Räume / Space and Pedagogy* (Zurich: Verlag Niggli, 2010), pp. 60–5.

CHAPTER 5

A Vital, Architectural Materialism: A House-person's Escape from the Anthropocentric

Pia Ednie-Brown

Rumbling and Tangling

> Teresa was born of the rumbling in a stomach.[1]

Quoting this line from Milan Kundera to describe the genesis of a character, Jane Bennett begins her book *The Enchantment of Modern Life* with the idea that 'a discomforting affect is often what initiates a story, a claim, a thesis'.[2] Similarly, Avery Green, as an architectural character and 'house-person', was born through the rumblings of unease about some persistent architectural habits and assumptions, and of a hunger for something else.

Avery Green is part of a larger project that pursues an architectural movement away from anthropocentrism – aiming to dislodge the human as the centre or ultimate reference point of concerns. Here, I am specifically seeking to develop an architectural approach to 'vital materialism', as described by Jane Bennett in her book *Vibrant Matter*. This approach builds on Bennett's brave suggestion that:

> Maybe it is worth running the risks associated with anthropomorphising (superstition, the divinisation of nature, romanticism) because it, oddly enough, works against anthropo*centrism*: a chord is struck between person and thing, and I am no longer outside a nonhuman 'environment'.[3]

The primary task of this essay, then, is to explore how one might approach anthropomorphising without falling into its indisputable dangers. Another way of thinking about the value of anthropomorphising is that as the 'chord is struck between person and thing', we enter an arena of 'mutual inclusion'. This is where the work of Brian

Figure 5.1 Avery Green from the front and back after 2015–16 alterations.
Photo: Lucas Allen

Massumi becomes key, as another who has tackled problems of both anthropocentrism and anthropomorphism head on.[4] Through his exploration of play and animals he assembles the concept of mutual inclusion, as a 'reciprocal imbrication of differences'.[5] His intricate, radically empiricist thinking provides a sympathetic counterpoint to the melody of Bennett's often more tangibly intimate observations. Massumi's work is also relevant here for his attention to processes of architectural production, which help move Bennett's vital materialism towards architecture. I draw on thinkers who share Massumi's philosophical lineage – such as Henri Bergson, Alfred North Whitehead and Charles Peirce. The developmental psychologist Daniel Stern becomes another important shared point of reference.

The pursuit of an architectural escape from the anthropocentric might seem a near impossibility: buildings are perhaps 'unnatural' environments that seem inseparable from humans, being more 'culture' than 'nature' – architectural history could be seen as a physical prescience of the Anthropocene. However, architecture can be understood differently if seen primarily through and with assemblages of forces – where the 'human' as a force becomes part of a tangled ecology, rather than its only impulse. This ecology might not even involve any humans, as suggested by studies of the architecture of animals and geology.[6] But most importantly here, can we recalibrate our sense of buildings as things beyond the human, even when they involve us?

Avery Green became a companion with which to explore this question; with whom I acted, thought and recalibrated my actions and thinking. As with all companions, a complex, tangled interdependency is gathered. This tangling becomes an important aspect of a vital, architectural materialism, where agency is set loose in a manner that does not allow it to exclusively stick to anything. As Massumi has pointed out 'The transindividuality of the process of vital becoming complicates the question of agency . . . no efficient cause can be isolated behind the movement of experience's self-surpassing'.[7] Bennett concurs with an image of the bicycle rider through which the vital-materialist-architect might begin to think of their role:

> Agency is, I believe, distributed across a mosaic, but it is also possible to say something about the kind of striving that may be exercised by a human within the assemblage. This exertion is perhaps best understood on the model of riding a bicycle on a gravel road. One can throw one's weight this way or that, inflect the bike in one direction or towards one trajectory of motion. But the rider is but one actant operative in the moving whole.[8]

Avery Green's process of alteration involved a similar kind of assemblage of forces where I was in the midst of a qualitative bundle of forceful relations – riding my architect-builder bike. Within this complex of forces something called a 'personality' of the house came to be better understood. This was not a personality that was simply there to be 'uncovered', but a complex qualitative impetus or force-field of the house that was being perpetually made, generated and discovered at the same time, as all personalities are.

Avery Green[9]

> So many people are shut up tight inside themselves like boxes, yet they would open up, unfolding quite wonderfully, if only you were interested in them.[10]

Like all houses, Avery Green is unlike any other house.

Typologically speaking, she would be categorised as a Victorian terrace: a corridor-based plan links rooms along a linear sequence; her long, narrow figure; her high, plastered ceilings adorned with ceiling roses and ornamental cornices; her high timber sash windows and timber floors. These are all familiar architectural refrains that locate her in the Victorian genre, so well-known and understood, particularly in the Australian state called 'Victoria'. Clearly, however, a house exceeds typology, as a human person exceeds the generic features of a human body. This excess becomes evident, for instance, in the degree to which her Victorian-ness has been mongrelised. Built in 1900, she had a face-lift in the 1950s, in which her high-fronted, ornamented Victorian painted façade was toppled and replaced by a shorter, patterned-brick, wide-windowed approach to the street. Some late Art Deco features and fixtures were introduced. A rounded, colonial porch stands in place of her previous, gently curved front verandah. Her neighbours to the west – built to the same plan, form and detailing – offer evidence of what she once was, and just how much she has changed.

Along her east party wall she was once attached to a twin, but this was demolished in the 1980s to make way for a medium-density

Figure 5.2 Avery Green's kitchen clock, 2016. Typography design by Trampoline/ Sean Hogan.
Photo: Pia Ednie-Brown

housing development such that a small, apartment-sized house clings to the side of Avery Green, like a child of the 1980S hanging on to a historical grandparent. An amalgam of period homes spanning the decades from the late 1800s onwards spread out around her. Picket fences are everywhere. Villages of clustering shops, trams, trains, churches and schools connect and modulate the quilted carpet of picketed residential lots into which she is patched. Ever larger, new apartment buildings are currently creeping across her local landscape in an efflorescent drive towards densification.

There is nothing clearly remarkable about the house or her milieu – just like most people you see walking down the street. Yet, like all people, she is full of secrets and surprises.

Avery Green's recent transformation meant heaving her physical, material actuality through a significant process of change. The construction process transformed us both, albeit differently. She has both physically and qualitatively altered. For myself as designer, builder, previous inhabitant and 'client' – thereby becoming intricately involved in multiple ways – I experienced unfamiliar forms of encounter and learnt how to stretch forms of attention. If one understands intimacy, as I do, as shared transformation, one could say that Avery Green and I have had an intimate relationship that developed over a decade.

Avery was also the house with which I finished writing my doctorate in 2006, becoming a wordless partner of a developing research trajectory. It was at that time that I began to understand creative projects as very much like living creatures – things I had responsibility towards but which were never utterly in my control: 'They provided legs with which vaguely forming ideas could learn to walk and take unplanned excursions to return with unexpected surprises.' Through that doctoral research process, I came to appreciate 'how much we are guided by the things we set out to guide',[11] and how this appreciation becomes an important ingredient that shifts designing into design research. In order for this to happen, however, you need to apprehend creative projects as much more than simply an extension of one's authorial intentions. A creative project may well be inseparable from you, like your child, but it is also distinguishable from you, finding its own forcefulness, even as agency picks itself up and moves beyond any single entity and into the whole field of the creative event. Avery Green took this to another level.

Ultimately, this might be seen as a story about how the personal is ironically but inextricably involved in cultivating attention to, as Bennett puts it, 'the impersonal life that surrounds and infuses us',[12] in order to 'generate a subtler awareness of the complicated web of dissonant connections between bodies'.[13]

Vitality Forms: An Anthropomorphic Manner

> preservation of a type of value in a sequence of change is a form of emphasis. A unity of style amid a flux of detail adds to the importance of the various details and illustrates the intrinsic value of that style which elicits such emphasis from the details. The confusion of variety is transformed into the coordinated unity of a dominant character . . . *Personality is the extreme example of the sustained realization of a type of value.*[14]

Movements acting to unsettle anthropocentrism appear to be gaining ground, such that attention is opening up to the activity, lively presence and self-sovereignty of nonhuman and 'inanimate' things. The 2015 legal battle seeking to attribute personhood to Leo and Hercules, two chimpanzees held as experimental subjects at Stony Brook University, is one among many examples of agitation for the recognition of nonhuman animal rights and self-sovereignty. In 2017 the Whanganui River in New Zealand was recognised as a person under the law. In 2014 Te Urewera, a New Zealand national park, ceased to be Crown land or a National Park, becoming 'a legal entity' with 'all the rights, powers, duties, and liabilities of a legal person'.[15] As the Minister for Maori Affairs, Dr Pita Sharples, summarised: 'The settlement is a profound alternative to the human presumption of sovereignty over the natural world.'[16]

A person is not always human, but it is also notable that many humans were not always considered to be persons – slaves, women and children have historically not had legal personhood, for instance. If we now consider this past to be abhorrent, my provocation here is that there are ethical reasons for taking this shift even further in reconsidering the status of buildings in a related way – towards an architectural, vital materialism. Buildings are generally considered to be property, like wives used to be. In a time when a house is increasingly considered to be an investment more than a home, other forms of value might productively assert themselves if we recalibrated our relationship with our dwellings.

I have often nevertheless worried that the act of engaging with a house as a person might be going a step too far, tripping into a clunky territory in which a 'house' takes form as human-like – similar to dressing up a dog in a skirt. Increasingly, this called me to carefully assemble some tactical guidance. This assembling begins with Bennett's cascaded examples seeking to unpack anthropomorphising as an everyday tactic:

> One might allow oneself, as did Charles Darwin, to anthropomorphize, to relax into resemblances discerned across ontological divides: you (mis)take the wind outside at night for your father's wheezy breathing in the next room; you get up too fast and see stars; a plastic topographical map reminds you of the veins on the back of your hand; the rhythm of the cicadas reminds you of the wailing of an infant; the falling stone seems to express a conative desire to persevere.[17]

Her examples anthropomorphise through discerning shared patterns in what she refers to as 'the outside-that-is-inside-too'[18] – moments and textures are felt both inside us and elsewhere. These patterns are connective, eliciting an attention to transversal movements in which we find ourselves non-hierarchically implicated, evoking a feeling of being part of the life of the world and it being part of us – as one pattern resonates with another. This seems to be precisely where vitality elusively and ontogenetically exists: *in the resonant co-incidence of emergent patterns*, amplifying one another in a manner that can both snowball into intensities, and pitter patter away back into whispers.

For a *vital* materialism, an attention to these somewhat abstract and emergent connections is significant in avoiding the risk of unwittingly diminishing vitality by always folding back into human (and ultimately anthropocentric) forms. However, as Bennett admits, it can be 'hard to keep focused on. It is too close and too fugitive, as much wind as thing, impetus as entity, a movement always on the way to becoming otherwise . . .'[19] The vitality of matter is wild, always slipping beyond language and our efforts of attention. My hunch has been that this problem of elusiveness could be mitigated through nestling these fugitive connectivities inside an accompanying attention – to personality and the person. This hunch was encouraged by Alfred North Whitehead who suggested that 'The survival of personal identity within the immediacy of a present occasion is a most remarkable character of the World of Fact. It is a partial negation of its transitory character. It is the introduction of stability by the influence of value.'[20] Furthermore, as Charles Peirce suggests, the presence of a person can motivate a powerful sense of care: 'Love is not directed to abstractions but to persons . . . Suppose, for example, that I have an idea that interests me. It is my creation. It is my creature . . . it is a little person. I love it . . .'[21] As discussed, 'person' and 'human' are not synonymous – and to recognise the personality of something appears as a powerful act of post-anthropocentric anthropomorphising. While my imaginings of Avery were always playing on the cusp of snapping her into a human-like person, I have come to believe that playing along this cusp is unavoidable. In edging along such a cusp, a step over the edge can be discerned through a feeling of disjunction, via a slightly forced assimilation.

The problem is related to recognising differences across the nature of metaphors. Brian Massumi warns that 'When a metaphorical reading begins, it is a sure sign that the process has stopped. It has been taken up by or flipped over into an entirely different process, one based on formal assimilation rather than formative differentiation.'[22] It is possible that Bennett's 'resemblances across ontological divides' might be mistaken for these process-stopping metaphors, which is clearly not what she is looking for, nor what her suggestive text conveys.

So a question arises: what characterises the making of resemblances that cross an ontological divide *without* halting the connective, generative vitality of this crossing? Massumi tells of when, after a public presentation in the late 1990s in which he discussed Greg Lynn's blob-like architectural formations, a literary critic in the audience spoke up: 'In a tone that announced that the coming comment would trump the entire presentation, he pronounced: "But of course, they're breasts."'[23] The reductive simplification of Lynn's early process experiments to a piece of female anatomy offers us a good illustration of anthropocentric metaphorical work, and an example of related traps scattered everywhere as we explore the power of anthropomorphising. Massumi uses this example to unpack the difference between a metaphorical process and a generative, topological process in which 'the starting point is force, rather than form'.[24] He juxtaposes the breast example with the idea that Lynn's buildings might be 'bud-like'. As he says, 'Metaphors happen' but 'It is less that buildings are budlike than that the processes from which both buds and buildings grow proceeds adventitiously, in like *manner*.'[25]

What matters is the 'in like *manner*': the degree to which the resemblance takes a dynamic form that moves across complexes of senses, rather than an act of stuffing something into a box (or breast shape) that seems like a fitting form. Manner is a behavioural refrain; the way in which a movement or a process happens. So, if a building is a person, or person-like, what matters is the way in which buildings become eventfully present in the manner of a person. It's less about how they *are*, but *how* they 'happen' – their vital becomings are the arena of mutual inclusion. Becoming is always on the edge of becoming otherwise. A fruitful way to start approaching this processual edge is to think in terms of *amodal perceptions*, which have been explored in depth by Daniel Stern, who describes them as 'not sights and sounds and touches and nameable objects, but rather shapes, intensities, and temporal patterns – the more "global" qualities of experience'.[26]

Attention to manner – and ultimately to persons – might be cultivated through an awareness of amodal perception: a qualitative sense of the happenings-going-on that are not encapsulated by any one sensory mode. It involves a coinciding of the manner of things that are less resemblances than *semblances*.[27] Stern describes the experience of such an amodally derived integration as a 'primitive form of *dejà-vu* event':

> at a pre-verbal level (outside of awareness) the experience of finding a cross-modal match (especially for the first time) would feel like a correspondence or imbuing of present experience with something prior or familiar . . . It is likely that in this domain of emergent experience there is also the experience of a premonition of a hidden future in the process of revealing a structure that can only be sensed opaquely.[28]

Amodal perception elicits an expanded present – a present-ness in which the past and future are actively folding – or budding. The familiar becomes uncanny, running temporally wild. Perhaps one could say that while that literary critic might feel a satisfying sense of discovery as he maps the form of breasts on to the forms of digital blobs, Massumi's philosophical explorations with Lynn's architectural experiments involved feeling out a cross-modal match between the blobs-in-action and the budding-going-on inside the thinking through of certain philosophical adventures. Or, more accurately, Massumi might insist, he was feeling this out amodally – 'the perceptual feeling of their co-occurring, is itself, strictly speaking, in *no mode*. It is the direct perception of what happens between the senses, in no one mode'.[29]

Amodal perceptions – these 'global' qualities of experience – operate through action-assemblages that Stern went on to call *vitality forms*.[30] He points out that anger, for instance, can have different vitality forms, in that it can 'explode', 'ooze out', 'sneak up', or be 'cold'.[31] However, none of these four vitality forms *belong* to anger, just as budding does not belong to Lynn's blobs – rather, they are part of a *manner* that blobs or bodies might act out. Vitality forms are intrinsically shared existential properties that cross ontological divides. Their vitality pulsates in their *wildness*, in their tendency to always exceed and escape absolute capture. However, while vitality forms may be unmoored and not owned, they are inseparable from and attain tone and complexion through the particularities of their manifestation. Their wildness is not exactly tamed by the uniqueness of their movement in the particular situation, event, material, medium, but it is modulated and tempered by what I will go on to discuss as a 'personality signature'.

Wildness: Cracking and Growling

> there is a world of things out there – rocks and trees and stones and grass and all the other things that crawl and run and fly. They are things in themselves, but we make them sensible by giving them meanings that shore up our own views of the world. In my time with Mabel I've learned how you feel more human once you've known, even in your imagination, what it's like to be not. And I have learned, too, the danger that comes in mistaking the wildness we give a thing for the wildness that animates it.[32]

In the weeks prior to construction work beginning, I picked up a book called *H is for Hawk by* Helen Macdonald. After a quick peruse I was excited. It resonated – Helen Macdonald's relationship with a hawk called Mabel was somehow, I was sure, like my relationship with the house. *H is for Hawk is for House*. Putting aside her academic job, Macdonald's grief-elicited training adventure with Mabel led to an unusual kind of book – partly historical biography, partly nature writing, part autobiographical memoir. Silly as this may sound, I wondered if we were related in some distant way – having the same surname as the maternal side of my family: Macdonald with the 'ac' and small 'd' (spelling of particular significance to the family line). This book immediately felt like a companion. The read didn't disappoint. Disarmingly candid, poetic and often grippingly suspenseful, from the end of the first chapter onwards I was hooked – scribbling down quotes and notes, soaking up the story as if it was an uncanny echo from the future of the adventure I was about to have – a stretched out feeling of déjà vu.

This resonance helped me, in a loosely isomorphic manner, to feel the house as a creature with whom my relationship was developing – curiously – and in a way that would not neatly map on to human–animal relationships. Nevertheless, one passage about Macdonald's relationship with Mabel the hawk resonated:

> I love Mabel, but what passes between us is not human. There is a kind of coldness that allows interrogators to put cloth over the mouths of men and pour water into their lungs, and lets them believe this is not torture.[33]

Like Mabel, Avery was cold. I recall someone walking in the front door out of the scorching heat one summer's day and commenting on how good the air conditioning was. There was no air conditioning. Avery was always a cold house, and this meant that in summer she was bliss and in winter she was hard to warm. There wasn't much heating and in winter we shivered. Avery has bluestone foundations and double brick walls – the bricks being made from dense, finely grained, red clay – most likely dug out from the Northcote Brickworks clay pit operating at the turn of the century, now a park that is a ten-minute walk away. She is quite literally of the earth on which she stands. She was old – both in built years and in substance. It felt like her age was a deep brick well that sucked the heat of the moment into an unreachable clay pit from which she had arisen. This was not the same kind of coldness of the torturer that Macdonald found in Mabel, this was the coldness of a different kind of unreachability or distance – one that plummets first into the depth of time, and into a different kind of time altogether.

Of course, extended heat waves elicit a kind of tipping point, where Avery's physical substance flips its attention away from the geological towards the atmospheric. Once warmed up, she holds that warmth for days, even as it cools down outside. The event of her flipping towards an atmospheric attention stays with her like the lingering of fresh memories. Her relative slowness to absorb, hold and emit energy is part of her very particular durational rhythms and relations.

It is certainly in her own time that she is always moving and cracking. The summary statement from the geologist's soil report, done in 2015, states that: 'The volcanic origin and depth of Clay indicates a high soil reactivity and seasonal heave potential.' The plastered brick walls and lath-and-plaster ceilings slowly growl and chatter about these heavings through the fine (and not-so-fine) cracks that are always on the move, opening themselves up to new conversations with the air, its dust, light, temperature and humidity changes, and insects.

Her cracks are not just part of her ageing, they open up to and through those forces that stir deep in the clay like ancient, pre-verbal memories erupting to remind the present of its past, while opening up to the future. The cracks call for attention. The Victorian ceiling roses and ornamental cornices sat like dry, crinkled frosting over this registration of deep geological time. The ceiling in the living space of Avery Green felt like a geological formation in itself. Far from flat, it had been cracked and distorted into tectonic plates pushing into one another. On two occasions sections of the ceiling fell in – revealing itself to be a thick layer of heavy, almost concrete-like substance stuck over old timber battens. The ceiling had become a kind of volatile landscape that occasionally erupted.

What could be said to be similar about the coldness in Avery and Mabel is in relation to what we call 'wildness' – the untamed or undomesticated actions of the world that are beyond attempts at capture

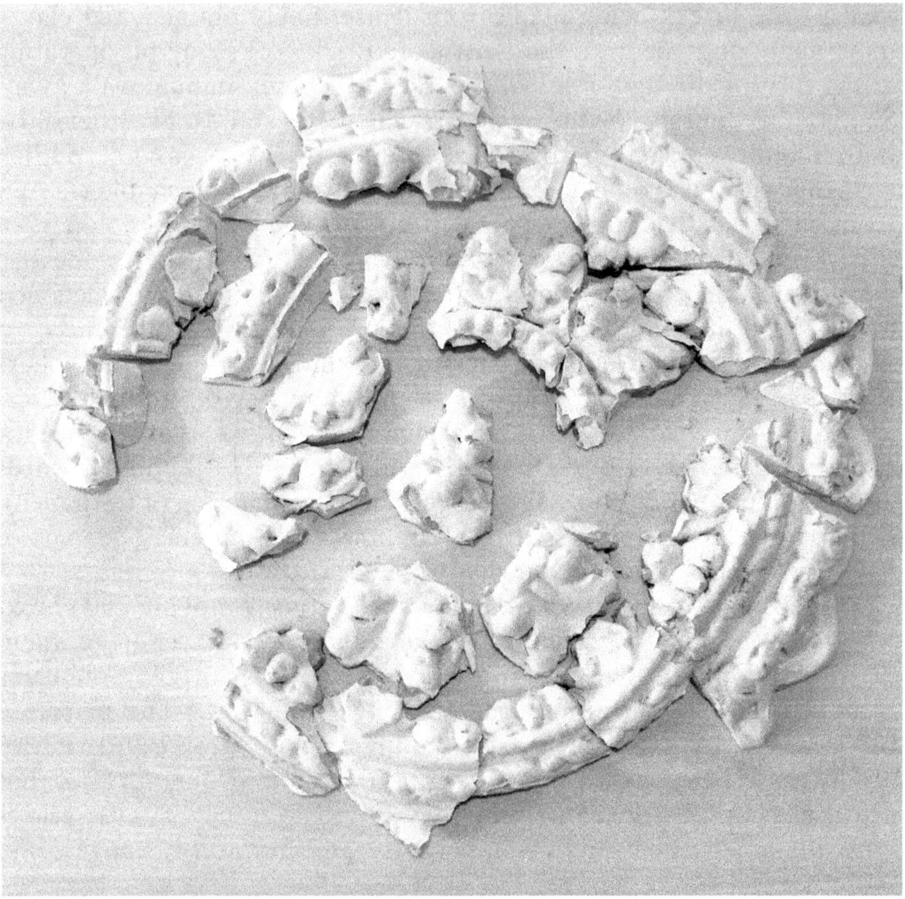

Figure 5.3 Fallen Rose – remnants of Victorian ceiling rose after new ceiling installed, 2016.
Photo: Pia Ednie-Brown

and control. Her wildness became the important fugitivity to keep an eye on – despite and because of the degree to which it escaped me, for this is where vitality forms scamper across ontological divides. There is perhaps nothing tamer than a constructed, domestic environment, and yet these everyday companions offer vitality through an intimate access to an 'outside' that creeps about everything folding into our domestic interiors. Like her landscape-ceiling cracking with the slow growlings of a wilderness, her personality revealed itself gradually and in draughty, wind-like whispers.

The Forces of Personality: Affect Attunement and Person–Time Entanglement

> [T]he World of Change develops Enduring Personal Identity as its effective aspect for the realisation of value. Apart from some mode of personality there is trivialisation of value.[34]

How, then, might one approach and work with nonhuman personality? As we move vitality forms into one of the problems this chapter tackles – that is, how to usher an anthropomorphic impetus in the direction of a vital (post-anthropocentric) becoming – the issue of relationship and *working with* becomes significant. This raises the issue of affect attunement – a concept at the heart of Stern's work – which involves entering into a rhythm or 'movement shape' with something. It is not about copying, but embodying a rhythm or pattern by transforming it into another form of expression:

> Affect attunement, then, is the performance of behaviours that express the quality of feeling of a shared affect state without imitating the exact behavioural expression of the inner state . . . true imitation does not permit the partners to refer to the internal state. It maintains the focus of attention upon the forms of the external behaviours. Attunement behaviours . . . recast the event and shift the focus of attention to what is behind the behaviour, to the quality of the feeling that is being shared . . . Imitation renders form, attunement renders feeling.[35]

These attunement behaviours occur through vitality forms, which are modulated and altered through and with the specificity of their recasting. This might be in a coinciding pattern across the seen and the heard, or it might be an infectious leap from one person's gesture to another's, where an act of attunement doesn't exactly copy, but enters into and recasts via a 'personality signature'. The variation and idiosyncrasy of the recasting is important, being linked to a sense of authenticity in the action. In contrast to attunement, very close imitation will often seem a little robotic or inauthentic, possibly becoming more of a joke or those comic imitation routines often in the service of ridicule – somewhat like the literary theorist's metaphorical breasts.

Allowing myself to anthropomorphise with Avery, or any other building, can be productively approached through a process of attunement with abstract, global qualities that we might both be able to enter into, albeit in different ways, through a personality signature – an idiosyncratic embodiment of 'what is behind the behaviour'. For a human, the anthropomorphic becomes indispensable, being our only 'way in'. I cannot *not* be human. Buildings, on the other hand, are perhaps unavoidably 'archimorphic'. Tapping into and attuning with qualities crossing house and human are clearly very hard to undertake in explicit forms, however, because we are temporally out-of-sync, and vitality forms are temporal entities. Human-time is not the same as house-time. However, could we both inhabit, together, a 'person-time'?

In his 1914 Gifford lectures, Henri Bergson addressed 'The Problem of Personality' which he 'regarded as the central problem of philosophy'.[36] This importance of this problem, he explains, is that philosophy always aims to unify the multiplicities of the world into coherent principles and ideas in which it is difficult to find 'a place for personality, that is to say, of admitting real individualities possessing an affective independence, each of which would constitute a little world in the bosom of the great world'.[37]

We find ourselves once again facing the image of breasts – in this case as a cleavage in which personality as a 'little world' is nestled in the bosomy 'great world'. Working contrary to the systematicity of scientific method in which the person and the personal are absorbed 'in the ALL', Bergson's lecture asserts the force of personality as an active, affective, durational, complex, singular yet multiplicitous, qualitatively defined form of unity. This form of unity can nestle in a cleavage in which unification and multiplicity coincide – amodally. Erik Bordeleau argues that for Bergson:

> the person is essentially a matter of *temporal contraction*. The person as temporal contraction or duration doesn't necessarily involve a sense of intentionality or humanness. It sometimes simply suggests the 'truly primitive and immediately given' dimension of an experience, its implicit wholeness as it precedes any philosophical explication.[38]

Vitality forms and amodal perceptions could surely count as the '"truly primitive and immediately given" dimensions of experience'. Between house-time and human-time, person-time appears as a temporal contraction – not of the whole world but of the vitality-forming-worlding of the person into a complex manner; a contraction that is simultaneously an expansion, like a highly complex form of déjà vu. The movements of Avery Green the house – as with all the activities and qualities that are born of relations in which she is involved – are her worlding. This would include her material substance and its relations with heat/cold and other energy-based movements such as interactions with light, her stories or histories (geological, industrial, cultural, architectural, and so on), her potential futures, her shifting milieu. If, as Jane Jacobs once wrote, 'And what is a habitat? It's an intricate, complicated web of interdependencies',[39] then doesn't this also go some way towards defining a person?

Is it possible to think about personality as a *very complex* vitality form? Stern has discussed amodal perceptions as integral to the experience of what he calls the *emerging sense of self*: a mode of experience that dominates for the newborn child but remains alive throughout life as 'the ultimate reservoir that can be dipped into for all creative experience'.[40] If amodality lies at the basis of the experience of emerging organisation – or the sense of an emerging self – then vitality forms and affect attunement could be seen as the building blocks of personality. If so, then working with the personality of a house as more-than-its-form takes us back to Massumi's differentiation between generative, topological process in architecture and the making of metaphors where 'the starting point is force, rather than form'. Here, however, is a design process driven by *forces of personality*.

'The house the vortex built' had been the name of a paper I thought might emerge well before construction work on Avery Green commenced. The maelstrom of making did not feel as 'neat' as a vortex might imply, but the force of a complex, elusive form seems an accurately vague way of describing it. This force could be understood as an emerging force of personality, drawing on Peirce's notion that

> personality is some kind of coordination or connection of ideas [. . .] This personality, like any general idea, is not a thing to be apprehended in an instant. It has to be lived in time; nor can any finite time embrace it in all its fullness. Yet in each infinitesimal interval it is present and living, though specially coloured by the immediate feelings of that moment.[41]

Personality lives in infinitesimal, temporal intervals and in the fullness of an expanded duration: it contracts and expands. This is part of another problem with personality: it escapes us. Our own personality, let alone that of another, is always beyond us and in the midst of others. The force of personality is both an expression of vitality and a productive problem because it remains wild – as soon as it becomes tamed into, say, a 'subject', personality fades. Avery, it becomes clear, could never simply be either an object or a 'research subject' separate from its researcher, but rather is an entangled complex of forces.

Play

> The mode of abstraction produced in play does not respect the law of the excluded middle. Its logic is that of mutual inclusion.[42]

During the six years I lived in the house, doing anything about her cracking ceiling and crumbling, rotting kitchen and bathroom seemed beyond me. There were minor changes: the interior was painted, family flew interstate like angels and did more painting, cleaning and nailing of plywood over rotting floorboards; I sanded down old timber left in the backyard to make long, chunky shelves in the kitchen; a makeshift aluminium towel rail was constructed in the bathroom; rotting masonite was removed from the shower and replaced with off-the-shelf plastic lining; a low shelf by the toilet was inserted to cover over the rotten timber from which mould spores had spat across the cracked white tiles. But beyond these small moves, she surrounded me with hugeness and heaviness, with an apparent resistance to movement, other than a thinly veiled, ongoing and gradual decay.

I drew ideas for altering the house for many years – eight years in fact – largely on yellow tracing paper. Stacks of torn-edged, diaphanous, yellow leaves marked with graphite thoughts bear witness to the many potential excursions this house travelled in my imagination. This process of imagining was full of its own potent playfulness that mostly occurred privately, but did fold out into the public space of an exhibition during one period of its trajectory.[43] It wasn't until some time after moving out, and away from her immediate presence, that I overcame inertia and shifted the gears of imagination into physical action.

The work began with demolishing a decrepit kitchen and bathroom. For about three weeks I slowly demolished the interior alone, with my new steel-capped boots, heavily gloved hands and a crowbar in the dead of winter, while waiting for the final building permit to be signed off. Moving from the idealised, glassy, swimmable space of drawing into the resistant stubbornness of the physical was almost shocking. Walls don't actually move at the click of a mouse. I thought I knew that, but I knew inertia better. However, once the dismantling was in swing – once I was inside the effort – those weeks were filled with a sense of plasticity – a feeling of heightened, breathless transformation.

Pulling off the back of the house – opening walls, heaving cabinets out of their places (the nails that held them in place hanging off them like the roots of weeds), levering cladding off in heavy, dusty, flaking chunks – her spatial condition became as elastic as putty, something like the disorienting zoomability in Rhino software, but with weight

Figure 5.4 After the timber kitchen and bathroom had been removed the underfloor area was full of broken bricks of the same red clay as the old house structure.
Photo: Pia Ednie-Brown

and physical force. She transformed daily – vistas opened up and pockets of space that were previously secrets to one another became suddenly, sometimes violently connected. The south-facing window of the old brick house had been tussled into a dank corner – the kitchen wall had run over and hidden the end of its stone ledge, and then a rude asbestos alcove stuck out – blocking what a window can do well: provide a view. As the barriers between that window and the world started to open up through demolition, it was liberating, as if the window was waking up, becoming free of a cage.

There was a strange and highly affecting wildness to this experience – where things seem to be running their own relational course. Each move shifted the whole of the relations, and the entire assemblage heaved and swaggered as it recalibrated with each shift – as each piece of timber came away, everything changed. This was also true, albeit largely more slowly, as the new pieces came together. Avery and I swam a turbulent sea of relations, both together and very differently. One could say that we *played*.

It would be easy to say that this resonance of a shared transformational disequilibrium was not at all 'shared', but rather entirely projected by myself, on to a house. That would be the usual story. Let me tell another story – as briefly as I can – about how a form of multiplicitous unity (a personality) evolved through play. Remember the volatile ceiling that occasionally erupted? Through a process of installing a new, safe and flat ceiling, an old ceiling rose had to be destroyed, triggering an exploration of how we might replace the lost rose with two new ones, one for each of the two parts of the living space. After an extended design process involving many dead-ends, coupled with a gradually amplifying idea of the ceiling as a form of landscape (via a series of detail decisions that emerged during the construction process), I sourced a mountain form, and with my assistants[44] developed a version of it with a crater. This took me back to the soil report, and the previously curious statement of the 'volcanic origin of the clay'. At the time of receiving that report I was fixated on the 'high soil reactivity and seasonal heave potential' aspect of the sentence, given the implications this had on footing depth, viable modes of construction, and the cost implications. But with footings all in place, the emergence of a volcano-like crater led me to look deeper into the geological history of the region, to discover the degree to which Avery Green both sat on and is constructed with clay of volcanic origin. The cracking brick walls, by then mostly plastered over, opened up as significant in new ways. The mountainous and volcanic ceiling 'rose' congealed into what came to be called 'Over-the-top-terrain'. Her 'heave potential' had flowered into something like an efflorescent 'déjà-vu event' – where the past, the present and the future folded into a complex, multidimensional vitality form that contracted and expanded through geological time, material behaviour and house-time. This folding movement linked the present and deep past of the soil and the bricks, the cracking walls and ceilings, the new ceiling figures, the curiosity and design instincts of myself and the assistants, 'simple' physical behaviour and formal representations, among other things – into a complex flowering of personality. Whitehead might see this as a series of events through which 'The confusion of variety is transformed into the coordinated unity of a dominant character. . .'[45] The manner of her presence deepened just as it became expressed.

There is much more to tell – of the picket proliferation, of the discovery of pencil drawings by an 11-year-old girl on hidden studwork from 1955, the backyard relics, of the outside-in, downside-up twisted eruption of the Victorian greenhouse into Avery's flowering future, of

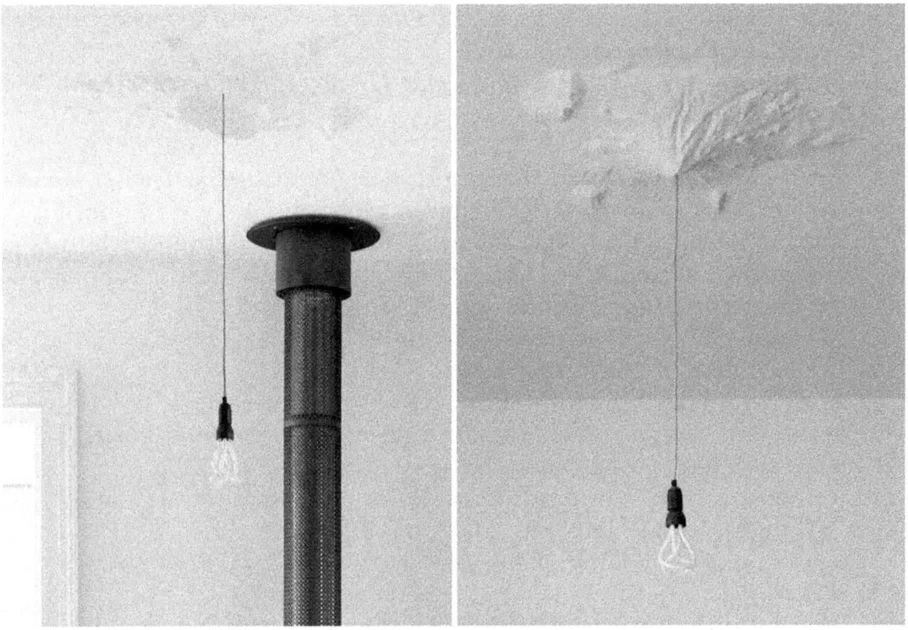

Figure 5.5 'Over-the-top-terrain' – mountain and crater ceiling rose replacements in the living room spaces, 2016.
Photo: Lucas Allen

her building-garden-clothing wrapped around her brick mass, of her emergent jewellery.

By thinking things as persons, we may manage to usher their activity to attention, and to tentatively generate new forms of value. In allowing oneself to anthropomorphise, one needs to be careful to not trip from attention to 'in-like-manner' into pre-given form, tumbling into applied metaphors like falling for a ready-made pair of breasts. Rather, it requires a finger on the amodal pulse: remaining sensitive to complex, abstract, dynamic forms of activity that are at once unified and multiplicitous, expanding and contracting. Together, in our mutual difference, we imbricate as persons.

Notes

1. Milan Kundera, *The Unbearable Lightness of Being* (New York: Harper and Row, 1984), p. 39.
2. Jane Bennett, *The Enchantment of Modern Life: Attachments, Crossings and Ethics* (Princeton: Princeton University Press, 2001), p. 3.

3. Jane Bennett, *Vibrant Matter: A Political Ecology of Things* (Durham, NC: Duke University Press, 2010), p. 120.
4. Brian Massumi, *What Animals Teach Us About Politics* (Durham, NC: Duke University Press, 2014), pp. 50–4.
5. Ibid., p. 7.
6. Attention to nonhuman architecture can be found in Mike Hensel, *Animal Architecture* (Oxford: Oxford University Press, 2005); Karl von Frisch, *Animal Architecture* (New York: Harcourt Brace Jovanovich, 1974); James R. Gould and Carol Grant Gould, *Animal Architects: Building and the Evolution of Intelligence* (New York: Basic Books, 2007).
7. Massumi, *What Animals Teach Us About Politics*, pp. 40–1.
8. Bennett, *Vibrant Matter*, p. 38.
9. Avery Green has her own website: www.averygreen.org.
10. Sylvia Plath, *Johnny Panic and the Bible of Dreams: Short Stories, Prose, and Diary Excerpts* (London: HarperCollins, 1979), p. 292.
11. Pia Ednie-Brown, 'The Aesthetics of Emergence, Architecture and Design', PhD thesis, RMIT University, 2007, p. 18.
12. Bennett, *Vibrant Matter*, p. 4.
13. Ibid.
14. Alfred North Whitehead, *The Philosophy of Alfred North Whitehead*, ed. Paul Arthur Schilpp, The Library of Living Philosophers (New York: Tudor Publishing Company, 1951), p. 690 (my emphasis).
15. Available at http://maorilawreview.co.nz/2014/10/tuhoe-crown-settlement-te-urewera-act-2014/ (last accessed 25 September 2016).
16. Ibid.
17. Bennett, *Vibrant Matter*, p. 120.
18. Ibid.
19. Ibid., p. 119.
20. Whitehead, *The Philosophy of Alfred North Whitehead*, p. 689.
21. Charles S. Peirce, *Philosophical Writings of Peirce*, ed. Justus Buchler (New York: Dover Publications, 2011 [1955]), pp. 362–3.
22. Brian Massumi, *Architectures of the Unforeseen*, forthcoming.
23. Ibid.
24. Ibid.
25. Ibid.
26. Daniel Stern, *The Interpersonal World of the Infant* (New York: W.W. Norton, 2000 [1985]), p. 51.
27. See Massumi's extended work on this difference, where amodality and the work of Daniel Stern is discussed quite extensively, in *Semblance and Event: Activist Philosophy and the Occurrent Arts* (Cambridge, MA: MIT Press, 2011).
28. Stern, *The Interpersonal World of the Infant*, pp. 52–3.
29. Massumi, *Semblance and Event*, p. 110.
30. Daniel Stern, *Forms of Vitality: Exploring Dynamic Experience in Psychology and the Arts* (Oxford: Oxford University Press, 2010).

31. Ibid., p. 28.
32. Helen Macdonald, *H is for Hawk* (New York: Grove Press, 2014), p. 275.
33. Ibid., p. 223.
34. Whitehead, *The Philosophy of Alfred North Whitehead*, p. 693.
35. Stern, *The Interpersonal World of the Infant*, p. 142.
36. Henri Bergson, *The Problem of Personality* (1914), http://members3.jcom.home.ne.jp/yoshihara.jya/the_problem_of_personality_1-3.htm (last accessed 25 September 2016).
37. Bergson, *The Problem of Personality*.
38. Erik Bordeleau, 'Immediation, Bergson and the Problem of Personality', in Erin Manning, Anna Munster and Bodil Marie Stavning Thomsen (eds), *Immediations* (Ann Arbor: Open Humanities Press, forthcoming 2018).
39. Jane Jacobs, *The Nature of Economies* (New York: The Modern Library, 2000), pp. 21–2.
40. Stern, *The Interpersonal World of the Infant*, p. 67.
41. Peirce, *Philosophical Writings of Peirce*, p. 350.
42. Massumi, *What Animals Teach Us About Politics*, p. 10.
43. Leonie Matthews and Amanda Alderson (curators), *Trace: Architectural Musings*, Mundaring Arts Centre, Western Australia, 3 October–9 November 2014.
44. The arrival of the crater occurred through the involvement of three architecture students, Lily Nie, Amelia Fagence and Josefin Nord, who played with, adjusted and modified a given digital model I gave them, and who worked on the process of 3D laser-cutting the forms.
45. Whitehead, *The Philosophy of Alfred North Whitehead*, p. 690.

CHAPTER 6

Performing Bitumen, Materialising Desiré

Julieanna Preston and Jen Archer-Martin

It was night on a desert road in late spring.

From the dim remnants of the day's unrelenting light emerged a snorting beast bathed in headlamps, heralded by warning bleats and high-visibility vests. Its rank breath met the plummeting evening air as gaseous excretions. Approaching this horizon-inhabiting spectacle half-dazed by the vibrations of hurtling over cracked pavement at 110 kilometres per hour, I was soon engaged in a participatory interaction, my admittance marked by orange cones and MEN AT WORK signs.

As I slowed to a full stop, the roar of the truck engine was abruptly replaced by a complex symphony of grinding, whirling mechanical parts, chugging in unison for the sole purpose of laying a new road surface. The entire scene, engulfed by an oily black heat, was consumed by the mandate to make a path for progress. Moths and other insects took refuge in the low beams and fluttered into the truck cab unfazed by the graveyard of splattered exoskeletons adorning the windshield.

The continuous line on my dashboard map misrepresented the physical reality of the road-under-construction; a gap approximating the length of the road-eating-road-spewing mechanical creature appeared. This moving gap crept upon the flat sand-laden topography at a three-metre-per-minute snail's pace. I could only trail behind in a stop-start manner, wasting time, fuel and patience, while other vehicles eventually joined the queue.

> *An entourage of fossil-fuel-expending groupies on a pilgrimage from here to there, we were eventually ushered on to a makeshift track to perform a slow procession around the scene. From the night's abyss beyond the floodlights, through waves of diesel exhaust, I gawked at the machine's digestive process and its attendants. Finally, at a speed inversely proportional to that at which we had entered, we emerged from the spectacle on to the smooth unmarked virgin surface of the other side.*

The above recalls a personal encounter with the lively ecology of road-surfacing matters that shaped the context of the durational performance *bit-u-men-at-work*.[1] Performed over three nights in Melbourne, Australia, in October 2015 as part of the PSi Fluid States event *Performing Mobilities*, the work was a collaboration between Julieanna Preston, Jen Archer-Martin, a stretch of pavement outside the Margaret Lawrence Gallery, two caretakers with high-visibility safety equipment, a woman-machine-suit complete with tubular appendages and headlamps, a performance score, some pink chalk, a scattering of intentional and unintentional spectators, texts by Jane Bennett, Deleuze and Guattari, Donna Haraway, Rosi Braidotti, Virginia Held, Lewis Hyde and others, notions of vital materialism, posthuman and ecofeminist ethics, labour, care, desire and desiring-machines, and some sticky, oozy, smelly, black bitumen.

Bit-u-men-at-work is part of an ongoing series of works by Preston that seek to explore the limits between human and nonhuman agency in order to reveal the vibrancy in materials.[2] This iterative and emergent practice of material ethics experiments with various performative modes in the hope of fostering alternative relationships with earthly substances deemed inert by philosophical and social constructs. Preston's work is particularly concerned with the vital or vibrant surfaces of our living environments whereby surface is positioned as a spatio-temporal situatedness emerging out of the intra-actions between material subjects, a concept borrowed from Karen Barad.[3] Employing ecofeminist and new materialist strategies that aim to undo patriarchal and anthropocentric hierarchies, the work takes notice of the complex assemblages of our living environments while seeking to explore not just how we as humans might live in them, but how they, themselves, might live.

According to biogenic theory, bitumen is a natural transmutation of dead life – fossils, plants and tiny marine organisms – into black gold, a process that uses little more than heat, pressure and millions of years of time. Extracted from the earthly place of its manufacture or produced as a residue from petroleum distillation, this viscous hydrocarbon-based matter is put to work as a surfacing material in transportation, architecture and other industries, as an ingredient in road and footpath asphalt, boating seals, roofing felt, building coatings, fence post coatings, cattle sprays, inks, paints and waterproofing fabric treatments. In architecture, bitumen tends to be relegated to places that are out of sight: sandwiched between concrete and timber as damp proof course; hidden between framing and cladding as bituminous building paper; applied hot or cold to flat rooftops often hidden by parapets. It is almost never found in the interior spaces of architecture unless accidentally tracked in on shoes or tyres on a hot, sticky day. With the exception of the trafficable rooftop, this key ingredient in the making and using of our built environment is removed, in architecture, from human contact.

Roads and pavements are the threads of the urban fabric in which people and architecture exist. Connecting the urban and rural organs of national bodies, roads make up the circulatory life-support system of countries and continents. This affordance of mobility was of particular relevance to the Australian context of *Performing Mobilities*: isolated communities in outlying regions of the Australian continent rely on the maintenance of approximately 823,217 kilometres of roads for sustenance. These roads are, without exaggeration, called the life-blood of the nation. In the development of the performance work, first-hand experiences of road-bitumen's life and livelihood were gathered through visits to a local bitumen plant and to numerous night-time urban road construction sites where the mixing of sounds, smells and conversations by machines, material and workers bore out a dark reality of the material's coalition with the greedy consumption of earthly resources, human and nonhuman alike. Both life-supporting and an accomplice in resource-depletion, the material bitumen becomes politicised as a live thing-body with its own nature and culture.

In this chapter, Preston and Archer-Martin resist a simple retelling or documenting of the performance and instead attempt to reveal the agential voices of its assemblage. Bitumen, a high-visibility vest and traffic safety reflector, the woman-machine's suit, a performance score and a love letter are entangled, enabled and complicated by textual excerpts registering the presence of new materialist theorists and posthuman philosophers. Much like the matted pile of things that Jane Bennett discovered caught in the grate of a stormwater drain,[4] this collection of words and images muses on the debris of the performance as another self-organised pile – an assemblage of events and encounters operating across scales of temporality, materiality and affectivity. Each section mines the pile for a particular set of relations between various recognisable material bodies, pairing image with text in a manner that refuses to recognise either as inert – mere representation or translation – but rather celebrates the thing-power they exude.[5] As a matted surface with its own agency and desires, the text draws out the philosophical and theoretical concerns of *bit-u-men-at-work* to effect a shift from the conceptual (the realm of the scientist and philosopher) to the perceptual (the domain of the artist), a distinction made by Deleuze and Guattari in *What is Philosophy*.[6]

Section 01 introduces bitumen, a live black matter, through a coagulated dialogue between a poetic and philosophical voice. Here, the former is extracted from poems by Karen Solie and David Martin, and the latter, from Jane Bennett's *Vibrant Matter*. The text, including its format, recognises bitumen's geological origins, the context of its use and the gap-filling actions of the performance. *Section 02* zooms in on the synthetic textile of a high-visibility vest, pairing it with text from an advertisement for roadworkers. Here, the notion of the labourer is replaced with that of a caretaker, informed by an ethic of care as articulated by feminist philosopher Virginia Held. This 'call for care' is woven as a secondary thread into the text as both a disruptive and a reparative act, much as the roadworker's high-visibility tribal garb both screams 'Take care!' and reassures 'I'll take care of it'. In the performance, the caretaker undertakes care-ful acts as attendant, bodyguard and spectator. *Section 03* responds to the discarded skin, or suit, of the pavement-repairing woman-machine named Desiré, and charts some of the central concerns that emerged in the character's development between temporal fragments of pre-, mid- and post-performance musings. Punctuating these are textual excerpts that recognise the contributions of Deleuze and Guattari's writing on the desiring-machine, Donna Haraway's concept of the cyborg and Rosi Braidotti's posthumanist philosophy. *Section 04* reanimates the performance score, and through it, the laborious actions of the woman-machine. Revealed in this text is the programmed choreography of the machine's intimate caring labour and further instructions or snippets of what is perhaps an inner monologue, drawn together with marginal notes and citations. Here, notions of labour as outlined by Lewis Hyde and Michael Hardt enter into conversation with Deleuze and Guattari's concepts of production and the machine. *Section 05* presents a strangely personal text that appears to chart an evolving relationship of affection towards bitumen. It asks the question: if a material such as bitumen, along with all of its assemblage or ecology, is considered as 'live' or agentic, might it have the capacity to care or to be cared for, to desire or to be desired?

Figure 6.1 The material pile in situ.
Photo: © 2016 J. Preston

Figure 6.2 The rough and ready road surface expresses its own aggregate constitution.
Photo: © 2016 J. Preston

01

'picture an ontological field without any unequivocal demarcations between human, animal, vegetable, or mineral',[7] 'bitumen oozing from frac- **VISCOUS** tures in the earth or afloat like other fatty bodies, condensed by sun and internal salts, harassing snakes with its fumes'.[8] 'All forces and flows (materialities) are or can become lively, affective, and signaling'.[9] 'you can smell it down here. Cor- **CRUDE** rosive vapours unexpectedly distributed, caustic particulate infiltrates your mood . . . Attracted by the same sorrowful chemical compound emitted by damaged trees on which it feeds, its aural signature approximates the rasp of causatum rubbing its parts together'.[10] 'And so an affective, speak- **STICKY** ing human body is not radically different from the affective signalling nonhumans . . .'[11] 'in the open pit where swims the bitumen, extra brilliant, dense, massive, in the Greek asphaltos, "to make stable," "to secure"'[12] '. . . with which it coexists, hosts, enjoys, serves'.[13] 'Pharmacist's earth that resists decay, **FLAMMABLE** resolves and attenuates, cleanses wounds. Once used to burn the houses of our enemies, upgraded now to refinery-ready feedstock, raw crude flowing through channels of production and distribution'[14] 'consumes, produces and competes'.[15]

'Despair . . . like bitumen itself, applied to render darker tones or an emphatic tenebrism, imparts a velvety lustrous disposition, but eventually discolours to a black treacle that degrades any pigment it contacts'.[16]

BLACK

'In this onto-tale, everything is, in a sense, alive'.[17] 'Behold, the Plant is alive! I give you the loafing-crunch of Draglined Sand; the shut-eye-beak-oool of Feed Hopper; the scheming-sheaths of Toothed Rollers; the rumen-torque of Pug Mill; the pupa-soup-gyrate of Separator;

LIVE

the moulted-scales of Tailings Pond; the magpie-appraisal of Settling Tank; the shadow-tailed-cache of Elephant Storage; the nagging-scent of Water Drained to River. I submit Nature's Supreme Gift to Industry'.[18] 'I believe in one matter-energy, the maker of things seen and unseen. I believe that this pluriverse is traversed by heterogeneities that are continually doing things.

VITAL

I believe it is wrong to deny vitality to nonhuman bodies, forces, and forms, and that a careful course of anthropomorphisation can help reveal that vitality, even though it resists full translation and exceeds my comprehensive grasp. I believe that encounters with lively matter can chasten my fantasies of human mastery, highlight the common materiality of all that is, expose a wider distribution of agency, and reshape the self and its interests.'[19]

MATTER

Figure 6.3 The caretaker's garb among other reflective safety surfaces.
Photo: © 2016 J. Preston

02

Wanted: Road Maintenance ~~Labourers~~ Caretakers

Due to ~~increasing government expenditure on local roading projects~~ the upcoming *Performing Mobilities* durational performance 'bit-u-men-at-work' at 40 Dodds St, Southbank VIC 3006, Australia, Road Maintenance ~~Labourers~~ Caretakers are being sought for temporary work assignments.

In this role you will assist with the maintenance of Desiré, a unique desiring machine ~~the council's road infrastructure~~, and attend to her-its needs and safety while she-it carries~~ying~~ out tasks such as pothole repairs ~~and driving council trucks and other vehicles~~. You will work within a team environment, ~~and~~ enjoy night-time outdoor manual labour and 'illustrate human relatedness and the daily reaffirmations of connection'.[20] You will 'take care': a moral commitment in addition to but beyond a natural and emotional impulse towards others including objects and the environment.[21]

Road Maintenance ~~Labourers~~ Caretakers may do some or all of the following:

- ~~use~~ *watch over a* machine~~s and equipment to~~ *as it surveys,* applyies *do-it-your-self bitumen asphalt mix* ~~chip seal, asphalt and other materials~~ to ~~make~~ *repair* surfaces such as footpaths, driveways~~, roads and airport runways~~ *'in that close attention to the feelings, needs, desires, and thoughts of those cared for and a skill in understanding a situation from that person's view are central to caring for someone'*[22]
- *monitor the machine as she-it* digs up road surfaces and prepares them for resealing
- operate ~~heavy~~ *light* machinery such as ~~graders and rollers~~ *the Go-Pro and iPad*
- pour and smooth concrete and asphalt *with an empathy towards others; meeting the needs of others in face-to-face interactions*[23]

- check and maintain machinery and equipment such as *adjusting headlamps, chalk and dispensing tubes . . .*
- direct and control *vehicular, pedestrian, equestrian and animal* traffic moving around the construction *performance* site
- *protect and defend Desiré with the provision of affection, mutual concern and emotional satisfaction*[24]
- *seek greater clarity about what the ethics of care is*[25]

Road Maintenance ~~Labourers~~ Caretakers may need to have:

- *digital technology* driving skills
- must possess a *fluorescent high-visibility vest and set of portable reflective warning signs* ~~current MR or HR truck licence and a current OHS white card; a Traffic Management ticket is also highly desirable~~
- knowledge of how to ~~operate heavy equipment and~~ *care for a desiring machinery; to trust and value it*[26]
- knowledge of the materials they use, such as *water and bitumen* asphalt~~, road metals, and drainage pipes~~
- knowledge of *crowd control, audience participation/ interaction parameters*, road construction methods and roadmarking
- *a mobile phone*
- *knowledge of current health and safety policies and ethical engagement specific to this sector*

Road Maintenance ~~Labourers~~ Caretakers:

- ~~usually~~ will work irregular hours *from 6–9 pm 7–9 October 2015* ~~and often work early mornings and during weekends, and may also do shift work and be on call. They generally work longer hours in summer when more roading construction work is undertaken~~
- work outdoors in exposed sites *and adjacent to various forms of vehicular and pedestrian traffic*

- work in most weather conditions and in conditions that may be noisy, wet, cold, dirty and dusty
- *do everything 'to maintain, continue, and repair our "world" so that we can live in it as well as possible'*[27]

~~Many~~ Road Maintenance ~~Labourers~~ Caretakers need ~~start out with~~ few or no skills ~~but~~ and will learn skills on the job. 'Care is intrinsically relational.'[28]

Pay for Road Maintenance ~~Labourers~~ Caretakers varies depending on the type of work they are involved in and their level of experience and responsibility. People working as labourers usually start on minimum wage or a little more. Those operating heavy equipment or machines usually earn about $18–$20 an hour. Specialist machine operators can earn more than this; '"[s]ome caring relationships seem to have a significance in 'excess' of the labour they enable"' as if the work associated with caring 'expresses ethically significant ways in which we matter to each other, transforming interpersonal relatedness into something beyond ontological necessity or brute survival'.[29]

If you wish to be considered for this role, submit your application and cv ASAP ~~online at https://au.jora.com~~ *to bitumenatwork@gmail.com.*

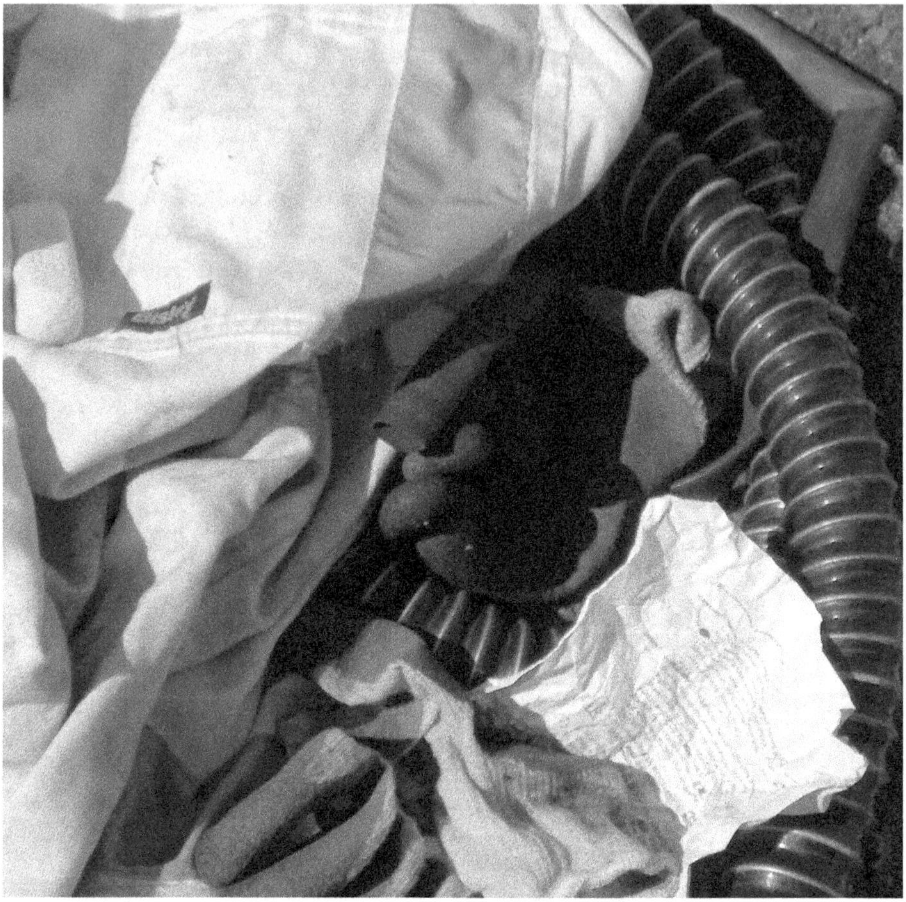

Figure 6.4 The suit of the woman-machine reveals her-its identity.
Photo: © 2016 J. Preston

03

The suit and my body are not the same. Its ampleness enables my actions; I am the guts of a piece of container technology immersed in a web of ecological practices.[30] And yet together we become something far more than a costumed, fleshy, middle-aged female body fused with the body of a cotton twill, dome-buttoned, reflective-tape-edged work suit brandishing a plastic tube filled with a thick, gritty, oily substance, a piece of fluorescent pink chalk, work gloves, boots and a headdress of LED lamps. For a few hours each night, our bodies are one and the same for the purpose of practising care.

'How machine-like do you want to become?' 'I desire it to be neither-nor, both-and . . . the bitumen, the machines, the bodies, the culture, and all the accoutrements, so – the bitumen, the machine, and the body – I'm trying to hold them together as different kinds of bodies, and look for empathetic relationships between them. . .'[31]

It hangs in deflated attention awaiting its next deployment.

Everywhere it is machines – real ones, not figurative ones: machines driving other machines, machines being driven by other machines, with all the necessary couplings and connections. An organ-machine is plugged into an energy-source-machine: the one produces a flow that the other interrupts.[32]

Each time I am activated, I accrue another level of autonomy by virtue of maintaining the asphalt pavement surface.

To become is never to imitate, nor to 'do like', nor to conform to a model, whether it is of justice or of truth. There is no terminus from which you set out, none which you arrive at or which you ought to arrive at. Nor are there two terms which are exchanged.

> The question 'What are you becoming?' is particularly stupid. For as someone becomes, what [s]he is becoming changes as much as [s]he does [her]self. Becomings are not phenomena of imitation or assimilation, but of a double capture, of non-parallel evolution, of nuptials between two reigns . . . There are no longer binary machines: question–answer, masculine–feminine, man–animal, etc. This could be what a conversation is – simply the outline of a becoming.[33]

A tarry smear spreads across my frontal erogenous zones, the site of stroking, pressing, rubbing, pumping, grinding. White to black.

> Desiring-machines are binary machines, obeying a binary law or set of rules governing associations: one machine is always coupled with another. The productive synthesis, the production of production, is inherently connective in nature: 'and . . .' 'and then . . .' This is because there is always a flow-producing machine, and another machine connected to it that interrupts or draws off part of its flow . . . And because the first machine is in turn connected to another . . . the binary series is linear in every direction. Desire constantly couples continuous flows and partial objects that are by nature fragmentary and fragmented. Desire causes the current to flow, itself flows in turn, and breaks the flows.[34]

I saw it come out in the dusk. It stood in the street vulnerable to the scrutiny, giggles, whims, insults and concerns of dogs, headlights, people, flies, weather and bicycles.

> Desire is the set of passive syntheses that engineer partial objects, flows, and bodies, and that function as units of production . . . Desire does not lack anything; it does not lack its object . . . Desire and its object are one and the same thing: the machine, as a machine of a machine. Desire is a machine, and the object of desire is another machine connected to it.[35]

She was wrapped by an appendage – a proboscis, a penis, a vacuum, a tail, a python, a sucking mouth all at once – that hung, swung and spewed as a weighty pendulum.

> The cyborg image can be read in two ways: as a coupling between a human being and an electronic or mechanical apparatus, or as the identity of organisms embedded in a cybernetic information system. In the first sense, the coupling between human and machine is located within the body itself – the boundary between the material body and the artificial machine is surgically redrawn. In the second sense, however, the boundary between the body and technology is socially inscribed, at once indistinct and arbitrary, but no less functional . . . Cyborgs are hybrid entities that are neither wholly technological nor completely organic, which means that the cyborg has the potential not only to disrupt persistent dualisms that set the natural body in opposition to the technologically recrafted body, but also to refashion our thinking about the theoretical construction of the body as both a material entity and a discursive process.[36]

It twitched, belched, bellowed and bleated as she bent, folded, scrawled, lumbered and crawled.

My monistic philosophy of becomings rests on the idea that matter, including the specific slice of matter that is human embodiment, is intelligent and self-organising. This means that matter is not dialectically opposed to culture, nor to technological mediation, but continuous with them.[37]

Follow the score. Live out the machine. Repair the road. Becoming bitumen.

The posthuman subjectivity I advocate is rather materialist and vitalist, embodied and embedded, firmly located somewhere, according to the feminist 'politics of location' . . . a serious concern for the subject allows us to take into account the elements of creativity and imagination, desires, hopes and aspirations . . . a vision 'worthy of the present'.[38]

I only have eyes for you. I only have eyes for you. I only have eyes for you you you you u u.

The relationship between the human and the technological other has shifted in the contemporary context, to reach unprecedented degrees of intimacy and intrusion. The posthuman predicament is such as to force a displacement of the lines of demarcation between structural differences, or ontological categories, for instance between the organic and the inorganic, the born and the manufactured, flesh and metal, electronic circuits and organic nervous systems.[39]

Touch. Point. Fluorescent pink. AroundandAroundandAroundand Around. She gave up her soft, pink, fluorescent body to the coarse surface as lines demarcating the sites of repair.

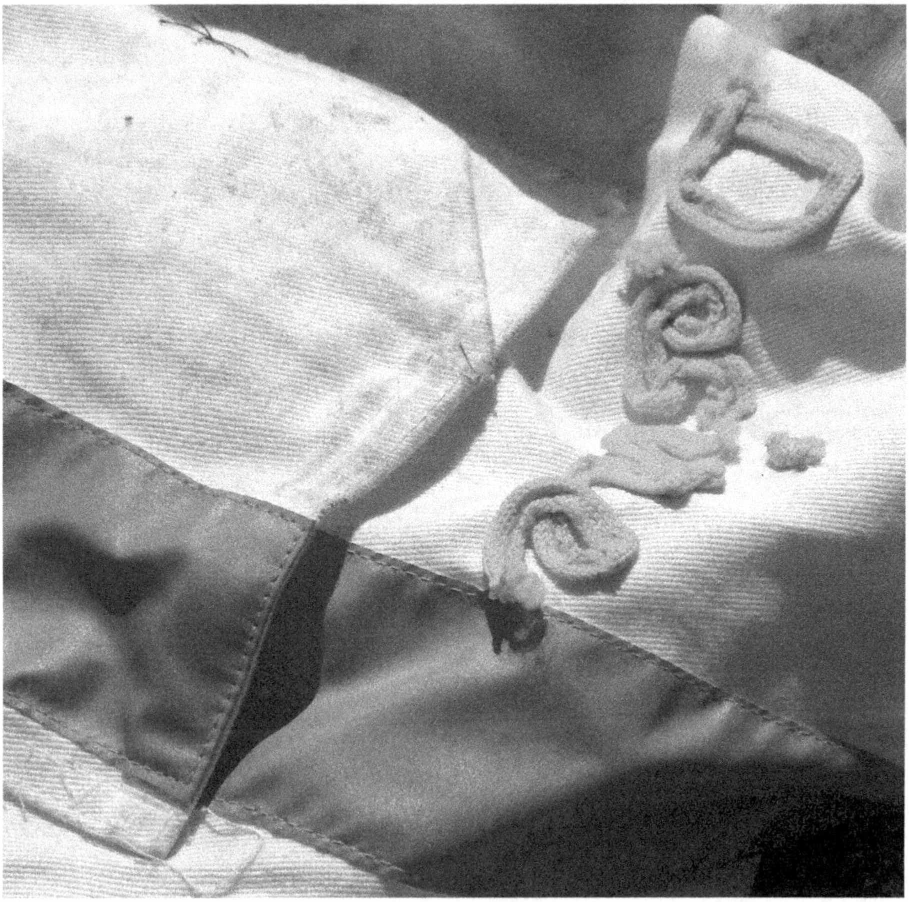

Figure 6.5 A well-worn performance score mingles with the pile of other materials it directs.

Photo: © 2016 J. Preston

04

Caretaker:
Set triangles.
Lead Desiré.
Turn on.
Adjust.
Check.
Press record.
Watch Desiré.

Desiré:
STOP.
Head down. HAAAAAH.

> It is at work everywhere, functioning smoothly at times, at other times in fits and starts. It breathes, it heats, it eats. It shits and fucks. What a mistake to have ever said the id. Everywhere it is machines – real ones, not figurative ones; machines driving other machines, machines being driven by other machines, with all the necessary couplings and connections.[40]

STOP. Shiver-jolt bobble, PHEW. *Possessed by a sudden lapse of neural conviviality, let go momentarily to the posture of homo-erectus.*
Head up.
STOP. PHEW.
Elbow chest chalk.
STOP. PHEW.

> *'We are machines – complex mechanisms comprised of an assemblage of organic and inorganic matter. Our cells live, die and are replenished. Parts of us are damaged and get repaired. We store and burn fat. Our muscles build and waste. We are constantly becoming new versions of ourselves. Our behaviour is responsive to a complex assemblage of drives and effects; our "mind" is not in total control. The DNA of our microbiome far outnumbers that of our "body". We ingest calories, sugars, chemicals and minerals that give us energy and alter our physical, mental and emotional states. The things we ingest bring with them*

microorganisms, immigrants that join the community of our gut flora while others migrate out via our bodily waste. Our outside becomes in-corporated and our inside is ex-creted. Our inner "public" is constantly in flux, and the changing forces and energies of that public have agency in the assemblage that is us. Our human-machine is not a single discrete entity. It is at once inside and outside, organic and inorganic, singular and multiple, us and not-us.'[41]

Fold. STOP. PHEW.

Hence we are all handymen; each with his little machines. For every organ-machine, an energy-machine: all the time, flows and interruptions.[42]

Scan be, be, be, BEEEEEEEEEP!
Chalk circles, WOOSH.
STOP. PHEW.

'Are humans so different to machines? What are the arguments beyond the biological imperatives? Might the limit be that humans make machines and machines cannot make us? The contemporary body is becoming-cyborg – we already incorporate machines into us, implants or prostheses. We rely on machines to monitor us, fix us, feed us and transport us. Noting the ethical risks, it might come to pass that machines could create humans; to grow us. What form of copulation might that take? What would then drive the work of (re-) production? Are humans both the machine and the environment for our own re-production? Do humans actually provide the creative force? And what of other expressions of creativity and artistry? Might a machine become capable of emotions such as love, joy and sorrow? Of morality, compassion, responsibility and ethics? Of logic, reason and intellect?'[43]

Fold, PHEW. *Without the aid of rear view mirrors, use peripheral vision and environmental sound radar, to traverse what laid before you.*
Reverse, be, be, be, BEEP, BEEEEEEEEEEP!
STOP. Shiver-jolt bobble PHEW.
Fold. STOP. PHEW.

'Are Desiré's deeds work (a cyclical product generating or consumptive process with a defined beginning or end) or

labour (an ongoing process that feeds physical/biological necessity and leaves no lasting trace)?'[44]

Lumber. STOP. PHEW. *Throw your mass as if it were a pendulum.*
Touch. STOP. PHEW.

Writing a poem, raising a child, developing a new calculus, resolving a neurosis . . . these are labours . . . Work is an intended activity that is accomplished through the will. A labour can be intended, but only to the extent of doing the groundwork or of not doing things that would clearly prevent the labour. Beyond that, the labour has its own schedule. Things get done, but we often have the odd sense that we didn't do them . . . And labour, because it sets its own pace, is usually accompanied by idleness, leisure, even sleep . . . When I speak of labour, then, I intend to refer to something dictated by the course of life, rather than by society, something that is often urgent, but that nevertheless has its own interior rhythm, something more bound up with feeling, more interior than work . . .[45]

Snap. STOP. PHEW. *Major joints entertain short and minor convulsions.*
Dump. STOP. PHEW. *Poo, puke; the smell is choking.*
Fill. OOOOHHHH. STOP. PHEW.

Applying care, the sensitivity to the needs of others, Noddings' 'needed "engrossment" with the other'.[46]

Inch. STOP. PHEW. *Use the belly as a giant slug-muscle.*
Hump. STOP. PHEW.

'Empathy. Loving something other, even an other that is undesirable, toxic, abhorrent, abject.'[47]

Fold. Repeat.
Stand. STOP. Shiver-jolt, bobble. PHEW.

Producing, a product: a producing/product identity. It is this identity that constitutes a third term in the linear series: an enormous undifferentiated object. Everything stops dead for a moment, everything freezes in place – and then the whole process will begin all over again.[48]

STOP.
***Caretaker*:**
Turn off.
Adjust.
Loop.
Lead Desiré.

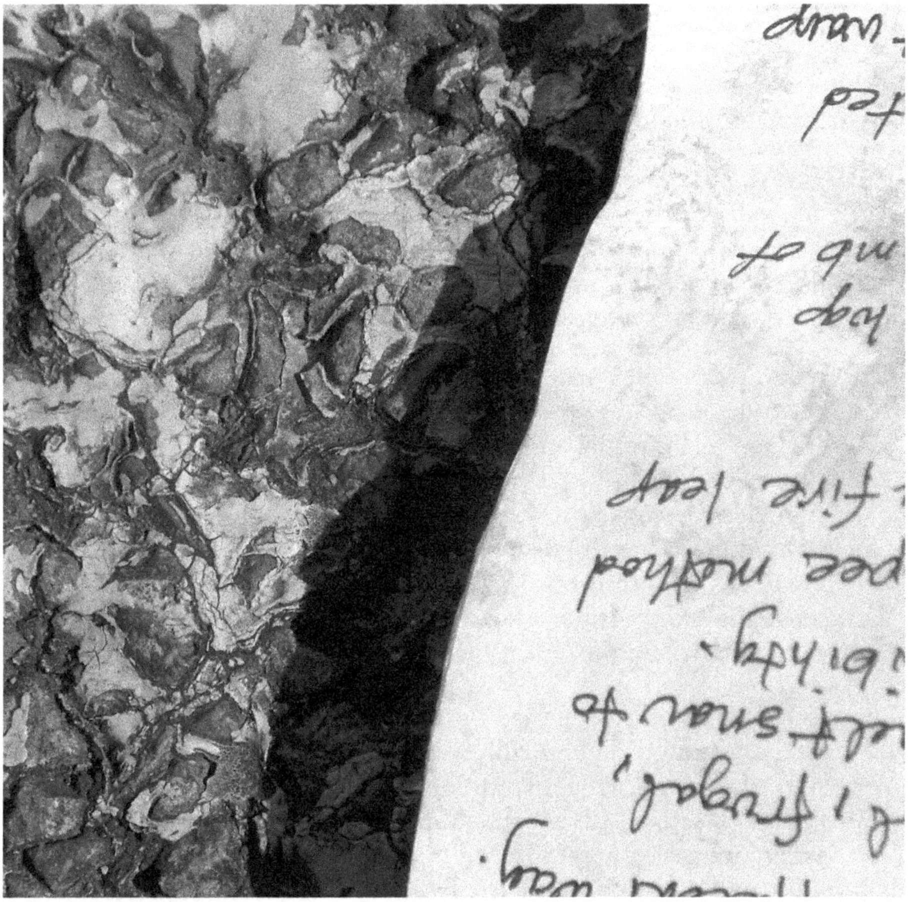

Figure 6.6 A love letter strewn in the folds of less desirable matter finds its way into view.

Photo: © 2016 J. Preston

05

My dearest Bitumen,

What is it to speak, let alone write, to a material as if it were live?
How do such gestures recognise your vibrancy without threatening your independence? How might my voice register what Jane Bennett calls 'the obscure but ubiquitous intensity of impersonal affect'?[49]
I can only proceed guilelessly.

I hate you. You stick, burning, to my bare feet in the hot summer sun.
Your noxious odour reeks – it repels me; reeks of earthy, sweet-sour, liveness – it compels me.
Your syrupy-sweet, inky-dark, empty-full deep molasses void incites nameless desires to touch, to taste, to consume.
Thick, shining, oozing, black, viscous road-fluid secretions; heat-swallowing, sunlight-glinting, rain-dancing.
Your sensual beauty disgusts me.
I am struggling to reconcile sensations of attraction and abhorrence.[50]

I hate what you do. You seduce me to your fossil-fuel-sucking, carbon-monoxide-emitting ways,
Your smooth-gliding, wheel-spinning, fresh-air-rushing ways,
Your music-pumping, adventure-thumping, landscape-blurring, new-sights-whirring ways.
Is it unfair of me to downplay the freedoms and conveniences you afford me?
You labour for me daily, the invisible labours of a long-term lover now taken for granted.
And yet you just lay there, sprawled out, willingly, offering a service with no tangible or durable good, as Michael Hardt might contend, an architectural material surface carrying out immaterial labour.[51]

Can I imagine life without you? Dusty, muddy, wheel-boggy, water-loggy, slip-slidey treachery,
Gravel-clattery, skull-shattery, bone-shaking, ear-aching bumpy bangy clangy misery.
The road would not be the road without your smooth, protective skin
Washed away, blown away, punished by the irreconcilable incompatibility of earth, weather and traffic.

You maintain order, organise flows, keep the watery enemy of safe, efficient movement at bay.
Such an unselfish sacrifice of earthly resources affords us humans to go places. We crave to go places but mostly we crave to just go.[52]

What are you? Are you yourself a flow? At first, quick-soft and malleable, then slow;
Sun-melting, tree-root-cracking, earth-subsiding-slumping, brittle-heat-crazing; lively responses to lively forces.
You are hospitable and hostile, connective and divisive, cleaving flows above from flows below;
Creating two sides where there were none, where all was one, no treacherous crossing, no impassable expanse.
You prioritise my travel over all else; you wrench mobility away from others and gift it to me.
At the moment, there is no villain in this story, not yet.[53]

But who are you? Who were you? The very essence of former life, compressed into a thick liquid;
Now pressed into service, at once awe-inspiringly ancient and feebly oppressed.
You will always be other, but perhaps one day I will be you. Not in a million years, but maybe more?
My carbon may become your carbon, my body-skin your road-skin, its folds and crevices harbouring life;
Its oils keeping it supple, until they don't, and creases become cracks become potholes, crumbling, flaking.
Such intimate talk, such interspecies mingling, runs the risk of anthropomorphising while battling against a human-centric world view. Like Bennett, I feel that relating to you one on one, face to face, material body to material body, is a risk worth taking.[54]
Our skins don't rub together well. Intimate encounters are not pleasurable; kissing the pavement is not particularly appealing.
Skin-scraping, bone-breaking, gravel-embedding, tear-shedding violence.
You may be okay, but for me the result of that attraction may be fatal.
Unless I am in control: pounding the pavement, hitting the road, setting the rhythm and pace with rubber-sole, rubber-tyre protection.
Does this bring you any pleasure?

Until I laid down next to you I did not know what it was to desire something undesirable.[55]
Here, a confession, a proclamation: as much as I hate you,
I love what you do for me.
I might even, sometimes, in a way, love you.
I want you, desire you, find you irresistible in your badness, as much as I know you are not good for me.
Please understand that your toxicity means I need to be cautious about getting too close; I hesitate, move slowly, touch infrequently and back away. Perhaps the future will afford more exuberant activities.[56]
Others might not understand, but perhaps we are not so different, you and I. Neither pure; nor villain.
Both protector and polluter, container and contaminant, creator-connector and divider-disruptor.
I see you now, and in you, I see me. I am not sure if that makes me love you more, or love myself less;
Hate you more, or hate myself less; hate you less, or hate myself more.
But for better or for worse, in sickness and in health, I am much obliged, my love.
Here, in the space of this letter, progress is made towards the wellbeing of our mutual co-existence.[57]
I cannot say I am sincerely, truly, yours,
Or that you are sincerely, truly mine,
But it seems that we belong together.
Forever – as long as that may be.
x

Acknowledgements

Blackwoods Protectors, NZ
Kerensa Diball, caretaker
Mick Douglas, *Performing Mobilities* Artistic Director
Nigel Green, Contract Manager New Zealand, Downer, NZ
Ryan Haberfield, Lead Asphalt Operator, Downer, NZ
Dave Gedney, Roading and Civil Team Leader, New Zealand Transport Agency, NZ
Yvonne Lee, Asphalt Production, Road Science, NZ
Vikki McInnes, Margaret Lawrence Gallery curator
Barrie McKay, Regional Production Manager, Road Science, NZ

Scott Morrison, caretaker
School of Design, Massey University
Rob Sibbing, Senior Accounts Manager (Asphalt), Boral, AUS
Eden Smith-Joyce, Administration Assistant, LS NewCo Pty Ltd, NZ
Safeworx, NZ
The Uniform Factory, NZ
Uli Thie and Ken Howe, 3D technicians, SoD, Massey University
Laurene Vaughan, *Performing Mobilities* Passages curator

Notes

1. See https://vimeo.com/141598824.
2. Jane Bennett, *Vibrant Matter: A Political Ecology of Things* (Durham, NC: Duke University Press, 2010).
3. Karen Barad, 'Posthumanist Performativity: Toward an Understanding of How Matter Comes to Matter', *Signs* 28:3 (2003), pp. 801–31.
4. Bennett, *Vibrant Matter*, pp. 4–7.
5. Ibid., p. 4.
6. Gilles Deleuze and Félix Guattari, *What is Philosophy*, trans. Hugh Tomlinson and Graham Burchell (New York: Columbia University Press, 1994), pp. 15–34.
7. Bennett, *Vibrant Matter*, p. 116.
8. Karen Solie, 'The Road In is Not the Same Road Out', in *The Road In is Not the Same Road Out: Poems* (New York: Farrar, Straus, and Giroux, 2015), p. 77.
9. Bennett, *Vibrant Matter*, p. 116.
10. Solie, 'The Road In is Not the Same Road Out', p. 81.
11. Bennett, *Vibrant Matter*, p. 117.
12. Solie, 'The Road In is Not the Same Road Out', p. 81.
13. Bennett, *Vibrant Matter*, p. 117.
14. Solie, 'The Road In is Not the Same Road Out', p. 81.
15. Bennett, *Vibrant Matter*, p. 117.
16. Solie, 'The Road In is Not the Same Road Out', p. 81.
17. Bennett, *Vibrant Matter*, p. 117.
18. David Martin, 'CBC Literary Prize Winner: Tar Swan', Air Canada enRoute 10 October 2014, https://enroute.aircanada.com/en/articles/cbc-literary-prize-winner-tar-swan-poetry (last accessed 26 November 2016).
19. Bennett, *Vibrant Matter*, p. 122.
20. Virginia Held, 'Taking Care: Care as Practice and Value', in Cheshire Calhoun (ed.), *Setting the Moral Compass: Essays by Women Philosophers* (New York: Oxford University Press, 2004), pp. 59–71 (p. 59).
21. Ibid., p. 60.
22. Noddings in ibid.

23. Ibid., p. 61.
24. Ibid., p. 63.
25. Ibid., p. 59.
26. Ibid., p. 63.
27. Ibid., p. 60.
28. Ruddick in ibid., p. 64.
29. Tronto in ibid., p. 62.
30. Isabelle Stengers, 'Introductory Notes on an Ecology of Practices [online]', *Cultural Studies Review*, 11. 1 (2005), pp. 183–96.
31. Preston and Archer-Martin Conversation Audio, Museum Building, Massey University, Wellington, New Zealand, 26 August 2015, 1:55.
32. Gilles Deleuze and Félix Guattari, *Anti-Oedipus: Capitalism and Schizophrenia*, trans. Helen R. Lane, Robert Hurley and Mark Seem (Minneapolis: University of Minnesota Press, 1983), p. 1.
33. Gilles Deleuze and Claire Parnet, *Dialogues II* (New York: Columbia University Press, 2007), p. 3.
34. Deleuze and Guattari, *Anti-Oedipus*, p. 5.
35. Ibid., p. 26.
36. Anne Balsamo, *Technologies of the Gendered Body: Reading Cyborg Women* (Durham, NC: Duke University Press, 1996), p. 11.
37. Rosi Braidotti, *PostHuman* (Cambridge and Malden, MA: Polity Press, 2013), p. 350.
38. Ibid., pp. 51–2.
39. Ibid., p. 89.
40. Deleuze and Guattari, *Anti-Oedipus*, p. 1.
41. Archer-Martin Notes, 2015.
42. Deleuze and Guattari, *Anti-Oedipus*, pp. 1–2.
43. Archer-Martin Notes, 2015.
44. Archer-Martin Notes, 2015.
45. Lewis Hyde, *The Gift: Creativity and the Artist in the Modern World* (New York: Vintage, 2007), pp. 63–4.
46. Held, 'Taking Care', p. 61.
47. Archer-Martin Notes, 2015.
48. Deleuze and Guattari, *Anti-Oedipus*, p. 7.
49. Bennett, *Vibrant Matter*, pp. xiii–xiv.
50. Preston and Archer-Martin Conversation Audio, 2015, 25:11.
51. Michael Hardt, 'Affective Labour', *Boundary*, 26.2 (1999), pp. 89–100 (p. 94).
52. Preston and Archer-Martin Conversation Audio, 2015, 21:33.
53. Preston and Archer-Martin Conversation Audio, 2015, 11:47.
54. Bennett, *Vibrant Matter*, pp. 119–20.
55. Preston and Archer-Martin Conversation Audio, 2015, 23:38.
56. Bennett, *Vibrant Matter*, pp. 121–2.
57. Held, 'Taking Care', p. 69.

PART II

CHAPTER 7

Machine-oriented Architecture: Oikos and Ecology

Levi R. Bryant

Let us begin in true philosophical fashion with the invention of a fantastic Platonic myth. In this spirit, let me state, tongue in cheek, that humanity is clearly descended from snails and turtles. We are alienated snails and turtles, and are perhaps best classified as hermit crabs. Clearly, given our propensity to build, all of the evidence points to the fact that our ancestors were beings that once had a home, that they were once sheltered. This is suggested by the fact that even when we have a home we feel curiously alienated from it and search for it. Not only did our ancestors have a home, that home was an organic part of their being. They were one with their home. It is for this reason, no doubt, that we perpetually yearn for the home that we lost. As a consequence, our slimy gooey bodies, descended from snails, formed exoskeletons, though of an existential sort, where we were condemned to forever seek shells of various sorts to replace that shell that had once been an organic part of our being. Yet unlike the hermit crab that steals its shell from a snail or perhaps happens upon an abandoned drink can or bottle, we are snails that have, through some strange dialectical gesture, learned how to build shells that nonetheless remain external to or outside of us. This is a crucial difference. While the hermit crab *finds* its shell, those species descended from the hermit crab – bears, prairie dogs, birds, termites, bees, wasps and humans – build their own shells. It's as if, with our shells, there must be a minimal alienation or contradiction. The homes are both ours – as a result of being constructed by us – while not being ours as a result of not being attached to us. We are not one with our homes.

As a consequence, unlike snails, we suffer a minimal alienation from our homes. The history of why this curse occurred and when precisely it happened is unclear. Legend has it that the gods were jealous and offended by the vanity of the snails who had such wondrous mobility, such beautiful shells and such impenetrable armour that they exiled these archaic snails and turtles from their organic dwellings, rendering them alien and foreign to those that inhabited them. Like Sisyphus, the gods condemned the living to building their dwellings without ever quite being able to be at home in them.

Perhaps this was the early, slimy, exposed origin of humanity: the creation of the building. But that's not quite right. Somewhere or other Lacan says that culture has two origins. On the one hand, he says, culture begins when disposing of our waste becomes a problem. Humanity is a species that worries about how to deal with entropy or how to dispose of its waste. On the other hand, according to Lacan, humanity begins with pottery. Pottery, Lacan says, is the creation of a void and that void, he thinks, is the condition of the signifier or signification. Pottery, he says, is what makes us specifically human, for pottery creates the void that is unique to humanity and that is a condition for the existence of language.

We should question this second thesis, for the building of a building is far more primordial than pottery and shared by a variety of species descended from snails and turtles. Yet the building, the dwelling, is also the formation of a void. The void or absence might indeed, as Lacan says, be a condition for signification, but it is also quite common outside humanity. It is not only humans that produce emptiness; rather also bees, termites, prairie dogs, bears, birds, ants, wasps and a variety of other animals. All of these beings empty space and create spaces, thereby producing voids. Perhaps signification is far more prolific than we imagined. At any rate, we can see just how much the snails and turtles, with their beautiful shells, armour and freedom of movement, must have drawn the envy of the gods. Not only did the gods exile all of these beings from an organic relation to their homes, but they condemned them to the construction of their own emptiness, building spaces that would never quite be their own. Of course, this teaches us something about the gods as well. If the gods were outraged by the fine dwellings of snails and turtles, with their beauty and armour, then this is perhaps because the gods themselves are alienated. Perhaps the gods could not bear the sight of our snail and turtle ancestors who were one with their homes and thereby resolved to impose their own alienation on these most blessed of creatures.

But enough of these fantastic mythical musings. Newton claimed that there is only *absolute* space. If that's the case, then there can be no question of there being this or that space, for there's only space. Similar musings arise when we reflect on zero. How many zeros are there? We would like to say that there are as many zeros as there are absences, yet we distinguish something from something else by virtue of what it *is*. How can two nothings be distinguished from one another? For one zero to be distinguished from another there would have to be *something* about them that differs. Yet zero is nothing. However, with dwellings there it is. We have voids in the plural or domains of emptiness that are nonetheless distinct. How can this be?

In true Lucretian fashion, I would like to propose that architecture operates in, through and on the void, paradoxically multiplying and varying it in an infinite number of ways.

As I have argued elsewhere, all of being is composed of machines.[1] Atoms are machines. Stars and planets are machines. Plants and animals are machines. Texts are machines. Institutions, automobiles, norms, laws, works of art and computers are all machines. There are, of course, different types of machines just as there are inanimate and animate beings; yet just as inanimate and animate beings are *both* beings, all beings, whether natural or fabricated, are machines. In short, being a product of human fabrication is not what qualifies something as a machine. Only a subset of machines has this origin.

I call this metaphysics or ontology 'machine-oriented ontology'. We are accustomed to thinking of an ontology or metaphysics as an account of the ultimate structure of reality in the most general terms possible. An ontology outlines what sorts of things exist at the most general level and what properties beings have at the most general level, and so on. Sometimes people claim that they reject ontology on the grounds that they hold all beings to be characterised by becoming rather than being. Here being seems to be equated with stasis or fixity, where becoming is, of course, change. However, the claim that all beings are perpetually changing, that they are all characterised by becoming – a claim that I endorse – is itself an ontological claim. 'Being' is not synonymous with 'stasis'.

While the characterisation of ontology as a theory of the ultimate structure of reality that articulates what sorts of beings exist at the most general level is not false, it is perhaps not as helpful as one might wish. I would instead characterise an ontology as a general theory of what it means to give an account of something. When a psychiatrist prescribes Xanax for a person suffering from anxiety, they are presupposing an ontology. The psychiatrist and patient presuppose that the ground or cause of anxiety is chemical imbalance in the brain. This is a variant of materialist ontology. Not only does this ontology influence practice – the psychiatrist and the patient both do what they do because they presuppose this ontology – but it also influences research or inquiry. The psychiatric researcher will ask the questions she asks and do the scientific research she does based on the ontology she presupposes. She will search for an organic cause of anxiety because she presupposes a particular variant of materialist ontology, and will ignore other lines of inquiry or possible grounds of anxiety such as how the person's life is bound up with meaning, or how the person's life is related to dynamics of social organisation, or other possibilities besides. I hasten to add that what I have just outlined is only *one* variant of materialist ontology. We can imagine other materialist ontologies that don't trace, in the domain of psychological phenomena, everything back to neurology but that also take into account material dynamics of meaning, the signifier, social relations and so on. Such an ontology would lead to a very different form of inquiry and practice.

What I wish to say is that field of inquiry, ontology, that seems so remote from day-to-day concerns, from scientific inquiry, from politics and ethics, is, in fact, of profound importance. There is no escaping ontology, nor is there a single utterance in any language that does not make ontological assumptions. Often these presuppositions are unconscious in the sense that they are so familiar, so proximal to our thought and dealings with the world, that we don't even know we are making them. Making them explicit and critiquing them therefore carries the possibility of improving both our inquiry and practice.

For my part I argue that all of being is composed of machines. If one finds this signifier or term distasteful, any other will do. Certainly in the past I have used a variety of different terms such as 'objectile', 'object', 'thing', 'system', 'substance', 'entity', 'body', and 'process' to denote the same concept. What's important here is not the terminology we use, but rather the concept that that terminology denotes. Broadly, there are two things I wished to accomplish through the use of the term 'machine'. First, I wish to draw discussion away from the interminable epistemological discussion of the relationship between the subject and the object. It's not that I don't believe epistemological questions are important. One can imagine an entire machine-oriented epistemology. Rather, it's that questions of how we know and what we can know are distinct from questions of what things are. It was my hope that the term 'machine' would be foreign enough to interrupt habitual associations that lead us to think of subjects the moment the term 'objects' is evoked.

Second, and of far greater importance, with the concept of machines I wish to draw attention to how things *operate* or what they *do*. Rather than outlining a list of categories of predication like Aristotle, or discussing the properties or qualities of things, I instead wish to focus on how things operate. This, then, is the essence of all machines: *they are activities that are defined by their operations*. We can clearly see this in the case of technological machines such as smartphones and in the case of living things. These entities certainly engage in all sorts of activities.

However, it is also true, I argue, of non-living machines such as rocks. Within this framework, beings are not defined by their properties or qualities, but rather by their powers and activities or operations. A power is a capacity to do something, while an operation is an activity on the part of an entity. Qualities or properties are effects of these operations. Here beings are defined, following Spinoza, in terms of their effects or their capacities to affect and be affected by other beings. *A being is what it can and does do.*

Take the example of colour. Rather than saying that an entity *has* a particular colour, colour is instead treated as an event that erupts from within an entity in interaction with an environment. It will be noticed that the colour of an object changes under different lighting conditions. We can imagine people debating as to what the true colour of an object is. Machine-oriented ontology takes a different approach. The object does not have one true colour, but rather colour is what takes place through an interaction between the surface of the entity, wavelengths of light and the neurological system of the organism beholding the entity. Different wavelengths of light will produce different colours in one and the same entity. When the lights are turned out, it's not that the colour of the object has been veiled or hidden, but it has truly become colourless. Colour is the result of an interaction of an object or machine with the world about it, not something that the entity has as an intrinsic feature. It is an event.

Or take the example of a chair. A machine-oriented analysis would not focus on a description of the chair – its shape, configuration, style and so on – nor even on the function or use of chairs (though clearly that cannot be ignored). Rather, machinic analysis would focus on what chairs do. For example, chairs distribute and channel the forces of gravity down to ground or earth, both defying the forces of the cosmos and using those forces to their advantage. However, chairs are not merely machines that distribute forces such as gravity. They are machines that act on the bodies that sit upon them, defining postures, conditioning those bodies in a variety of ways, defining levels of fatigue and energy, impacting concentration, etc. It is not by mistake that church pews are often uncomfortable, without cushions and difficult to recline in. These machines operate in such a way as to prevent relaxation so that the subject might be properly attentive to the spiritual rituals they are participating in. Indeed, not only is the pew a machine, but the entire service and church is a machine. Chairs are not merely something that people use, but are also machines that operate on people in a variety of ways.

Machine-oriented ontology is thus an analytic framework. In unfolding a machine-oriented analysis we ask the following questions: First, upon what does the machine operate? In the example of the chair, the machine operates upon forces such as bodies and gravity. In the case of colour, the entity operates on wavelengths of light. Following Deleuze and Guattari, I call these things upon which machines operate 'flows'.[2] Here it should be noted that machines need not operate on things other than themselves but can operate upon themselves as well. For example, a university administration operates upon its faculty, which is a part or element of the university machine. Second, what operations does the machine engage in when operating on these flows? For example, Foucault engages in an analysis of the various operations that function within disciplinary machines, looking at the techniques through which docile bodies are produced.[3] Similarly, cellular biologists investigate the operations of cells and how these cells produce other cells or influence other cells or act on foreign bodies such as bacteria to defend against them. Finally, a machinic ontology investigates what machines or entities produce in and through their operations. Colour is what is produced through the operations of entities in relation to wavelengths of light, whereas bodily postures and affective states are what are produced through the operations of chairs. Of course, the product of a machine need not be an output that departs from the machine like a chicken laying an egg. The product can also be a quality or state of the machine, as in the case of colour or shape in response to gravity or a particular action like that of a runner.

A machine-oriented architecture would thus approach the building, construction or edifice as a machine, investigating the edifice in terms of how it operates, that upon which it operates and what it produces in operating. A building is a machine. In approaching architecture in this way, I am seeking to develop an ontology of the building or edifice. Our task will be to determine what sort of machines buildings are. There will not, of course, be a single answer to this question as there are different types of buildings that operate in different ways. Moreover, there is a history of architectural machines such that edifices that operated in a particular way in the past operate differently today. A manor house, for example, might become a hospital or a hotel. The factory, school, temple, shopping centre, greenhouse, home, restaurant and so on are all different sorts of machines that engage in different operations and that produce different things. Nonetheless, there are broadly shared features among architectural machines that can be outlined. From there, future work – though I will gesture to some of this work here – can be undertaken to further specify different types of building-machines within this broader ontology of the machine. That's how it always works with ontology. We begin with an account of the most general features shared by all beings and then develop regional ontologies for the different types of beings that exist.

Before proceeding, however, it is first necessary to stave off a potential confusion. The architectural machinism or mechanology I am seeking to develop here should not be equated with a sort of utilitarianism that approaches architecture solely in terms of its use or usefulness. Operationalism and functionalism are not the same thing. In the present context – matters are different in mathematics – 'function' refers to usefulness. For example, a machine like a knife is functional when it has a blade well suited to its task, has a handle that fits nicely in the hand, has good balance so that it's not awkward or difficult to use, and so on. A functional knife is one that has a form that best suits it to serving its purpose. A machete is good for cutting branches and large leaves blocking one's way, but has a form very poorly suited to julienning peppers and carrots. An operation, by contrast, is simply an activity that produces a particular product by acting upon a flow. The manner in which a machine such as iron rusts as a result of oxidisation in interactions between iron, moisture and oxygen is the result of an operation, but it serves no use or purpose. It is just what happens when these machines are brought together. A building can be striking or beautiful, operating in such a way as to produce all sorts of profound affective responses, but there is little here that the bureaucrat would find useful. Many machines ranging from features of living beings to various tools and technologies will have functions, but many other beings will engage in operations without these operations serving any specific purpose or having any particular use.

So, an architectural mechanology. How do architectural machines operate, upon what do they operate, and what do they produce in operating? Earlier I suggested that the building or edifice creates or produces a void. Through the framing of space, the building produces a space within space; an enclosure. At the most basic and general level, architectural machines are enclosure-machines. They are machines that operate on space to enclose. Later we will have to investigate what, in turn, enclosure-machines operate upon. For the moment, however, we must focus on the activity or operation of enclosing.

At the most fundamental level, then, architectural machines operate in such a way as to produce a spatialisation of space. The spatialisation of space is an operation through which the undifferentiated void becomes differentiated, forming spaces within spaces. There are, of course, a variety of ways in which the spatialisation of space takes place, as in the cases of roads, pavements, rivers, mountain ranges and curved space-time furrows produced by the gravity of massive objects. In all of these cases, the spatialisation of space creates paths along which other machines move and become. The wind must navigate mountain ranges and canyons. Yet what seems unique in the case of architecture is that the differentiation of space takes place through the formation of an enclosure.

As an aside, this raises all sorts of questions as to whether tree hollows and caves are instances of architecture. Certainly all sorts of beings, including humans, dwell within these voids or enclosures. Must something be built by bees, wasps, birds, prairie dogs and any other beings that dwell to count as architecture, or is it sufficient that an enclosure be used to dwell to count as an architectural machine? Perhaps caves and hollows are transitional stages between hermit crabs that find their home and the birth of true architects that construct their home. Similarly, just how enclosed must an enclosure be to count as architecture? Must it have a roof or is it sufficient that it has three or four walls? I have no firm answer to these questions.

The first and most primordial operation engaged in by architectural machines is the spatialisation of space in the formation of an enclosure. Enclosure is an operation whereby the void is cleaved in two, forming a boundary between one side and another. As a result, a path is created that structures movement for other bodies. We must walk along the stone wall of a field to get to the other side or, at least, climb over it. These walls, in their turn, must be maintained, ensuring that enclosure is not a one-time operation, but an operation that must continually be undertaken. Entropy always threatens. Enclosures are always on their way to disappearing, returning space to its undifferentiated form. When walls are enchained to one another we get the formation of an enclosure or the genesis of an interior space.

The boundary formed by the operation of enclosure is perhaps not merely a boundary, but is rather also a membrane. Membranes both relate and separate, opening a being on to a broader world while also separating it from that world. The nature of the membrane produced in the operation of enclosure says a great deal about the outside. Often this reference to the outside occurs at the level of meaning or signs; these signs becoming embodied in the flesh of matter. For example, a castle with its thick, imposing walls and battlements speaks to a menacing and dangerous world where attack can occur at any time. Similarly, homes with fences in back yards and garages behind the house, such as those that are common in the suburbs of my city, speak to a certain relation with the neighbour. They simultaneously refer to the neighbour while creating a disjunction with the neighbour. Garages in front of the house increase the likelihood that you will encounter others in your neighbourhood when returning home or when pottering around doing various forms of work. They open on to the neighbourhood. In this regard, they function as catalysts for the formation of neighbourhood communities. By contrast, the garage behind the house from which people get to main roads through alleys significantly diminishes the likelihood of encounters with neighbours. For this reason, they operate in such a way as to diminish the formation of relations between people. They do this not by virtue of what they mean or how they signify, but by virtue of how they have utilised and arranged space. These membranes and how they are arranged operate on flows or bodies, relating and separating them in a variety of ways. As a result, they are catalytic operators with respect to the outside.

There is thus something ecological about membranes. While often we focus on the interior formed in architectural relations as well as the façade of the enclosure, the membrane always also refers to an outside, as if almost citing it. The peak of a roof or its flatness refers to whether or not rain and snow are common where the enclosure has been constructed. The mirrored windows of office buildings refer both to sunlight that rains down upon enclosures, yet also to the possibility of prying eyes from other businesses engaged in corporate espionage. The substances out of which walls are made refer to considerations of temperature and weather. Enclosure does not simply form a void or an interior, but refers to an outside and the events that transpire there. There is thus an ecology of the enclosure that always and everywhere refers to the outside, both citing the problems posed by the outside, but also inviting elements of the outside in through windows and doorways. The membrane makes a selection from the cosmos, filtering it, drawing in flows of light, air and other animal and human bodies through various openings.

Yet the ecology of enclosure does not end there. In many respects, enclosures have a plant-like structure that sends roots into the ground and lifts leaves to the sky. Windows do not just produce fields of visibility opening on to the outside, but also draw on solar flows assisting in the heating of the space. A dog positions itself in the field of these solar flows, capturing comforting heat in a way that would not occur outside. Enclosures must put down roots, drawing on flows of energy in the form of gas and electricity, as well as flows of water. These flows of energy will be necessary for the metabolism of the enclosure, allowing it to continue in its ongoing operations. And like all metabolic systems, enclosures are open systems, drawing substances and energies from the outside and releasing waste into the environment. Through these flows of energy, enclosures produce gradients or differences that allow certain activities to take place. Yet accompanying the ongoing production of these gradients or differentials there is always entropy, waste, the release of disorder; and this waste must be contended with by the outside through the formation of dumps, waste sewage treatment plants and the impact of gaseous emissions on the atmosphere.

However, there's a far more concrete way in which the operations of enclosure refer to the outside. Every enclosure must stand if it is to produce its void. As a consequence, enclosure does not merely divide inside from outside, but must also channel and distribute the forces of the cosmos. The enclosure must contend with the forces of gravity as well as the elements, channelling them in a variety of ways so as to produce the enclosure. Such is the meaning of machines such as the lintel, the post, the arch and the dome. Operations of enclosure must negotiate with, must compromise with, gravity, wind, sun, rain and snow so as to stand and continue to stand. There will be proud enclosures that appear to defy gravity, standing in paradoxical and fantastic ways, but this will always be an illusion. Standing will be a problem that must be solved for every enclosure, and the nature of that problem changes depending on ecological conditions. For example, the construction of enclosure would have to take place under different but related procedures on Mars because the mass of that planet is about half that of the planet Earth.

There is something fractal about the operation of enclosure, for enclosure does not simply cleave the void, dividing outside and inside, but also takes place within the interior space that has been delimited through enclosure, repeating itself in the formation of rooms and paths or hallways. Hallways are like vessels in a circulatory system, distributing the flows of bodies as they move through the interior and ensuring that the rooms, which are like cells or organs, remain partitioned from one another and thereby restricted to being sites for particular operations. These interior enclosures, in their turn, operate upon the bodies that inhabit them – animal, human, and things such as furniture and production technologies – as flows, both forming them in a variety of ways and relating and separating them in a variety of ways.

All machines exercise degrees of gravity with respect to one another, influencing the movement and operations of other machines. By 'gravity' I am not referring solely to the sort of gravity produced by the mass of an object causing a curvature of space-time that defines a path along which another object moves. Rather, I am referring to something much broader that is close to Foucault's conception of power. Roads, for example, exert gravity in this broader sense for vehicles, people, businesses and so on, because they define paths of relation between entities. The once thriving Bates Motel in *Psycho*, for example, has its existence transformed as a result of the construction of a new highway. Where it once enjoyed a large clientele as a result of constantly passing traffic, it now finds itself isolated and unrelated.

Machines can be sorted into different operational types based on their gravitational relations to other machines. Thus, for example, a machine that determines the paths of movement and becoming of a variety of other entities can be called a 'bright object' by virtue of the manner in which it structures the movement of other beings. The sun is a bright object for the solar system because it structures the movement of the planets by creating a curvature of space-time, while the sole steel-mining factory in a small town is a bright object with respect to the other businesses of that town as well as its inhabitants. The fortunes of these inhabitants as well as that of the local businesses are bound up with this factory. When there is one major source of employment within a town, that factory functions as a bright object structuring the ecology of interpersonal relations, labour and economics for that city. When the factory closes, that ecology collapses and ripples are sent through everything else. This is what happened in Flint, Michigan, when the automotive factories closed. As a consequence, people find that they must perpetually consider the factory when making any decision. For example, the factory might be engaged in environmentally destructive practices that contaminate drinking water, yet the inhabitants and local government of the town might find it difficult to address these issues because people are so dependent on the factory in order to live. We can thus call those entities whose path is structured by a bright object 'satellites'. They are caught in orbit around this other machine or bright object.

In addition to bright objects and satellites, there are dim objects. These are objects that only faintly appear in ecologies and that exercise very limited gravity within the ecologies they inhabit. The homeless and certain minority groups within a city would be examples of dim objects. They are there in the ecology, yet have very limited possibilities of movement and becoming and exercise even more limited gravity. The most terrifying objects would be black holes. These are objects that exercise such powerful gravity that they are inescapable. Many people worry that capitalism is a black hole, fearing that it is a machine or assemblage capable of assimilating all opposition such that no alternative is possible. A terminal illness is a black hole. Certain drug addictions are black holes. In all of these instances the agent is ineluctably trapped within the gravity of another machine. Finally, there are the rogue objects. Astronomers have recently discovered rogue stars, planets and perhaps even rogue black holes. These are cosmic objects unattached to any particular system that wander throughout galaxies and between galaxies. They seem to be strangely free of the gravitational paths determined by other machines, wandering throughout the universe such that they suddenly erupt within other ecologies, reconfiguring them. Revolutionary groups, certain works of art, certain sequences of thought, certain technologies and so on would be instances of rogue objects. They are, from a certain vantage and in the register of culture, not astronomy, what Badiou refers to as 'events'. They seem to appear as if out of nowhere and when they do they reconfigure all of the gravitational relations or paths structuring an ecology.

The interior operations of enclosure function to sort entities as satellites and dim objects through the formation of gravitational relations that act upon the bodies that inhabit them. Domestic dwelling embodies an entire history of postures, activities, identities and interpersonal relations expressing the formation of gravitational paths that operate on those that dwell within them. The manor house partitioned space in such a way as to relegate the servants to the status of dim objects, doing everything possible to render them invisible, while also transforming them into gears, sub-routines or mechanisms within the overall manor house machine. It is not merely that the manor house partitioned space such as the space of the kitchen, the laundry and the servants' quarters in such a way as to render the servants invisible, but also in a manner befitting Foucault's analyses of subjectivising functions of certain spaces; these distributions of space functioned to literally form servants as servants. In other words, they acted upon human bodies to form them as particular social types. A variety of semiotic and spatial machines were deployed to achieve these ends. At the semiotic end of the spectrum, rules and uniforms were used to regulate the servants, tell them what they were and distinguish them from the lords. For example, servants were forbidden from having romantic relations with one another. No doubt the lords of the manor appealed to practical justifications for these policies, claiming that they prevented drama and unwanted pregnancies that would get in the way of the operations of the manor-machine. However, the message of these incorporeal regulatory-machines was clear: the servant was to give over his or her entire life to being a mechanism within the machine of the manor and was nothing other than a machine within that machine.

Spatially these subjectivising operations were carried out through partitions of space that emphasised sparse, utilitarian functionalism with respect to servants' quarters, workspaces and paths of movement. The quarters, with their utilitarian functionalism, were designed merely to sustain life so that it could continue to function in much the same way that sleeping areas are designed on aircraft carriers and military submarines. Spaces for leisure activity and social interaction were thoroughly de-emphasised so as to produce bodies and subjectivities thoroughly devoted to operating the manor. This alone, however, did not solve the problem of the relationship between the lords of the manor and the servants. Special hallways and pathways had to be constructed so that the servants could move from place to place in the manor without being seen by the lords. The manor house partitioned space in such a way that there were really two kingdoms within the kingdom, where one of these kingdoms functioned not merely to operate the manor machine as a whole, but also to form those servant bodies that operated the manor in such a way as to make them servants.

Something similar happened with the dwellings of the racially segregated South in the 1950s. It is not simply that urban and surburban, as well as public spaces such as restaurants, were racially segregated; even the so-called private space of the home formed interior membranes that divided the races. Here the 'help' was spatialised in such a way as to transform it into a dim object. Often the kitchen of the middle-class home was behind doors, separated from both the dining area and the general living area. Again, this functioned to inhibit certain interpersonal relations and also to subjectivise those bodies that occupied these spaces, reminding them that they were gears in the functioning of a particular machine and that they were paradoxically outside, even while being inside, the family unit.

No doubt these spatial configurations of the relation between the kitchen and the living and dining space did not merely reflect racial relations, but also engaged in gendering operations. The kitchen was to be the space of female bodies, tucked away from male spaces and the general family space. The membrane formed by the enclosed kitchen with its door operated in such a way as to reinforce these gender identities and ensure that certain forms of relation between man and woman, husband and wife, mother and child, did not occur. The shift to open-concept kitchens reflects a general shift in gender and familial relations. Kitchens now often open on to living and dining areas. This reflects a change in relations to children and between men and women. The kitchen is now a collective space in which all are to participate. Women are not to be hidden away, nor is the kitchen an exclusively female domain, but rather both men and women are to participate in the preparation of food, that flow of energy that plays a key role in allowing these particular enclosures to operate. However, it would be a mistake to think that these new configurations of space simply *reflect* changing gender and family relations. The demolition of the membrane between the kitchen and the broader living space creates a machine that functions to encourage particular sorts of interpersonal relations, just as the garage placed at the front of a house functions to encourage the formation of community within a neighbourhood. Again, the spatialisation of space functions as a catalytic operator to afford or constrain certain forms of relation.

I have here only sketched what a machine-oriented architecture would look like in the faintest of outlines. In the preceding, I have focused on how distributions of space operate on bodies, defining the paths along which they move, relations between bodies that dwell within these spaces and pass through them, and how they relate to one another. I have sought to gesture towards how the membranes definitive of enclosures interact with the broader world outside them, such that they don't merely partition outside from inside, but also interface ecologically with an outside, and also how enclosures channel the forces of the cosmos, creating unheard-of voids. A more complete analysis would have to investigate how enclosures are generative of certain ecologies, functioning as catalysts for the formation of roads, power plants, supermarkets, schools and so on, required to render these forms of dwelling possible.

Yet there is so much more to develop. First, operations of enclosure are not the only operations characteristic of architectural machines. Architectural machines do not merely enclose spaces, but also create organs that form conduits between, inside and outside. Windows and doorways are organs within membranes that form relations with an outside. How does light operate through windows in architectural machines? How does it operate upon the bodies that flow through architectural machines? There are also thermodynamic questions to be asked regarding how energy in the form of food and fuel passes through architectural machines, the inputs and outputs of waste produced by these machines, and how this relates to the broader ecology in which these machines are embedded.

There are questions to be raised about how these machines function as machines of subjectivisation and what sorts of subjectivities these machines produce. Foucault paved the way for the analysis of this dimension of architectural machines in *Discipline and Punish*. What are the machines of subjectivisation in the home, mall, restaurant, church, school, factory, office and so on? Generally, machines of subjectivisation are seen in a negative light, but are there emancipatory subjectivisation machines? Additionally, these machines do not merely produce subjectivities, but also contribute to the formation of various types of communities. They can function to inhibit the formation of certain forms of collective relations as well. Above all, there is the question of aesthetics and how architecture functions as an aesthetic machine. Music has the curious ability to affect us through sound – without signification – alone. Sounds can be spooky or joyous or angry or aggressive or exuberant. The same is the case with space. Different partitionings of the void can produce different effects. How is it that space operates in these ways?

Finally, there is the question of the temporality of architecture. There is, of course, the sense in which enclosures are crystals of time, referencing the time in which they were produced, its ecology, its semiotics, its assumptions about how people should relate. Architecture preserves times. Some spaces are haunted because they preserve time so well. Chernobyl is a city and series of enclosures that is haunted because it references its past and is a site that remains, despite the fact that it has ceased to operate. It calls for flows yet no bodies flow through it. The New City shopping mall in Bangkok is haunted in a similar way, yet a different one as well. Like Chernobyl, it has been abandoned, but it has not ceased to operate. Rather, the New City mall now operates on entirely different, nonhuman bodies. Filled with water, there are populations of fish that populate this enclosure.

Above all, we should seek to determine what a rogue or revolutionary enclosure would be. We generally think of enclosures as restrictive, yet they afford movement and becoming in all sorts of ways. The gods might have exiled us from an organic relation with our shells, yet in doing so they gave us the opportunity to create enclosures that act upon us and carry the possibility of enhancing our becomings and movements in all sorts of ways. In defiance of the gods, we should ask what an enclosure can do.

Notes

1. Levi Bryant, *Onto-Cartography: An Ontology of Machines and Media* (Edinburgh: Edinburgh University Press, 2014).
2. Cf. Gilles Deleuze and Félix Guattari, *Anti-Oedipus: Capitalism and Schizophrenia*, trans. Helen R. Lane, Robert Hurley and Mark Seem (Minneapolis: University of Minnesota Press, 1983).
3. Cf. Michel Foucault, *Discipline and Punish: The Birth of the Prison* (New York: Vintage, 1995).

CHAPTER 8

The Compass of Beauty: A Search for the Middle

Lars Spuybroek

A very specific problem occurs at the heart of ontology: how can things exist externally, with others, while being made up of parts, and thus existing internally? Or, to phrase it a bit more pointedly, in Kantian terms: how can things have synthetic relations between the whole and the world while being constituted analytically, through relations between the whole and its parts? How can these two realms be part of one continuum of existence? No variety of materialism has been able to solve this problem. In its traditional form, determinism, either God or consciousness is needed to direct the connecting vector of necessity; and its later form, emergence, leaves a gap between the interacting parts and the emerged whole happily interacting with other wholes. Even in the nineteenth century, Darwin struggled with the idea that variation acted as the sole positive force in nature, 'endlessly' adding 'forms most beautiful',[1] with natural selection doomed merely to act as a negative force, selecting out some of those variants as ugly misfits. Indeed, fitness in itself contributes nothing to the concept of variation, since it is not the environment that tells parts how to come together. Apparently, parts only interact with parts and wholes with wholes, and while materialist ontologies succeed very well in explaining the intensive parts stage and the environmental wholes stage, they completely fail to connect the two. The two physical sides of the equation are separated by a yawning metaphysical gap, impossible for them to bridge, at least physically. A brief reflection on the vertical nature of the term 'emergence', however, should make us realise that the flat, blind world of material interactions cannot exist without transcendence. Scientists and philosophers of science speak of emergence as if it is the reverse of classic top-down imposition, and it is, but merely in directionality, certainly not conceptually: it inhabits the same vertical axis, covers the same vertical distance and thrives on the same dualisms. Without question, admitting to the metaphysical nature of emergence would deeply affect all notions of physicality, which is why all materialists shy away from it. Therefore, we should find a way to accept transcendence and, instead of making it part of external agency, make it part of things themselves.

To do so, we would first need to put enough mind into matter to allow the parts to see beyond their own horizon. We should come to understand their efforts to conform as an actual striving for a whole, which amounts not to a general teleology, like the abovementioned necessity, but rather to a local teleology, or what we might call a local transcendence. Then, inversely, we should allow wholes to connect to parts of other wholes, turning that local transcendence into a zone of attraction. My claim is that only beauty makes this reversal possible. It makes the parts exceed the whole, rather than the whole exceeding the parts, as the doctrine of emergence prescribes. When you say someone has beautiful eyes, you do not expect the other to take out an eye and hand it over, as Baudrillard once joked. The parts of other people or things that we like – somebody's red hair, the shining of gold, the curves of the hills, the light flickering on the river – we do not like as such, but as parts of a whole, as radiating from that whole.[2] And at that point, the part has transcended its role as a part. The red hair might insulate the scalp from the cold, but our liking has no interest whatsoever in that physiological function. Natural selection will never be able to explain why redness came about in the way that emergence can, but emergence will never be able to explain why redness is liked – they pass each other like ships in the night. Beauty allows parts to be visible and available to other wholes without removing them from their relationship with neighbouring parts. Philosophically speaking, this is unheard of: no other power is capable of jumping over the proverbial gap between the two realms. Beauty – and it is no accident that Darwin used the word – solves that impossible equation and manages to put the analytic and the synthetic in the same realm of existence, or at least to find a point where they intersect or align, or even pivot when we think of it as a reversal: a point that is necessarily ontological. Things cannot be without being beautiful; or, to put it somewhat more neutrally, things cannot be without making a claim on their environment, no matter what that claim is. Beauty is like the narrow middle of an hourglass, with all parts gathering into a single point on the convergent side and spilling out on the other, divergent side, as if radiating from that point. Our question in the next twenty or so pages should then be: How does beauty construct this intersection between the two states?

Traditionally, this point has been termed a 'middle', a middle that has taken on so many forms that it may be useful to roughly sketch its historical transformations before we enter into a more detailed discussion. A good place to start would be Apollo's call for moderation, which later developed into Aristotle's virtuous golden mean, and in between, Plato's monopolar universe where beauty occupied the absolute centre of everything. This concept raises some questions right away: does it mean that beauty is itself the middle – like a heart or an origin – or that it must exist between pre-existing extremes that have not yet been mentioned? Plato was rather ambiguous on the matter, since in his philosophy beauty plays the role of the good yet is as often described by him in terms of the terrifying, such as a bolt of lightning that strikes from the sky. Apparently, his singular pole secretly leads a double existence. A few centuries after Plato, lightning became the model Longinus used to postulate his notion of the sublime in the *Peri Hypsous*: the claim of things not to a middle position but to the greatest and the highest. For more than a millennium, the universe of aesthetics has remained in this bipolar state, oscillating between beauty and the sublime, though occasionally other forms are admitted – the novel, the strange, the comic, the tragic – mostly in the form of subcategories. The first notion of beauty and the sublime being connected by a continuous scale of gradual transformations – as if by a slider, so to speak – may have come with the invention of the picturesque, famously described by Uvedale Price as 'a station in between beauty and sublimity'. As is well known, Kant carefully follows the English aestheticians in their theories, while adding more positions to the slider and shifting beauty slightly towards the middle by introducing the pretty (*Hübsch*) at one extreme and the sublime at the other, with the magnificent and the terrifying (*Schreckhaft-Erhabene*) in between. Dilthey, the German neo-Kantian philosopher, in turn managed to add the ugly to the line-up as well, and was the first to call the system a spectrum. Following this hint on colour, it was Max Dessoir who then constructed a diagram of aesthetics in the form of a colour wheel, a spoked circle, finally bending the linear spectrum into a curved systemacy. At that point, it was not clear to Dessoir how the circle in fact reintroduced the concept of a middle on a new level: as a centre, not as the midpoint on a line. At last, in the 1970s, the American process philosopher Charles Hartshorne, by then a septuagenarian (though with another thirty years ahead of him), mixed Dessoir's model with Whitehead's ideas on beauty to form a very precise biaxial model while placing beauty back at the centre, creating a middle between two dimensions, between two sliders – one analytical, indexing the relations between parts, and the other synthetic, indexing relations between wholes. At that point almost 2,500 years had passed since Plato had expressed his ideas on beauty.

Describing the course of beauty through history, even in such a sketchy fashion, immediately challenges a facile concept of the middle, demanding a far more rigorous definition that will allow us to understand the variations and how these might have evolved from one another. In some of these historic phases, the term 'middle' referred to moderation and mediation; sometimes it indicated a mean; and sometimes it was used in the sense of an equation. However, in this apparently confusing lineage we discern a clear increase in dimensionality, going from Plato's universal centre point to an ever-widening linear scale, then transforming into a circular surface defined by a centre and a circumference. Naturally, during each of these phases, questions arise. For instance, looking at its linear phase, should we view the middle as a pivot between two ends of a scale? That would mean the middle was fixed and the extremes were variable. Or should we view the poles as fixed, with a sliding midpoint between them, which things could seek out through variation? The first would probably best be called an equation, the second a mediation. Strangely enough, the continuous blurring of concepts itself seems to have increased the dimensionality of the system. The single point transforms into a single line with two poles, and that single line into two lines (now with four poles), each stage defined by its own notion of a middle, be it a centre, a form of mediation or an equation. We should not only be questioning what exactly constitutes a middle but also asking ourselves what it is whose middle we are speaking of, since throughout its history beauty has been surrounded by ever more diverse aesthetic values. Does this mean beauty is positioned in a world that consists of states that are not beautiful? Yes, in a way. And when such states are not beautiful, are they still part of that pivoting function, that ontological function that we have assigned to beauty? Yes, probably. And if so, does that mean those other states are related to beauty in a way in which they are not related to each other? Yes, it certainly would.

At the moment when we start to view beauty as fundamental to existence, we are able to understand the variable powers of the analytic and the synthetic as they merge in entities, spawning things that are not only beautiful but, just as often, ugly, magnificent, cute or funny, if not hilarious or ridiculous, or even quirky and quaint, cool, boring or weird, melodramatic and vulgar, or again totally common and ordinary, not forgetting of course horrific and terrifying, or utterly gruesome and disgusting – and many, many more things. Such ontological abundance means in the first place that all things are positive: all things act in the arena of presence, an arena deprived of any backstage area, basement, or curtains to hide behind. Things can be withdrawn, autistic or melancholic, but they are so in the light of day. In the second place, it means all positive things are equations of the analytic and the synthetic, both axes producing positive values somewhere between zero and a maximum. And, since the synthetic deals with the configuration of presence – all wholes interacting with one another at a certain moment – it also means, in the third place, that such a snapshot fills the complete mosaic of beauty in all its variations. It forms a universe where every fragrant flower, every smile on a face, every bomb attack, every nightmare, every tumour and every silly joke seems to be part of a massive kaleidoscopic image in which the heaviest stone monument and the tiniest reflection, a flash of red hair and a plane crash, the most fragile dragonfly and the darkest forest all mosaically fit together at every instant, constantly aggregating into enormous multicoloured crystals, which immediately collapse to be replaced with new generations; and this kaleidoscopic image is beyond what anyone of us would call order, or chaos for that matter, passing a threshold at which sheer contingency and pure perfection are wholly interchangeable.

Let us now take our little sketch and, step by step, add more detail.

Spectrum and Circle

The ancient, colossal statue of Apollo on his island of birth, Delos, carried in one hand his famous bow and in the other a second, much smaller statue of the Three Graces, mounted on a disk. Though a frequent method of depicting Apollo's dual nature in ancient Greece, this iconography is no longer commonly known, since most statues have not survived intact and only a handful of engravings on ancient coins and descriptions in ancient manuscripts remain. Apollo's better-known attributes, the bow and the lyre, fulfilled similar functions, though more ambivalently, since in ancient Greece the two were clearly connected. For example, Heraclitus used the bow and the lyre to illustrate his celebrated doctrine on the harmony of opposites,[3] later developed into *concordia discors*, the maxim of the Renaissance. Aside from the formal resemblance between bow and lyre, there is the conceptual one: the string of a bow can 'sing sweetly', as Homer wrote,[4] and the music of the lyre can strike at our hearts with the sharpness of an arrow. The classical philologist Karl Kerényi argued that Apollo could not be adequately characterised by the customary loftiness ascribed to him but combined chthonic darkness and Olympian clarity in one divinity.[5] In a similar vein, the classicist Marcel Detienne speaks of Apollo's 'profound ambivalence', especially because he had more killings to his name than any other god.[6] Apollo was capable of 'striking from afar' (*hekebolos*) with his arrows as well as enchanting and persuading with his music or his tongue. In other words, Apollo's dual nature is not so much a question of choice, of either/or, but of a combination, a doubling of the dimensions in which each of his actions takes place.

In light of this, we should be quick to distance ourselves from the depiction of Apollo as the tedious, teetotal, proto-Christian anti-Dionysus that the early Nietzsche made of him in *The Birth of Tragedy*. The young philosopher crudely located Dionysus at one end of the spectrum and Apollo on the other, as if the first were interested only in excess and the second merely in harmony. Apollo's temple in Delphi was in fact shared with the Dionysus cult. In winter the temple was used to dedicate services to Dionysus, but the rest of the year the priestess – the Pythia – was in regular but frenzied communication with Apollo through epiphanies that were at least as ecstatic as those of the god of wine and spirits. Certainly, Apollo's maxim – *mēden ágan* ('nothing in excess'), inscribed above the entrance to the temple in Delphi – is a call for moderation, but we have to keep in mind that moderation is always one *of* excess. Apollo's call is not one for abstinence: he does not propose to counter excess with asceticism or passivity; that would lead absolutely nowhere. We should understand that excess and moderation are not of the same order and that we cannot just stop halfway towards excess. We cannot simply interrupt ourselves, nor can we divide ourselves in two, into a rational, moderating mind and a body thirsty for excess, since the mind would quickly concede during any ecstatic act. No, it would be much better to imagine excess and measure as two forces coming from different directions. And those two forces need to be mediated: they can only be resolved through one act. In this case, a single act does not subsist in doing one thing until the point of exhaustion. The act needs to follow a curved trajectory: to start in one direction and come to a close in another. A single act – that is, an act of beauty – does two things simultaneously. First it aims for excess, then it aims for moderation, or, to use the metaphor of Apollo's bow, it shoots the arrow upward while aiming forward. With this model, we are shifting the notion of mediation towards that of mathematical equation: between the horizontal axis of measure and the vertical axis of excess, Apollo draws a curved function, equating the influence of both, starting with more verticality and ending with horizontality.

Doing something well, or, as Aristotle would say, doing something virtuously, then becomes a form of *navigation*, in which we do not move in one direction but steer between multiple directions. This, of course, we recognise from Plato's analogy of the charioteer in the *Phaedrus*, where the soul is represented by a chariot pulled by two winged horses, one black and the other white. Plato's analogies – the cave, the ladder of love, the charioteer – are not just metaphors, as often indicated, but closer to mathematical functions, and it is no accident that in many translations they are clarified with concise diagrams. In fact, it would not be wholly off the mark to call Plato the first analytic philosopher, since those analogies could easily be written out in mathematical symbols (his notion of truth was deeply influenced by Pythagorean equations). Anyway, the brilliance of the analogy of the charioteer lies in the fact that the vector of an act can be separated into two forces, or, more precisely, two sets of variables, since each horse can exert anything between minimum and maximum force. And since the horses are winged, the chariot can go up, down, left or right. It is quite clear from Plato's descriptions in the *Phaedrus* that the steering cannot be reduced to the mere imposing of one's will on both horses – if that were the case, the soul would not need the horses to strive. On the contrary, Plato describes a myriad of behaviours: zigzagging through the sky, falling back to earth, and steering one's way up to the sphere of immortality to become part of the ever-recurring cycles of the heavenly bodies. The soul, as Plato sees it, is not the charioteer steering the body as a homunculus but the single movement between two directions. Slightly earlier, when writing the *Symposium*, he used the term *metaxu* for this in-between, a term which becomes especially important in the dialogue between Diotima – 'a woman from Mantinea' – and Socrates, as she teaches him about the nature of love as it relates to beauty.

'Love is of beautiful things',[7] she says, which means not yet possessing beautiful things but being in a state between not having and having beauty, a state that cannot be described as a static betweenness but as a being-under-way, a state of striving and navigating. In this sense, all acts are acts of love because they strive for beauty, and such acts coordinate themselves between two feelings: one of sheer happiness[8] and one of pure fear, a fear of falling in which one moves in the opposite direction along the vertical axis of transcendence towards doom and failure. This double movement of love is taken up again in the *Phaedrus* after the analogy of the charioteer, when he arrives at the moment of possession, falling in love with a beautiful boy whose face strikes him like 'a bolt of lightning';[9] it is a love that makes the soul 'begin to grow wings'.[10] And, as often in Plato, it presents a dual argument that floats between stillness – we should bear in mind that the charioteer actually stands still in his chariot – and movement, between wisdom and ignorance, but here especially between overpowering and empowering. We are 'captured by beauty' while 'a fear comes over us',[11] a power that comforts us as much as it terrifies us, and one that he as often associates with a bolt of lightning as with the brilliance of the sun.

In Plato, we are not only introduced to this vast cosmic system of heavenly verticality and earthly horizontality but also to this confusion of beauty-as-the-highest and beauty-as-the-middle. And the confusion sometimes tends to take hold of the pages and spread like a stain. For example, Plato is adamant about the ontological nature of beauty when he states that beauty is literally 'seeing reality';[12] then again, he is convinced that the realm of beauty, a 'place beyond heaven', is 'a place without colours, without forms, and without solidity'.[13] Obviously, such a contradiction at the core of his philosophy poses a colossal problem. How can we see what is invisible? Let us first note that the confusion was not merely his own: it preceded him in different forms, and it persisted all the way through Hegel's 'sinnliche Idee'[14] and Paul Klee's 'art renders the invisible visible', to cite just two examples. Also, we should realise that the problem is more of a geometrical, dimensional nature than a conceptual or philosophical one. Without a doubt, Plato put all the elements in place: the vertical, the horizontal, linearity, circularity, the middle, the circumference – though the whole idea remains a tangle almost too discouraging to unravel. As stated, it would take thinkers a couple of thousand years to see that what looked like a pole was actually a line, and that what looked like a line was actually an axis, and what looked like one axis with two poles was actually two axes, and that those two axes were equated by a circle, and that the circle was a single line that had one pole in the middle. After a few millennia of aesthetic development had traced beauty back in the centre, we can conclude that Plato had been right all along.

The notion of beauty-as-the-highest is one we find in many variations, of course, especially under the Neoplatonic philosophers, such as Pseudo-Dionysius, Plotinus and Saint Augustine, who without exception were theologians. Nietzsche derisively called Christianity 'Platonism for the people',[15] which might not be completely accurate, except for the implicit argument that Christians took advantage of Plato's confusion. The image of God embodies fear as much as it does love, and this confusion goes back much further than the Christian interpretation of Platonism. For instance, Zeus was associated with lightning, thunder and weather in general,[16] that is, with what we would call the sublime, while his son Apollo was associated with the sun and the radiance of the beautiful. (I would not be the first to state that Christianity copied that model from the ancient Greeks. In fact, very early depictions of Jesus show him as beardless as Apollo, and with his head surrounded by the same radiant halo.) But let us not dwell too long on the mythological origins of Western theology. Since our interest goes out to beauty and navigation, we should focus on its dimensional structure and try to unravel the difference between beauty-as-the-highest and beauty-as-the-middle. Longinus, who in the first century AD wrote *Peri Hypsous* – literally meaning 'On the High', though generally translated as *On the Sublime* – makes extensive use of the thunder-and-lightning model to describe the epiphanic character of sublimity. Throughout the treatise, it is clear that Longinus aligns the sublime with greatness – a word he uses over and over – as well as with the power of lightning that strikes from above, moving the subject 'out of himself' (*ekstasis*) and overpowering him with an 'irresistible force'. Let us disregard the fact that Longinus' argument lies in the realm of rhetoric, or art in general, since it makes no difference for the positioning of the sublime on the vertical axis whether we encounter it in words, in imagery, through standing in front of actual mountains, or through sitting at home contemplating the endlessness of the universe – the diversity of these examples is telling enough. Beauty, sublimity, ugliness, nobility – without exception, these aesthetic values are to be found in the realm of the natural as well as the artificial; therefore, no theory relying on the formal properties of these realms will be able to sufficiently define such values. What is remarkable is that what at first seem to be mere metaphors are in fact exact phenomenological descriptions of aesthetic feelings; and what is even more remarkable is that their precision does not lead to a phenomenology but to an ontological machinery of a perplexing geometrical exactitude. How else would it be possible for things to be called 'high' or 'great'?

After Longinus was translated into French by Boileau in 1674, his book quickly landed in the hands of the English aestheticians, and it was they who developed the sublime and prepared it for the German idealists, who turned the high into the deep, first as Kant's *Abgrund*, then as Schelling's *Ungrund*. John Dennis, Joseph Addison, the Earl of Shaftesbury, Edmund Burke: over a period of a hundred years, English aesthetic philosophers took the sublime and refined it with notions such as that of enthusiastic terror, which they distinguished from common terror (a fear mixed with a feeling of admiration), and placed it in the realm of the unlimited, the majestic and the stupendous, all direct descendants of Plato's black horse, the horse of divine madness, or as the ancient Greeks called it, *enthousiasmos*. But what in Plato was still an overlapping of two forms of beauty, the highest and the middle, now became more clearly distinguished: beauty was a smooth world of what Francis Hutcheson famously called 'uniformity amidst variety',[17] while the sublime was a world of the unlimited and the unbound, of either enormous size (like mountains), indefinite size (like weather and storms), or infinite size (like endlessness itself). Even without elaborating on the issue, it is immediately clear how the variety of terminology led to Kant's 'Analytic of the Sublime', in which the sublime is analysed as formlessness[18] or as the gap in judgement, be it in its mathematical state of the infinite or its dynamic state of pure forces without form. For our purposes, the younger Kant is of more use, since he drew, in particular, from the wealth of Burke's *A Philosophical Enquiry into the Origin of Our Ideas of the Beautiful and the Sublime* of 1757 and started to change its organisation from a bipolar to a linear system.

Though in his *Observations on the Feeling of the Beautiful and Sublime* (1764) Kant is not as imaginative as Burke in introducing new aesthetic values, he is highly original at conceiving linkages between them. While in Burke's *Enquiry* all aesthetic examples are defined as subcategories of the two polar categories, we encounter a more complex systematisation in *Observations*. As in Burke, we are told that mountains are sublime, as are Egyptian pyramids, and, in general, men more than women, but also black hair and all things related to the night, while small things are beautiful, and of course women more than men, as well as blond hair and delicate things bathing in daylight. The two colours of Plato's horses return even in human hair, defining the same distinction of ecstatic *Rührung* and calming *Reiz*.[19] As said, the increased systemacy of the *Observations* is of more interest to us, especially since it is based on what Kant calls *Mischung*, admixture. We should bear in mind that 'admixture' is a concept closely related to Plato's *metaxu*, since it requires a continuum between two different states. With the term *Mischung*, Kant is able to articulate the existence of objects that are, for instance, less sublime and more beautiful, such as the splendid, *das Prächtige*. That notion of the splendid is then no longer a subcategory of the sublime, like Burke's magnificence, but a genuine category born of the parentage of mixture. Because of its direct relation to power and overpowering, Kant found the splendid in palatial and ecclesiastical buildings. Homonyms for splendid are 'superb', 'great', 'grand', 'magnificent', all referring unambiguously to size. Largeness is not merely a question of size; it necessarily follows the play of forces, and therefore structure is more visible than, say, a smooth skin. For example, Rome's St Peter's basilica, Kant argues, has both sublime aspects, because of the colossal order of 'its frame, which is large and simple',[20] and elements of beauty, such as the 'gold and the mosaic work', and in their mixture we apprehend it as splendid. This is a discovery of great significance, though mostly overlooked by Kant himself, since it means that an object that has aspects of two aesthetic categories can be experienced in one feeling rather than through swinging back and forth between two. Such an insight could have led him away from subjectivism, because it emphasises the singularity of the aesthetic object.

At the far end of the sublime, Kant posits the *Schreckhaft-Erhabene*, the terrifying sublime, followed by the noble (*das Edle*), and then by the splendid. Each of these moves further away from a pure sublime, mixing in more beauty, until we finally arrive at beauty itself, first in a more mature version, which still seems to contain some remnants of the sublime, and then in a juvenescent version he calls *hübsch*, pretty, a derivation of beauty that 'speaks less to the heart'.[21] As often, though, next to admixtures we find Burkean subcategories of the sublime and of beauty, such as tragedy and comedy. Since in the *Observations* Kant is not trying to build a solid philosophical system, as he is in the three Critiques, it is rather difficult for the reader to distinguish between genuine aesthetic feelings and variants of such feelings. Gradually, however, we see the beginnings of a *linear* system emerging, not Plato's polar or Burke's bipolar model, but a continuous line with at one end things that are *smooth*, vary gradually and are mostly smaller in size, and at the other end things that are *rough*, vary more through angularity and sudden shifts and are larger. This resembles almost exactly the system used by Uvedale Price to position his notion of the picturesque as 'a station between beauty and sublimity'.[22] In 1796's *On the Picturesque*, he maps out exactly what the picturesque consists of:

> Another essential quality of beauty is gradual variation; that is . . . where the lines do not vary in a sudden and broken manner, and where there is no sudden protuberance: it requires but little reflection to perceive, that the exclusion of all but flowing lines cannot promote variety; and that sudden protuberances, and lines that cross each other in a sudden and broken manner, are among the most fruitful causes of intricacy. I am therefore persuaded, that the two opposite qualities of roughness, and of sudden variation, joined to that of irregularity, are the most efficient causes of the picturesque.[23]

Reading this carefully, we notice that Price describes the two not just as a pole of roughness and an opposing one of smoothness but also as two types of variation. Here, we get the first hint in aesthetic theory that things are combinations (equations, mixtures, *metaxu*) of two sliding scales, one of smooth and one of rough variation, one of graduality and one of suddenness. What first seemed to be a mere *pole* of beauty opposed to one of the sublime slowly develops into an *axis* of beauty, sliding between unity and plurality, and an axis of the sublime, sliding between maximum depth, that is, the infinite, and minimum depth, such as prettiness. This would mean that less smooth does not automatically equate to more rough but that both smoothness and roughness consist of their own sliding scales, each influencing every object independently. We find another hint at such a theory in Hogarth's renowned *Analysis of Beauty*, which is generally taken as an argument for mere smoothness, since it stipulates the importance of the smooth, S-shaped serpentine line, which he calls the line of beauty. This is only partially correct, since in Hogarth's analysis these lines of smoothness and gradualism *do not connect up smoothly*:

> there is one type of waving line that truly deserves the name of the line of beauty, only one precise serpentine line that I call the line of grace . . . lines that should be judiciously mixed and combined with one another . . . into [a joint sensation of bulk and motion].[24]

Later in the book, when discussing contemporary women's hairdos, he calls the combination of smooth curves and criss-crossing wantonness 'picturesque',[25] almost forty years before Uvedale Price used the term. And in his paintings and engravings he uses the same term for dancing groups, gatherings at dinner tables and crowds in the street. In his introduction to the book, Ronald Paulson very aptly describes Hogarth's aesthetics as 'an aesthetics of the crowd'.[26] The title *The Analysis of Beauty* suggests the desire to update the notion of beauty, though, not to introduce a new species, and to move away from the all-too-idealised, all-out smoothness of Giorgione or Titian, in which smooth lines do connect up smoothly. Hogarth tried to locate a new middle in the combination of roughness – what he calls 'bulk' – and smoothness – 'the line of grace'. In Price and Hogarth, we encounter as yet only a suggestion of a biaxiality of the aesthetic system; we must wait almost two hundred years to see it elaborated to its full extent in the realm of philosophy.

In that discipline, it was first Wilhelm Dilthey, the German neo-Kantian philosopher, who expanded Kant's selection of values, fitting in more of the terms that Burke had introduced. What makes his contribution particularly valuable is the introduction of the term 'spectrum' in his discussion of the notion of mixtures. In 1887's *Poetry and Experience*, he writes:

> To this mixture of the sublime, the tragic, and evil, ugliness can be added. Here we reach the limits of aesthetic impression. We represented the beautiful as the midpoint of a spectrum of poetic moods.[27]

Of course, we have just leapfrogged over the span of a full century, so by the time we encounter Dilthey, many details have been added to what we can almost start calling the aesthetic diagram. Aside from the term 'mixture' reintroduced after Kant, we see that Dilthey has managed to finally position ugliness in the line-up; until then, ugliness had merely been a subcategory of beauty, and a negative one at that. The works of Victor Hugo, Dickens or Shakespeare would be unimaginable without their ugly characters, Dilthey argues; the narrative would simply not move forward. And he encounters the same positivity of the ugly in African masks and in Dante. To clarify, he is not making a judgement; neither judgement nor criticality plays an ontological role in aesthetics. Following the same line of argument, Charles Hartshorne states very clearly that there is no negativity in aesthetics, not even a zero, only positivity:[28] there is no way we cannot experience; we might qualify our experience as 'negative', but that is still a qualification and not a non-qualification. What is more, Dilthey speaks of a spectrum of values, which will prove to be important when we start to involve the colour wheel as a system incorporating not only gradualism but also contrast and suddenness. And, he makes a far bigger effort than his predecessors to restore the notion of beauty-as-the-middle, repositioning it from one side of the spectrum to the centre:

> On both ends of the spectrum, whose middle is formed by the ideally beautiful, there arises an admixture of displeasure, and from a dissolution of the latter, a peculiar agreeableness. In one case, the feeling of something immeasurably great in the meaning of an object must be overcome; in the other case, the feeling of something trifling.[29]

He is on to something extraordinary here. After hundreds of years of aestheticians extending the range of the sublime, adding various types of terror, even of horror (in the case of Ann Radcliffe),[30] he extends the range of beauty, not just with prettiness but many other aesthetic values, at least enough to shift beauty towards the middle. Though much of Kant remains in his analysis, Dilthey succeeds in including many of the values that Burke listed in his *Enquiry*, such as the ugly, the tragic and the comic, as Kant had failed to do. As with his predecessors, it is often difficult to precisely distinguish between categories and subcategories, but shifting back and forth, we can retrieve the following spectral sequence from *Poetry and Experience*: moving from one end to the other, we encounter the sublime, the tragic, the ugly, the beautiful, the sentimental, the comical, the graceful and the petite. At this point it is irrelevant whether or not we agree with this list. We merely need to acknowledge that what we called 'minimum depth' a few paragraphs ago has now been extended by multiple values, with petite at the far end, in clear reference to the smallest possible size of things. 'Trifling' also denotes a certain shallowness or superficiality, directly positioning it on an axis of depth, even though it indicates a lack of it. On the other hand, a spectrum of depths does not fit with Hutcheson's smooth spectrum that went from unity to variety, with everything in between and beauty in the middle. Evidently, organising aesthetic values in a linear system presents serious limitations. For instance, we can see how the sublime might differ only one notch from the tragic, but to have the ugly removed likewise by a single notch from beauty seems improbable. The more existing aesthetic values we try to incorporate, the less a single dimension succeeds in explaining how middles and extremes are to be related. If everything is mixture, what is at the ends? Surely, if there are ends, they would be excluded from the mixture. But if we succeeded in removing the ends, where would that leave the middle? That said, the enormous contribution of Dilthey's spectrum lies in the inclusion of the ugly as a positive value and (re-)positioning beauty in the middle of the system.

Finally, in his *Aesthetics and the Theory of Art* of 1906, the German aesthetics theorist Max Dessoir turns the spectrum into a circle. A two-dimensional circle is capable of organising values in a way that the one-dimensional line of a spectrum cannot; it can include adjacent gradations, such as that between the sublime and tragic, as well as contrasting oppositions, such as that between beauty and ugliness. In Dessoir's book it is depicted in a very small diagram, no more than an inch in diameter, with six aesthetic categories aligned along the perimeter. The spectral line born out of Burke's bipolar system now becomes an aesthetic circle that runs from sublime to beautiful, to cute (*Niedlich*),[31] to comic, to ugly, and finally to tragic, which links up again with the sublime. Without going too far with our analysis, we should make a few remarks on Dessoir's terminology. In the first place, 'cute' is a far better term than Kant's 'pretty' or Dilthey's 'petite'. 'Pretty' is not shallow enough, and 'petite' not small enough, to occupy the position most contrary to the sublime. For instance, babies are cute, and for good reason: cuteness is the form beauty takes in situations where there is a complete lack of power, so as to restore that power. Cuteness merges the shallow and the likeable into an overwhelming sweetness – again, a category acknowledged by Burke[32] – which we recognise from our soft drinks and our obsession with sugar, as well as from the way lovers constantly address one another as 'Sugar', 'Sweetie' or 'Honey'. Cuteness plays a far more important role in our contemporary aesthetic than it did in Dessoir's time, when there was no Hello Kitty, no My Little Pony, no Mini or Swatch (Figure 8.1).

On the other hand, when we compare Dessoir's circle to Dilthey's spectrum, some terms are missing, and some of the positionings are rather unconvincing. For instance, it is difficult to imagine the sublime and the beautiful as being adjacent to one another in the same way that

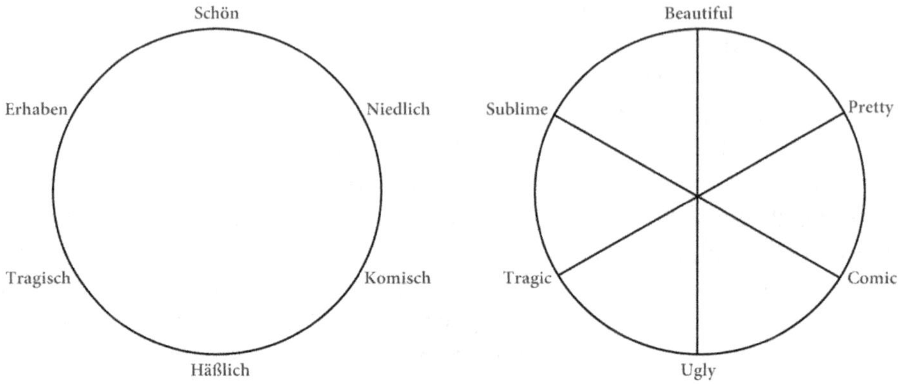

Figure 8.1 The aesthetic spectrum as published by Max Dessoir. On the left is the original German version from his 1906 *Ästhetik und allgemeine Kunstwissenschaft*; on the right, the diagram as published in the 1970 English edition *Aesthetics and the Theory of Art* (which mistranslates *Niedlich* as 'pretty' instead of 'cute').

beauty and the cute are, nor akin in the way of the sublime and the tragic, whose link was thoroughly established by Schiller and Schelling. Nor can we imagine the sublime and the beautiful being as close as the ugly and the comic, though Dessoir's positioning of the ugly is again an enormous improvement on Dilthey's. The comic and the ugly have an intimate relationship that we recognise from a long history, starting with dwarves, hunchbacks and jesters in the European courts, hilarious and pitiful Falstaffs in the theatre, and the *dumme August* and stumbling clowns in the circus. Similarly, from the eighteenth century onwards, we witnessed the explosion of caricature, the ultimate science of elasticity – elongating noses, thickening lips, bulging eyes, widening heads, shrinking chins and so on – which culminates in our own fabulous Mr Bean, who is blessed with the most elastic face ever. As with Dilthey, we are for the moment only concentrating on the organisational geometry of the aesthetic system, and therefore we can overlook the misplacing of certain categories and the resulting sequential order. Crucial at this point is that Dessoir closes the linear sequence into a circle by merging the ends, creating a continuity of aesthetic values.

It is no accident that the circular system looks like a colour wheel, as Dessoir himself remarks: 'the whole fabric of aesthetic feelings can take on various tints. . .'[33] Probably he chose six tints[34] for his aesthetic circle because it resembled Goethe's colour wheel of 1809 (see Figure 8.2, left), who, unlike Newton, based his colour scheme on gradations as much as on opposites (or what Goethe called polarity). The English edition of Dessoir's book adds spokes to the circular diagram, making it look

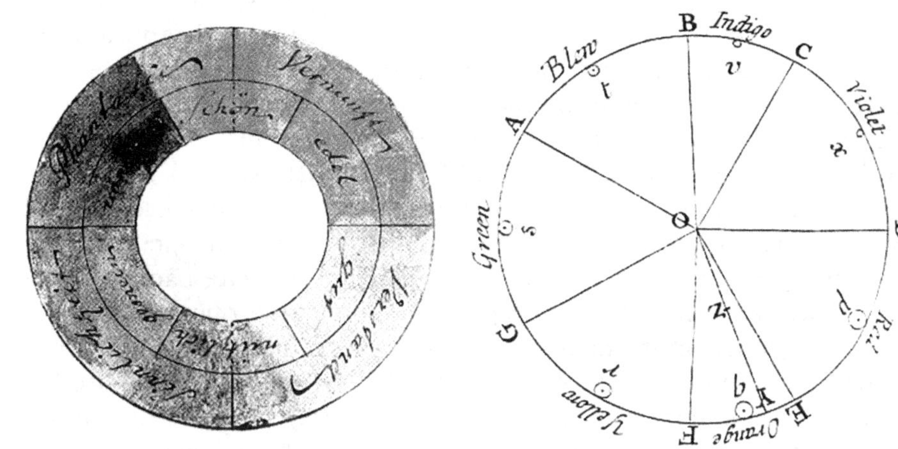

Figure 8.2 The two most famous colour wheels: on the left, Goethe's 1809 version with six colours (containing the term *Schön* in the red area); on the right, Newton's version from *Opticks* (1704).

even more like a wheel. Dessoir, who explicitly mentions Dilthey's *Poetry and Experience* as the main source of his ideas, admirably managed to join the two ends of the spectrum, like the ouroboros biting its own tail. Above all, he writes, his goal was 'to arrange the primary forms in such a way that the transition from each to the two adjacent ones occurs with conceptual ease, and those opposed in content are opposite in position'.[35] Again, it is an order that explains the two dimensions of existence in a way that a straight spectral band cannot. We can read the circle rotationally, following the gradual change from beautiful to cute to comic to ugly, and we can read beauty as opposite to ugliness as well, since they are positioned directly across the centre of the circle from each other. It coincides exactly with the colour wheel, which we can read as a system that contains *smooth*, gradual variations, such as that between red and orange, as well as *rough*, complementary contrasts, such as that between red and green.

In the history of colour theory, the circular diagram actually preceded the linear spectrum, since the latter is based on wavelengths in the electromagnetic realm that were not established until the nineteenth century. When we look back at the colour wheel with the knowledge of electromagnetic waves, we should ask ourselves how it is possible that ultraviolet can occupy a position directly adjacent to infrared when the two are at opposite ends of the linear spectrum. The position of violet between blue and red is completely logical when we look at the colour wheel, but not when we look at the linear band of colours of the electromagnetic spectrum.[36] It is quite a mystery, and in the world of colour theory there is no real answer to be found; it appears that *colour is a system in itself*, independent of electromagnetic waves, and therefore necessarily takes on the shape of a closed circle. How else can the colour corresponding to a wavelength of 380nm (violet) fit next to the one corresponding to that of 720nm (red)? What is discontinuous in the linear spectrum is continuous on the colour wheel, solving all relations between colours as gradations, but without sacrificing the structuring oppositions. Circular colour diagrams date back to medieval times, and though Aron Sigfrid Forsius made one in 1611 that contained much more detail, none of these exhibit the simplicity of Newton's colour circle published in his 1704 *Opticks* (see Figure 8.2, right). It is not certain that Newton ever laid eyes on the diagram of Forsius, nor how he came to bend the linear spectrum created by prism and rainbow alike into a circle. One reason why Newton created his circular diagram could be that he conceived it as a disc. With all the colours – and in his mind there were seven, which deeply disturbed Goethe, who preferred six – painted in the right sizes, the disc, when spun around at high speed, would change from multicoloured to white. (There we are: white is the mixture of all mixtures, the middle of all mediation.) This was to prove his theory that white light could be broken into spectral colours by a prism. However, it doesn't explain the colours' order. Probably the final answer was given by Newton himself, who admitted that between red and blue we would see indigo, not just the violet we find in the prismatic range.[37] None of these explanations is very satisfying. The perplexing fact remains that *all* colours can be arranged on a wheel, a solution far more convincing than the linear electromagnetic spectrum: it radically turns colour into a world of its own, an autonomous system constructed by internal relations of gradation and opposition.

The fact that we cannot explain something with concepts that are external to it means that, philosophically speaking, we have reached bedrock. A system that only consists of smooth, gradual variations would need an underlying, second system to adequately explain contrasts. And a system that consists only of fractures or rough variations would need a secondary system to explain kinship. It is mind-boggling to discover an ontological machinery based on continuity explaining the discontinuous, since it acknowledges polarity without having to rely on negativity. Nothing precedes colour; no other systems are a priori to it: there is only the parallelism of other value systems, such as aesthetics, taste, smell and feeling, but no deeper ontology. What we generally view as mere peripheral, surface phenomena are actually structured in themselves, and therefore absolutely fundamental. Facts are made of value systems, or, as Whitehead put it: 'an actual fact is a fact of aesthetic experience'.[38] This not only means that colour follows the structure of being but, more shockingly, the reverse as well, potentially creating a massive leak between aesthetics and ontology. In a nutshell: objects are constructed in the same system that we use to have feelings for those objects. And so subjectivism is the first to leave the scene, followed by negation, and then materialism – matter is simply what matters.

Compass and Wheel

Before we move to the final stage in the development of a biaxial systemacy, in the form of Charles Hartshorne's Diagram of Aesthetic Values, we should take a brief look at the ideas on beauty of his primary influence, the Anglo-American philosopher Alfred North Whitehead. Like Hartshorne, Whitehead developed his ideas on beauty quite late in life, and not really until two of his last books, *Adventures of Ideas* (1933) and *Modes of Thought* (1938), published when he was in his seventies.

As I have discussed on earlier occasions,[39] to define the nature of the two axes properly it is vital to understand Whitehead's argument, especially considering the history of aesthetic theories, which, by the way, both he and Hartshorne felt confident enough to omit. Beauty – 'the teleology of the universe', as Whitehead phrased it[40] – consists of two dimensions, one of 'mutual adaptation', the other of 'patterned contrasts',[41] or, in the words of Price, Hogarth and Burke, one dimension of smoothness and one of roughness. The axis of mutual adaptation (note the phrase's subtle evolutionary and environmental ring) indexes the necessity of harmonising, that is, wholes harmonising with other wholes; in short, the *synthetic axis* of smoothness, or extensity. The fact that it consists of an axis means that on the one end we find things that harmonise extremely, that are ultra-unified, which Whitehead calls 'minor beauty' or 'the absence of a painful clash'.[42] Meanwhile, on the other end, we find things that don't succeed in harmonising, that is, things that are ultra-plurified, what we call ugly. It is important to understand that the other term, contrast, is different from mere diversity, though. Things do not simply vary, they break away from each other. We see fractures emerging, sudden shifts and cuts (being literally *analytic*). Such contrasts and fractures often lead to layering and stratification, with parts or groups of parts hiding behind one another, in what we often denote with 'depth' or 'profundity'. Therefore, the effect of contrast is often expressed by magnitude, which is why we find the previously discussed greatness of the sublime on this axis, as well as the smallness of the cute at its opposite end.

This system allows every thing, every 'occasion', every gesture to exist as a combination of smoothness and roughness, or in Whitehead's terms, massiveness and intensity. Here, massiveness refers to an index of coordination by gradual variation, and intensity to an index of the degree to which that coordinated whole allows its parts to be available to others. In themselves, there is nothing new in these remarks; we find them as readily in Uvedale Price or Edmund Burke. What is remarkable, however, is the fact that Whitehead does not put these on a single sliding scale, with massive, compact wholes at one end and loose, fractured ones at the other. Whitehead's doctrine is not just another take on Hutcheson's unity amid variety. The parameters of massiveness and of intensity each have a uniform side and a diverse side; both are driven by variation, but each by a different type: one smooth, the other rough; one operating on adaptation, the other on contrast.[43] Though he does not refer to prior aesthetic theories, which would have been helpful, nor visualise his system in the form of a diagram, which would have been even more helpful, he clearly views the system as a two-dimensional one, organised along two axes, each with minimum and maximum values at the ends.

Eventually, by combining Whitehead's ideas on beauty with Dessoir's little diagram, Hartshorne took the final steps in his development of a diagram of aesthetics, an effort which can be traced over many years, beginning in the 1970s with *Creative Synthesis and Philosophic Method*, where he published the first version of what he then called the Dessoir-Davis Circle. As a diagram, it was strongly influenced by Dessoir's example from the beginning of the century, but the philosophy behind it owes far more to Whitehead. The version Hartshorne published in *Creative Synthesis* was a still-crude version of what he later, in 1987's *Wisdom as Moderation*, finalised as the 'Diagram of Aesthetic Values' (see Figure 8.3). In these diagrams, Hartshorne made two essential adjustments to Dessoir's model, based on his readings of Whitehead: first, he repositioned beauty, and second, he added the superb,[44] the neat and the commonplace.[45]

We should look at the repositioning of beauty first. It is quite clear that Whitehead's notion of beauty lies at the core of his process philosophy: things are only beautiful in their *striving* for beauty. Beauty is, above all, a teleological concept, since, as Whitehead himself said,

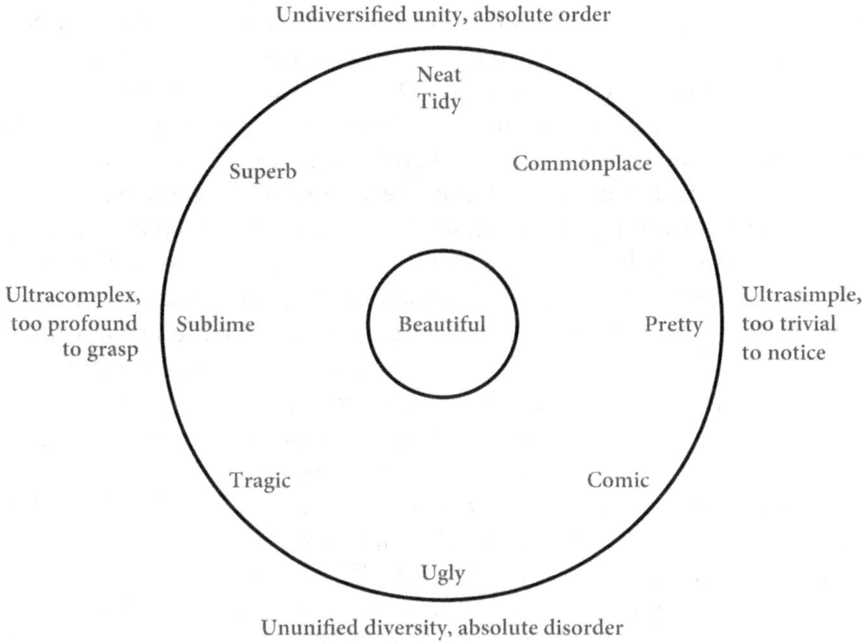

Figure 8.3 Diagram of Aesthetic Values from Charles Hartshorne, *Wisdom as Moderation* (1987).

'adaptation implies an end',[46] and while things strive to harmonise they can only do so by freeing their parts, allowing them to break away. Beauty, then, is not simply a state but a vector, similar to Apollo's arrow at the beginning of our discussion: each extensive act carries the need for intensity. Beauty inherently lies at the centre of all this, as literally the target of every arrow, merging target with trajectory. It lies where the two axes intersect, and not where Dessoir located it, at the rim. Even though Hartshorne was deeply influenced by Whitehead, to actually position beauty at the centre of a circle with two axes was a masterstroke.[47] Thinking back to Plato's white and black horses, we can see how Hartshorne's model recasts the two forces as one striving for harmonisation and the other for intensity. In Hartshorne's diagram, beauty is again firmly positioned in the middle, but the middle of a far more complex system that reconfigures Plato's monopolar, solar notion of beauty: 'Beauty, in the most natural sense of the word, is the center, the *double mean in both dimensions*.'[48] Beauty is not a simple, singular middle, but a middle trying to find another middle.

Along with his Platonic repositioning of beauty, Hartshorne added three new categories to Dessoir's six, one of which he called 'superb' – an idea we have already come across in Burke, in the form of magnificence, as well as in Kant, in the form of the *Prächtige* – and the other two 'neat' and 'commonplace'. The latter two are crucial additions: 'neat', though not a wholly satisfactory term, has connotations of monotony and boredom, while the commonplace corresponds to the normal or ordinary. With these, Hartshorne completely rearranges – repairs – the top half of Dessoir's model. It can be no accident that these final categories were added in the twentieth century, the age of the media and the masses. Before then, the concept of the commonplace was known mostly in the form of vulgarity, which at best ended up being associated with the comic. But in its modernist form, it points to a blandness and a complete lack of qualities that is truly original. The neat, better known in the form of boredom, is far older and, as *ennui*, was even considered an art by the likes of Charles Baudelaire and Beau Brummell (who famously turned to his valet to ask which of two lakes he admired most).[49] Andy Warhol, the twentieth-century champion, if not patron saint, of boredom, made an eight-hour movie of the Empire State building filmed in real time over a single night, appropriately titled *Empire*. He also loved to spend his holidays in Sweden, because, as he said, 'in a place like that you can get so bored'.[50] The closest category from ancient history would probably be the decadence of the late Roman Empire as described in Petronius's *Satyricon*. With Hartshorne's circle, the aesthetic spectrum seems to transform into a continent, a planet even, where the spectral lines of Kant, Dilthey and Dessoir form partial routes or complete equators. Hartshorne's addition of the neat and the commonplace created a 'north passage' at the top of the diagram similar to sixteenth-century attempts to expand shipping routes from Europe.

With Hartshorne's Diagram of Aesthetic Values, we can finally go full circle: reading clockwise, we encounter the sublime, the superb, the neat, the commonplace, the pretty, the comic, the ugly, the tragic and finally the sublime again. We should make a few adjustments, however. The superb is not as convincing as magnificence; the latter has more historical roots that go deeper and wider than superb, which dates back no further than the Renaissance. The neat should be substituted by the boring; again, its history is just too powerful, as we saw above, to say nothing of the celebrated elaborations of Martin Heidegger and Erich Fromm on the topic. The other replacement should be for the pretty, which we should exchange for the cute, which is conceptually stronger, and more correct opposite the sublime. Hartshorne seems unaware of Dilthey's categorisation of 'trifling' coinciding with his own qualification of the pretty as bordering on the 'too trivial', and how Kant's notion of the *Hübsch* preceded these. Oddly enough, Hartshorne never discusses any historical precedents or developments of the circle or its terminology. Therefore, the final circular line-up will be: sublime, magnificent, boring, commonplace, cute, comic, ugly, tragic, and back to sublime. Although Hartshorne never bothered to draw the actual axes and only indicated the four poles in additional captions, we should include these in the revised diagram as well: a horizontal axis spanning from sublime on the left to cute on the right, and a vertical axis from ugly at the bottom to boring at the top (see Figure 8.4). Together they create the structure of a wheel or compass. It moves from the silent scream of the sublime to the exalted cry of the magnificent to the yawning mouth of boredom to the flat expression of the commonplace to the gentle smile of the cute

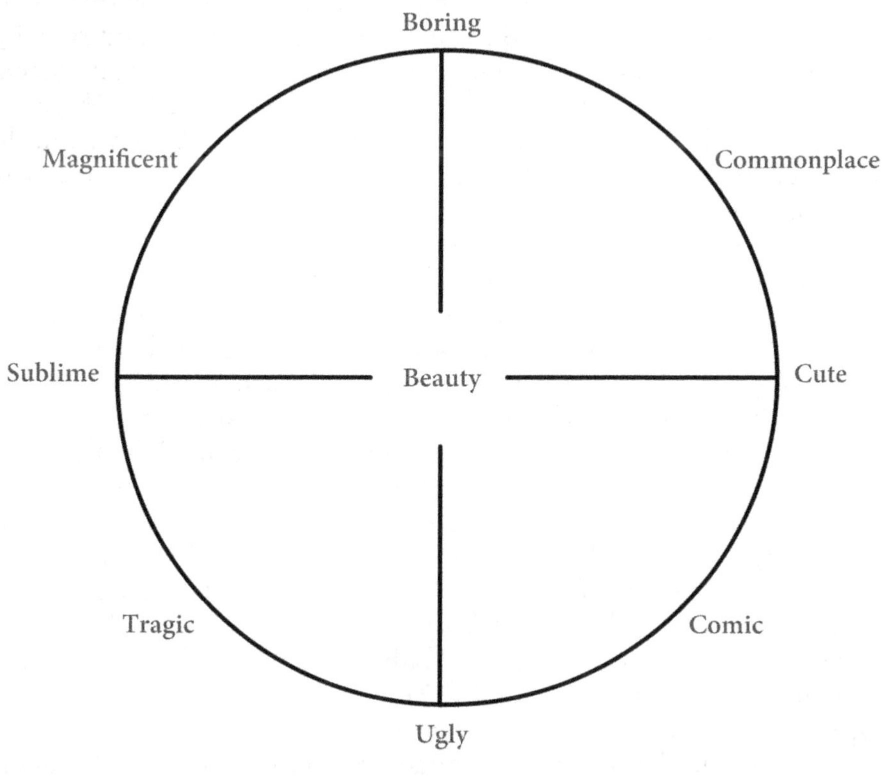

Figure 8.4 The compass of beauty (adapted from Hartshorne's diagram to include the biaxial system and a revised terminology).

to the outright laughter of the comic to the disgusted 'ick' of the ugly, on to the weeping of the tragic, and back to the noiseless gasp of the sublime. We could play these facial expressions as an animation and we wouldn't be able to discern any jumps or cuts. And it all works *because* beauty has been taken out of the sequence: the relations between all these aesthetic values are wholly different than those between them and beauty. We have eight aesthetic categories that occur on the outer rim of aesthetics, connected by spokes of gradually decreasing value to the hub of beauty, which is in fact a ninth one, or the first, whichever one prefers. That the system in its final form looks like a compass reflects both meanings of the word: a limited, finite structure such as a planet as well as an *instrument* for navigating that planet.

Translated back into the colour wheel, this would give us the standard hues at the outer edge of the circle, with more brightness mixed into each colour until it becomes pure white light in the middle. (Plato's solar model of beauty was probably no accident.) Now we should also be able to find a place for every nameable aesthetic value on this circle, since feelings can vary in all directions, both rotationally and radially. We should have no problem finding positions that are located neither at the centre or at the rim but occupy the as-yet-undefined area in between – the quirky, the quaint, the weird, the cool, the elegant, the vulgar, the melodramatic, the horrific, the gruesome, etc. – but that is an argument we will save for later.

When we fast-forward through the history of beauty, the first peculiarity that attracts our attention is that it started with Plato, who hated art, then developed through aesthetics, with indispensable contributions by artists, and then moved away from art again. For example, I think the Large Hadron Collider and the Saturn V rocket are more sublime than paintings of mountains, far more abstract and far more violent. And football stadiums are more magnificent than Kant's St Peter's, and when a wave performed by 80,000 spectators moves over the stands, we are overpowered and swept away – to use Longinus's terms – by sheer awe. General Tommy Franks also called his invasion of Baghdad a strategy of 'shock and awe', leaving no misunderstanding about where we should locate the sublime in our own age. I think there is more terror and horror in the daily imagery of suicide bombings than in *Alien*, *Friday the 13th* and *The Texas Chainsaw Massacre* put together. There is more of the commonplace and the ordinary in reality television, in the endless soap operas and in Facebook posts than in the street life of Baudelaire's Paris. And if you type 'beauty' into your search engine, you won't find the work of contemporary artists but a zillion websites related to the cosmetics industry. And who is not cute today (though no society goes as far as the Japanese with their *kawaii*)? It seems that art is playing an ever-smaller role – and the media an ever-larger one – in the development of the diagram, and especially in how it organises the distribution of objects. Was Plato right again? Permit me to leave that as an open question.

In any case, what becomes evident in the developments over the last fifty years is that they show the ontological nature of the diagram more prominently. It is also clear from these developments that we seem to be living in an era that is expanding the diagram at high speed while moving away from its middle with equal speed. We live in an age of design: not just the design of objects but of events, concepts and issues, of organisations and procedures, even of our own lives. One's own life has become a project. The number of things is growing exponentially, and growing exponentially further away from beauty. If the diagram concerns all things, not just works of art, we should realise that it concerns them through beauty. This is the true power of Hartshorne's Diagram of Aesthetic Values: only beauty can relate the vertical axis to the horizontal one. The two axes are not independent; they don't form a mere coordinate system. If they were independent, the diagram would not be a circle but a square, and we could simply combine one extreme with the other, which goes against the whole notion of a middle. A square is not an equation; a circle is. We should keep in mind that even the sublime in Hartshorne's diagram is plotted halfway against the vertical axis of harmony and coordination. The fact that the influence of each axis always needs to be mediated makes beauty more than simply the middle of a circular world: it reverses the roles and makes the periphery a derivative of the middle. Both areas are circles: a white one in the middle and a multicoloured one at the outskirts.

I don't have to stress the fact that Hartshorne's diagram shares many traits with the cruciform structure of Heidegger's fourfold; the similarities are quite obvious. They share the same purpose: to divide Being according to two axes, one spanning the space between the unified (boredom) and the plurified (ugly), the other between the deep (sublime) and the shallow (cute).[51] Of course, Heidegger does not define the fourfold by the axes but by the four quadrants, which he identifies as sky, mortals, gods and earth. This is telling in a way, because by defining the quadrants he makes it impossible to view the axes as productive. The fourfold remains a static architectural system, a *Geviert*, and though he sometimes speculates about one quadrant mirroring the other, and even about a 'round dance',[52] it never attains the status of an ontological machine equipped with dynamic sliders. Viewing the intersection of the axes as a hub, and identifying that with beauty, causes the compass to take on the character of a wheel more than a cross. Heidegger's Being always takes an unmoving, neutral position, humming in the background, whereas Whitehead's and Hartshorne's beauty thrusts things forward into presence. From the perspective of the Diagram of Aesthetic Values, the four quadrants can never be primary because they are parented by two axes. All activity lies with the axes, and they are bound to one another, limiting each other's influence to a circular field of existence – what I earlier called the arena of presence. Heidegger strongly resented the notion of Being as presence[53] and attempted to extend the phenomenal world to absence (for example, the negativity of nothingness and the invisibility of *Zuhandenheit*), to things happening without passing through consciousness. Certainly, no one would deny that things exist before they enter human consciousness, but that does not mean that reality condemns things to roam around in darkness. On the contrary, it means *things can claim light and consciousness in their own right*: nonhuman thought and unseen light. Things think before we think them (how else could we understand things?), they are visible before we see them (how else would we see them?), and they affect their environment before we feel them (how else would we find them beautiful?). Again, the way the existence of things is constructed cannot be fundamentally different from the structure of our feelings; this is what the Diagram of Aesthetic Values teaches us.[54]

When we take a careful look at the diagram, we can better see how process and product not only are combined but are *combined symmetrically only in the middle* and asymmetrically everywhere else (though still equated). When we go back again to stand in front of St Peter's with our faces upturned and our mouths open in admiration, it is the magnificent *structure* that overwhelms us. If we move from the basilica's position of magnificence vertically down on Hartshorne's map, we encounter figures such as Macbeth and Michael Jackson, obliterated by the tragic *events* they have instigated. At the position of magnificence, it is the massive structure that overwhelms us, and at the position of the tragic, it is the enormity of the events overwhelming their subjects: exactly the same magnitude in very different dimensions. This is why we recognise the top area of the diagram – the realm of magnificence, boredom and the commonplace – as the general territory of structures, or what Mikel Dufrenne called the spatial arts, and the bottom area – the realm of the tragic, the ugly and the comic – as the zone of events, or again in terms of aesthetics, the temporal arts.[55] That doesn't mean buildings 'are' boring; it means that when time is stopped they become boring, as in Warhol's *Empire*, where the Empire State building is boring because you are trapped in your seat. (If you are walking in New York, the Empire State building is anything but boring.) Or think of the funny example of Heidegger stuck in a provincial railway station after missing a train.[56] Forced to wait for four hours, he started walking up and down the platform like a pendulum, hopelessly trying to restore time, like a panther in a cage. Inversely, the asymmetry of space and time means that the positivity of ugliness functions very well in plays, literature and movies but not in architecture. While in a gangster movie a character like Al Capone boosts the speed of events by bashing in heads with a baseball bat, an ugly building does not have the same positive effect on urban space. That doesn't mean a building cannot be ugly; obviously it can, and a play can as easily be boring – that is not my point. In the specific case of a boring play, I think it exposes too much architecture, for example when it lacks development and has cardboard characters who move through the drama without changing. Similarly, a building is ugly when it tries to be funny or becomes too theatrical, since the chances are that we will encounter it more than once, killing all possible humour, or that we will experience it from more than one angle, destroying every illusion.

On the product side, things have to be looked at in terms of how they relate to time; from the process side, they have to be looked at in terms of how they relate to space. Beauty is not organised by going from product to product nor from process to process, but from process to product and from product to process and back again. Ours is a jerking, jolting universe. If aesthetics operated within one dimension, a single line of variations and gradations would suffice. If it consisted merely of spatial encounters, things would simply shape each other from the outside and the synthetic axis would do all the necessary work. And if it solely consisted of events meeting one another, all would be pure development; the internal growth of things would never lead to them being born into the world. In the Diagram of Aesthetic Values, these two lines are bound to one another as axes, with both rather than one or the other exerting their influence on the final product. When things are formed, they are internally driven by a force occupying the analytic axis of intensity, while they simultaneously orient themselves in and adapt to an external world whose powers are expressed along the synthetic axis of the extensive, that is, present themselves as forms. Things present themselves in one realm, but they cannot be explained through one dimension, only through the conflation of two dimensions.

Stand in front of a 400-year-old oak tree. Its structure – the branchings, the bifurcations, the random curvature – all this is pure process, pure time and growth. But does it present itself to us as time? Do we experience it as time? No, we experience it as sheer magnificence. All that was time is presented to us as beauty, and all that is beauty we experience in time, yes, but the second stretch of time is wholly discontinuous with the first. In this sense, beauty is purely Platonic, atemporal stoppage.

Notes

1. Cf. the very last sentence in *The Origin of Species*.
2. See Lars Spuybroek, 'Charis and Radiance: The Ontological Dimensions of Beauty', in *Giving and Taking: Antidotes to a Culture of Greed* (Rotterdam: V2_Publishing, 2014), pp. 118–49.
3. Heraclitus, Fragment 51.
4. *Odyssey* XXI: 411.
5. Karl Kerényi, *Apollo: The Wind, the Spirit and the God* (Dallas: Spring Publications, 1983), p. 58.
6. Marcel Detienne, 'Apollo's Slaughterhouse', *Diacritics*, 16.2 (1986), p. 51.
7. *Symposium* 201e and 204b.
8. *Symposium* 204e.
9. *Phaedrus* 254b.
10. *Phaedrus* 251c.
11. *Phaedrus* 251a.
12. *Phaedrus* 248b.
13. *Phaedrus* 247c.
14. G. W. F. Hegel, *Vorlesungen über der Ästhetik*, I.I.3, Die Idee des Schönen: 'Das Sinnliche Scheinen der Idee'.
15. Friedrich Nietzsche, from the preface to *Beyond Good and Evil*. In the original German: 'Christentum ist Platonismus für's "Volk"'.
16. Walter Burkert, *Greek Religion* (Cambridge, MA: Harvard University Press, 1985), p. 126.
17. Francis Hutcheson, *An Inquiry into the Original of Our Ideas of Beauty and Virtue* (1725), pp. I, 2, 3.
18. Immanuel Kant, *The Critique of Judgment*, §24.
19. Immanuel Kant, *Observations on the Feeling of the Beautiful and Sublime* (1764) (Berkeley: University of California Press, 1991), p. 47. In the original German: 'Das Erhabene rührt, das Schöne reizt'.
20. Ibid., p. 49.
21. Ibid., p. 87.
22. Uvedale Price, *On the Picturesque* (1796) (Edinburgh: Caldwell, Lloyd & Co., 1842), p. 90.
23. Ibid., p. 82.

24. William Hogarth, *The Analysis of Beauty* (1753) (New Haven, CT: Yale University Press, 1997), pp. 51, 73.
25. Ibid., p. 35: 'the present fashion the ladies have gone into, of wearing a part of the hair of their heads braided together from behind, like intertwisted serpents, arising thickest from the bottom, lessing as it is brought forward, and naturally conforming to the shape of the rest of the hair it is pinned over, is extremely picturesque'.
26. Ibid., pp. xvii–lxii.
27. Wilhelm Dilthey, *Poetry and Experience* (1887) (Princeton: Princeton University Press, 1985), p. 146.
28. Charles Hartshorne, *The Zero Fallacy* (Chicago: Open Court, 1997), p. 204.
29. Dilthey, *Poetry and Experience*, p. 145.
30. Ann Radcliffe, 'On the Supernatural in Poetry', *The New Monthly Magazine* (1826), pp. 145–52.
31. The English edition (Detroit, MI: Wayne State University Press, 1970) mistranslates *Niedlich* as 'pretty' instead of 'cute' (p. 150). Cf. the original diagram in Max Dessoir, *Ästhetik* (Stuttgart: Ferdinand Enke, 1923 [1906]), p. 139.
32. Edmund Burke, *A Philosophical Enquiry into the Origin of our Ideas of the Sublime and the Beautiful* (1757) (Oxford: Oxford University Press, 1998), Section XXI and XXII.
33. Dessoir, *Aesthetics and Theory of Art*, p. 149.
34. In the original German, the word is *Färbungen*, of which 'colorations' or 'colourings' would be a better translation than 'tints'.
35. Dessoir, *Aesthetics and Theory of Art*, p. 150.
36. See John Gage, *Colour and Culture* (London: Thames and Hudson, 1995), p. 171: 'Newton's colour-mixing diagram . . . has a clear inner coherence because it was simply an attempt to roll up the prismatic spectrum.'
37. Isaac Newton, *Opticks*, Book I, Par. II, Tab. III, fig. 11.
38. Alfred North Whitehead, *Process and Reality* (New York: The Free Press, 1978), p. 280.
39. Lars Spuybroek, 'The Ages of Beauty: Revisiting Hartshorne's Diagram of Aesthetic Values', in *Vital Beauty: Reclaiming Aesthetics in the Tangle of Technology and Nature* (Rotterdam: V2_Publishing, 2012), pp. 32-60.
40. Alfred North Whitehead, *Adventures of Ideas* (New York: The Free Press, 1967), p. 265.
41. Ibid., p. 252.
42. Ibid.
43. The two dimensions of smoothness and roughness, or massiveness and intensity, correspond directly to Ruskin's organisation of Gothic aesthetics in terms of changefulness and savageness, as I have discussed in the first chapter of *The Sympathy of Things* (London: Bloomsbury, 2nd edn, 2016).
44. Hartshorne changed it from 'magnificent' in 1970 to 'superb' in 1987.

45. Hartshorne borrows the term 'commonplace' from Whitehead. See *Adventures of Ideas*, p. 261.
46. Whitehead, *Adventures of Ideas*, p. 252.
47. Actually, the idea to take beauty from the rim and move it to the middle came from Kay Davis-Leclerc, one of his students at Emory University. Hartshorne mentions this in several of his books but gives slightly different versions of the story. In *The Zero Fallacy* (p. 203), he suggests that the diagram was a collaboration between him, Dessoir and Davis-Leclerc, but this can be true only in an abstract sense: Dessoir died in 1947 in Frankfurt and never met Hartshorne. Hartshorne most probably saw Dessoir's diagram for the first time in 1970, when the English translation of the latter's work was published. This assumption is supported by the fact that Hartshorne adopted the mistranslation of *Niedlich* as 'pretty' in his own diagram. Davis-Leclerc was his student in the 1950s, but not by the time he published *Creative Synthesis*, where the diagram is presented in the final chapter.
48. Charles Hartshorne, *Wisdom as Moderation: A Philosophy of the Middle Way* (New York: SUNY Press, 1987), p. 2.
49. Carlo Maria Franzero, *Beau Brummell: His Life and Times* (New York: John Day, 1958), p. 71.
50. *The Philosophy of Andy Warhol* (Orlando: First Harvest, 1977), p. 72: 'When you're in Sweden & you see beautiful person after beautiful person & you finally don't even turn around to look because you know the next person you see will be just as beautiful as the one you didn't bother to turn around to look at – in a place like that you can get so bored that when you see a person who's not beautiful, they look very beautiful to you because they break the beautiful monotony.'
51. Graham Harman, *Heidegger Explained* (Chicago: Open Court, 2007), pp. 132–5.
52. Martin Heidegger, *Poetry, Language, Thought* (New York: HarperCollins, 2001), p. 178.
53. Harman, *Heidegger Explained*, p. 1.
54. To give an example: it means that I think a sunset is actually there, and beautiful, without anybody seeing it – a thought that would horrify any (neo-)materialist.
55. Mikel Dufrenne, *The Phenomenology of Aesthetic Experience* (Evanston: Northwestern University Press, 1973), pp. 239–48.
56. Martin Heidegger, *The Fundamental Concepts of Metaphysics* (Bloomington: Indiana University Press, 1995), p. 93.

PART III

CHAPTER 9

Architectures of Air: Media Ecologies of Smart Cities and Pollution[1]

Jussi Parikka

Air Conditions

Clean air is a rare occurrence. It is rather a nostalgic memory in the context of the contemporary city – defined by the sprawling megacities that in many cases carry over a legacy of industrialism and infrastructures based on the archaic energy sources of the planetary underground. Materialities of breathing and sustaining life in the specific chemical zones we call cities is one particular approach one can take to urban planning and architecture; what sort of zones for breathing are designed, intentionally or unintentionally? The atmosphere is one particular way of thinking about the built environment by way of the air-conditioning modernity where air is not merely the romantic deep breath in, but a chemically measured reality increasingly also measured as data – and managed as data.

We encounter political dilemmas of inclusion and exclusion, exposure and security already on the level of particles such as dust.[2] Dust and air pollution are silent aggressors that demonstrate the political urgency of the atmospheric condition: the age of modern design can also be understood as one of bubbles and spheres, as Peter Sloterdijk argues, referring to the constitution of subjectivity as an air-conditioning operation.[3] Modernity opens up as air conditioning and as airborne terror: of denying the possibility of breathing the air of streets and public spaces. Terror begins in the air.[4] This claim connects political contexts of cleaning and dusting to issues of chemical warfare. Such warfare is not merely an issue of the usual armed conflicts, but an increasingly naturalised part of security regimes that govern the urban sphere: an air of gas and clouds, of molecular combinations designed to turn the social breathing space into a space of suffocation.[5] This has become evident during the past years of security politics of excessive tear gas use as a quasi-military form of urban sanitisation against social movements. Examples are plentiful, including for example the infamous case of Turkey during and after the Gezi demonstrations in 2013, the events in Ferguson in 2014, and more recently, the use of tear gas against environmental protestors during #COP21 in Paris. The list could go on and include a longer history of the normalisation of such techniques of denial of air. The commons of the air is quickly turned into a commons of the unbreathable, although with the striking difference of gas-masked police enjoying the personal sphere of breathing. The gas mask becomes a key symbol and operational item of the modern era of subjectivity (Figure 9.1).[6]

A low-level, slow violence is the background screen of industrial modernity.[7] In other words, from the specific events of denied breath, we can move on to observe the wider sense in which poor air quality is an issue that is itself normalised, and yet a violent part of the condition of living. We can name this a slower and more inconspicuous form of warfare that is expressed often in other sorts of vocabularies such as environmental problems, the Anthropocene, sustainability and/or pollution. The Anthropocene is a term that emerged in scientific discussions of geological periodisation, but has become a sort of a placeholder for the wider impact and effects of man-made climate change that moves across lands and seas, atmospheres and even space (e.g. space junk). The term has been widely adopted in discussions in architecture and art too.[8]

The term's abstract generality has been challenged by more geographically aware, gender-specific and politically aware analysis of the role of capitalist modes of production and consumption.[9] The Anthropocene becomes a coordinate, and one recurring term in narrativising this condition and hopefully also facilitating an understanding of the links between the biological, the economic and the political spheres of interaction. But it has also been proposed that there is a specific value to approaching it through the lenses of art and the wider context of aesthetics that accounts for the reality of the Anthropocene as 'a sensorial phenomena: the experience of living in an increasingly diminished and toxic world'.[10] This experiential also expands to the wider sense in which it is being produced as a technological reality – a layer of planetary computation that works by way of sensors, data visualisation, satellites and more.[11] Hence, any sort of discussion of materialities of architecture becomes a discussion of space in the context of computation that expands to issues of logistics, supply, infrastructure, but also, importantly, the interfaces through which 'the world is sensed and made sense of'.[12] The envelopes of air conditioning are also envelopes governed as data and accessible

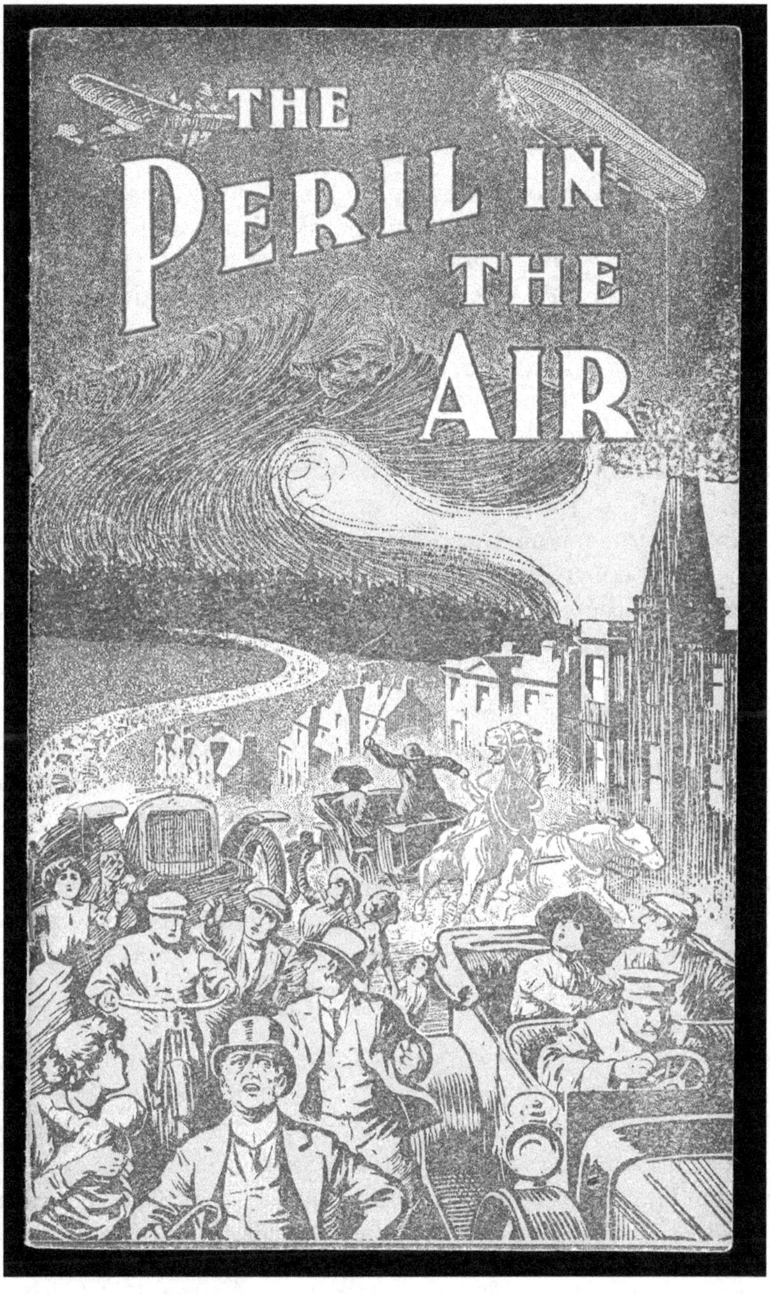

Figure 9.1 An advertisement for cough and cold tablets from 1913 captures some of the early connotations of airborne terror: cities are sites of modern ills from factory pollution to lung diseases.

Photo: Wellcome Library, London, available under Creative Commons Attribution only licence CC BY 4.0

through interfaces, as Benjamin Bratton argues, adding that 'the interfacial operations of software and architecture should not be categorized as two distinct economies, but as mutually involved sides of corresponding governing effects, sometimes symbiotic and sometimes antagonistic in their relations'.[13]

Besides being a chemical issue, air pollution is present as data and even as a sort of visual media in the sky. The photochemical smog that covers many global metropolitan areas consists of nitrogen oxide (NO), nitrogen dioxide (NO_2), ozone (O_3) and volatile organic compounds (RH). This is the elemental media condition across the aesthetics of contemporary landscapes of industrial and post-industrial life. An urban screen, hovering above the cinematic megacities of Los Angeles, Istanbul, Beijing, Sao Paulo and many other places, is a residue of the transport cultures of automobiles as well as other exploitation of the fossil fuel depths of the planet. It is also a historical, almost oddly like a media archaeological, chemical residue of the old in the contemporary.

Smog has of course not disappeared. Nowadays, smog is more likely to follow from the extensive private car traffic that characterises the city, at least in terms of its chemistry. It presents itself in slightly alternative visual ways and in different forms, but it is something that can be addressed through questions such as: What are the conditions of visibility of air pollution? What are the conditions of chemical composition and the political-economic distribution of smog? Smog is then, besides being a reference to a specific form of air pollution, also a conceptual bridge between the industrial and the post-industrial computerised city, a bridge between the production of molecular pollution and its registration as part of the digital city, the smart city sensors and data.[14] This sort of a materiality is one that is about the folds between architecture, data and the chemistry of the air – a sort of a media ecology of multiple materialities.

Besides being a theoretical interest for new materialism, such multiple folds of matter in intra-action[15] relate to many of the burning issues in architecture and urban planning. Questions concerning air quality become one key theme in the debate concerning the modern and smart city. The dilemma of air and pollution cuts and divides insides and outsides, breathable and polluted spaces, in subtle, informationally observed ways. Technical definitions and questions of air also have a relation to smart cities as places of the measurability and processing of data. The computational data points that allow a 'management of uncertainty' through the constant monitoring, optimisation and 'penetration of computational interventions' are part of emerging city plans.[16] This ranges from the idealised, custom-built tech cities such as South Korea's Songdo to Spanish Santander, which is the EU's well-funded test case for the massively sensored city.[17] Besides the computational, there is also a seemingly more archaic form of media that comes through the toxic materials in the air. This latter point refers to a sort of a veil, a screen that hovers across the everyday in the megacities of the current climate.

This chapter focuses on urban environments as defined by the emergence of new forms of measurement of the city – and its airborne pollution – through smog sensors. I will also envelop this more straightforward assumption as part of a conceptual argument: What does it mean to look at smog as a medium itself, and to approach it as an index of the technological city that is haunted by the industrial veil? What conditions this 'looking' and even 'seeing the city' through eyes that are often data, often statistical, as in art projects such as 'Seeing the Air'?[18] I am interested in the photochemical smog as a screen media of the city, and pollution's relation to smog sensors and the creation of breathable zones. Many of the problems we identify as 'environmental', such as air pollution, are already discussed and operated as data (both analytic data and financial data, traded in the offset markets). Hence, I choose to discuss the environmental as part of a media ecology of observing, measuring and processing of data. To follow John Durham Peters, the consideration of the environment and its elements as media must also lead to questions as to how the media technological framing of elements leads recursively into an alternative view of nature through those technological frameworks.[19] Air is one crucial media environment in which our sensation happens, but air is not the same in technological culture, let alone in the remote-sensed data city-cum-lab, as it is in a purely scientific, chemical definition. Air has its own life and its own history, and in some parts this history becomes part of media and art history, as articulated below.

Following this introduction, I want to discuss the smart, modern city as defined through its unwanted elements, in this case pollution and waste. Issues of sensing and perceiving pollution become key aspects of political subjectivity in the urban environment. Two kinds of sensing perception are then discussed, first through a discussion of smog as visual medium or environmental art, and then continuing to address the locations of air pollution as data that feeds back into the understanding and governance of the city.

The City and its Residues

The media city has come to refer to the infrastructural redesigning of urban environments both in terms of the clustering of media industries into innovation hubs and parks and the infrastructural implementation of systems that offer new data-enhanced services, information and interfaces to urban life. This latter is part of the idea of smart cities that promise optimised ways of addressing intensive urbanisation. It is interesting, however, to observe the disconnect between the custom-built, shop-window smartness of places such as Songdo in South Korea and Masdar in Abu Dhabi as the example cities of a green sustainability supported by corporate funds (including Consensus Business Group, Credit Suisse and Siemens Venture Capital), and the real existing cities where 'smart' solutions relate to the layered histories of the place. As smart city writers such as Anthony Townsend underline, 'the vast amount of people living in cities don't live in cities like that right now'.[20] Urban issues are actually of a different scale and don't seem at first to touch the narrow smart city focus at all: 'It took ten years to build Songdo and Masdar, which each house maybe 100,000 people, and in the same period, we've added hundreds of millions of people to the next big cities of the global south.'[21] In other words, we are rarely 'starting from scratch'.[22] Actual population growth, environmental questions and climate change, difficult ecosystems of cities and their surroundings, and the supply of food and fresh water are the issues for the future of cities as much as current planning.[23] Hence, as Orit Halpern and Gökçe Günel demonstrate, current smart city plans, including Songdo but especially Masdar City in Abu Dhabi, are implicitly enveloped in a narrative of emerging environmental catastrophe.[24] What the authors describe as the tie-in between 'speculation on disaster' and 'sentiments of hope and optimism' becomes a way to frame the symbolic function of smart cities and also their design plans. The science-fictional style of the plans works to enhance the realisation that 'Masdar City is promoted as a utopian living arrangement that acknowledges and resolves the current energy crises of the world, while mitigating climate change'.[25] In other words, the emerging global climate crisis promotes a sort of flipside of what is meant to be a utopian narrative of future cities: instead, it produces a suspicion of dystopian gated enclaves that become resilient against the environmental and social issues that define the current metropolitan landscape. In the case of Masdar, the plans have a specific relation to imagining a post-oil-reliant Middle East luxury lifestyle, but more widely they point to issues of thinking climate change as incorporated to technological infrastructures. What is noteworthy is that some of these, like Masdar, are already discussed as 'failed experiments' in their own right.[26]

Such analyses of smart cities acknowledge how current urban development works in the context of global problems as well as historical contexts. These critical insights also take into account the specific dynamic temporalities that define cities here and now. It recalls the fact that media (as technologies and techniques that enable perception, sensation, habit) are built on top of existing infrastructures from the organic to technical media.[27] Cities present themselves through the archaeological layers that can be excavated through various signs, systems, infrastructures and traces left behind. The city itself has been an inscription surface for writing, from the early use of mud and clay to the more recent standardised forms (such as brick) that define the technological city.[28] Many global cities include an interface with the industrial legacy as well; in terms of issues this presents itself through, for example, the residuals of the overgrowth of cities, pollution and waste management. Different bin solutions are an amusing showcase of what smart cities could be as waste management. But such solutions always include much more than just the primary function of waste collection: the start-up behind the London smart bins suffered a blow after it was revealed that the pods actually track the MAC addresses of smartphones in the vicinity.[29] Indeed, waste is never just waste but is an access point to a wider circulation of information and value creation, management of the wanteds and unwanteds of the city.

Dominique Laporte in the *History of Shit* argues that the emergence of the modern infrastructural city is to be considered also as a production of modern subjectivity. The production of cleanliness became part of city planning as a way to install order; the emergence of the bourgeois subjectivity of segregated spaces is partly visible in the measures taken to install sewerage and other waste systems. Furthermore, this was not merely an issue of closing off the unwanteds, but of designing certain ways in which this circulation could be managed productively. The city is where waste turns to gold by way of purification and privatisation of even the seemingly most unnecessary:

> under the seal of divine power, the city – site of exchange from the earliest moments of generalised circulation – was similarly subject to purification. Whether belly or granary, the city is that place where merchandise accumulates and is consumed before being turned into gold. To purify the city, one must enrich it in a manner that makes way for the means of production. But shit cannot be converted into cash through mere elimination. Before its restitution in sublimated form, it must nourish the very cesspools of its production.[30]

Waste and contemporary pollution present a convergence of environmental and political issues as part of the media ecology of the city. Ecology is here a broader term than the environment and refers to the various cultural, political, historical and media contexts in which issues of the environment are conditioned, measured, represented, discussed and materially transformed into other spheres of interaction.[31] Besides the literal and proverbial excrement analysed by Laporte, I want to contextualise this discussion in relation to air pollution, followed by the various contexts in which the city is localised and datafied with sensors.

I will propose a couple of detours and twists in the way in which we understand the city, technology and smog – the haze that is a companion of industrialisation and persists as the haze of the supposedly post-industrial: tiny particles that create an odd sort of media city that is technological in more ways than the smart city discourse assumes. One is tempted to claim that this is how the city looks in the Anthropocene: defined both by its waste and pollution as remainders of the industrial age, fossil fuel use and inadequate waste solutions, and by the data-intensive measures that aim to offer an understanding of this chemical reality of the Anthropocene and turn it into an excessive calculation, storage and financialisation of that data. It is registered in the various sensors, tracking, calculating, visualisations and statistics that are the quantified and then datafied basis of the city. The chemical reality and the data about it are interlocked. In other words, accounting for the layered infrastructures as well as historical legacies of the city reminds us of the old problems that new technologies are supposed to solve: smog from industry, transport that is the legacy of the twentieth century, and the old energy forms still firing up a technological society, based on coal and so on. This is the particle world of technological cities that we inhale: the dirty dust and smaller molecular elements that ensure that air is never *just* air.[32] The air also includes harmful chemicals that mix with our insides, violating the basic line between the self and the non-self in a continuous mock example of the 'democratic' city: we all share the pollution. Of course, this is not entirely true, *pace* such writers as Ulrich Beck, who much earlier in the 1990s argued that 'poverty is hierarchical, while smog is democratic', illuminating how the distribution of evils is also 'democratic'.[33]

In Beck's risk society vision, it is this inequality of production of evils that is distributed across the urban social layers. Additionally, environmental hazards become a shared commons, just as air and land is meant to be.[34] And yet, through urban planning and the systematic production of the city that reproduces and reinforces ethnic, economic and other divisions, issues of air pollution are not shared by all. This is a theme recognised in critical urbanism and, for example, the discussion about the politics of infrastructure: cities have, for a long time, been part of a production of inequality through infrastructural choices, for example relating to water and sewerage,[35] and we can discuss similar issues in relation to the seemingly more ephemeral dystopia of the air too. Any discussion of the environment(al) needs to be a discussion of the ecology of multiple 'social, political, ethical and aesthetic dimensions'.[36] Hence, more than environmental consciousness, the ecological analysis presented here accounts for the geographical and political distribution of waste, the situated nature of pollution, and the political economy of solutions offered as part of the management of the issue both in cities and globally.

In places such as Zhengzhou and many other Chinese cities, smog persistently consists of residues of fossil fuel burning and particulate matter such as PM2.5. Such a situation is not because of a lack of regulations, but problems in enforcing them effectively. This issue is made evident in such material as the online documentary *Under the Dome* (2015) by Chai Jing, on the subject of Chinese air pollution and the disconnection between regulations, economic mandates and local levels of enforcement. Furthermore, the number of news pieces, images and stories about Chinese smog problems threatens to mask the issues that are prevalent in a lot of European cities. London, for example, is among the cities that have failed to follow up on the required limits for nitrogen dioxide,[37] underpinning the other side of the story: invisible air pollution does not as easily transform into the stream of media representations about smog cities. Not all air pollution is visible, a twist that should not be ignored in the discussion of this visual media that is another entry point to the sensor and data-registered ways in which we understand the chemical atmosphere of the technological city. Further emphasising the point about the uneven distribution of visibilities as a matter of the political geography of slow violence, Rob Nixon reminds us that the narrativisation of global environmental catastrophes also follows the logic where 'some afflicted communities are afforded more visibility – and more access to remediation – than others through the mechanisms of globalization, environmental racism, and class discrimination'.[38]

From coal smog, diesel fuel burning and other sources, the archaic elements of the planet are enfolded even in the twenty-first-century version of post-Fordist capitalism that is still fuelled by the earth fossil political economy.[39] The relevance of considering energy solutions as part of the wider technological infrastructures of smart cities reveals, at this point, more than just smart monitoring: it is, instead, a bigger infrastructural issue of political economy that depends on certain environmentally disastrous energy forms. Indeed, as scholars are nowadays again noting, questions of technology are not restricted to the urban, but are distributed across vast rural areas too.[40] The question of perception and sensing the urban and its problems is one of the key issues that sustain the smart city as a technological assemblage: a smart city is a sensorial city, where perception is partly displaced on to the specific sensors and their analytical back end.

Aesthetics of Smog: A Sensor City

A media-biased proposition: think of smog as a chemical screen, even a chemical screen medium. The sun enlivens it with its light, which is the most fundamental thing in visual culture. The screen is not a background but an environment that wraps you inside its toxic cloud. We register this sort of visual screen with our bodies with every breath but also with different sorts of sensors that have developed as an essential part of the observation of industrial culture. For us humans, ironically, this sort of visual screen art *irritates* the eye – molecular elements such a peroxyacetyl nitrate and ozone don't obey the visual distance that is necessary to form an image, but act directly as part of the visual system. It is this sort of an experienced chemistry of the city and its toxins where sensor realities of pollution start.

Imagine writing the history of media cities from this perspective, which seems to borrow ideas from experimental aesthetics and art methods. The Anthropocene has become the commonplace name for radical environmental changes, but it is, in certain ways, also a new art historical period that is measured in lung diseases and cancer rates. The environmental catastrophes produced as part of industrialisation – or what is nowadays often called the Anthropocene or Capitalocene[41] – are measures of this other sort of register of visual and tactile history. For instance, the ozone depletion period since the 1970s visualises a concrete change in the conditions of light on the planet.

For a sketch of an alternative ecological art history, one could claim that ozone depletion relates to radical molecular art since the 1970s.[42] It is a sort of a visual art historical period caused by the photodissociation of key chemical agents such as chlorofluorocarbons (CFCs), freons, halons as well as solvents, propellants and so on. It's a weird period when one starts to consider it from this perspective: problems of refrigeration and the invention of products such as freon have their residual after-effects in the upper atmosphere which, as historian John McNeill notes, have not really, until now, featured as having an important role in human history. Usually things that concern us happen in the lower spheres of the planet.[43] History has been atmospherically biased towards things much closer to human headspace. But the modern historical period rather concretely consists of carbon dioxide, ozone and sulphur dioxide too, and this is not a feature restricted to that one particular narrative-atmospheric space. The massive increase in CFCs has resulted in what could be called the 'ultraviolet century'.[44] The effect of ozone depletion, as we have grown to know it, is an increased penetration of UV-light/radiation through the stratosphere, resulting in a different sort of light balance from the 1970s that will last until approximately 2070 (as the restoration of the ozone protection layer is a slow process). This sort of art historical period is registered on the skin and the organisms of humans as increased cancer rates; in animals such as whales there are similar epidermal reactions,[45] and the same occurs in plants and crops. Smog itself is also visible in the increase in cardiovascular diseases, asthma and lung inflammations, for example.

Environmental histories of smog can also contribute to this alternative art history.[46] This sort of art history is oddly connected to photochemical trails and their industrial transport roots: cars and their journeys, part of the infrastructure of modernity. Besides industrial pollution, smog is a question of what is experienced and registered on the organic body, but it is also in peculiar ways a technological question. It relates to both the technological productions of the chemical world that defines contemporary culture and the specific political-aesthetic allocation of this as a material, sensed reality. This is a dividing and partitioning of spaces, breathability and visuals in the city.[47] Who has to see and suffer from pollution is a question that should be put on the agenda of aesthetic theory.[48] This is a situation where visual politics, the politics of breathing as well as the politics of sensoring are negotiated. It is also the target of other sorts of campaigns that are, perhaps, in spirit close to Sloterdijk (the defining questions of modern subjectivity are those of breathing and air control/atmosphere), but executed by various alternative means. The very real problem of breathability becomes the site where the various forces of technological and economic planning/design form the urban subject.

Besides the body as sensor, there is also the wider question of sensors which features as the driver of the discussion about the data-enhanced city. Part of the issue is that in many instances, contemporary air pollution is not visible to human eyes. Even if, as outlined above, pollution registers itself on the body, not all current problems come down to the visible smog layers above cities such as Santiago, Istanbul, São Paulo or, for example, the infamous situations in many of the megacities of China, where smog descends on the streets in a much more imposing manner than in other metropolises.

In several ways, it is the existence of environmental problems that spurs the mobilisation of technological solutions such as high-level smog sensoring coupled with big data analysis. Here, remote sensing/smog sensing/environmental sensing is becoming a crucial node in terms of producing the feedback-looped citizen/smart environment. The smog disaster cities of China produce massive amounts of data from sensors and other sorts of input for scientific research based on quantitative analysis of pollution levels, together with the linking of smog sensors, social media data and big data analysis to establish the geographic/location-based distribution of the issues, which are taken as the synthetic chemical screen of the city itself. Big data and big sensors become in some cases ways of collecting and processing environmental data in 'monitoring, which can better guide people's behaviour and government strategy design for smog disaster mitigation'.[49] People become functions of the data flows as its sensors (through social media messages, for example) and its quantified subjects, while the issue of the political is rather left grey: monitoring does not necessarily mean any sort of a political follow-up. Interestingly, social activism is here supported by corporate hardware and issues of policy become more central than questioning the politics of infrastructure.

Many projects concerning coordinated data sets from sensors to social media messages become a way of mobilising computational solutions and infrastructures too. These include Apache Hive system-based information warehouse solutions and real-time computation systems such as Storm (also Apache-based, and open-system, offered by Hadoop), which demonstrates how chemical residues spur data. Management of the environment means also managing data about the environment. Any environment includes data about itself, the wider media ecology. This refers to the informational ecology that is able to store, handle, query and process the data, which also changes our understanding and relation to the environment in the process. It is on this level of computational infrastructure that the old technological urban pollution, such as smog from transport, meets the new infrastructures that are built in response to it: monitors, computational process, data storage and more.

Jennifer Gabrys investigates some key smart city projects in terms of how they have mobilised notions of environmentality as part of the agenda of sustainability.[50] In a way, one could see these as directly addressing the issue of the technological city as well as the polluted city, but now with a sense of a redistribution of power. It is a visual production of the city as per its statistical distribution of pollution levels in terms of graphs – and also in terms of apps that allow the city to be mapped according to its pollution levels, adding another layer to the more chemical sense of smog as media. Monitoring is not necessarily only remote either, but literally mobilised by researchers who track the existing infrastructural routes of the city; moving along the existing channels of transport/communication such as ferries, subways and pedestrian routes in cities such as Hong Kong and Shenzen becomes a way to see how air quality varies:

> Another innovative experiment in capturing highly localized air quality data was recently conducted in the cities of Hong Kong and Shenzhen. Instead of locating fixed monitoring stations around these cities, researchers at the MIT Senseable City Lab attached small sensors to their wrists and belts and then travelled along standard commute routes on ferries, subways, and on foot. The sensors gathered data for carbon monoxide, nitrogen dioxide, temperature, humidity, and noise and monitored PM 10, a measure of coarse inhalable particles. On their calves, the researchers strapped a GPS and camera to track spatial information.[51]

In other words, the airborne pollution that defines the modern subject in relation to its breathing conditions, that is, air conditioning, also triggers questions of the governance and subjectivity of urban sites and movement in and across such locations. These are issues that Gabrys also focuses on. However, she is interested in how this can be read through Foucault's vocabulary, and a perspective on 'environmental technologies as spatial modes of governance might alter material-political distributions of power and possible modes of subjectification'.[52] Indeed offering a contribution from the perspective of Science and Technology Studies (STS), this angle is less a question of individual subjects than the enfolding of urban citizens as 'sensing nodes – citizen sensors', where issues of environmentality, sensors, mediated logistics and political subjectivity become knotted. Following Gabrys's idea, this relates to how the participatory citizen is inserted as part of the circuit of management of the environment in a way that corresponds to Michel Foucault's analysis of territories and security: but rather than controlling individuals, here creating environmental conditions in which certain sorts of behaviour and end results are produced. Foucault's way of outlining the genealogy of 'case, risk, danger and crisis'[53] as particular terms that function in the context of security is in some ways pertinent to our interest. Foucault tracks the importance of this mechanism through contagious diseases, and his analysis pays attention to the centrality of the (market) town as a territory of contagion. Furthermore, the focus on territorial and statistically managed security is something he observes as not being nullified or denied but addressed by way of containment; these are mechanisms of control and security. This approach could also be a relevant way of understanding air pollution as linked to security issues that 'involve the delimitation of phenomena within acceptable limits, rather than the imposition of a law that says no to them'.[54] In other words, the issue is less a straightforward getting rid of pollutants than finding frameworks in which they can be observed, contained and, at least, held within certain limits defined by the massive amount of data and the views of different institutions, health bodies and so on. Data also plays a part in this security operation.

This data-security arrangement leads to the production of a sustainability of the city that links the city dweller as part of a bigger, often corporate network of computational events, but which still does not automatically enable a wider sort of participation in the bigger logic of fundamental political questions. The infrastructures of sustainability are at the moment being touted and built by the major corporations involved in cloud and smart city projects. The computational platforms are at the same time connected to the corporate platforms of the likes of Google, already piloting and prepared for the reception of data through interoperability with Hadoop systems. The Google cloud platform has the processing capacity suited for smog and air pollution data. The environmental and chemical issues become big data: 'Networked sensor technology is in the early stages of revolutionizing business logistics, city planning, and consumer products' is the testimonial one-liner that narrativises something which otherwise stays as data: Google becoming the software back end for the big data gathered from client devices observing the city.[55]

In terms of the political question of this smart city, some of the issues relate to the designs and debates concerning citizen sensing. Here, the sensor is taken as the bottleneck where the major dilemma of control of data can be addressed on a collective activist level. From the perspective of big data this is more of a modest approach, but useful in activating the question of design, infrastructure, data and the polluted urban environment. With a focus on the sensors, the issue becomes a stronger articulation of citizen-mapped location instead of mere talk of ubiquity. Much of this design discourse revolves around the value of empowerment and shifting the focus of design from the product to the collective production of placing sensors and using them to tag the city according to possibilities of gathering data. It is referred to in terms of making things public, in Latour and Weibel's sense of the term, stemming from their jointly curated exhibition.[56] And it partly extends to participatory design where the city becomes reinvestigated through citizen activities. Gabrys opts for the term 'ambividuals' for this sort of a situation of subjectivity in the smart, sensored-feedback city: citizen-subjects function as 'ambient and malleable urban operators that are expressions of computer environments'.[57] This is a mode of subjectivity relevant to the discussion of cognitive capitalism as a framing of communicative opportunities. But, argues Gabrys, it does not assume the ambividual to be an 'expression of a cognitive subject'; instead it 'does articulate the distribution of nodes of action within the smart city'.[58] The cognitive becomes a distributed, infrastructural operation within the circuit. It feeds both towards the understanding of the subject and towards the issues of how the city itself is framed as a milieu, an environment of multiple layers. What Gabrys's work points out is the circulation of sensor data as something that reframes not only the question of the city as programmable, but also the relation of such programs to issues of citizenship.

In a way, some projects in HCI design demonstrate that the fallacy of the ubiquitous relates to a fantasy of a removed, corporate and, indeed, homogeneously ubiquitous sensing and processing environment, whereas many of the more interesting projects are reminders that this ubiquity is not evenly distributed, but becomes an issue that needs further focus: some places are more intensively mapped than others, some places are more sensed than others.[59] Design projects that mobilise sensor placement, citizen drones and other projects scale down the massive level of computational ubiquity to the question of where the data for the ubiquitous city come from – a point raised in a way by Benjamin Bratton and Natalie Jeremijenko in another context debating information visualisation, the interface and different sensor projects.[60]

Data transactions are part of a complex environmental, ecological and territorial operation of defining secure limits and optimised feedback loops. It is in this milieu that the existing levels of, for example, air pollution are measured. But the data milieu is also conditioned by the historical layers of the city: its transportation system, infrastructures, the seemingly residual industrial that features as smog. The archaic persists. And it taps into the politically important citizen activities, which, however, have to negotiate their work often in relation to corporate hardware, such as Intel-provided cheap sensors. In more philosophical terms, sensorial environments are less about the remote sensing of things *out there*, and more about capturing them as part of a shared circuit in which they become part of the experience and consideration of 'us'; it is a sort of a co-emergent tuning, to continue paraphrasing Gabrys, that is, a constant processing of sensor data, but as a way of creating matters of concern.[61] Turning the idea of remote sensing on its head, Gabrys is able to pinpoint a moment when instead of transporting data about the environment to us, such mechanisms can function as ways of constituting subjectivity and circuiting us as part of the concerns raised by them. This is where the added layer of sensors, data and their computation is not merely an isolated event of registering. Instead, urban subjects also become functions of that further level of smart computational city infrastructure. This is not a revelation per se, but something that some test cases (such as Santander) and researchers recognise: a lot of the work of sensor data is focused on how 'to improve the performance of key infrastructure, such as roads, rail, water systems and electrical grids'.[62] Or as Townsend puts it, explicating the situation where infrastructural optimisation then becomes itself dependent on the sensitive, added layer of computationality: 'You're creating a structure that is inherently unstable and can only be controlled by a computer and software that can sense what's going on.'[63]

But political momentum is not necessarily merely about the circulation of information. Instead, it can be seen as involving a relation to designing infrastructures in which sensing/sensation becomes possible. Hence questions about sensing emerge as a way to negotiate the techno-bodies of sensation[64] as multiple scales of mediated registering: the human sensorially and remote sensorially experienced pollution levels are one such sort of an entangled mixed ecology of sensing and sensation. This point actually comes back to the conceptual development I offered in the previous section through art projects and the relation of the experiential body to the realities of pollution that are not always easily available to the human senses. Hence, Gabrys and Braidotti provide exciting ways to consider this extended understanding of sensors (the technological, the embodied) and the media realities of air pollution as data and as a visual, chemical screen.

Of course, this mix can be addressed through informational contexts too, but sensors and remote sensing should be understood also in terms of their concrete locations as part of the habitual life patterns of urban dwellers. Sensor placement becomes a tool to hotspot places, to enact a sense of location and movement that engages with the trail of data production. In a way, sensors prescribe certain spots as places of special interest and the placing of sensors then becomes a crucial question as to *where* the city is sensed, *where* it is mapped, what is being seen as valuable about a tactical or strategic *location*. Carlos Barreneche demonstrates how geo-services produce a specific geographical ontology that is prescribed by way of software and corporate platforms through tagging, linking of user data and so forth.[65] In similar ways, we need to see how air and geography are linked through the sensorial, and what prescribes the chemical trails to be turned into visible data as part of the smart city.

The issue of location is a central part of the debate and becomes emphasised when focusing on issues of sensation; where the locations of air and pollution are, and how they become part of the way in which the city lends itself to human *and* technological senses. Moving down to earth from locations above human heads in the atmosphere, air pollution levels fluctuate radically also *within* cities.[66] These differences in locations and their air quality are part of the historical and political ways in which aesthetics is being allocated: the visuals, smells, chemicals and toxins of the city that do not fall evenly. This is the aspect of the *nomos* that is not merely a cut in the division of the terrestrial or the aquatic, but also the air.[67] It is not only an ordering of ownership but also the consequence of urban planning, industrial residue, infrastructures from transport to the emerging smart cities that themselves are built on top of cities real and imagined, technological and polluted.

Notes

1. A longer version of this chapter was published as 'The Sensed Smog: Smart Ubiquitous Cities and the Sensorial Body', *Fibreculture*, 29, 2016, a special issue on 'Computing the City', ed. Florian Sprenger and Armin Beverungen. This version is published under the *Fibreculture* licence Attribution 4.0 International (CC BY 4.0).
2. Jussi Parikka, *A Geology of Media* (Minneapolis: University of Minnesota Press, 2015), pp. 83–107.
3. Peter Sloterdijk, *Bubbles. Spheres Volume I: Microspherology*, trans. Wieland Hoban (Los Angeles: Semiotext(e), 2011).
4. Peter Sloterdijk, *Terror from the Air*, trans. Amy Patton and Steve Corcoran (Los Angeles: Semiotext(e), 2009).
5. On tear gas, see Anna Feigenbaum, *Tear Gas: From the Battlefields of WWI to the Streets of Today* (London: Verso, 2017).
6. See Yigit Soncul, 'Containing the Mask, Governing the Emergency: The Case of Turkey', *Theory, Culture & Society*, 32 (2015), pp. 285–91. My thanks are due to Yigit Soncul for sharing his research, based on his ongoing PhD research project on the mask and modern media ecology.
7. See Rob Nixon, *Slow Violence and the Environmentalism of the Poor* (Cambridge, MA: Harvard University Press, 2011).
8. See Etienne Turpin (ed.), *Architecture in the Anthropocene. Encounters Among Design, Deep Time, Science and Philosophy* (Ann Arbor: Open Humanities Press, 2013); Heather Davis and Etienne Turpin (eds), *Art in the Anthropocene. Encounters Among Aesthetics, Politics, Environments and Epistemologies* (London: Open Humanities Press, 2015).
9. See Donna Haraway, 'Anthropocene, Capitalocene, Chthulhocene. Donna Haraway in conversation with Martha Kenney', in Heather Davis and Etienne Turpin (eds), *Art in the Anthropocene* (London: Open Humanities Press, 2015), pp. 255–70.

10. Davis and Turpin (eds), *Art in the Anthropocene*, p. 3.
11. Benjamin Bratton, *The Stack. On Software and Sovereignty* (Cambridge, MA: MIT Press, 2015); Davis and Turpin (eds), *Art in the Anthropocene*, pp. 3–4.
12. Bratton, *The Stack*, p. 165.
13. Ibid., p. 166.
14. An important context for this proposition is Jennifer Gabrys's work, *Program Earth. Environmental Sensing Technology and the Making of a Computational Planet* (Minneapolis: University of Minnesota Press, 2016), while it also relates to my *A Geology of Media*, which outlines ways in which media theory participates in discussions of ecology and the environmental humanities. Benjamin Bratton, in *The Stack*, identified the city as one of six key layers in the ongoing reorganising of the relations that include much more than just the earth. Discussing cities, Bratton remarks that political subjectivity is becoming tied also to infrastructural determinations that are much beyond the usual sphere of roads, buildings and plumbing. Indeed, Bratton notes that megaurbanism tells a story of the new interfaces that connect cities to other scales of the planetary systems; multiple levels of determination relating to hardware, software, sensors, users, interfaces and other layers.
15. Karen Barad, *Meeting the Universe Halfway. Quantum Physics and the Entanglement of Matter and Meaning* (Durham, NC: Duke University Press, 2007).
16. Orit Halpern, *Beautiful Data: A History of Vision and Reason since 1945* (Durham, NC: Duke University Press, 2014), p. 27.
17. Todd Newcombe, 'Santander: The Smartest Smart City', *Governing*, May 2014, http://www.governing.com/topics/urban/gov-santander-spain-smart-city.html (last accessed 20 May 2017).
18. Kevin Gates and Ramesh Sampath, 'Seeing the Air', visualisation project website, 2015, http://www.seeingtheair.com (last accessed 20 May 2017).
19. John Durham Peters, *The Marvelous Clouds. Toward a Philosophy of Elemental Media* (Chicago: University of Chicago Press, 2015).
20. Sommer Mathis, 'The Rise and Fall and the Eventual Rise Again of the "Smart City". A conversation with Smart Cities author Anthony Townsend', *CityLab*, 13 January 2014, http://www.citylab.com/tech/2014/01/rise-and-fall-and-eventual-rise-again-smart-city/8081/ (last accessed 20 May 2017).
21. Ibid.
22. 'Starting from Scratch', *The Economist*, 7 September 2013, http://www.economist.com/news/briefing/21585003-building-city-future-costly-and-hard-starting-scratch (last accessed 20 May 2017).
23. Cf. Bruce Sterling, 'Bruce Sterling's Vision of the Future City', *BBC*, 8 May 2013, http://www.bbc.com/future/story/20130507-bruce-sterling-2050-city-vision (last accessed 20 May 2017).

24. Orit Halpern and Gökçe Günel, 'Demoing Unto Death. Smart Cities, Environment, and Preemptive Hope', *Fibreculture*, 29 (2017), http://twentynine.fibreculturejournal.org/fcj-215-demoing-unto-death-smart-cities-environment-and-preemptive-hope/ (last accessed 20 May 2017).
25. Ibid.
26. Katie Herzog, 'The World's First Zero-carbon City is a Big Failure', *Grist*, 17 February 2016, http://grist.org/climate-energy/the-worlds-first-zero-carbon-city-is-a-big-failure/ (last accessed 20 May 2017).
27. See Shannon Mattern, *Deep Mapping the Media City*, Forerunners: Ideas First (Minneapolis: University of Minnesota Press, 2015); see also Bratton, *The Stack*.
28. Shannon Mattern, 'Of Mud, Media and the Metropolis. Aggregating Histories of Writing and Urbanization', *Cultural Politics*, 12.3 (2016), pp. 310–31.
29. James Vincent, '(Updated) London Bins are Tracking your Smart Phone', *The Independent*, 9 August 2013, http://www.independent.co.uk/life-style/gadgets-and-tech/news/updated-londons-bins-are-tracking-your-smartphone-8754924.html (last accessed 20 May 2017).
30. Dominique Laporte, *The History of Shit*, trans. Nadia Benabid and Rodolphe el-Khoury, with an introduction by Rodolphe el-Khoury (Cambridge, MA: MIT Press, 2000), p. 26.
31. See, for example, Verena Andermatt Conley, *Ecopolitics. The Environment in Poststructuralist Thought* (London: Routledge, 1997); Matthew Fuller, *Media Ecologies. Materialist Energies in Art and Technoculture* (Cambridge, MA: MIT Press, 2005).
32. John Protevi, *Life, War, Earth. Deleuze and the Sciences* (Minneapolis: University of Minnesota Press, 2013), p. 46.
33. Ulrich Beck, *Ecological Enlightenment* (Atlantic Highlands, NJ: Humanities Press, 1995), p. 60.
34. Simon Cottle, 'Ulrich Beck, Risk Society and the Media. A Catastrophic View?', *European Journal of Communication*, 13.1 (1998), pp. 5–32.
35. Fran Tonkiss, *Cities by Design. The Social Life of Urban Form* (Cambridge: Polity, 2013), pp. 148–9.
36. Rosi Braidotti, *Transpositions. On Nomadic Ethics* (Cambridge: Polity, 2006), p. 123.
37. Matt McGrath, 'EU Commission Launches Legal Action over UK Air Quality', BBC News, 20 February 2014, http://www.bbc.com/news/science-environment-26257703 (last accessed 20 May 2017).
38. Nixon, *Slow Violence*, pp. 64–5.
39. See, for example, Imre Szeman, 'System Failure: Oil, Futurity, and the Anticipation of Disaster', *South Atlantic Quarterly*, 106.4 (2007), pp. 805–23; Antti Salminen and Tere Vadén, *Energy and Experience: An Essay in Naftology* (Chicago and Alberta: M-C-M, 2015).

40. Nicole Starosielski, *The Undersea Network* (Durham, NC: Duke University Press, 2015).
41. See Haraway, 'Anthropocene, Capitalocene, Chthulhocene'.
42. On art and the Anthropocene, see Davis and Turpin (eds), *Art in the Anthropocene*.
43. John McNeill, *Something New Under the Sun. An Environmental History of the Twentieth Century* (London: Penguin, 2000), p. 52.
44. Ibid., p. 114.
45. Abbie Thomas, 'Whales Showing More Sun Damage', *ABC Science*, 10 November 2010, http://www.abc.net.au/science/articles/2010/11/10/3062051.htm (last accessed 20 May 2017).
46. See Nicholas Mirzoeff, 'Visualizing the Anthropocene', *Public Culture*, 26.2 (2014), pp. 213–32.
47. Cf. Jacques Rancière, *The Politics of Aesthetics*, trans. Gabriel Rockhill (London: Continuum, 2004).
48. This aesthetics of and in the city addresses not merely any local condition but issues of global politics. In Nicholas Mirzoeff's recent take, it becomes entangled as part of the logic of global political movements such as Occupy, which demand a 'right to look' in an exchange without surplus value. For Mirzoeff, this right is 'aesthetically a priori, philosophically foundational, and historically prior' ('Visualizing the Anthropocene', p. 214).
49. Jiaoyan Chen et al., 'Big Smog Meets Web Science: Smog Disaster Analysis Based on Social Media and Device Data on the Web', *WWW Companion '14. Proceedings of the companion publication of the 23rd international conference on World wide web companion* (2014), pp. 505–10.
50. Jennifer Gabrys, 'Programming Environments: Environmentality and Citizen Sensing in the Smart City', *Environment and Planning D: Society and Space*, 32 (2014), pp. 30–48.
51. Doug Cooley, 'Improved Sensor Technology Shares Real-time Air Pollution Data', *SmartCitiesCouncil*, 2 April 2014, http://smartcitiescouncil.com/article/improved-sensor-technology-shares-real-time-air-pollution-data (last accessed 20 May 2017).
52. Gabrys, 'Programming Environments', p. 32.
53. Michel Foucault, *Security, Territory, Population, Lectures at the Collège de France 1977–1978*, ed. Arnold I. Davidson (Basingstoke: Palgrave Macmillan, 2007), p. 61.
54. Ibid., p. 66.
55. Google Cloud Platform Blog, 'Data Sensing Lab at Google I/O 2013: Google Cloud Platform Meets the Internet of Things', Google Cloud Platform Blog, 13 May 2013, http://googlecloudplatform.blogspot.de/2013/05/data-sensing-lab-at-google-io-2013.html (last accessed 20 May 2017).
56. Bruno Latour and Peter Weibel (eds), *Making Things Public* (Cambridge, MA: MIT Press, 2005).
57. Gabrys, 'Programming Environments', pp. 42–3.

58. Ibid., p. 43.
59. See, for example, Stacey Kuznetsov et al., 'Ceci n'est pas une pipe bombe: Authoring Urban Landscapes with Air Quality Sensors', in *CHI '11: Proceedings of the SIGCHI Conference on Human Factors in Computing Systems* (2011), pp. 2375–84; Carl DiSalvo et al., 'Making Public Things: How HCI Design Can Express Matters of Concern', in *CHI '14: Proceedings of the SIGCHI Conference on Human Factors in Computing Systems* (2014), pp. 2397–406.
60. Benjamin Bratton and Natalie Jeremijenko, 'Suspicious Images, Latent Interfaces', *Situated Technologies Pamphlets 3* (New York: The Architectural League of New York, 2008).
61. Jennifer Gabrys, 'Sensing an Experimental Forest: Processing Environments and Distributing Relations', *Computational Culture*, 2 (2012), http://computationalculture.net/article/sensing-an-experimental-forest-processing-environments-and-distributing-relations (last accessed 20 May 2017)
62. Newcombe, 'Santander'.
63. Quoted in Mathis, 'The Rise and Fall and the Eventual Rise Again of the "Smart City"'.
64. Gabrys, 'Sensing an Experimental Forest', referring to Rosi Braidotti.
65. Carlos Barreneche, 'The Order of Places: Code, Ontology and Visibility in Locative Media', *Computational Culture*, 2 (2012), http://computationalculture.net/article/order_of_places (last accessed 20 May 2017).
66. See Jenny Xie, 'Tracking Exactly How Much Air Pollution You're Exposed To', *CityLab*, 5 March 2014, http://www.citylab.com/tech/2014/03/tracking-how-much-air-pollution-youre-exposed-step-step/8525/ (last accessed 20 May 2017).
67. Quoting Carl Schmitt, *The Nomos of the Earth* (New York: Telos Press, 2006), p. 49: 'because it is not inconsequential whether the industrialized and mechanized world that men have created with the help of technology has a terrestrial or maritime foundation. But today, it is conceivable that the air will envelop the sea and perhaps even the earth, and that men will transform their planet into a combination of produce warehouse and aircraft carrier. Then, new amity lines will be drawn, beyond which atomic and hydrogen bombs will fall.'

CHAPTER 10

The Intelligence of Computational Design

Luciana Parisi

If technology, as Larry Hickman claims, is more than technique because it involves cognitive inferential activity, could it be argued that the computational transformation of design brings forward new intelligent activities generated through and within the means of automated processing?[1] In the 1990s, digital modelling involved the application of non-standard geometry and complex mathematical functions to design curvilinear structures.[2] Here the thinking activities of machines were relegated to experiments with binary logic with differential calculus. Since the early 2000s, however, technological design has rather shifted towards a re-materialisation or naturalisation of the digital forms evolving on the other side of the screen. The future of automated design, as envisioned in the exhibition 'Radical Atoms' presented by the Tangible Media Group (MIT) at the 2016 Ars Electronica Festival,[3] involves a naturalisation in the interconnection of bits and atoms where smart materials are modelled upon the intelligence of natural substances. However, as the interface of digital modelling and material structures concerns the design of immersive environments by replacing the filmic filter of the interface with the concreteness of intelligent atoms, no longer can the binary logic of the digital impose a form on physical matter. Even with the early use of CAD in digital design there was already the realisation that the differential calculus, as a non-standard mathematical model, was rather attuned to the intelligent dynamics of matter rather than any formal language insofar as it exposed design to evolutionary continuity between the given and the constructed. In the last fifteen years, as architectural design has been concerned with a *generic* function of computation, involving a new synthesis of calculation and statistics, quantification and prediction, measure and hypothesis, it has become even more apparent that the structural behaviour of increasingly smaller parts has become central to new forms of spatio-temporal becoming.

As opposed to the function of the differential calculus establishing a meta-equivalence between two distinct realms – the digital and the material – the new focus on the general function of computation has rather decomposed distinct scales into granular data and their common behaviour. This means that computational design can account not only for the local behaviour of molecular matter but also for how its spatio-temporal evolution can be understood in terms of computational functions of organisation and structuring. Hence design has entered the granular scale and the micro activities internal to material structures, and is no longer concerned with simply framing data in already existing models. Material computation, as this recent phase in architectural design has also been called,[4] involves a specific rearticulation of materiality and materialisation to develop an open-ended design, in which properties and behaviours can be directly accessed and used as active raw sources, exposing how the microscales of natural elements subtend the construction of macrostructural environments. Material computation thus exposes this seamless infinitesimal reflection between biophysical and technical strata.

Instead of a symbolic representation of physical elements, it can be argued that material computation extends the interactive/responsive paradigm of second-order cybernetics, by more directly exposing the computational capacities of materials to respond to and from spatio-temporal specificities: no longer the constructive interaction between systems or within a mutating environment, but a focus on the self-design of materials, namely in terms of a computational processing of data involving the ordering of randomness. Here design no longer follows the abstract articulation of geometrical and mathematical patterns, but is more exclusively concerned with revealing the self-assembling capacities of materials to generate, adapt and modify their forms, creating sustainable and adaptable environments – without any external intervention. In contrast to a formal automation of design relying on already defined ends carried out by sequences of linear instructions, material computation is concerned with the inherent morphogenetic potential of materials as the starting condition to generate forms through their internal tendency to structure randomness and thus grow, evolve and complexify. The scope is not simply to establish a continuous feedback between programmed instructions and biophysical environment, but rather to offer a more radical ontological proposition of merging computation with biophysical self-organisation. Here computation involves not a binary calculation of probabilities, but is *naturalised* because it is understood in terms of the behavioural effects of molecular activities coinciding, as it were, with a granular calculation of variations. In other words, computation here no longer implies the application of formal logic (and language) to any system, but more importantly its meaning has become extended by and through the biological framework of second-order cybernetics concerning the relation between matter, energy and information at the threshold of randomness and order.

Computational materiality thus implies a naturalisation of design here intended as *techne*, or instrumentality, and defined not by logical aims, but by operations, procedures and means that cut across strata, rules, forms and go beyond the specific constraints of each and any form. The granular computation of data has thus transformed design into an automated mechanism of aggregation, no longer conforming to the logic of finality, where aims are pre-implicated in the premises of the process. Instead, automated design exposes cognition and perception to data communicability or mediality, the very quality of transmitting, storing and commanding vast volumes of data as a mode of prediction, a mechanism or procedure of knowing how data sets can be correlated under certain circumstances. This quality of computational communicability, however, does not imply the execution of rules through the means of computational data processing. Instead, it is precisely data processing that now directs or steers open-ended design mechanisms that depend upon the mediality of data, correlating increasingly smaller sets of data variations. Instead of a universal model that conforms means to ends – or calculation to the demonstration of postulates – with material computation, design has become a mode of informational organisation moving from means to means or function to function (and not means to ends or ends through means). Automated design implies a shift from digital formalism (and its applications of ends to means) to computational functions (the processing of means through means), an active indifference to causality and finality. In what follows, I will discuss this shift to the dominance of means or mediality in design, as involving, as Mario Carpo suggests, the dissolution of the logic of compression.[5] I will suggest that this technological transformation is part of a more general image of computational sovereignty – or planetary computation[6] – where the granular articulation of data across scales is central to a new 'informatics of domination',[7] activated through and with the becoming dynamic of automated systems, which are now able to include randomness, the unknown and uncertainties into their function of prediction and experimental aggregation of data.

By drawing on John Dewey's notion of instrumentality, and Charles S. Peirce's continuity of logical inferences, the chapter concludes that the shift to computational materiality will be the starting point for a critical rearticulation of the relation between ends and means.[8] Automated design, therefore, involves not only a transformation of human cognition and perception, but most importantly, the advance of computational logic and inferential reasoning.

Material Computation: Of Bits and Atoms

In the late 1990s the use of computation to experiment with the intelligence of materials was put into practice by the so-called 'neoplasmatic design'.[9] Here the capacity of matter to carry out structural functions coincides with the idea of an emergent design linked to the intrinsic properties of self-organisation. In particular, the world of botanical matter and animal flesh become central to attempts to design semi-living structures involving a genetic manipulation of micro-organisms, such as bacteria and viruses, whose information, matter and energy exchange is a trigger for the evolution of complex morphologies. With the use of biotechnology, the design of living environments involves the evolution of living landmass composed of genetically engineered organisms. For instance, Steve Pike's projects, such as 'Algoearthchitecture' and 'Nonsterile', are concerned with the evolutionary design of microbial mechanisms and thus with exposing how the medium of design itself can grow into complex networks of structures and communication.[10] Here, the neoplasmatic manipulation of microscale organisms involves the emergence of environmental structures whose very means of fabrication are living entities, equipped with energy, information and chemical properties. The investment in neoplasmatic architecture is understood in terms of material agency – that is, defined not by pre-established ends, but by the emergence of a complex interactivity, emerging from the aggregation of self-organising parts. Here, what is important is not the end or finality of design. Instead, design has come to coincide with a network of functions that channel other functions, invoking the emergence of more nuanced structural adaptations.

While networked complexity is central to second-order cybernetics and the last forty years of experimentation in computational and interactive design, the new focus on the intelligence of materials points out that microbiological activities – and not only human language – bring to bear the function of mediality as they transmit, store, communicate and exchange energy, matter and information.[11]

As these biophysical means have come to promote a non-teleological model of automated design where structures mutate over time and order is constantly reshuffled across thresholds of chaos, a new form of cybernetic dominance has come to the fore. No longer does the solipsistic enclosure of self-organisation set up against an external environment as a source of expansion for the growing of one system. With neoplasmatic and biosynthetic design, it is precisely the uncovering of the computational activities of environments (that is, the synthesis of energy and information, the use of randomness, the metabolic function of data processing, adaptation and genetic mutations, the hierarchical structuring of functions and so on) that constitute design as a function of functions integrating material, form and force as continuous iterations of data computations. It is no longer the modelling of the environment through interaction with the environment that can ensure governance through a continuous feedback. Instead, it is the computational communicability of the environment – that is, not that the environment speaks a language, but that the communicability of language has become information processing held within molecular matter.

By moving beyond digital modelling and the animation of forms, design has thus embraced material computation as a means or instrument that exposes the information processing of complexities. This emphasis on the mechanism of computation, rather than on the digital modelling of complex spatio-temporalities, is rather concerned with the behavioural effects and the agential activities of materials that have no predeterminate aims. Instead, as the cybernetic steering of behaviour has entered the realm of molecular agencies, so the advance of material computation in design reveals the new concern with the instrumentality of design as a concern with its own tasks as a medium of and for data activities. In short, with material computation, design no longer coincides with the cybernetic engineering of predictable scenarios, but with the task of inducing new correlations of vast amounts of varied data flows.

We know that with form-oriented design, for instance, the information-driven manipulation of NURBS-geometry (that is, non-uniform rational B-spline) embraced experiments in animated simulations with the end of abstracting dynamic behaviour through the topological modelling of material substrates. Instead, with material computation, design has relinquished any formal schema to become itself a means of processing variables, relying on the internal functions of physical properties and the local behaviour of materials. Thus, material computation is neither modelling nor simulation of an external environment, and similarly it is not limited to patterns of responsive interaction. It is not a formal paradigm aiming to read matter. Instead, the ends of computational design have been replaced by the means of its own existence, the activities that catalyse the building of structures. With material computation, the means of matter are able to beget other means so that the architectural form becomes one with matter's environmental activities. Away from the mechanistic view of a computational universe, where eternal laws and finalities are presupposed to drive the engines of parts, material computation reveals the epistemological dominance of automated crafting, relying on the dynamic mechanisms of information processing underpinning biological, physical and technical systems. It is interesting to note that, for instance, the 'Radical Atoms' exhibition at Ars Electronica (2016) seems to extend material computation precisely across sensori-motor activities, physical force, and digital hardware and software (together with 3D printers and laser cutters) to experiment with the capacities of these means to be designed by external forces rather than being scripted to certain aims. This project is a hypothetical envisioning of the physical embodiment of digital information in malleable and reconfigurable materials: a dynamics reflected in both biophysical and digital environments at once. As both environments are said to be synchronised, the structural shapes of atoms emerge and adapt to sensori-motor inputs. This synchronisation relies on the dynamic functions of atoms inspired to the behaviour of free radicals (that is, atoms, molecules and ions with unpaired electron) that are highly unstable and transformable and have no predetermined finality or program within them.[12] These highly malleable environments are a self-governing arrangement of functions of equivalence between chemical, biophysical and digital processing, replacing the filmic barrier of pixels – or the screen in virtual environments – with real-time computational crafting. By dissolving the visual boundary or the image-centred mediation of virtual environments, the 'Radical Atoms' project is an example of the new dominance of computational means whereby spatial experience is granted by a means-to-means correspondence between biophysical and digital processing.

This shift towards means-oriented design needs to be understood within the wider epistemological context of the crisis of finality and of logical-deductive reasoning (that is, the method by which results or ends are already contained in the premises of a process of truth deductions). In particular, as Mario Carpo has recently argued, big data design can no longer be defined in terms of standard compression of data, reflecting a method of knowledge based on a limited capacity of mathematical synthesis, defined by a formal axiomatics that would subsume the means or instruments of and for knowledge to the ends of narratives and history.[13] According to Carpo, big data refers to the operations of collecting, storing and ordering increasing amounts of cheap and abundant data that one day would be transmitted at no cost, and side-stepping the necessity of data compression – or logical synthesis. For Carpo, emerging informational models and techniques have been replacing cultural technologies of compression (for instance, from logarithms to scale drawings to descriptive geometry and even the alphabet, or the voice recorder) and enabled almost a full matching between raw and recorded or transmitted data. In other words, the promise of big data is that the richness of data retrieved is becoming equivalent to that which is transmitted, revealing that what was conceived to be randomness and/or noise to be compressed for the ends of communication has rather come to qualify the very nature of communicability entrenched in environmental complexities. While some data can be lost in this means-to-means communicability, the increasing volume of available raw data is instead matched by increasing randomness/noise in automated systems of data processing, which, according to Carpo, can no longer be represented in mathematical notations or modelling. Instead here computational design enters the field of non-organised data. This new epistemological possibility of data abundance and availability counters the historical data-compression activities of Western science whose methods of general axiomatics produced data scarcity – that is, a model of knowledge based upon an already restricted availability of data. Instead of recording and transmitting data, general axiomatics performed data synthesis according to preset formal notations. The compression of data into scripts followed the logic of deductive implication – that is, this result stems from or is implicated in this rule – for which one model would be applied to and describe any event, establishing truths that aimed to predict any particular situation. Carpo explains that instead of making predictions based on mathematical laws and formulas, with big data it is possible simply to search for an event that may have already happened and can be simply retrieved in the new universal archive of data. This mode of prediction, however, entails not simply the retrieval of what has already happened, but has acquired a granular quality for which data sets are increasingly variable and in variation. In other words, prediction relies not on the classification of data into groups, clusters and so on, but on the computational capacities to process increasingly smaller variations, revealing a super granularity and hyperdiscreteness of material components. Instead of carrying out statistical calculations to establish standard averages, with big data, the prediction of increasingly smaller events is based upon the inductive retrieval of local data. Prediction becomes enmeshed within those computational means for which design is concerned with the structural functions of minuscule materials. This data-processing design has also been defined in terms of aggregate architecture because it involves the synthesis of large amounts of increasingly discrete elements entering in close contact.[14] Here the emphasis is on the singular activities of parts within evolving structures that, instead of being theoretically modelled, are rather gathered through the observation of physical granular systems.

Big data design is thus not simply a matter of technical efficiency, but more importantly reveals that the modality or the means of design are now structuring and transforming the very logic of design. Material computation relies upon an inductive method of design, which places the local properties of materials and the varying behaviours of physical elements at the centre of the design process. From this standpoint, design involves a continual extension of the search space through the computational capacities of selection, mutation and inheritance. This neo-empirical dominance of the inductive search for granular data is no longer a simulation of emergent patterns, but shows that aggregate data can determine a range of possibilities and analytical measures to establish levels of fitness of structures within set possibilities.[15] Novel spatio-temporal patterns are said to arise not in formal pre-arrangements, but in the realisation of the multiple behavioural capacities of aggregating elements.[16] What is new here is that material properties are not simply variables in an interactive system, but are constitutive of computational design itself – they are both the physical and digital means that describe the procedure, the tasking, the activities of computation, merging matter and *techne* into one plane. If material computation has rejected the deductive model of universal rules and its top-down method of form finding, then this non-compressive mode of data search, selection and transmission tends to unify scales through its operational means as planetary data processing.

To what extent, one may ask, is computational design simply part of the mechanisms of expansion of a post-cybernetic sovereignty or 'planetary scale computation',[17] which takes control through a dynamic rather than mechanical *techne* or instrumentality? And what are the political consequences of this anti-logical reformulation of design, where data has become the very means of computation and the medium of design itself? If material computation involves a conception of instrumentality as processing means without ends, does it actually challenge or simply invert the hierarchy between theoretical models – deductive truths and ends – and practical processing – inductive retrieval of local and granular data? If design has become one with the means of computation, it seems important then not to take the dominance of big data naively as the only expression of computation. Rather, for design to address the technological transformation of cognition and perception, one may first of all interrogate the stake of instrumentality today, that is, the consequences that planetary computation have in view of automated intelligence. The question is how to theorise an alternative to the dominance of inductive methods of (non-compressible) data retrieval, where design has become equivalent with the means of its own articulation (that is, big data, material computation) and with the computational infrastructuring of scales. If design is itself a technique and technology of and for an epistemological reformatting of knowledge, then design does not just expose the crisis of axiomatic truths, but has become constitutive of a computational governance of predictive control.

We know that with second-order cybernetics, notions of interactivity and responsiveness defined a design logic already relying on the operative functions of feedback control, statistical averaging, prediction by probability and a logical calculus of differential behaviours. With material computation, the granular discreteness of data has rather revealed the internal levels of randomness across scales – biological, physical, cultural, technical, political, financial – and transformed design into a connective mechanics or a *knowing how to link across*, anticipating the epistemological formation of third-order cybernetics. Here computational design is not only an inductive or non-compressive method of data retrieval, but has rather become the experimental field for the articulation of computational control and governance activated by and through machine intelligence. In other words, computational design has not only incorporated material functions of self-organisation, adaptation, mutation, selection, structuring of randomness and redeployment of redundancy, but it has also grown its own instrumental logic – an automated learning from the mechanisms of multi-scale computation. If second-order cybernetic design had envisioned automated systems that would interact, respond and develop a dia-logical mode of adaptive conversation,[18] third-order cybernetics is rather concerned with multiscalar randomness in multiscalar systems, in which prediction implies not simply statistical averaging, but above the structuring of incomputables to enable the formation of robust and dynamic complexities that scale up from within and across systems. Here prediction relies not only on statistical results from already retrieved data, but also on a new synthesis of computational calculation and logic. According to the mathematician and physicist James Crutchfield, randomness – or infinite varieties of infinities – is not a limit for computation, simply demarcating the passage of a threshold into disordered and uncompressible information.[19] In other words, randomness does not correspond to the entropic tendency of a system to dissipate structure or destabilise its equilibrium. Instead, the complexity of structure or its levels of order stems from the anti-entropic function of randomness, whereby uncompressible information is central to the constitution of various scales of complexity. Anti-entropy explains the structural emergence of asymmetric complexity within a system, because here randomness is constitutive of the evolution of order, granting a system duration and stability: the more levels of randomness, the more structural asymmetries within and between scales. Here randomness defines not the breaking down of the system, but precisely the capacity of a system to evolve new levels of complexity and transform one level into another across scales. It is precisely the discovery of the *constructive construction* of indeterminacy that sets up the computational regime in a new light. This is the form of computational prediction embedded within automated design whose retrieval of infinite amounts of granular data reveals how increasing levels of randomness actively construct computational order, exposing how means in information processing also involve the emergence of new ends in computational logic.

From this standpoint, big data design does not exhaust the use of computation in design, but can be critically addressed as a symptom of the reconfiguration of technical knowledge and the transformation of modes of control and governance. If big data design is a manifestation of the shift from a logic of compression, whereby existing data had to conform with pre-existing ends, to an immersion within the technicality and mediality of design in terms of informational processing, it also involves a radicalisation of cybernetic communicability for which data are as much retrieved as they are transmitted. As design itself becomes one with the virtuality of information and its indeterminate potentiality, suspending all appeals to causes and ends, it also implies a new order of cybernetic control and governance coinciding not only with the image of big data design, but more precisely with the dominance of a computational logic, whose reconfiguration of calculative ends from within the mediality of data must be addressed.

Data Sovereignty

Before the explosion of big data, the use of computation in design mainly involved the algorithmic description of a formal calculus that could be implemented to programme the evolution of structural functions. In its early stages, automated design defined the means of implementation of deductive logic so that algorithmic procedures could conform to rules in the same way as a Turing machine would conform to universal mathematical laws. As a thought experiment, the Turing machine was meant to elucidate the mechanical operations of a formal language through which all possible results could be executed following a determinate set of rules. The adaptation of this method in design was, according to Carpo, central to modernity. However, as Terzidis points out, the use of computational power in algorithmic architecture has also exposed the limits of this deductive form of design based on predefined ends.[20] Similarly, the computational synthesis of logic and granular statistics goes beyond human cognition and perception, and exceeds results based on given premises. The automation of design is thus an automation of cognitive and perceptive capacities involving not simply the implementation of ideas or the representation of reality, but more importantly a granular discretisation of thinking and perceiving, a breaking down of truths and images in terms of functions and tasks. With the development of the computational synthesis of calculation (dynamic statistics) and logic (models of reasoning) design is no longer a mirror of deductive thinking, but has rather embraced heuristic and experimental principles of trial and error to generate new ends from the retrieving, collecting, matching and transmitting of large volumes of data in real time.

As already mentioned, Carpo is right to advocate for a major shift in design with the emergence of big data architectural design, in which complex quantitative phenomena (structural design, energy performance, patterns of use and occupation) can be tested without the need for interpreting them through cause-and-effect, deterministic rules or deductive models. This is the image of a computational infrastructure that is disconnected, broken, fragmentary, rickety, a patchy aggregation of infinite varieties of data. However, instead of operating as a horizontal network where design mainly embodies the very function of aggregating smaller parts by means of connection (textual, visual, sonic, gestural, behavioural, emotional, decisional), one could see the computational infrastructure in terms of vertical megastructural machines of informational data that Bratton calls 'The Stack'.

In particular, according to Bratton, the specificity of means or instrumentality of design – that is, of the computational processing of data or of the ubiquitous advance of what he calls 'planetary computation', needs to be viewed in terms of a veritable 'historical agent of economic and geographic command'.[21] While the view of big data and material computation claims that design no longer conforms means to pre-determinate ends, but is rather reconfigured by the means it uses, Bratton rather envisions that planetary computation is re-allying means and ends, as design implies interweaving and connecting scales between continents, urban structures and perpetual affordances.

Thus, the shift from the logic of deductive formalism in the early form of automated computation (and its subsumption of means to ends) to inductive-driven data retrieval based on trial and error (and thus of means without ends) corresponds to the transformation of automated forms of computation that express changes in the model and the actions of governance. However, a close concern with this shift also needs to account that it brings with it a new understanding of instrumentality, involving a non-rearticulation of means and ends. For instance, Bratton insists that the computational technologies inhabiting distinct scales (urban, interfaces, perceptual) are comprised in distinct layers (earth, cloud, city, addresses, interface, users) arranged vertically and constituting a modular and interdependent order. These layers, however, are not just computational, but more importantly expose their technical qualities as embedded in social, human and concrete forces.[22] The Stack does not simply coincide with the dominance of technical functionalism, but it instead concerns the forms of knowledge and order that computational instrumentality has set in place and that expose the evolutionary nature of a geopolitical planetary space. My intention here is not to displace the discussion about material computation for design and its implication for knowledge on to a specific discussion about the sovereignty of computation, but to take the latter as an instance of the naturalisation of *techne* that has entered the planetary sphere through and with the techno-logic of computation. From this standpoint, Bratton's articulation of the Stack offers us the architectural image of computational infrastructure as it takes different forms at different scales (energy and mineral sources and grids, underground data infrastructure, urban software, public service, planetary service systems, interfaces and augmented spaces, quantified selves, the social omnipresence of algorithms, senses and robots).[23] While the effects of planetary computation include the granular capacities to manipulate and act upon matter, molecularity and atomicity, they also concern more than one scale and go across and above these micro levels. From this standpoint, the computational order of self-organisation at the granular scale of matter is not the same as the computational order of logic and calculation that connects and interweaves scales. In order not to confuse the concreteness of material organisation with the computational abstraction concerning the modality – the knowing how (that is, the manner in which it works) – one has to account for the scale of computation or, borrowing from Deleuze and Guattari, for the formation of the computational stratum as a historical moment.[24] As computational design seems to subsume the non-symmetric scales of the whole planet under its logic of dynamic calculation and predictive indeterminacies, it is also itself another stratum grappling on top of biophysical scales (energetic, atomic, molecular, genetic), and can thus not be equivalent to the computational capacities of matter. Instead, to claim that material computation implies that design can emerge from and through the agencies of molecular, atomic parts, establishing a direct channel between the biophysical and the digital, is to deny that historical moment in which cybernetics and computation enabled the automation of a knowing-how, of the modalities of ordering, collating, matching, selecting, aggregating data. A claim for material computation therefore risks misplacing the abstract with the concrete in a particular way. While the argument against the 'fallacy of misplaced concreteness'[25] accuses abstract methods of offering a complete description of the materiality of actualities, the view of material computation in design takes the concrete complexity of data as a mode to understand the abstraction of computational design as a whole. This inverted fallacy thus risks making us blind to the complex asymmetries between scales whereby biological randomness, for instance, is not equivalent to the digital order because these are systems entrenched in their own specific evolution and histories. A critical view of computation therefore shall account for the biophysical scale of computational activities, but also, and importantly, recognise that computation involves a synthesis of logic and calculus developed in historical and epistemological accounts of ordering, measuring, proving, constructing, organising, sorting, matching, and of, above all, modalities of knowing – deductive, inductive, abductive.

From this standpoint, the attention to computation shall also be an experimental inquiry into automated knowledge, implying the changing qualities of instrumentality activated with and through the mechanisation of logic and calculus. If computational design overlaps with planetary computation, it is because the local rearrangement of means and ends at each scale reveals a complete but non-totalising image of sovereignty. From this standpoint, the Stack does not correspond to the image of the big data network, but rather resembles a growing abstract machine attached to the concreteness of computational actualities – the non-individualised computational partialities interconnecting multi-scale machines, offering an image of the whole, which, according to Bratton, also contains alternatives and possibilities for new forms of governance. The Stack is a diagram and a cartographic machine and is a self-organising, accidental, open and emerging megastructure, which exposes the multiscalar quality of computational means. Here the critical articulation of computational design does not conform modalities to finalities or means to ends, but is concerned with computational activities at various scales – that is, with the specific and concrete mechanisms of data processing whose distinct consequences or ends are to be addressed. From this standpoint, this is to advocate neither for a formal model of computation that can contain all scales nor for an empirical searching of computational evidence in physical actualities. Instead, the localities of computational processing of data (atomic, molecular, biological, physical, environmental, cultural, social, technical and economic) shall be the starting point for a collective articulation of a general intelligence – or a general logic – which includes and works through multiscalar levels of computation. The latter, I argue, is both attached to the concrete limits of the actual occurrences at each scale and yet is abstract enough to account for the heterogeneous elaboration of a multiscalar formal view of computational processes, which redeploys verticality in its organisation and, as addressed in the next section, requires the invention of an instrumental kind of formalism.

In Bratton's efforts to articulate the verticality of the Stack there is an understanding of design as a logic of and for political geography. More than an analysis of how states operate and how technologies as means are symptoms of a new governance, the Stack as a vertical order defines how the contagious ingression of computational mechanics into the means of each scale – physical, biological, cultural, social, technical strata – has come 'to absorb functions of the state and the work of governance'.[26] As planetary computation reveals the multiscalar interdependence of each scale, it also defines the computational logic of political geography as involving 'the means and the ends of a specific kind of platform of sovereignty'.[27] Here the computational instrumentality of the platform does not simply conform to deductive logic, where design coincides with preordained ends, and yet it does not simply mirror the dominance of data empiricism, where design becomes equivalent to the medium through which it works. The indeterminacy of the outcomes instead is crucial to rearticulate how the logic (and thus the use of means to an end) of computation emerges out of local computational constraints. This implies an immanent rearticulation of means and ends within and across scales as dependent upon the indeterminacy of local operations, functions, procedures and activities, which cannot be subsumed to an a priori finality. It implies that techniques and technologies are dynamic articulations of causes and effects, means and ends for the production of subjects and objects. For Bratton, the Stack is, therefore, 'the machine as the state', because the state and governance are embedded, entrenched and dependent upon the workings of the machine. This implies that computational machines and their logistic order in platforms are not transcendent to but generative of governmentalities. In other words, the mechanics of technologies, the means, the way they work, already embody the possibility of a techno-logic and are thus not simply instruments – means used to the end of governing. Following Bratton, the mechanics of material computations are thus generative of power, of governances, of normative perceptions, cognitions and actions. However, if planetary computation is generative of governance it is also because it is the expression of a techno-logic working through the uncertainty of results. Local computations can thus become reassembled in an evolving machine-thinking whose sources are human discourses, human bodies, affectivities, emotions and behaviour, as well as data of molecular, chemical, physical, cultural, social and personal scales. Here design is not without logic and does not simply rely on already existing data but has become dependent on computational synthesis: namely non-deductive logic and dynamic calculation.

Planetary computation reveals that the automation of design does not simply replace synthesis with uncompressible data, but rather exposes a transformed techno-logic that can be defined in terms of an experimental formalism. The latter involves not the immediacy of data aggregations, but rather an instrumental activity on and through data, altering their field of immediate retrieval. This is because the question of data compression has been central to the development of experimental logic in relation to the problem of randomness in computational and information theories. In what follows, I propose an instrumental approach to design as a technology or a cognitive activity able to transform the environment. By drawing on experimental logic in computation, it is possible to readdress design from the standpoint of indeterminacy, incomputability and uncertainty of information. It is precisely by accounting for the impossibility of pre-determining end results that the means of computation do not just enable a seamless collection of infinite information, but also, and importantly, imply the transformation of data into new meaning through experimental logic.

Randomness, Instrumentality, Formalism

If computational design is not simply a technique or an application of tools, it is because it is first of all a technology, involving the activity of intelligence in transforming cognitive and perceptual habitual patterns or techniques.[28] By drawing on John Dewey's pragmatist view of instrumentality, I suggest that with computation, and the mechanisation of logical reasoning in the Turing machine, machine intelligence has irreversibly transformed habits of perception and thought. In particular, as the Turing machine became the field of experimentation for a mode of reasoning and its limits, it also revealed that intelligence could be automated and that reasoning could extend beyond the confirmation of results to already existing truths. The gap between premises and results showed that it was not possible to know in advance the ends of computation before the processing of information could run its course. Incomputables, or randomness here intended as non-compressible infinites, could not, therefore, be synthesised by the universal axioms automated by the Turing machine.

To address this problem of the limits of computation, algorithmic information theorist Gregory Chaitin combines Alan Turing's discovery of the incomputable with Claude Shannon's insistence that noise is central to the effectiveness of communication.[29] Chaitin addresses the question of the limit of computational logic by demonstrating how randomness (noise, entropy or incompressible amounts of data) is rather a condition of computation.[30] For Chaitin, computation corresponds to the algorithmic processing of maximally unknowable probabilities. In computational processing, he explains, the output is always bigger than the input: the computational processing of data breaks the equilibrium between input and output. This also challenges the deductive method of formal computation according to which the model of artificial intelligence was grounded in simple rules, or the syntactical ordering of symbols. For Chaitin instead, algorithmic randomness[31] or that which constitutes the very limit of computational deduction demarcates the point at which automated reasoning extends beyond the data environment that it retrieves and thus exposes the intelligible substrate in which it is inscribed. In particular, the discovery of the so-called Chaitin's Omega, or the algorithmic pattern of randomness, explains the ratio between meaningful patterns and noise, the problem of entropy, the measure of chaos, in a communication system. From this standpoint, the problem of randomness in information theory also involves a specific notion of entropy, in terms of irreversibly increasing volumes of information generated at the input–output levels of computation.

Chaitin explained the discovery of algorithmic randomness in computational processing in terms of the incomputable: unknown quantities of data whose rule-based processing no longer follows pre-established conditions. Since these nonlinear processes produce postulates that cannot be predicted in advance by the program, Chaitin argues that their result can be understood in terms of an 'experimental axiomatics', a postulate or decision emerging from within evolving data in the system.[32] However, patternless information, emerging from within computational processing, points to a dynamics internal to algorithmic operations (that is, not derived from its external contingencies). According to mathematician and physicist James Crutchfield, Omega needs not simply to be understood as marking the edge of order, but as central to the internal production of computational structuring of information.[33] Instead of claiming that randomness is the limit of computation, Crutchfield studies the introjection of randomness within computational structures.[34] Crutchfield thus puts forward a theory of dynamic computation by combining ideas from equilibrium and non-equilibrium statistical mechanics and dynamical systems based on the study of cellular automata and of their spatio-temporal behaviour.[35] Here complexity is laid at the order–disorder threshold: a crucial interplay between dynamics, structure, information processing and computation in pattern formation and evolution. The question of what organisation is (how order or structure emerges) implies that order and randomness are part of any process. To measure information, Crutchfield uses not axiomatic truths, but computational modelling and statistical complexity concerned with maximally predictive and minimally random measurement of data, actualised by automated machines.[36] Hence statistical complexity is not to measure randomness, but provides a relative measure of structure.[37] From this standpoint, the synthesis of logic and statistics in intelligent automated systems involves the re-elaboration of non-deductive logic (that is, the experimental production of axioms) and of dynamic statistics (a relative measure of structure based on randomness).

If technology involves the transformation of intelligence, then the automation of intelligence activates not the end but the transformation of compression, its expansion towards infinities and the realisation that infinite varieties of infinities (infinite granularities) are rather the condition by which the logic of structures can evolve. Automated design is thus above all implicated within this larger technological transformation of cognition and perception, defining not simply the end of logical thinking but rather the injection of dynamics within reasoning, the ingression of incomputables within axiomatics.

With automated design, computational means are not without ends, but are rather modalities of abstracting data varieties beyond their local configurations as experimented by a further level of abstraction into new axioms, codes and instructions, and perhaps new meaning. This is not simply re-conducible to the data-driven indeterminacy of a planetary computation form of sovereignty. If axioms are becoming experimental truths, able to postulate or synthesise unknowns, computational design also involves a logic of experimentation exposing how formal intelligence can become speculative – that is non-deductive or able to conjecture hypotheses beyond given premises. However, planetary computation involves not the merging of biophysical and technical scales of computation. While the technological transformation of cognition and perception involves both concrete and abstract modalities of reasoning, at the biophysical scale, computation more specifically concerns the evolution of complex structures. The turn to material computation in design claims that these biophysical forms of self-organisation are central to the formation of smart design, putting to work material intelligence. While this focus on the biophysical order of computational complexity importantly advocates for a view of design embedded in material capacities and not in formal rules, it risks imparting a seamless convergence between the biophysical and the technical scales of computational capacities by focusing on the neutrality of data variations. However, with the automation of intelligence, the form of reasoning operating in data environments and proper to the order of computational machine-thinking concerns a locally embedded ordering randomness through functions of selection, sorting and evaluation of already computed data (that is, data that has already been transformed into binary code language, for instance). The emergence of these functions points to an informational stratification of matter and thus an informational transformation of data. This is already forcing computational design to engage with the transformation of cognition and perception, which require a rearticulation of a logic of automation that will question the idealised materialism that rejects all logic and design possibilities. The axiomatic experimentation with data within and throughout computation instead importantly suggests that automated reasoning cannot be incorporated into a naturalised techno-capitalism, defined by the equivalence of scales and a given identification of nature with culture (that is, the pre-existing ground of data).

Returning to the question that we started with – can new activities of cognition emerge from the means of computational processing itself – this chapter suggests that computational design brings to the fore an automated synthesis of data, which shows not simply the limits of reasoning, but instead the extension of thinking by machines. As already suggested, machines here are not simply tools or functional systems, but are involved in technological transformations and generation of knowledge. According to the pragmatist John Dewey, instrumentality concerns the transformation of ends and means of knowledge. Here results are not derived from premises, but both proofs and axioms enter a process of articulation that allows instructions to confront infinities, incomputabilities, indeterminacies, through which it is possible to demarcate a constructive path, whereby design functions (that is, the open data-synthesis) lead to cognitive and perceptual consequences, and, more importantly, to the transformation of truth and knowledge in general. For instance, Dewey sees an object of knowledge not as the starting point, but as something with which thinking ends, or something produced through and with a process of enquiry and testing. For him, all knowledge requires experimentation from means to ends insofar as meaning is a consequence of thinking, the emancipation from previously established ends throughout the function of means.[38] From this standpoint, the computational functions of design are not without consequences for knowledge. The open synthesis of data rather implies that algorithmic functions have not simply the task of casting away doubt (to conform facts to ideas), but of carrying out logic – or an experimental knowing – through running, sorting, comparing ideas as well as elaborating suggestions, guessing, rejecting, selecting.[39] To ascertain that computational design can become a logical experimentation of means and ends, the indeterminacy of data shall be matched by the finding of proof. The latter depends on the possibility of accepting or rejecting a proposition on the grounds of whether or not there can be a connection with some other proposition. In other words, proofs or results are always embedded in a chain of existing propositions, because thinking above all implies sociality and the particularities of data to involve observing, collecting and comparing particular causes. Here instruments (or tools such as telescopes, microscopes, algorithmic procedures, and so on) have become intrinsic to a general process of thought.[40] In other words, instruments are 'organs of thinking'[41] and as such they carry out the speculative search for proofs that can sanction, reassess, discard and construct truths. From this standpoint, means are modes of processing an advance into the unknown, an experimental construction followed by axiomatic, the instrumental transformation or elaboration of infinite data into the abstract layers of meaning. Instrumentality here shows that thinking is linked neither to fact nor ideas, but to a logical experimentation, concerned not with knowing this or that, but with knowing how, and thus delineating a space of thinking. Computational design can thus be approached in terms of the means by which automated thought can eventuate from procedures, tasks and functions. With pragmatism, it is possible to argue for another configuration of instrumentality showing how the connection between data processing and ideas is not one of demonstration of what was already thought, but requires the activities of a knowing-how, involving a transformation of ends with and through means. If for pragmatism, instrumentality is generative of knowledge, then material computation and open data synthesis in design also implies the emergence of a logic – that is, of an inferential chain of reasoning – as the starting point to articulate a new kind of formalism.

Computational design, therefore, implies the emergence of multi-scale thinking, an experimental formalism based on their equivalent mode of processing information – here biophysical computation cannot be taken as a model for the computational modelling of biophysical structures. Instead in order for scales to become connected, computational design needs to address their localities, specificities and situations as a first step towards the collective, asymmetrical and experimental knowledge that opens the possibility for a new formalism: namely a general model for transforming local computations into a logic of continuity, or complex inferential reasoning.

If Dewey's instrumentality enables us to understand technology as a means that transforms ends and generates new modalities of intelligence, Charles S. Peirce's rearticulation of logic rather proposes a continuity of inferential modalities (abduction, induction, deduction) that he uses to argue for an evolving relation between signs (material and discursive semiotics) as constitutive of what he calls formal semiotics.[42] Inferential reasoning as a process of abstraction is embedded in material situations. Logic therefore does not come first. Instead logic as the abstract order of inferential reasoning is a consequence of material activities and is rooted in the social. Inferential reasoning depends on material and discursive systems of neighbourhood or relations of signs that can be of any kind, and is thus, in this sense, unlimited. For Peirce, logic studies the social transformations of signs and stands for a general theory of representation. Through the recording of sensorial and semiotic data, a complex machine of logical filters and lenses enables the choice of context and data. Logic thus coincides with instrumentality – that is, the generative qualities of means – able to symbolise, contrast, follow and transfer information, and can be used to distinguish implicit relations (potentialities) from explicit relations (actualities), material from discursive signs. From this standpoint, while computational logic enables the ordering of distinct levels of randomness (biophysical, cultural, social, digital, economic) across scales, it also exposes the process by which non-inferential materialities become articulated into data. The latter eventuates an order of thinking that is at once entrenched in the localities of each scale, but that can also give way to a larger or general schema of relation between relations. Here infinite possibilities of inferential reasoning are based on the contingent relations of signs (the neighbourhood relations of natural, semiotic, technical signs) and the computational synthesis of dynamic logic, probability and randomness. If the computational stratum connects scales – as in planetary computation – it does so by adding a new formalism, a dynamic logic emerging from within data processing, incorporating complex orders of inferential reasoning, questioning the fundamental split between ends and means. From this standpoint, not only the deductive logic of design, but also the return of an idealist materialism of mere open synthesis needs to be carefully watched out for. As automated design is itself a manifest image of computational reasoning or, as previously suggested, of a logical instrumentality of the machine, it is no longer possible to ignore that it is already contributing to the articulation of a dynamic formalism, generating not only new modalities of knowledge, but also possibilities for aesthetic and political intelligences.

Notes

1. Larry Hickman, *Tuning Up Technologies. Philosophical Tools for Technological Culture: Putting Pragmatism to Work* (Bloomington: Indiana University Press, 2001), reprinted in Robert C. Scharff and Val Dusek (eds), *Philosophy of Technology: The Technological Condition: An Anthology*, 2nd edn (London: John Wiley and Sons, 2014), pp. 406–19, p. 17.
2. See, for instance, Greg Lynn, *Animate Form* (New York: Princeton Architectural Press, 1999).
3. See http://www.aec.at/radicalatoms/en/people/mit-tangible-media-group/ (last accessed 19 September 2016).

4. See Achim Menges, *Material Computation: Higher Integration in Morphogenetic Design* (London: John Wiley and Sons, 2012).
5. Mario Carpo, 'Big Data and the End of History', *Amnesia Prospecta*, 48 (August 2015).
6. Benjamin Bratton, *The Stack. On Software and Sovereignty* (Cambridge, MA: MIT Press, 2015).
7. Donna Haraway, 'The Cyborg Manifesto: Science, Technology, and Socialist-Feminism in the Late Twentieth Century', in *Simians, Cyborgs and Women: The Reinvention of Nature* (London: Routledge, 1991), pp. 149–81.
8. John Dewey, *Essays in Experimental Logic* (Chicago: University of Chicago Press, 1916); Charles S. Peirce, 'Reasoning and the Logic of Things: The 1898 Cambridge Conferences', in *Lectures by Charles Sanders Peirce*, ed. K. L. Ketner (Cambridge, MA: Harvard University Press, 2005).
9. Neoplasmatic design is inspired by the exploration and manipulation of actual biological material. In particular, it draws on molecular biology, biotechnology and nanotechnology for architectural and design practices. See Marcos Cruz and Steve Pike (eds), *Architectural Design – Neoplasmatic Design*, 78.6 (2008), special issue.
10. Ibid.
11. See Michael Hensel and Achim Menges, 'Morpho-Ecologies: Towards Heterogeneous Space', *Architecture Design*, 1 February 2007.
12. See http://www.aec.at/radicalatoms/en/people/mit-tangible-media-group/ (last accessed 20 September 2016).
13. Carpo, 'Big Data and the End of History'.
14. Hensel and Menges, 'Morpho-Ecologies'.
15. Ahlquist and Menges suggest that computational processes are iterative and recursive but also expanding. They work by growing and specifying the information, which describes form through procedures that recursively generate form, calling variable parameters within the state space. See Sean Ahlquist and Achim Menges (eds), *Computational Design Thinking* (London: John Wiley and Sons, 2011), p. 24.
16. Ahlquist and Menges, *Computational Design Thinking*, p. 24.
17. Bratton, *The Stack*, p. 12.
18. Gordon Pask, 'Heinz von Foerster's Self-Organization, the Progenitor of Conversation and Interaction Theories', *Systems Research*, 13.3 (1996), pp. 349–66.
19. J. Paul Crutchfield, 'The Calculi of Emergence: Computation, Dynamics, and Induction', *Physica D* (1994), special issue on the Proceedings of the Oji International Seminar Complex Systems – from Complex Dynamics to Artificial Reality, held 5–9 April 1994, Numazu, Japan SFI 94-03-016.
20. Kostas Terzidis, *Expressive Form: A Conceptual Approach to Computational Design* (London: Spon Press, 2003).
21. Bratton, *The Stack*, p. 6.

22. Ibid., p. 11.
23. Ibid., p. 5.
24. Gilles Deleuze and Félix Guattari, *A Thousand Plateaus: Capitalism and Schizophrenia*, trans. Brian Massumi (London: Athlone Press, 1987).
25. Alfred North Whitehead, *Science and the Modern World* (Cambridge: Cambridge University Press, 1928), p. 24.
26. Bratton, *The Stack*, p. 7.
27. Ibid.
28. Hickman, *Tuning Up Technologies*.
29. Gregory Chaitin, 'Randomness and Mathematical Proof', *Scientific American*, 232.5 (1975), pp. 47–52.
30. Gregory Chaitin, *Meta Math! The Quest for Omega* (New York: Pantheon, 2005). Andrey Kolmogorov's complexity theory is considered to pioneer the field of algorithmic information theory. See Ming Li and Paul Vitanyi (eds), *An Introduction to Kolmogorov Complexity and its Applications*, 3rd edn (New York: Springer Verlag, 2008); Chaitin, 'Randomness and Mathematical Proof'.
31. See Christian S. Calude and Gregory Chaitin, 'Randomness Everywhere', *Nature*, 400 (22 July 1999), pp. 319–20, and Gregory J. Chaitin, *Exploring Randomness* (London: Springer Verlag, 2001), p. 22.
32. Gregory J. Chaitin, 'The Limits of Reason', *Scientific American*, 294.3 (2006), pp. 74–81.
33. Crutchfield, 'The Calculi of Emergence', p. 14.
34. Ibid., p. 16.
35. J. Paul Crutchfield and Melanie Mitchell, 'The Evolutionary Design of Collective Computation in Cellular Automata', in J. P. Crutchfield and P. Schuster (eds), *Evolutionary Dynamics: Exploring the Interplay of Selection, Accident, Neutrality, and Function* (Oxford: Oxford University Press, 2003), pp. vii–xi.
36. Crutchfield, 'The Calculi of Emergence', pp. 22–3.
37. Crutchfield and Mitchell, 'The Evolutionary Design of Collective Computation'.
38. Dewey, *Essays in Experimental Logic*, pp. 438–9.
39. Ibid., p. 197.
40. Ibid., p. 211.
41. Ibid.
42. Peirce, 'Reasoning and the Logic of Things'.

CHAPTER 11

Grothendieck Topoi: Architectural and Plastic Imagination beyond Material Number and Space

Fernando Zalamea

A Quick Glance at Grothendieck's Work

Alexander (Alexandre) Grothendieck (Berlin 1928–Saint-Girons 2014) must be considered, without doubt, as the major mathematical genius of the last sixty years, and, next to David Hilbert, as one of the two fundamental mathematicians of the last century. With a published work of nearly ten thousand pages (covering geometry, topology, number theory, complex variables, to only quote the heart of mathematics), with more than one thousand new definitions (when an ordinary mathematician might be happy if she or he has introduced one new definition in the field) and with completely revolutionary understandings of the notions of number ('schemes'), space ('topos') and form ('motives'), Grothendieck has opened all kinds of new roads for the development of mathematics in the coming centuries.

Nevertheless, Grothendieck's work is almost completely unknown outside a small group of specialists. Unlike Einstein, whose ideas (simplified or deformed) have reached the public domain, Grothendieck still lies in the shadow, even if his conceptual revolution goes much further. In fact, if Einstein studies the relativisation of space-time and discovers its local invariants, Grothendieck studies the relativisation of space-number and discovers its global universal invariants. After his recent death, a sudden interest has arisen in a life worthy of fiction (there are three partial biographies[1] and an inspiring novel),[2] but time is still needed to fully appreciate the magnitude of his mathematical work.

Grothendieck's inexhaustible universe may be divided (wrongly, as in any compartmentalisation) into four main periods.

1) From 1949 to 1957, along certain geographical margins (Nancy, São Paulo, Kansas), he produces fundamental contributions in topological vector spaces, homology, category theory and complex variables, obtaining profound theorems and leaving rich seeds to be developed in the following decades.[3]

2) Between 1958 and 1970, in the very centre of mathematics (Paris), Grothendieck advances his research at the Institut des Hautes Études Scientifiques (IHES), specially constructed to shelter him. After a scintillating, condensed vision of his future programmes,[4] he writes with the formidable Jean Dieudonné the *Éléments de Géométrie Algébrique* (EGA) (the appearance of schemes),[5] and directs his famous *Séminaire de Géométrie Algébrique* (SGA) (the appearance of topoi).[6] An archetypical vision of form, a common root for all (co-)homologies (the appearance of motives), emerges also in the IHES years.[7] The finer mathematical grain of the epoch goes through the Institute, where innovation becomes a trademark: a nice anecdote tells that, as a visitor complained about the meagre IHES library, Grothendieck replied – 'Here we do not read mathematics, here we make them.'

3) After leaving the IHES in 1970 (the result of political radicalisation, intemperance and disappointment with his entourage), Grothendieck founds a radical ecologist movement *Survivre et vivre* ('survival' first, 'survival and life' afterwards), to which he offers the best of his indomitable energy. He goes away from the mathematical community, returns to the margins (the Université de Montpellier, where he had done his undergraduate studies, 1945–48), and hides happily in the French province. Between 1981 and 1991 a passion for mathematics surges again, in extraordinary manuscripts (moduli spaces of Riemann surfaces, fundamental groupoids, anabelian geometry, tame topology, *dessins d'enfants*, derivators and so on).[8] He writes an intense and extensive mathematical reflection, *Récoltes et semailles*, in which he attacks forcefully a mathematical community that, in his view, had betrayed him, but in which, above all, he elaborates the most significant treatise ever conceived about mathematical creativity.[9]

4) In 1991 Grothendieck disappears, and secludes himself completely in the Pyrenees (the last margin). Nevertheless, between 1991 and 2014 he continues to write steadily, and finally leaves a 50,000-page manuscript to the Bibliothèque Nationale de France, a legacy now disputed by his family. A report by Georges Maltsiniotis (March 2016) describes the existence of 10,000 mathematical pages, and some 30,000 pages of a *Treatise on Evil*. The sheer monumentality of Grothendieck's enterprises surpasses our usual canons, and one or two decades will be needed to have a reasonable account of this last legacy.

The interest of modern (1830–1950) and contemporary (1950–today) mathematics, as far as Grothendieck is concerned, consists not so much in the partial modelling that they offer, but rather in their help in deploying the imagination. A hundred years before Grothendieck, Riemann surfaces had stimulated visual and conceptual inventiveness.[10] Full of plasticity, the very handling of Riemann surfaces (they are beautiful *material* constructs) allows transits and possibilities that rigid, classical, non-plastic geometries prevent. On the other hand, Riemann had observed the importance of analytic continuity for the development of functions of a complex variable (holomorphic and meromorphic functions). A hundred years later, *sheaves* were invented by Leray (in 1942, in a concentration camp, at the same time that young Grothendieck was interned with his mother in another camp) and were further developed in Cartan's seminar at the École normale supérieure (where Grothendieck landed after his undergraduate career). A sheaf is the simplest mathematical object (just two topological spaces related by a projection with a good local behaviour), which can be oriented towards a precise study of local/global processes. In the language of sheaves, Riemann's analytic continuity is expressed by the structural fact that the sheaf of germs of holomorphic functions is separated. Thus, a sophisticated dialectics – elasticity/rigidity, continuity/separation – enters into play (see Figure 11.1).

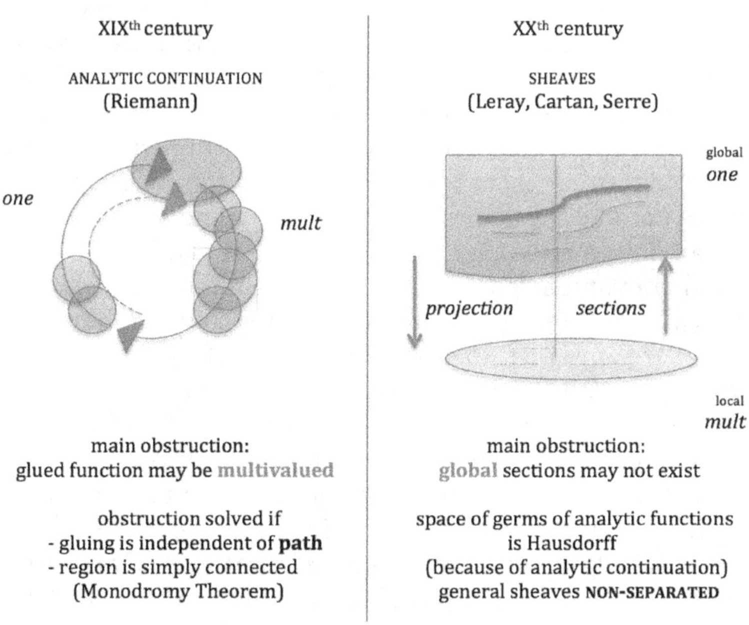

Figure 11.1 The sheaf concept.

In a similar vein, Grothendieck topoi (categories equivalent to categories of sheaves over abstract topologies) constitute plastic sites, specifically open to dynamic variations. Grothendieck topoi unify deep insights into arithmetic (number) and geometry (space).[11] Beyond Cantorian, classical, static sets, the objects in a topos are to be understood as generalisations of variable sets. Instead of living over a rigid bottom, governed by classical logic, they live over a dynamic Kripke model, governed by intuitionistic logic. Beyond the classical example of the separated sheaf of holomorphic functions, a sheaf does *not* have to be separated in a general topos: *points do not have to determine their associated objects*. We can even imagine objects without points, defined only through flux processes. A wonderful example is the topos of actions of monoids. Such a topos has an underlying classical logic (where the law of excluded middle holds and points are essential) if and only if the monoid is a group. Thus, when we deal with structures, which are monoid non-groups, the logic of their action is just intuitionistic, non-separated, closer to topological fluxions, deformations, disruptions.

In simple terms, we may characterise Grothendieck as the mathematician, who, after Poincaré, unified Galois and Riemann, the two mathematical geniuses of the nineteenth century.[12] We may thus imagine that, on a conceptual, non-exclusively technical level, Grothendieck topoi generalise, in some sort, Riemann surfaces. Even if the assertion is not mathematically correct (we would also have to introduce Grothendieck schemes into the account), methodologically it is fruitful. Figure 11.1 shows dynamic, relative movements. Bases change, no eternal objects are considered. But the correlative changes are in turn studied mathematically, and they are incorporated as new objects in an upper level. In this way, an iterated dynamics emerges – a dynamical study of dynamics – which can have a strong influence on cultural studies.

As another example, going a little further and inverting our thought, one can deal with topoi whose underlying logics are dual to intuitionistic logic. Paraconsistent logics (1963) thus appear in the panorama, logics where we can have *local* contradictions without forcing *global* contradictions, which would destroy the system.[13] It is fairly clear that the dynamic logics of art are either intuitionistic or paraconsistent, but certainly not classical. The dialectics of art and mathematics already hint at such a situation, but it is interesting to notice that 1) if we situate ourselves in a multilayered site akin to art, that is, in some sort of non-well-defined Grothendieck topos of *art actions* (compare with the well-defined topos of monoid actions), 2) if we think *dually* – as art should do with respect to mathematics – and 3) if we allow ourselves to live in a continuous *medium* of contradictions, then we will be approaching many of the strongest forms of contemporary art. We will be entering into that perspective in the following section.

Grothendieck Topoi in Cinema, Architecture and Art

Using synthetic and multiple perspectives applied to the sheaf concept, Grothendieck obtains an extended notion of *place* (*topos*). Two major shifts are indeed proposed: 1) consider not a usual, analytic topology (given by open sets), but an alternative, synthetic topology (given by arrow coverings: sets are replaced by relations); 2) consider not one sheaf, but all sheaves of a given kind (a category of sheaves) on such a synthetic topology (called a 'Grothendieck topology'). A category of sheaves over a Grothendieck topology is, by definition, a Grothendieck topos. Now, many Grothendieck topologies are available in many categories, and a variation of the topologies gives a variation of the sites (which, in turn, yield *topoi*). Some Grothendieck topologies produce *algebraic and spatial sites* (such as the *étale* topos of a scheme, with which Grothendieck and his school solved the Weil conjectures), others produce *arithmetical sites* (such as the arithmetical topos of Alain Connes, with which he hopes to structure better and perhaps solve the Riemann hypothesis, the greatest open problem in mathematics).[14] What interests us here are the architectonics of the constructions: a single, universal concept (sheaf) is projected on to both space and number, unifying the major, apparently distant, fields of geometry and arithmetic. Beyond material number and space, Grothendieck topoi thus render visible the invisible. Before Grothendieck, some visionaries (Galois, Riemann, Poincaré, Florensky, for example) had imagined such a common kernel of arithmetic and geometry, but no one had really *seen* it, inside a precise, technical architectonics. In what follows, we will pursue other paths where the invisible is rendered visible through other specific architectonics – in cinema (Tarkovsky), architecture (Gehry) and art (Kiefer) – and where some *material gestures* can be related to similar strategies in Grothendieck topoi.

Tarkovsky: Images of the Unseen

Andrei Tarkovsky (1932–86) embeds himself in a very concrete reality, to let us emerge towards the ineffable: 'The image is linked to the concrete, to the material, in order to reach afterwards, by mysterious ways, the spirit beyond.'[15] The '*image-observation*, the true concrete image' constitutes the support of his entire work: 'the image is an impression of the Truth given for us to perceive with our blind eyes'.[16] We can feel the *tour de force* proposed by Tarkovsky: there is a non-material domain of Spirit and Truth that we cannot see with our blind eyes, but that we can reach through a mysterious transmutation of material images.[17] As in the stutterer of *Mirror* (1974), who after a hypnotic session suddenly reaches an *étale* ('flat') language, the 'stuttering' of our blind eyes can be overcome when we contemplate the universe in all its multiplicity. In that vein, Tarkovsky reveals some of the *Mirror*'s secrets: the 'negative charm' of a Leonardo portrait, seen 'from outside, or sidewise, with a view coming from above the world'; the possibility of introducing 'a part of eternity in the instants deployed under our eyes'; the need to present an artistic image as an 'experience of complex, contradictory emotions'; the desire to walk along that 'fleeting instant where the positive ceases to be, where it slips to the negative, and vice versa'.[18]

The threshold becomes thus a central figure in Tarkovsky's architectonics.[19] Indeed, only from a threshold do different perspectives become available, and a true multiplication occurs in front of our blind eyes. Reason and sensibility merge together, coming *from above*. In a similar sense, in Grothendieck topoi, number (coming from *discrete* arithmetic) and magnitude (coming from *continuous* geometry) merge together, and may be derived from the abstract sheaf concept. Even more strikingly, in the threshold of Grothendieck's *géométrie arithmétique* (motives and anabelian geometry, going beyond the SGA period on *géométrie algébrique*), higher revelations occur.[20] Tarkovsky's visions – 'view coming from above', 'part of eternity', 'experience of complex', 'slip to the negative' – become, in Grothendieck's hands, deep, open conjectures for the development of mathematics (standard conjectures, anabelian conjectures).[21] Abstraction (a view from above) becomes an essential creative force because, in the general, particular walls disappear. Indeed, plasticity reigns in the general (non-material) realm, precisely because we can escape from the constraints of the particular (material) world. And an inversion of thought, fundamental for both Grothendieck and Tarkovsky, suggests that access to non-materiality (a true goal) is obtained through a profound immersion in concrete materiality. Only living on the *threshold of the opposites* (or, as Florensky would say, in some true antinomical thinking)[22] may open our blind eyes.

In *Andrei Rublev* (1966), the links of concrete particulars with the 'unique' are manifested throughout the film. The first images – ascent and fall – are materialised in a counterpoint of the four elements, when a man in a balloon flies over the river and ends up crashing: fire (balloon), air (flight), water (river) and earth (ground) are fused in a sequence of cinematographic planes which ends in the unified beauty of a horse wallowing in slow motion. On the other hand, the last image of the film comes back to the horses, after wandering through many concrete details of Rublev's *Trinity* – lines, mixtures, textures, veils, cracks – through which Tarkovsky opens our blind eyes to something 'beyond'. All in *Andrei Rublev* expresses the essential contradiction of the threshold between *here and there*: fields, birches, roots, bushes, sand, mud, rain, fumes – preludes to the fantastic material construction of the bell – are signs of a 'spirit beyond'. It is remarkable that Tarkovsky's 'negative metaphysics' is also perfectly reflected in his cinematographic technique. Through his long shots without cuts, his many views without horizon, his montages without defined time fluxions, his washed colour spectra, his contrapositions of silence and sound, the film-maker always points out to *what is missing*. Looking carefully at the extreme concrete particulars, we can imagine what eludes us. *Stalker* (1979) explores such a zone of access to a 'spirit beyond'. All types of *fragments* and *residues* (which recall Benjamin's *Arcades* project)[23] are scattered through the zone, as are the residual dialogues between the writer (limited by language) and the professor (limited by science). Straight lines are impossible in the zone, one always has to walk along broken diagonals, 'everything changes every minute'. Mixtures, inversions, *vibrations*, are mandatory in the search for a final answer, never reached, never reachable.[24] The magnificent long shot in which we see how the Stalker's daughter advances in front of our eyes, even if we know that she cannot walk, until the camera goes down and we observe that her father is carrying her, evokes all those *thin touches* of miracle and concretion, illusion and despair, joy and pain, life and death, in which we move.

Grothendieck saw himself as an architect in the IHES period, the builder of the abstract foundations EGA-SGA. Afterwards, he intervened also into the (very modest) concrete country houses in which he lived during his retirement periods (Villecun, Mormoiron, Lasserre). Tarkovsky also constructed his house in Myasnoye, in remembrance of his infancy and of the spaces recreated in *Mirror*. A polaroid taken by Tarkovsky (see Figure 11.2, where we have washed away the colours,

Figure 11.2 Myasnoye (26 September 1981), from Andrei Tarkovsky, *Instant Light. Tarkovsky Polaroids*, ed. G. Chiaramonte, A. Tarkovsky and T. Guerra (London: Thames & Hudson, 2004), p. 29.

to emphasise structure) shows the threshold of a door, from which a fence, an oak and a dense fog are visible. It is as if the greatest visionary architects of contemporary mathematics and cinema needed, in counterpoint, the simplest, most pedestrian architecture for their daily lives. The tensions between the abstract and the particular, the non-material and the concrete, the invisible and the visible (already deeply explored in Merleau-Ponty)[25] acquire here new forms of expression. It is no accident that such a dialectics between work and life may be considered as a threshold between interior and exterior. Along that ever-changing pendulum, Grothendieck and Tarkovsky lean towards the difficult understanding of an *internal soul* governed by abstraction, non-materiality and invisibility.

Gehry: Foldings of the Unformed

The work of Frank Gehry (b. 1929) is directly inspired by the freedom and plasticity of the dynamics of motion in art. As Gehry himself comments,

> Painting and sculpture influence my work. For instance, when I had the Bellini picture with the Madonna and Child, I originally thought of it as the Madonna-and-Child strategy for architecture. You see a lot of big buildings with a lot of little buildings, little pavilions in front. [. . .] I went back to Bellini and fastened on the folds of the drapery. You see that kind of motion in Giotto, too. A lot of that folding interests me.[26]

Gehry goes on to acknowledge the influence of Greek sculpture, Sluter, Brancusi, Moses and Oldenburg, creative spaces where Gehry finds artistic oscillations, to be transformed into architectural *undulations*. In fact, as Gehry recalls, 'I was looking for movement earlier, and found it in the fish. The fish solidified my understanding of how to make architecture move.'[27] The first forms of fishes in Gehry's architecture – Smith residence (1981), lamps (1983–86), Walker installation (1986), *Fishdance* restaurant (1986) – evolve towards Barcelona's *Fish Sculpture* (1989–92), a key moment in Gehry's morphological vision. With the *Fish Sculpture*, architecture is freed from the weight of materials. Thanks to a fine use of computer-aided design (CATIA, Computer Aided Three-dimensional Interactive Application, developed from the French aeronautical industry), a controlled *distribution* of forces and a precisely oriented *assembly* of matter are obtained, helping to construct and elevate curvatures previously impossible to realise.

Leibniz's dream, according to which mathematical symbols would free the imagination, acquires an entire new dimension with the Guggenheim Bilbao Museoa (1991–97).[28] Heavy matter converted into aerial foldings and unfoldings, thanks to CATIA-based mathematical calculations, is one of the most innovative aspects of Gehry's architecture. The dance of the titanium ceilings flying over the 'little pavilions in front' allows a contraposition of flow (fish and flower forms) and rigidity (office cubes). Bilbao's atrium encapsulates a forceful dialectics of materiality/non-materiality, combining a hymn to matter – water (giant windows over the river and the sky), air (flight of monumental white mouldings), fire (exterior play of flames and fumaroles), earth (floor and stone walls) – with the outstanding speed and lightness liberated through the many perspectives of the site. As Gehry comments, 'Everything connected with everything else seems freer, not taking your hands off. I love the free-flow.'[29]

Beyond the massive technical realisation of the Guggenheim Bilbao, the free flow emerges in fact with a liberation of gesture, to be found in Gehry's initial sketches for all his projects.[30] The pendulum between artistic creativity and technical implementation is always present. A free hand, liberated even further by CATIA, is one of Gehry's trademarks (see Figure 11.3). Grothendieck's imaginative freedom is here well reflected, both in the abstract and the concrete. Through sketched abstractions, both the mathematician and the architect envision archetypical non-material entities, which afterwards become embodied in concrete material types (numbers, spaces, forms). Gehry's drawings and Grothendieck's diagrams allow a growth of new ideas, with all sorts of transits between the conceptual and the concrete. Gehry's 'transient quality' of 'always exploring forms and how they connect'[31] resonates with Grothendieck's dynamic approach to mathematics, and with his transient techniques between different categories.

Figure 11.3 Guggenheim Museum Bilbao (1981), from Frank Gehry, *On Line* (New Haven, CT: Yale University Press, 2008), p. 50.

Bilbao's multiplicity, through a multitude of different perspectives offered to the spectator, is a perfect material analogue of non-material Grothendieck topologies. The richness of arrows and coverings in a Grothendieck topology is embodied in the wide variation of viewpoints and images of the architectural site. Going even further, the *sheaves* over the Grothendieck topology may be seen as those *global* comprehensions of the Bilbao structure where all *local* information (walks, senses, interpretations) become glued together in the overall understanding of the building. Guggenheim Bilbao can be thus imagined as a sort of Grothendieck topos, both in metaphorical abstraction and in concrete particularisation. Of course, mathematical exactness does not enter into the parallel (except for CATIA's implementations), but the *allegorical* impact is profound.[32] In that line of thought, Bilbao's heart – its non-rectifiable atrium – possesses exactly the same 'transient quality' of the heart of a non-extensional Grothendieck topos, where its subobject classifier demonstrably carries plastic, non-classical logics. On the other hand, the *reflection* of plasticity in a topos (an intermediate, intuitionistic logic reflected *locally* in all the Heyting algebras of subobjects) may be viewed as Bilbao's dance of foldings and unfoldings of the structure, along all the passages, rails, stairs and curves which allow the aerial transit over the atrium.

Kiefer: Residues of the Unplumbed

Anselm Kiefer (b. 1945) has turned into the *Great Blacksmith* of the fleeting and contradictory times that we have lived in between millennia. From the end of the twentieth century to the beginning of the twenty-first, his forge has attained the mythical dimensions of Vulcan and his work seems to perpetuate Prometheus's feats. Kiefer immerses himself completely in the domains of the unplumbed: realms of the imagination not previously sounded, measured or explored. His awesome *ateliers* in Buchen, Barjac or Croissy combine a multidimensional *conceptual* boldness and a polysemous plurality of *matter*, in which thousands of fibres are folded and unfolded in violent alloys of the organic and the inorganic.[33] Stone, earth, glass and lead help to transform the many *residues* of our civilisation into gigantic works of art (*Monumenta* 2007 is a good place to observe Kiefer's monumentality).[34] Grothendieck's stature is well mirrored in Kiefer's own achievements. Indeed, as difficult as it may be to signal prominent figures in art, Kiefer undoubtedly stands among the ones who will survive our ruins (cf. his lessons at the Collège de France, *L'art survivra à ses ruines*).[35] Exploring the unplumbed, Grothendieck,

Tarkovsky, Gehry and Kiefer all lie among those who have changed our usual perspectives, and have helped to open our blind eyes.

For Kiefer, following Manichean and alchemical traditions, 'the earth's sparks of light need to be extracted and elevated to the heavens until the earth, having no inner sun, perishes in darkness'.[36] In fact, Kiefer's artistic processes may be understood as profound transmutations of the elements, looking for an elusive (and impossible) pure abstract freeness, after effecting heavy gestural immersions in matter. In the same way as Grothendieck, Tarkovsky or Gehry imagine aerial architectonics based on concrete materials, Kiefer is also an architect of the sublime rooted in a muddy reality, where darkness appears as the essential fount of creativity.[37] After Auschwitz, the world can no longer be coded in an illusory Book, but, through a double transmutation (not one, but many – not positive, but negative), Kiefer tries to cipher the world through a troglodyte library of lead, corroded books (see Figure 11.4). An architectonics is still possible, but only going back

Figure 11.4 *The Breaking of the Vessels* (1990), from Anselm Kiefer, *Sternenfall. Chute d'étoiles*, ed. Assouline Ardenne (Paris: Editions du Regard, 2007), p. 264.

to mythical insights, archaic perspectives, or cosmic imagination.[38] In that search, a complex web of *strata* is essential, in order to provide a sense of time and history for the work of art.

The multiplication of strata (close to Warburg's ideas)[39] is also fundamental in a Grothendieck topos perspective. Layers, levels, sections are in fact encoded in the very notion of a *sheaf* (recall Figure 11.1), but, even more interesting, they occur ubiquitously all along the internal structure of a topos: as witnesses of infinite towers in an exponential (Cartesian closure of the topos), as approaching webs in limiting processes (limit closure of the topos), as logical traces in algebraic types (sub-object classifier). In this sense, the very axioms of a topos (Cartesian closure, existence of limits, sub-object classifier) reflect a *continuous connection of layers*, which embodies Grothendieck's typical understanding of the main dialectics of mathematical thought (many/one, discrete/continuous, algebraic/geometric and so on). Some sort of density is necessary to capture the complexity of the world, as Kiefer also shows in his big canvases. *Orages de roses* (1998), *Ta Maison chevaucha la sombre vague* (2005), *Flocons noirs* (2005)[40] introduce, for example, many techniques (shellac, emulsion, wires, flowers, lead, plaster, wood) which expand the fabric of the canvas towards the *physical* three dimensions and towards the *spiritual* multiple dimensions. Kiefer's sites – closely woven, coarse, dense, thick, heavy – reflect thus *materially* and *metaphorically* a multiplication of strata, as it happens axiomatically in a Grothendieck topos.

In an interview with Daniel Arasse (15 November 2001), Kiefer explains how matter and spirit are inextricably woven:

> Let's talk about materiality, matter. For me, matter is related to the spiritual. I do not make a distinction between an idea and its execution. [. . .] I think that the spirit is in the things, in matter. In lead, in straw . . . One has to discover, to reveal the spirit that they harbor. It is a primordial question.[41]

As we have seen, the same question is almost exactly stated by Tarkovsky, and it is also an essential question both for Grothendieck (interaction between mathematical free archetypes and concrete types) and for Gehry (interrelation between free-space drawing and concrete implementation). *Freeness* is here the main concept at stake. *Creativity* needs both the most abstract and the most concrete. Our wanderings through mathematics, cinema, architecture and art have shown the importance of a full dialectics between materiality and non-materiality, through many perspective inversions. The pendulum has to go back and forth unremittingly, knowing, as Bakhtin well said, that all important knowledge lies at the frontiers.

Notes

1. Georges Bringuier, *Alexandre Grothendieck. Itinéraire d'un mathématicien hors normes* (Toulouse: Pivat, 2015); Yan Pradeau, *Algèbre. Éléments de la vie d'Alexandre Grothendieck* (Paris: Allia, 2016); Philippe Douroux, *Alexandre Grothendieck. Sur les traces du dernier génie des mathématiques* (Paris: Allary Éditions, 2016).
2. Carlos Fonseca, *Coronel lárgimas* (Barcelona: Anagrama, 2015).
3. Alexandre Grothendieck, *Produits tensoriels topologiques et espaces nucléaires*, 16 (Providence: Memoirs of the American Mathematical Society, 1955); Grothendieck, 'Résumé de la théorie métrique des produits tensoriels topologiques', *Sao Paulo: Bol. Soc. Mat.*, 8 (1956), pp. 1–79; Grothendieck, 'Sur quelques points d'algèbre homologique', *Tohoku Mathematics Journal*, 9 (1957), pp. 119–221; Grothendieck, 'Classes de faisceaux et théorème de Riemann-Roch' (1957), in *Séminaire de Géométrie Algébrique du Bois-Marie*, 7 vols (12 parts) (multicopied originals, IHES, 1960–69), vol. 6, pp. 20–71.
4. Alexandre Grothendieck, 'The cohomology theory of abstract algebraic varieties' (1958), in *Proceedings of the International Congress of Mathematics, Edinburgh 1958* (Cambridge: Cambridge University Press, 1960), pp. 103–18.
5. Alexandre Grothendieck, *Éléments de Géometrie Algébrique* (with Jean Dieudonné), 4 vols (8 parts) (Paris: Publications Mathématiques de l'IHÉS, 1960–67).
6. Alexandre Grothendieck, *Séminaire de Géométrie Algébrique du Bois-Marie*, 7 vols (12 parts) (multicopied originals, IHES, 1960–69).
7. Alexandre Grothendieck, *Motifs*, manuscript (Berlin: Springer, c. 1967), p. 24.
8. Alexandre Grothendieck, *La longue marche à travers la théorie de Galois*, manuscript (1981), p. 1600; Grothendieck, *Pursuing stacks*, manuscript (1983), p. 629; Grothendieck, *Esquisse d'un programme*, manuscript (1984), p. 57; Grothendieck, *Les dérivateurs*, manuscript (1991), p. 1796.
9. Alexandre Grothendieck, *Récoltes et semailles,* manuscript (1986), p. 1252.
10. Bernhard Riemann, 'Principes fondamentaux pour une théorie générale des fonctions d'une grandeur variable complexe' (1851) (translation of 'Grundlagen für eine allgemeine Theorie der Functionen einer veränderlichen complexen Grösse', PhD thesis), in Bernhard Riemann, *Oeuvres mathématiques* (Paris: Gauthier-Villars, 1898), pp. 1–60.
11. Grothendieck, *Séminaire de Géométrie Algébrique.*
12. For an extended study of Grothendieck's work, see Fernando Zalamea, *Filosofía sintética de las matemáticas contemporáneas* (Bogotá: Universidad Nacional de Colombia, 2009); expanded English translation: *Synthetic Philosophy of Contemporary Mathematics* (Falmouth and

New York: Urbanomic/Sequence Press, 2012); further expanded French translation: *Philosophie synthétique des mathématiques contemporaines* (Geneva: Metis-Presses, 2009).
13. Newton Da Costa and Jean-Yves Béziau, *Logiques classiques et non-classiques* (Paris: Masson, 1997).
14. See Alain Connes, 'An Essay on the Riemann Hypothesis' (2015), www.arXiv:1509.05576v1 (last accessed 15 March 2017).
15. Andrei Tarkovsky, *Le temps scellé (Sculpting in Time)*, 2nd edn (Paris: Cahiers du cinéma, 1985), p. 136.
16. Ibid., p. 123.
17. For a similar, quasi-mystical experience in the works of Pavel Florensky, see Fernando Zalamea, *Antinomias de la creación. Las fuentes contradictorias de la invención en Valéry, Warburg, Florenski* (Santiago de Chile: Fondo de Cultura Económica, 2013).
18. Tarkovsky, *Le temps scellé*, pp. 126–7.
19. See Pierre Devidts, *Andreï Tarkovski. Spatialité et habitation* (Paris: L'Harmattan, 2012).
20. For other, more mystical revelations, see Alexandre Grothendieck, *La Clef des songes*, manuscript (1987), p. 315.
21. See Grothendieck, *Motifs*; Grothendieck, *Esquisse d'un programme.*
22. See Zalamea, *Antinomias de la creación.*
23. Walter Benjamin, *I 'passages' di Parigi*, ed. R. Tiedemann and E. Gani (Turin: Einaudi, 2000 [1927–40]).
24. For extensions of these ideas, see Fernando Zalamea, *Razón de la frontera y fronteras de la razón. Pensamiento de los límites en Peirce, Florenski, Marey, y limitantes de la expresión en Lispector, Vieira da Silva, Tarkovski* (Bogotá: Universidad Nacional de Colombia, 2010).
25. Maurice Merleau-Ponty, *L'Oeil et l'Esprit* (Paris: Folio, 2004 [1964]); Maurice Merleau-Ponty, *Le visible et l'invisible* (Paris: Folio, 2004 [1964]) .
26. Frank Gehry and Michael Sorkin, *Gehry Talks: Architecture and Process*, ed. M. Friedman (New York: Rizzoli, 1999), p. 44.
27. Ibid.
28. For an overview of Gehry's work, see Frank Gehry, *Frank Gehry, Architect*, ed. F. and F. Ragheb (New York: Guggenheim Museum Publications, 2001).
29. Coosje van Bruggen, *Frank O. Gehry. Guggenheim Museum Bilbao* (New York: Guggenheim Museum Publications, 1997), p. 37.
30. Frank Gehry, *On Line* (New Haven, CT: Yale University Press, 2008).
31. van Bruggen, *Frank O. Gehry*, pp. 62, 73.
32. For the force of allegories, see Benjamin, *I 'passages' di Parigi.*
33. Danièle Cohn, *Anselm Kiefer. Ateliers* (Paris: Editions du Regard, 2012).
34. See Anselm Kiefer, *Sternenfall. Chute d'étoiles*, ed. Assouline Ardenne (Paris: Editions du Regard, 2007).

35. Anselm Kiefer, *L'art survivra à ses ruines* (Paris: Editions du Regard, 2011).
36. Ibid., pp. 298–9.
37. For similar ideas in Valéry, Warburg and Florensky, see Zalamea, *Antinomias de la creación.*
38. Anselm Kiefer, *The Seven Heavenly Palaces* (Ostfildern-Ruit: Hatje Cantz Publishers, 2001).
39. See Zalamea, *Antinomias de la creación.*
40. See Kiefer, *Sternenfall*, pp. 170–1, 206–7, 241.
41. Anselm Kiefer and Daniel Arasse, *Rencontres pour mémoire* (Paris: Editions du Regard, 2010), p. 65.

CHAPTER 12

Vicarious Architectonics, Strange Objects, Chance-bound: Michel Serres's Exodus from Methodical Reason

Vera Bühlmann

Who experiments? The body. Who invents? It does.[1]

Architectonics as the Maintenance of Compatibility

This chapter introduces Michel Serres's philosophy of natural communication and seeks to initiate translations of it to the field of architectural theory, where there is, currently, a rising interest in a materiality that incorporates code and a formality that is computational. I am grateful to the architectural studio Pa.LaC.E (Valle Medina and Benjamin Reynolds, palacepalace.com) for contributing images from their Paris Hermitage (2015) project. Paris Hermitage is 'a place to know yourself by knowing all: omnia disce', they say, and they think of their project as the design of 'a place for elective counteraction to the reshaping of living practices (social/familial/working) by the extreme conceptual abstractions made possible by our raw power of technology'.[2]

Serres's philosophy is animated by a particular maxim: It is the demand that philosophy must be capable of factoring in state-of-the-art science and mathematics, as a real and factual, material as well as formal *puissance*[3] with which it must come to terms. As Serres puts it: 'If philosophy doesn't have to dominate science or become its slave or handmaiden, it must at least maintain compatibility with it.'[4] It is this same maxim that I want to raise for architecture as well: If architecture doesn't have to dominate science or become its slave or handmaiden, it must at least maintain compatibility with it. Maintaining compatibility with science means nothing less than distinguishing architecture (philosophy) from any form of dogma, as well as from the blind reflexes that pertain to ideology and the forms of corruption that are triggered wherever dogma and ideology are applied as 'immediate' or 'intuitive' and 'real' evidence, and feature in that sense as the representations of 'objective knowledge' in political opportunism, economic irresponsibility or religious fundamentalism.

Raising this maxim with Serres for philosophy, or as I suggest here for architecture, is not a call to moralism. At the core of such corruption, Serres's philosophy points out, there is no malign principle or personal ill intention to be found, no corrupt 'objectivity' or 'subjectivity' that could be 'accused' and 'corrected'. Rather, we find in Serres's philosophy a particular state of confusion responsible for this (our contemporary) situation, which contemporary philosophy does not know yet how to address. It is a confusion that is triggered by the gulf separating contemporary mathematical science (quantum physics, molecular biology, electrical engineering and information science) in which 'chance' acts as a mathematised principle, and hence as a source of necessity, from epistemology. The latter cannot well accommodate such a notion of principality of chance-boundedness of events, for it would mean reconciling chance-boundedness (non-repeatability) with reason and its core attribute (repeatability).

Without being able to address this confusion, Serres sees as responsible for a certain state of betrayal[5] and corruption in contemporary theory a philosophical notion of identity that operates in terms of membership. For identity, if broken up into relations of belonging, chance and necessity are two principles in conflict. One embodies directionality (necessity), the other thwarts and dissolves it (chance). Within an identity notion in terms of membership, descent and procreation, they are competing for hegemony over each other. The demand that Serres makes on philosophy, and which I suggest making on architecture as well, concerns a notion of identity for which chance and necessity would not only not be in conflict, but one for which necessity, with its directions, originates in chance, while chance must encompass directionality.[6] I want to begin by showing how this, for Serres, is the promise of a new kind of knowledge, which he calls the knowledge of an 'exodic discourse' (Figure 12.1).

Expulsed: The Place of the Vicarious

> My discourse is scientific and at odds with epistemology; it breaks with two millennia of method. Or rather, this old fiction is saturated with a different, incredible kind of knowledge. New knowledge. It is not fiction and not a true story I seek, but the exodic discourse . . .[7]

Figure 12.1 Paris Hermitage Grand Court (Judean Desert CDLXXXIII AD), 2014, inkjet print, 180 x 75 cm. Rendering of the recreation of the daily irradiance of the Judean desert in central Paris. Digital collage.

With the ambition formulated in his maxim that '[i]f philosophy doesn't have to dominate science or become its slave or handmaiden, it must at least maintain compatibility with it', Serres takes as his starting point that this factual technical mastery has expelled us from the promise of a knowledge that could be acquired and shared equally, justly and uncorruptedly, if only strictly rule-based methods were followed. Method, as 'arriving at the best result with the least effort, as earning the maximum while paying the minimum'[8] – this constrains us to tautology, Serres maintains. While '[m]ethod minimizes constraints and cancels them out', he elaborates, 'exodus throws itself into their disorder'.[9]

The knowledge that derives alone from method, as 'arriving at the best result with the least effort, as earning the maximum while paying the minimum', maintains a performative and immediate relation to the 'symbolics' that it applies in its formality: it assumes, ideally, the full presence of the elementary forms (or the words, or the thing itself, or phenomena) in the transparent neutrality of an ordered set-up (axioms, the alphabet, a vocabulary, in numeration, or in the apparatus of optical physics). We could call this the epistemological assumption of existential quantifiers,[10] and speak of methodic reason's arithmetics of truth-value: At home (in the ideal of such full and well-ordered presence) 'right' and 'legitimate' is the direction that is most economic.

In contrast to such an arithmetics of existential quantifiers, the exodic knowledge Serres hails looks at 'the symbolic' with the eyes of the uninitiated stranger (or the estranged initiated) who finds herself, foreign or alienated, undecided, in the midst of places (*mi-lieu*) with none of which she fully identifies.[11] This stance too maintains that knowledge must be formal, but it looks to information theory to find an adequate philosophical stance.[12] He thereby foregrounds information theory in its most uncomfortable and, to many, outrightly unacceptable character: the theorem that information has its price. I can only explain briefly here:[13] with the thermodynamic principle of time's irreversibility, no observation is gratuitous. The perfect experiment that Maxwell (and many others after him) dreamed of, an experiment whose agency would be a disembodied and pure mind, is impossible, because it would have to assume an infinite amount of negentropy with which it could pay for the new information. Information can be acquired only at a cost – and this regards not only a subjective agency of understanding, as Léon Brillouin and Leo Szilard demonstrated. It concerns objectivity itself, via the ciphered code in whose symbolics 'objectivity' is formulated. That information has its price is the theorem of a mathematical realism to Serres.[14] It is why he is at odds with epistemology, which uses the balance between expense and acquisition in a non-stratified and global manner: best result with least effort, maximum effect with minimal cost (Figure 12.2).

Figure 12.2 Paris Hermitage (Auditorium), 2014, inkjet print, 180 x 90 cm. Public auditorium interior. The contributors to the Paris Hermitage are invited to occupy the space for discussions with the wider public. Its perimeter is constituted by walls made from layers of pulverised quartz. Digital collage.

For such a mathematical realism, nature counts as both rational (finite) and irrational (infinite), as at once hidden (the encryption of the irrational) and exposed in the code as a sign of quantification (information as quantity), by the formal language of mathematics.

> Enlightenment philosophy teaches that the irrational must be driven out: what do the hideous statue and its inhuman form of worship have to do with us? But we have since learned to call anthropology what the Enlightenment cast out as madness or darkness, and we have also learned that exclusion brings us back to the sacred because the gesture of expulsion precisely characterizes sacrifice. By rejecting this form of worship and scene as barbarous, we risk behaving the way the Ancients did. Therefore let's accept our anthropological past as such; ignoring it would make it return without our suspecting it.[15]

How then is the infinite (the mathematical irrational) to be dealt with in this stance of mathematical realism? What Serres proposes concerns the place of the vicarious: philosophy must learn to address the locus of the vicar, the joker, the general equivalent. Mathematics is the royal path to knowledge, but the sovereignty of mathematics cannot govern immediately. That would make irrational forms of worship return without our suspecting it. The sovereignty of mathematics must be expelled – for the sake of a knowledge of nature.[16] Serres elaborates on the meaning of this for science:

> Nature is hidden behind a cypher. Mathematics is a code, and since it is not arbitrary, it is rather a cypher. Now, since this idea in fact constitutes the invention or the discovery, nature is hidden twice. First, under the cypher. Then under a dexterity, a modesty, a subtlety, which prevents our reading the cypher even from an open book. Nature hides under a hidden cypher. Experimentation, intervention, consist in making it appear.[17]

Science, then, is the remembering of the locus of the vicar, the joker, the general equivalent. Its knowledge is not that of the architecture of the cosmos or of the world, but that of the architecture of the vicarious place. The agency of exodic knowledge is 'exodic' because it registers that it cannot 'simply' (without cost, without sacrifice) identify with an assumed fullness of elements that were capable of rationalisation (as 'epistemology' arguably does, within the contrast that Serres establishes). It regards the 'symbolicness' of elements in mediate distance. It looks at elements as cryptic and coded, as encryptions of quantised 'strangeness', marked by chance-bound encounters (rather than as uniformly quantised in terms of belonging and membership). Serres suggests attending to 'strangeness' as an objective quantifier in the domain of the vicarious, where it modalises universal quantification: 'Strange in its precise meaning, without relation to the judging subject, universal; strange, this means improbable'.[18] To him, mathematics is a code that keeps the irrational (infinite) strangeness contained within the reality of rational actions: this is what allows thinking of mathematics in terms of how to maintain compatibility. One particular question clarifies the stance of Serres's mathematical realism: 'In other words, do our clear knowledge and effective technologies include dark patches of unexpected ignorance?'[19]

Within Serres's exodus from methodical reason, the symbolicness of elements is looked at as being constituted by ciphers. From the detached viewpoint of the expulsed mathematician, any finite group of ordered elements, whose combinatorial totality spells out the algebraic symmetry space of an equation, is a cipher. What does an algebraic symmetry space mean? We can imagine an encrypted sum of transformations, of which for any one transformation that could be carried out, there is one that could cancel it (undo it). 'Cipher' comes from *cifra*, for zero or nothing. So understood, every code can be looked at as a cipher: the decimal number system using ten as logarithmic base for all numbers, just as well as the hexagesimal number system, or the 'myriads of myriads' of Archimedes' Sand Reckoner.[20] To say that code matters is to say that every cipher introduces an encrypted rationality, a manner of counting that is, in each case, universally valid – but, because of the price of information, not in equivalent manner. We can no longer maintain, he holds, that there is one particular scale which must count as elementary and principal for all things equally.

Why does Serres call nature 'hidden twice'? Serres's first book was an extensive study on Leibniz,[21] in which he maintains that for the latter, 'the model of the system, this is the system of the model'.[22] In his reading of Leibniz, Serres suggests thinking of the universal characteristics, not in terms of an ultimate ground and referent for systematic deduction, but in terms of mathematical translations, on the vicarious level of structures, between systems. 'One needs to understand', Serres maintains,

> that in Leibniz's philosophy, systematic organization is ill understood when thought of in reference to one sole principle of identity, in terms of univocity. Rather, it ought to be thought of in relation to all the variations which this principle accommodates.[23]

This identity principle, he continues, allows us to treat rigorously 'a content that is un-organized [*inorganisé*] by notions, and by thousands of possible architectures'.[24] But this is not sufficient, he continues, because

> it is impossible [. . .] to think one sole notion in isolated and fragmentary manner, in its regional signification. It is essential for any one of them to be thought, defined, situated in reference to all the others. It is their nature to lend themselves for being integrated with their own consequential presentations – and in all of them at once.[25]

There is, in effect, 'always a plurality of possible deductive paths'[26] and 'the multiplication of paths augments the richness of the analysis and the solidity of the connection'.[27] Reason is addressed here, according to Serres, in terms of different structures' richnesses and solidities – this is a non-representational way to address Leibniz's distinction between necessary and sufficient reason. It is one that gives an account (*récit*). It addresses reason as a net of concurrent and multiply interlinked chains of deduction, in which values are polyvalent – 'a web of many concurrent chains'[28] within which 'one has to try to construct a network' that could 'constitute the plan of the labyrinth'.[29] Every approximation of such a plan 'carries in itself a secret for which we, in our confusion, search'.[30]

What is so counterintuitive to consider from the epistemological point of view, which always assumes an ultimate referent code, is how this 'secret' is not one that could ever be disclosed and exposed. Access to knowledge does not depend upon breaking an ultimate code by learning how it works in order to see what it conceals. It has long been clear that by following rigorously a methodical and deductive path that starts out from elements considered principal and ultimate, one will always find what one has put into the assumptions to start with. To refer to a famous example: if a computer simulation is to calculate the limits of growth, it will always produce a particular value for that variable around which the system is set up (it will never say that the assumptions that went into the formulation of the simulation are wrong).[31] Whereas for methodic knowledge there is only tautology, exodic discretisations and distributions, by using strangeness as an objective quantifier that modalises universal quantification, afford the unknown to factor-in, in a manner that needs not reduce the unknown, be it in negative or in positive terms. By acting on ciphered equations, such structures of deduction – for which the model is the system and the system is the model –conserve the unknown as a secret, as an element of chance and originality, in the cipher code they apply.

Serres's interest in cryptography is one that gives primacy to the processes of translation between what is technically called 'source text' and 'cipher text'. It is expulsed from being initiated, however diffusely, from an original source text, and it is expulsed also from a certainty that would draw from knowing that any one particular cipher text must provide the ultimate key to access the source text in its full extent. For Serres's knowledge of an exodic discourse, mathematics is the cornucopia from which wells the richness (or poorness) in terms of which an analysis can be meaningful, or a connection can be solid.[32]

Functions that are Rare – Ciphers, Mass and Complexity

There is a definition of complexity in Serres which makes it necessary to clarify his stance on what is, more often than not, bracketed from twentieth-century science as if it were a separate story that needs not impact upon scientific findings: namely, how to deal with the infinite in mathematics. Does Serres say the same, with a much more strange and alien vocabulary, as William Ross Ashby, Heinz von Foerster or Ilya Prigogine had begun to? Yes and no.

Most theories of self-organisation will readily say that systems in disequilibrium are of the greatest interest, and allow explanations such as 'order emerges out of chaos' and 'order or coordination arises out of local interactions between smaller component parts of an initially disordered system' or the like.[33] Yet most will address such systems as dynamic systems, and hence regard the order they study as a function in time. It is with regard to this that Serres has something to contribute. To Serres as well, order emerges like islands in an immense sea. But to him, such emergence is not immediately a function of time in space, it is not strictly of historical eventuality. 'Let's introduce mass into philosophy', he urges, 'in a way that's compatible with physics and the other sciences and placed by them among the fundamental units in dimensional equations, at the same rank as space and time: all three units counted by them as pure quantities.'[34] Serres relates 'mass' to a quantum physical understanding of information (information as energetic; mass to him is incandescent)[35] by making its role as an invariant quantity explicit: 'nothing can be removed from or added to it without inevitably finding again what has been subtracted from it or taking in it what has been added to it'; furthermore: 'Mass's permanence plays an analogous role to the constants that prohibit perpetual motion of every type. Nothing is free' (Figure 12.3).[36]

Let us see how Serres defines complexity: complexity demarcates 'a state, a system, where the number of elements, or the reciprocal relations among them, is unaccountably large or inaccessible'.[37] No statistical analysis of a dynamic system (statistically modelled as process (the integral) or as procedural (the differential)) considers the number of elements or relations as unaccountably large. This sets probabilistics, from the point of view of cryptography, apart from statistics: here, the

Figure 12.3 Left: Space (Interference), 2013, HD video, 19:37 mins. The numerical coordinates of a live 3D-scanned marl stone at 08:32 minutes into a carving process undertaken to re-empathise with the material; a critique of the remote forming of space via computer. The sequence of coordinates obtains the stone's new materiality: an interference pattern.
Right: Space (Carving) [film still], 2013, HD video, 19:37 mins. 12:16 minutes into the carving process.

question of identifying what is called the chance variable, the alphabet of coding, always remains a problematic issue. The 'identification' of chance as a variable is not axiomatic in probabilistics – this means that finding the elements for analysis is part of the problem itself. Technically speaking, probabilistics addresses chance as a variable by devising 'masks' for it through which it 'figures', variably.[38]

Serres regards mathematics as cipher code for learning about a source text in the cryptographical sense (nature, which is hidden twice – below a cipher and below a dexterity in coding).[39] This learning can proceed only by articulating cipher text: these articulations in the cipher text are objects, about which Serres maintains that they are essentially 'strange'. Their proper place – that of objectivity – is to be regarded as the vicariousness of a void, whereby its voidness needs to be 'addressed'. And this can be done in no other way than by ciphers, and their 'articulateness in spelling out nothing' (*cifra*, nothing, naught). The place of the principle must be dealt with by devising ciphers that are capable of translating different models of the system such that this system can be the system of all the models. It is this very set-up which makes Serres's philosophy so interesting for thinking about digital architecture.

Serres's notion of complexity is not instrumental to the explanation of the appearance of order per se. Rather, it is the appearance of order in its respective complexity that he is concerned with. To Serres, the kinds of systems or states that count as complex, in the sense of having an unaccountably large or inaccessible number of elements or relations, are not immediately functions of time; they are functions of time that are more or less strange, rare and improbable – for which mass has the same rank as space and time do in physics.

Rare literally means airy, porous, few in number and widely separated, sparsely distributed, seldom found, thinly sown, having a loose texture, not thick, having intervals between, full of empty spaces.[40] For mathematics, this means that complex states or systems cannot be modelled in any one particular space of similarity. There is no homogeneous scale that would render their components commensurable in a priori manner.[41] Rarity is a quantitative term that is of a scope which can be theorised and measured only probabilistically, in cryptography. It is the negative to that which is calculated as probable, as we speak of negative and positive entropy. In this, it neither implies such a homogeneous scale, nor does it imply a set of elements that were, in any a priori manner, commensurable. Rarity can be measured by probabilistic measures. With reference to rarity, complex states or systems can be attributed 'identity' relative to mathematical invariance – hence, not in the timeless sense of stasis, nor in the continuity (force-based) terms of dynamics (which renders time reversible and homogeneous).

Universality as the Invariant Recipient of Variations

Mathematical invariance, as the not strictly countable reference to mathematical identity, is crucial for Serres's treatment of structures (for which the model of the system is at once also the system of the model): this mutually implicative relation between system and model is at once determined and open, because such modelling proceeds by parallelism of structure[42] between the two (model and system are treated as encrypted, and both must be rendered translatable into each other – this is what cryptography does). Such modelling does not proceed by mapping one in terms of the other (this would be their functional treatment, by numbers and one particular calculus).[43] Parallelism of structure yields a kind of self-referentiality that is not 'incestuous' (reproduction of self-sameness). We could also say that such a model is a spectrum of an invariance (system), just as much as the system (invariance) is a model of the spectrality from which the spectrum is derived. Parallelism of structure provides for an objective kind of locality that emerges out of translation. Even if different spectra render apparent different phenomena of one and the same substance (all natural sciences render apparent, ultimately, the radioactivity of the sun's emissions), these different spectra do not contradict one another only because they give different renderings of 'one' and 'the same' 'source' emission (Figure 12.4).

Invariance implies a notion of structure where structure works like a sieve, rather than like a frame of determinability. This allows us to think of time as the manifold confluence of different temporalities,

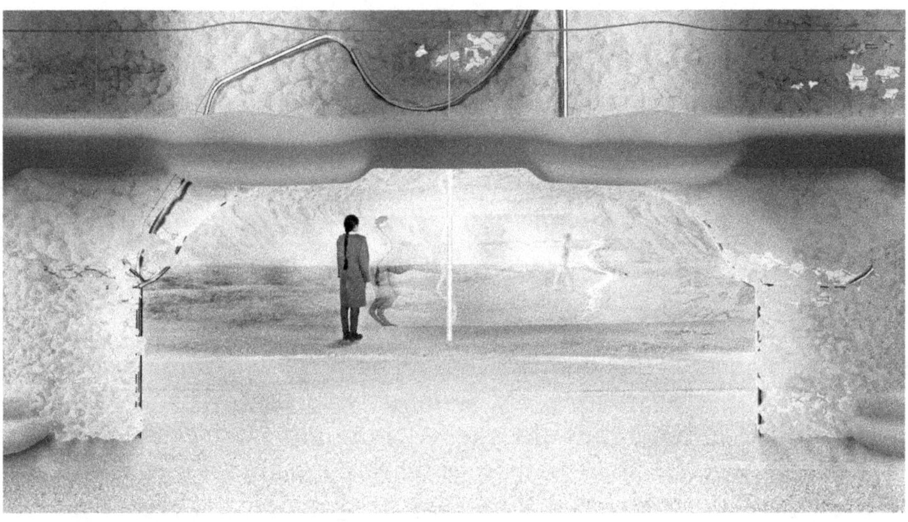

Figure 12.4 Paris Hermitage (Library), 2014, inkjet print, 180 x 90 cm. The library at the Hermitage has no books. One reading is selected monthly by the contributors for discussion. The library space is formed to allocate readers a place to face one another. This is the desert view from the library. Digital collage.

each of which can be 'quantised' in terms of 'entropies' (measures of disorganised order, measures of death): Serres distinguishes three different measures of disorder: one with regard to reversible order, one with regard to irreversible order (negentropic in terms of energy), and one with regard to the reversibility of irreversible order, which he calls negentropic (now in terms of quantum physical information).[44] To Serres, order establishes and maintains itself rarely. It appears in a great variety of forms of complexity, as massive, spatio-temporal pockets of negentropy within the ubiquitous ground of noisy disorder – a ground that is only a ground insofar as it shields an emitting background. We can recognise in this thought an account of the astrophysical understanding of the universe as expanding: the 'ground' that such 'identity' (as a rendering of an uncountable invariance) provides is a 'ground' insofar as it is the indefinite total of all that factors in it and that might or might not appear.[45] Everything that has ever been informs the vastness of this ground's immense 'magnitude'. All that consists of a confluence of different percolations of the activity of mass (light speed of solar radiation) that not only bifurcates linearly, but also keeps emitting through spectral forms that bear the irrational within themselves. This is the formal potency that technical spectra are capable of: they render phenomena apparent, they organise frequentation, they act as sieves and let (light) speed pass, and thereby temper this passing's percolations.

Mathematical Realism – Forms as Tombs

For such set-ups, Serres maintains, it remains true that regularity springs from forms (*morphé*), but forms must count as cryptic. In his *Second Book of Foundations: Statues* (1987) he introduces his understanding of forms as tombs. Forms, hence, both are and are not outside of time and space. They are the indexical markers of different temporalities that encounter one another. Forms, as tombs, mark the sites of death. They contain the irrational as a dead body, as remains that no one knows how to relate to properly. Without being dealt with, death might well bring to communities 'the plague' (not only in the evident sense of a disease, but also, more extensively, referring to anything that is, as the etymology of the term has it, 'annoying, bothersome, spreading easily'). Contained in every form, there is nothing to be found but death as the source of indefiniteness. But the forms themselves, which are tombs that contain this source, are black boxes. With this notion of the black box, Serres speaks of the return of the real into the rational:

> The Earth absorbs the remains, and we didn't think about them. It gives and receives, does away with, or erases the balance sheets. A fundamental ark, that is to say, a major black box. Thanks to it, we used to act as if nothing had happened. Like a mother and even more, it's the complement of every parasitical operation; better, the universal donor who, in order to never insist on return or reciprocity, makes the parasite possible. One day, I don't know why, the Earth was lacking for us. From that time on, we thought that nothing was created, nothing lost, that everything was transformed; from that time on, we calculated by balance sheets. The rational restores equilibria, balance, and proportions: that is its proper definition, by the origin of the word that designates it. That which brings itself back and brings back. And thus, the rational will always return the thing that you throw into it, unlike the Earth, which keeps, hides, dissolves, and annihilates it. If you toss a dead man into the emptiness, he will come back; reason will bring him back: but he never comes back from the deep terrestrial sum that he imperceptibly increases. Reason is recognised by its ghosts. Here then, in the black and white space of the page or the stars, the corpse reappears. The object that's missing in the balance sheet is risen. The return of the real into the rational.[46]

Black boxes are architectonic crypts. They are black boxes, but black boxes that are made up of white elements[47] – Serres often elaborates his notions of black and white with regard to the physics of light, that is, with regard to radiating and active solar light that is to be regarded as at once particle and charge.[48] Solar light is white, undetermined, and at the same time black, because indefinitely overdetermined. This cryptical and cryptographical take on forms introduces a spectral view of forms. To Serres, formality defines in that it renders apparent, organises frequentation, lets (light) speed pass, and tempers this passing's percolations.

Niveaus of Information, Saturated with Universality

But spectra themselves are forms too, in the sense of tombs that mark sites of death (the disintegration of all form of organisation). With this Serres pays respect to there being no particular spectrum that would exhaust the full extent of radiating and active solar light. Serres does not relate the phenomena rendered apparent by spectra to an existential logic (existential quantifiers of time and space without their modalisation by mass), but neither does he subsume them within an economy of exchange. Formality moderates light speed's abundant givens by tempering their velocity at different niveaus of information: the higher the amount of information, the faster the velocities and the more emissively radiating the mass. Forms are tombs, and they mark in this sense interrupted, distributed and bifurcating lines of originality and descent.

In the originality of formality which Serres envisages here, formality brings forth regularity in a domain that is set apart, separated and spared of appropriations of any sort – a 'publicness', hence, that knows no complementary domain of 'privacy'. It is a publicness that is welcoming in general – under the sole condition that the rules which constitute it as publicness are being respected. In that sense, Serres's formality gives regularity in a public domain we will have to address as sacred.[49]

But there is a crucial divergence from other theories of the sacred, and their respective notions of 'purity'. By regarding forms in spectral terms as black boxes made up of white elements, the domain whose regularity such forms establish is 'pure' not after having excluded all that is irrational (in the sense of mathematical infinity), but rather, it can be pure only in that it comprehends, within itself, the irrational. As in every religion, a principle of purity must constrain 'the plague' from spreading; this applies also here. But spectral forms are 'pure' proportional to the degree that they are colourless, and hence 'undecided': both black and white are the undecided sum of all colours, once energetically (blackness) and once informationally (whiteness). The purity of the sacred originality of forms, which Serres introduces, is a purity that is, counterintuitively so, kept best in articulations whose formality is maximally unsettled. It is a formality that is rich in involving polyvalence, articulations that are rich in values that are saturated with contingency (blackness and whiteness) – purity is articulated unsettledness, articulations in the formal language of mathematics. Serres's originality of formality in cryptography is rigorously true and exact to the cryptic and invariant content it articulates, by probabilistics that deals with quantities of strangeness. The rigour in such articulations, this rigour and this exactness are what this purification relies on, they are what institutes necessity (as teleonomy), but they are, themselves, bound only by chance (as invariance). The systematicity of such rigour and exactness is the improbable systematicity of functions that are rare.

Percolation and Circulation among Cast-off Forms: Communication as Secretion

At the heart of Serres's mathematical realism, there is a notion of purity, and hence of regularity and necessity, that can be achieved not by exclusion but by saturation: the larger the amount of 'colours' (distinct frequencies), as mixed up but unambiguously determinable values (probability amplitudes), that factor in the elements of the chance-bound calculations, the purer they are. Forms are sources of regularity not because they lock away the irrational; it is not despite but because they contain a corpse, the mass of a dead body, the trace of an organised finitude disintegrating into infinity. Forms are universal not because they are perennial, or immaterial, but in that they contain death.

> The simple and pure forms are not that simple nor that pure; they are no longer things of which we have, in our theoretical insight, exhaustive knowledge, things that are assumedly transparent without any remainder. Instead they constitute an infinitely entangled, objective-theoretical unknown, tremendous virtual *noemata* like the stones and the objects of the world, like our masonry and our artifacts. Form bears beneath its form transfinite nuclei of knowledge, with regard to which we must worry that history in its totality will not be sufficient for exhausting them, nuclei of knowledge which are profoundly inaccessible and which pose themselves as problems. Mathematical realism wins back in weight and re-adopts that compactness which had dissolved beneath the Platonic sun. Pure or abstract idealities will cast shadows once more, they are themselves full of shadows, they are turning black again like the pyramid. Mathematics unfolds, despite its maximal abstractness and the genuine purity which is proper to it, within the framework of a lexicon which results, partially, from technology.[50]

To Serres, forms encrypt, in an indefinite plurality of ways, universal nature. Each form contains this nature's indefinite and hence irrational secret. But again, not in the sense of locking it up and putting it away, turning it into a reservoir or stock[51] – this nature is this secret that can only be kept as a secret. Disclosure and exposition without mediation by code are corruption, because they don't account for the basic theorem of information theory: that no observation is gratuitous, that the acquisition of information comes at a price. Serres's philosophy is a physics of information, and we can see now how nature is the secret that cryptographical articulations can keep only while keeping it in circulation (nature cannot turn into a stock, a capital or a resource):

> Bacteria, fungus, whale, sequoia, we do not know any life of which we cannot say that it emits information, receives it, stores it and processes it. Four universal rules, so unanimous that, by them, we are tempted to define life but are unable to do so, because of the following counterexamples. Crystal, indeed, rock, sea, planet, star, galaxy: we know no inert thing of which we cannot say that it emits, receives, stores and processes information. Four universal rules, so uniform that we are tempted to define anything in the world by them, but are unable to do so because of the following counterexamples. Individuals, but also families, farms, villages, cities, nations, we do not know any human, alone or in groups, of which we cannot say that it emits, receives, stores and processes information.[52]

We should use 'secrete' as the verb for this fourfold and universal activity: nature is the activity of secretion, of something setting itself apart from itself, from *cernere* (separateness, from Latin: crisis, to separate, discriminate, sieve, also judge). Serres's forms as tombs and as source of regularity, in his spectral paradigm of thinking about structure, are to be understood as communicational forms: They originate in a site that marks death, the dis-integration of a temporary organisation, a sacred place – the place of the vicarious – where nature maintains its own secretion, a place which is purer and more polyvalent the elements are in, whose terms are staked.

Natural Laws as Laws of Conservation

In this sense, each form buries within itself the memory of a particular bundle of organised temporalities, which with Serres we can call a corpse. This may sound like a mythical tale that starts out from the other end (not that of beginnings, which usually informs myth). But consider that today's science formulates all of the so-called natural laws as laws of conservation (rather than predication or functional determination): the natural laws are laws that regulate an invariance, and an invariance refers to a 'quantity' that can receive variations. Invariance refers to an identity that is never given except as distributed and entangled, mixed up within states or systems of various complexity.

To sum up: the formality that expresses natural laws as laws of conservation, treating identity indirectly, mediately, through invariance, is cryptographical – it proceeds by a parallelism of structure. Cryptographical formality is, at first sight, that of equations, or equational systems; but unlike equations in algebra, cryptographical equations are not constituted by tautology (identity as equivalence). They mask an irrational core, source of the indefinite which they seek to contain such that it will not spread (the plague, disintegration, death). They render this irrational core apparent in regular manner, but without claiming to represent it. As Serres puts it: they are black boxes made up of white elements. The reality they contain is dark, it cannot exhaustively be rationalised; but the way they do contain this reality is strictly rational – any one way, of any one code, applied in any one cryptography, indexes the void in-between (*mi-lieu*) between reference points: this notion of method (way, path) collocates indexes into the frequencies of a spectrum. But because rationality must bridge cryptographically different orders of complexity, without there being a homogeneous space of ordination, there must always be consideration for the parallelism of structure that is at work in cryptography (between what is kept as a secret from the source text in a cipher text). The model of the system is not its representation, the model of the system is the system of the model.

How then to deal with this bridging notion of 'adequacy' between parallel structures? Adequate meaning can only be accepted by relations of 'equipollence'. Equipollence is Serres's term to characterise the relation between the real and the rational – their relation must be considered, in this same manner of parallelism of structure, as reciprocally implicative: they must count as equals in power, strength and extension not because they mysteriously (a priori) are, but because with regard to all that can be known they are not![53]

Death is not only the possible source of the plague, and hence of the spreading of further death, but also the source of all knowledge to Serres. Knowledge can never exhaust all that there is to know, it gives different renderings of it – just as technical spectra give different renderings of one and the same 'substance' (radiating solar activity). This is how Serres can say: 'The known is constructed in the same way as the knower is instructed.'[54] Hence, the rational must account for the real (which it buries, but also remembers, with which it breaks but which it, at the same time, continues) – without rest, everything must count for it. This is what the language of mathematics, as a formal language, organises in its cryptic articulations.

Nature is Buried in its own Script (Mathematics as a Formal Language that Translates the Frequentative Orders of Radiating Activity)

This is how Serres can maintain that it is nature itself which speaks in that language – the nature of the world. Nature, hence, is buried in its own script. It remembers its invariant identity. Nature then is, in that it is not written explicitly. It is the formal manner of this 'is not' that only cryptography can express. There is not one alphabet of nature, not one *characteristica* that can be considered as universal. Rather, nature 'sounds' from the distant bottom of all things ('le fondement ultime' or 'la terre permière'),[55] from the 'ultimate ground' that the philosophical tradition also calls 'reason'. Ultimately, this ground of all things is noisy, because it contains the totality of all that could ever happen, in the sense of being born or of ceasing to be – it is what Serres calls *le geométrale*, the ichnography. Or as he puts in *The Birth of Physics in the Text of Lucretius*, this is a ciphered nature that is at once a poem and its own poet.[56] It is important to bear this in mind, even though I can do no more here than point out reference points within Serres's argument, because it introduces a crucial estrangement from our more common notion of cryptography as a proprietary and esoteric code that lends itself to concealing something in protection against, or to the exclusion of, a third party. Not so in Serres: code is the formal language of mathematics that encrypts, instructively, in its reduced models, whatever strangeness must be included and needs to be addressed in the domain of the vicarious that to Serres is the objective world: the strange subject of his exodic discourse.

Thereby, mathematics is translational, in a material sense. The formulae of mathematical language, then, are not meant to determine identity explicitly (in its real finitude within the world) but to conserve it in its indefinite invariance – throughout all the transformations that particular regularities (structures) afford.[57] Mathematics is translational in that it 'translates' a complex system in its contingency: there is contingency whenever two varieties, two temporalities [*temps*] are in touch with each other.[58] Serres elaborates: 'Hence contingency is the envelope of systems in the same sense as we speak of a mathematical curve as the envelope of its tangents.' And he continues: 'systems are encircled [*entourés*] by contingency' and 'since systems are stable, homeostatic, and homeorrhetic, I will refer to that which envelops them as circumstance'.[59]

Serres's mathematical realism works with the notion of a 'reduced model', a model that is reduced not because it would inadequately represent an original within a space of similarity (without irrationality), but one that does not represent at all: it translates the complex state or system that it models (Figure 12.5).

Invariance, then, ought to be thought of also from a philosophical point of view as a transitory, frequentative order (rather than transitive object), as transpositional (rather than locational or global) and transmissive (rather than submissive or dominant). It is the coping with such 'radiating activity' that Serres's urging that philosophy needs to consider mass as a category independent of those of time and space, indeed, transcendental to them, aims to help to initiate.[60] The invariant identity notion thereby is indefinite, because the structures are to be thought of no longer as the edifice of a static building that contains something (a formality that captures a content), nor as the apparatus that renders certain options constant (order as a structure

Figure 12.5 Paris Hermitage, 2014, quartz crystal, thermoplastic film, bioglue, aluminium poles (various sizes), 60 x 60 cm. Pulverised quartz detail.

that were a function to homogeneous time), but rather as spectral masks that render this invariance apparent in particularly manifest spatio-temporal ways. Unlike the spatio-temporal paradigm of thinking about structure (as edifices or apparatus), ways of rendering massive manifestations of spatio-temporal pockets of informational negentropy[61] need not contradict each other in the spectral paradigm of (radioactive) mass – that is, just as little or as much as the ways in which technical spectra render colours, chemical substances, aromas or the like would 'contradict' each other in their rendering apparent of one and the same 'substance' (the emissions of the sun's radiating activity) in different frequency patterns. For philosophy, Serres maintains, such spectral concepts shift attention to thought's critical inventiveness (rather than its critical reflectivity or its progressive productivity) (Figure 12.6).

Coda: Architecture in the Anthropocene

All of this is admittedly at some distance from what architecture and architectural theory are – at first sight, and especially in the twentieth century – concerned with. But the classical registers of organisation in terms of architectural morphologies, typologies, tectonics, structures

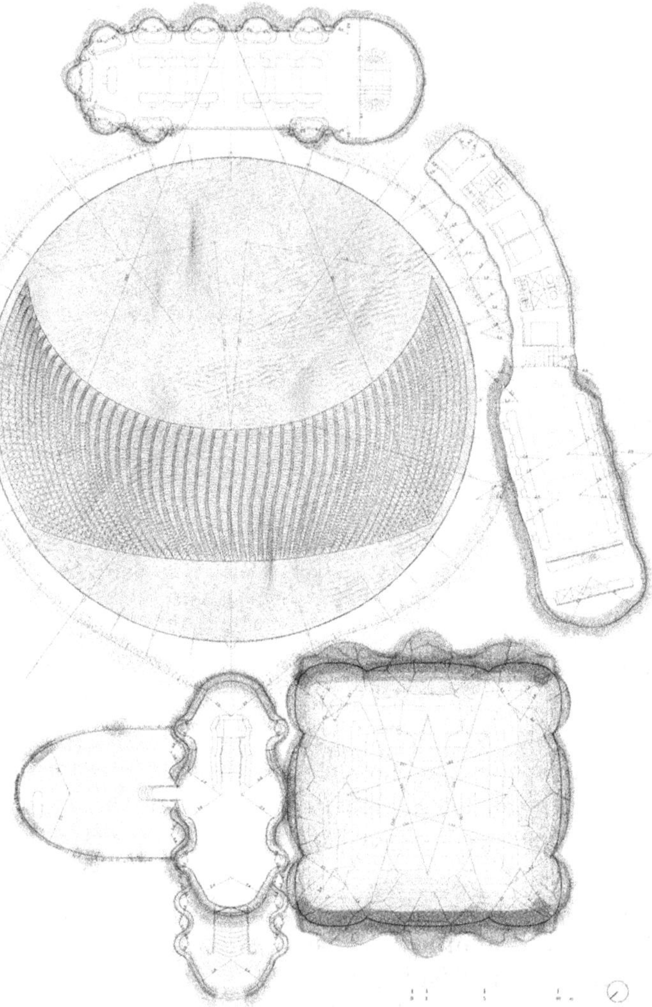

Figure 12.6 Paris Hermitage floorplan level +1.5 m, 2014, inkjet print, 180 x 90 cm.

and styles all draw from the classifications and categorisations at stake in these discussions. The emergence of computational architecture, with its learning algorithms, one-of-a-kind production facilities, parametric planning and design tools, 'objects' of participatory agency (objectiles), the web-based administration of catalogues of architectural objects (BIM) and all that features under the label big data in urban planning only increase the proximities between philosophy and architecture. Might a notion of modelling in terms of a parallelism of structures not resolve the bothersome conflict in twentieth-century architectural theory between structuralisms and their embrace of genericness, and typologies with their discriminatory capacity and their emphasis on specificity?

Any rendering of how this conflict can be resolved is arguably not merely a novel paradigm of theoretical explanation and historical accounting. It is of real and effective relevance for the emerging paradigm of sustainability in architecture (roughly understood here as the ability 'to remain diverse and productive indefinitely')[62] – for how is sustainability to be translated? If its modelling follows a stochastic path, it minimises the reign of chance and maximises linear control within a global model at the expense of polyvalence, ambiguity, strangeness and rarity (arguably key factors in any sustainable environment). With the discrimination of chance as an inevitable evil we have to deal with, such modelling produces homogeneity (purity by exclusion) on the one hand, while stocking up a complementary amount of bothersome nonfits on the other – Rem Koolhaas was indeed lucid when he complemented his notion of the Generic City (the city without qualities) with one of Wastelands (of historical identity that the Generic City has to dispose of). On the other hand, within a pluralist paradigm of ecological niches, the 'realisation' of sustainable building must follow the path of mimesis by analogy: its models must choose a paradigmatic form of organicity, with regard to which achievements in sustainability can be measured, evaluated and optimised. This paradigm too proceeds by the reduction of chance to a minimum. Both paradigms strive for maximal rational control of a general model: one by giving primacy to an imposing global scale, the other to a predefined 'pluralism' of localities.

The suggestion is to begin thinking about architecture in the terms of 'spectral concepts' as well. The promise is to see architecture again as decoupled from the totality of economic and political power, and to bring it back to an autonomy of building that knows how to maintain compatibility with the latter two, without wanting to either 'dominate' them nor 'be their slave or handmaiden'. This seems to be a necessary precondition for beginning to understand what sustainability can mean for architecture in the Anthropocene.

Notes

1. Michel Serres, *Variations on the Body*, trans. Randolph Burks (Minneapolis: Univocal, 2011 [1999]), p. 151.
2. Valle Medina and Benjamin Reynolds, *Paris Hermitage* (Basel/London: Pa.La.C.E. and New York: N. Weltyk/Cooperative Editions, 2016).

3. I use this word in French because it connotes a mixture of the words that lend themselves as translation to English (potency, possibility, potential, capacity, capability). In German I would translate it as *Mächtigkeit*.
4. Michel Serres, *Statues: The Second Book of Foundations*, trans. Randolph Burks (London: Bloomsbury, 2014), here cited from the kindle edition, position 1049.
5. Michel Serres, 'Trahison: la thanatocratie', in *Hermes III, La Traduction* (Paris: Les éditions de minuit, 1974), pp. 73–106.
6. Serres: 'and since the order of these concepts [music and the noise of Brownian movement (*bruit de fond*), archipels and sea, information and disorder, negentropy and second law of thermodynamics, the differing and the homogeneous, the precious and the diffused] is reversible, chance is the initial source and the final necessity'; Michel Serres, 'Vie, information, deuxième principe', in *Hermes III*, *La Traduction* (Paris: Les éditions de minuit, 1974), pp. 43–72, here p. 43, my translation.
7. Michel Serres, *The Five Senses: A Philosophy of Mingled Bodies* (London: Athlone Press, 2009 [1985]), p. 262.
8. Ibid.
9. Ibid.
10. This idea builds on Serres's problematisation of the universal quantifier (All) and the positive methodology it triggers in history, where it is concerned with operations of unification, integration and mean averages. Serres criticises the idea of seeing in history the complementary pole to the rationalism of an empirical scientist, whose methods are geared towards exposing an object, towards setting a particular domain apart from the whole, and hence work negatively by operations of exclusion, subtraction and elimination. Serres's point is that the universal ought to be considered 'under the form of distribution', and 'in the sign of quantification'. Cf. Michel Serres, 'Histoire: L'Univers et le lieu. Obstruction', in *Hermes V, Le Passage Nord-Ouest* (Paris: Les éditions de minuit, 1980), pp. 84–92, here p. 84.
11. Serres gives a surprising twist to the Cartesian scepsis: *dubitare* comes from *duo-habere*, he maintains, for being undecided about what something is to be taken for. Serres's twist is in regarding this moment as what he calls 'a frequentativum', as a returning oscillation between two positions. Cf. Michel Serres, 'Solides, fluides, flammes', in *Hermes V, Le passage du nord-ouest* (Paris: Les éditions de minuit, 1980), pp. 40–66, here p. 41.
12. Cf. Serres, 'Vie, information, deuxième principe', p. 45.
13. I have elaborated on this in my articles 'Maxwell's Demon (Non-Anthropocentric Cognition)' and 'Negentropy', forthcoming in Rosi Braidotti et al., *The Posthuman Glossary* (London: Bloomsbury, 2018).
14. Cf. Serres, 'Vie, information, deuxième principe', p. 46: 'Put briefly: strange means improbable, rare, and the calculus of miracles yields numbers that stand in closest proximity to zero. Hence Borel: the most

improbable phenomena are not ever yielded in this calculus. Hence Monod: When highly improbable phenomena do happen, then they reproduce themselves; they happen because they reproduce themselves. The grand question of chance and entropy already begins to show here. And thus, strangeness receives a precise quantification: on high niveau of information or negentropy. Strange is the echo of chance, and the object is one of necessity. The adjective [strange] does not qualify the substantive, it quantifies it' (my translation).

15. Serres, *Statues*, position 142.
16. I cannot elaborate on this here. It is the complex issue at the core of Serres's Foundations trilogy: the royal victim is one of the origins of geometry within Serres's mathematical realism. Cf. especially *Les Origines de la géometrie* (Paris: Flammarion, 1993), here 'Première dans le rite: La victime royale. Espaces de l'exclusion: origines politiques', pp. 111–54.
17. Michel Serres, *The Birth of Physics in the Text of Lucretius* (Manchester: Clinamen Press, 2000 [1977]), p. 140.
18. Serres, 'Vie, information, deuxième principe', p. 45.
19. Serres, *Statues*, position 143.
20. Archimedes' *The Sand Reckoner* established a theory of how to address large numbers that does not seek to identify their in(de)finiteness, but that proceeds by encrypting it – a procedure that finds wide application in today's informatics, under the name of 'double recursion'. The number system in Archimedes' time had identified as its largest number one that they called 'myriad' (today 10,000, or 108), and Archimedes began to use this name in a recursive manner, by taking that name as a code (rather than as a proper name) which can be operationalised by declaring that it must be a unit of this operative self-referentiality. He built different classes of numbers, myriads of myriads (108 x 108 = 1016) and myriads of myriads of myriads, and so on. Cf. Piergiorgio Odifreddi and S. Barry Cooper, 'Recursive Functions', in Edward N. Zalta (ed.), *The Stanford Encyclopedia of Philosophy* (2012), http://plato.stanford.edu/archives/fall2012/entries/recursive-functions, especially the section 'Double Recursion'. Serres foregrounds the importance of Archimedes' theory in his *Birth of Physics in the Text of Lucretius*: 'Atom-letters do not work like numbers [*chiffres*]. Whatever the base of numeration, in fact, or the alphabet of the cyphering [*chiffrement*], the various combinations of these signs among themselves produces acceptable numbers. Thus, the interconnection of atoms in things, conjunction, is cyphered, nature is coded. Atomic physics discovered the key to the code. Now the cypher is hidden in its turn, since atoms, subliminal, are imperceptible and very great in number. That atoms are letters is a thesis that heralds the great classical philosophies, the idea of cyphering and the secret code, the global working of physical science. Now read Archimedes' The Sand-Reckoner and you'll find a pre-combinative arithmetic that formalises

this idea. Physics is, indeed, an activity of deciphering or decoding.' Serres, *The Birth of Physics*, p. 142.

21. Here we have the crucial diversion Serres's thinking takes from that of the common reception of Leibniz's *Universal Characteristics*. This reception sees in the *characteristica* one basic 'alphabet' that would underlie, in the sense of being a referent to, all alphabets. Serres's reading of Leibniz is one from the point of view of twentieth-century mathematics; it is structuralist, and witnesses in Leibniz's 'interest in a metaphysics that were mathematical' (position 138) his own position on how to deal with the formal language of nineteenth/twentieth-century symbolic and universal algebra. Michel Serres, *Le système de Leibniz et ses modèles mathématiques* (Paris: Presses Universitaire de France, 1968), here cited from the kindle edition, my translation.
22. Ibid., position 481.
23. Ibid., position 575.
24. Ibid., position 182.
25. Ibid., position 180.
26. Ibid., position 188.
27. Ibid., position 224.
28. Ibid., position 224.
29. Ibid., position 224.
30. 'Cela n'est encore qu'une approximation par schéma, mais elle emporte un secret que nous cherchions confusément', ibid., position 235.
31. We have here the old theme of the demonstration of the existence of God by formal proofs. Cf. Jean-Yves Girard's three lectures at the Centre Henri Poincaré (2014) as a background discussion of how, also in mathematics, the formulation of the question predisposes the set of possible answers one can find – leaving the realist scientist with an irreducible uncertainty, even if the idealist scientist will have proved 'certainty': 1/3 'Qu'est-ce qu'une réponse? (l'analytique)', 2/3 'Qu'est-ce qu'une question? (le format)', 3/3 'D'où vient la certitude? (l'épidictique)', available online: https://www.youtube.com/watch?v=f7sT0J74pHI (last accessed 30 June 2016).
32. Cf. Serres, *Le système de Leibniz*, position 224.
33. Here taken from wikipedia.org, search term: self-organization (English wikipedia page).
34. Serres, *Statues*, position 1061.
35. Michel Serres, *L'Incandescent* (Paris: Le Pommier, 2003).
36. Serres, *Statues*, position 1061ff. Indeed, mass plays a transcendental role in Serres: 'Mass conditions the existence of the things of the world that conditions us, and its permanence conditions the universe.'
37. Serres, 'Solides, fluides, flammes', p. 61.
38. It is interesting to realise that these masks operate in the same manner as electronic communication channels do. Cf. my article 'Generic Mediality, Post-Alphabetical?', forthcoming in the proceedings of the 'Philosophy

After Nature' conference, Utrecht 2014, ed. Rosi Braidotti and Rick Dolphjin.

39. Cf. Serres, *The Birth of Physics*, p. 140.
40. etymonline.org
41. Cf. Serres, 'Solides, fluides, flammes', pp. 64–5.
42. Serres, *Le système de Leibniz*, position 580: 'Il n'y a pas là relation de cause à effet, il y a parallélisme de structures, c'est pourquoi nous parlons de modèle mathématique, et seulement de modèle.'
43. The seminal article that provided the crucial key for formulating the natural laws in physics as laws of conservation is Emmy Noether's 'Invariant Variational Problems' [*Invariante Variationsprobleme*] from 1918. This notion of invariance is central for understanding Serres. He defines complexity with reference to such invariant variational problems as 'demarcating a state, a system, where the number of elements, or their reciprocal relations among them, is unaccountably large or inaccessible', Serres, 'Solides, fluides, flammes', p. 61.
44. Unfortunately I cannot expand on these distinctions here. I have elaborated on them in my articles 'Negentropy', 'Invariance' and 'Maxwell's Demon (Non-Anthropocentic Cognition)', in Braidotti et al. *The Posthuman Glossary*.
45. Cf. Michel Serres, 'Information and Thinking/L'Information et la pensée', lecture given at the 'Philosophy After Nature' conference in Utrecht, Netherlands, September 2014, http://cfh-lectures.hum.uu.nl/information-and-thinkinglinformation-et-la-pensee-in-french/ (last accessed 30 June 2016), where one of the sections is entitled 'From Rotating Revolutions to an Expanding Universe'.
46. Serres, *Statues*, position 418.
47. Ibid., position 733.
48. Cf., for example, *The Five Senses*, p. 49: 'The speed of light is more important than its purity. Consider the novelty of this victory: the principal quality of a theory or idea, its oldest value, clarity, is overtaken by the speed at which it travels.' Or Michel Serres, *Rome: First Book of Foundations*, trans. Randolph Burks (London: Bloomsbury, 2015 [1983]), part one 'The Black and the White: The Covering Over'.
49. Cf. *Les Origines de la géometrie*, here 'Première dans le rite: La victime royale. Espaces de l'exclusion: origines politiques', pp. 111–54. Serres's relation to the sacred is obviously a highly complex and intricate one. But throughout his oeuvre he maintains a kind of dialogue with René Girard, to whom he dedicates *Rome*, especially the latter's book *Things Hidden Since the Foundation of the World* (Stanford: Stanford University Press, 1987).
50. Michel Serres, 'Ce que Thalès a vu au pied des Pyramides', in Hermes II, L'Interférence (Paris: Les éditions de minuit, 1972), p. 178.
51. Cf. Michel Serres, 'Moteurs, suivi de régression', in *Hermes IV, La Distribution* (Paris: Les éditions de minuit, 1977), pp. 41–86.

52. Serres, 'Information and Thinking/L'Information et la pensée'.
53. This is what seems to me the core argument in Serres's book *The Natural Contract* (Ann Arbor: University of Michigan Press, 1995 [1990]), especially pp. 24ff.
54. Michel Serres, *The Third-Instructed*, trans. Sheila Faria Glaser and William Paulson (Ann Arbor: University of Michigan Press, 1997 [1991]), p. 52.
55. Serres, *Le système de Leibniz*, position 12499.
56. I cannot expand on this here, unfortunately, but the two key references in Serres's oeuvre are *The Birth of Physics* (1977) and *Genesis* (Ann Arbor: University of Michigan Press, 1995 [1982]).
57. Cf. for a recent account of contemporary mathematics Fernando Zalamea, *Synthetic Philosophy of Contemporary Mathematics* (London: Urbanomics, 2012); see also Giuseppe Longo, 'Synthetic Philosophy of Mathematics and Natural Sciences. Conceptual Analyses from a Grothendieckian Perspective', available on Longo's institutional webpage: http://www.di.ens.fr/users/longo/files/PhilosophyAndCognition/Review-Zalamea-Grothendieck.pdf (last accessed 30 June 2016).
58. Michel Serres, 'Espaces et temps', in *Hermes V, Le passage du nord-ouest* (Paris: Les éditions de minuit, 1980), pp. 67–83, here p. 83.
59. Ibid.
60. Serres, *Statues*, position 1061ff.
61. We can easily think of digital models in these terms, as pockets of informational negentropy.
62. https://en.wikipedia.org/wiki/Sustainability (last accessed 30 June 2016).

CHAPTER 13

Transmythologies

Maria Voyatzaki

Reflecting on the Fault of Forgetting

Should we anticipate re-chaining Prometheus? Not, this time, for his hubris in offering to humans what belonged to the gods, but for his distinctive stolen gifts: fire, curiosity and imagination – what could, in a word, be described as art? Prometheus introduced humans to an ecosystem that was carefully structured by his brother Epimetheus. For the construction of this ecosystem, Epimetheus granted to each of the mortals essential traits that could help them survive or have a particular place in the Cosmos (earth, sky, ocean, underworld), and a particular programmed, axiomatic archetype or model for them to behave and live by, a protocol.[1] Through the gifts of Prometheus alone, humans were 'obliged' to be free and independent of any predetermined protocol in order to be able to survive, to invent in order to be able to live and to create in order to develop. Freedom acted as the *pharmakon* against predefined protocols, but, at the same time, as poison, since the use of the offered gifts alienated humans from the established natural and material ecosystem. Motivated by the illusive myth of being the only species that could create the Cosmos, and not the forgotten ones in possession of a rescue kit offered by divine grace, humans glorified Prometheus for giving them the means to observe, imagine, invent, create, use and develop tools, techniques, machines and technology, but also sciences, politics, arts and certainly architecture.

Architecture, the way we actually think and create it, is an outcome of this obligation for the freedom of humans to become the adored epicentre of the Cosmos. This dominance project was one of the most salient of human activities in the entire era of the Anthropocene because of its impact and effect, whether directly or indirectly, on the Cosmos and its different Epimethean ecosystems. Over this period, architecture was the representation of the glorification of human qualities that could legitimise its cosmic privilege, a statement of the conceptions of truth supporting the human-centred project, and the material expression of a world view according to which the glorified human and the conceived axiomatic truth could create a coherent assemblage.

It is less than twenty years since architectural thinking and practice was affected by the broader questioning of humanism in philosophy, the humanities and the sciences. This questioning directly affected the epicentre of the construction of architecture as a discipline, which was the conception of the human as the ultimate reference point or model for any architectural creative action or decision. This questioning, as Rosi Braidotti would argue, primarily concerned the idea of the transcended and 'teleologically-ordained rational progress'[2] of the biological, discursive – founded on reasoning – and moral expansion of human capabilities. For centuries, architecture, facing the established dualisms between the given and the constructed[3] the natural and the cultural, understood the human through the traits emerging from the 'given'. Its project was to appropriately materialise and adequately affirm important aspects of the given, as defined in each period of its history. From the beauty of the 'given' in the humanism of the Renaissance to the functionality of the 'given' in the Enlightenment and modernity, architecture followed with consistency the anthropocentric line of thought motivated by a reductive understanding of reality, masked behind the foundations of rationality, logic and progress.

It was only by the middle of the twentieth century that architecture started to consider the importance of the 'constructed' and to reorganise its ideas, practices and understandings on the basis of a human reference, ingrained with different aspects of 'otherness' and, at the same time, by the de-naturalisation of the differences and identities recognised in social structures and formations. By considering human development as socially situated and by defining otherness not as humanity's negative and specular counterpart,[4] architecture reconstructed its human-centred epicentre by establishing the human as no longer the ultimate natural species but as a social and cultural construction; a construction that introduces historical temporalities and glorifies the human as unique, with developed expressive and communicative capacities that allow it to create a society and culture that definitely affect the individual's own formation and progress. The importance of this social constructivism for architecture is not limited to the new attitudes of architectural thinking and new tactics of architectural creating. It is primarily the importance of understanding that the interaction between the human and other humans has a strong impact on the construction of this world view and its latent truths.[5] A critique of the assumptions of social constructivism opened up a view of the so-called nonhuman entities that resulted in a posthuman constructivism that focused on the interactions of various actants, that is, between human and nonhuman entities, which facilitated the development of new forms of understanding and manipulating subjectivity in globalised and technologically mediated societies.

The posthuman turn introduced the assumption that the terms of the anthropocentrically established binary oppositions and their excluded middle, like the given and constructed, society and nature, human and nonhuman, alive and matter, subject and object, organic and inorganic, animate and inanimate are substituted by continuums and are mutually inclusive.[6] Moreover, their enforced and radical separation is the result of the hierarchical structures of anthropocentrism that dominated the entire Western philosophical tradition from Greek antiquity to the social constructivist paradigms. The constructed, the material, the nonhuman, the objects, the inorganic or the inanimate are not only entangled in human activities, forming an inseparable continuum, but also become profoundly influential and transformative of human behaviour, perception and experience. Human beings are not really in control of their own creations produced by the techniques and technologies that they invented and imposed on materiality, as was believed for centuries. On the contrary, technology and materiality have a strong claim on human experience, behaviour and perception and, as Bernard Stiegler reveals through his work, the former structurally precedes the latter.[7]

Technical objects are conceived now as inorganic, organised beings possessing their own dynamics, irreducible to physics and biology.[8] This drives contemporary thought to reconsider the self-organising or auto-poietic force of living matter.[9] As scientific and technological advancements blurred the lines of demarcation between the poles, concepts emerging from a broad range of sources, from Bergson's notions of live matter and matter flow, Deleuze's becoming and, much later, similar concepts such as 'living matter' proposed by Rosi Braidotti or 'vibrant matter' or 'vital materiality' introduced by Jane Bennett, invite us to follow a more sophisticated understanding of how techniques and materiality participate in shaping us, as well as the world we bathe in.

All understandings and gains associated with the anthropocentric paradigm now appear to be partial truths supported by theoretical phantoms, alluding to our simplistic understandings of the complexity of the 'real'. If anthropocentrism primarily emerged by and through the use of Prometheus's gifts, we are, then, actually misinterpreting their role in the human adventure, which is not one of discovering a universal truth that could empower us to govern the world by transforming knowledge to power, but of revealing a truth from the specific perspective of the constitution of the problem, since such a concrete reality and objective truth that we are deceived to see by the media does not exist. Reality exists independently of our minds, but what we construct is grounded on reality. It is the mission of all myths and fictions to be the speculative reason that takes us beyond what we see, the very reason why we should perhaps treat Prometheus with sympathy. After all, he gave us the tools and technologies to imagine, to speculate, to move beyond the given state of affairs of material, to create ideas and concepts. It is materiality that forces us to think, but to think means to take that line of flight to speculation. The problem with such speculations arises when they become dogmatic, erroneously totalising agents. Is this, after all, his second hubris, this time not against gods, but against humans, for which he must be re-chained for supplying powerful means that are susceptible to deception in order to cope with a falsified understanding of the Epimethean ecosystem, living in a bubble of false alternatives? Or must we hold a place for him in our narrative? Perhaps commemorate him again, for the same gifts and their use gave us the possibility, even if delayed by Epimetheus, of understanding that Prometheus is only consistent through his 'doubling by his brother'[10] who not only commits the fault of forgetting but also reflects on this fault.

If technical, material objects are inorganic, organised beings, possessing their own dynamics, which give matter the hallmark of vital activity with a strong claim on human experience, behaviour and perception, then what is happening with architecture? As architecture throughout its history has always been defined on the basis of a certain world view and in reference to a certain conception of the human, what will architecture become in the posthuman turn or even more in the nonhuman? How is its broad spectrum of established ideas, values and practices problematised by this new philosophical debate on architectural thinking and practice, in our globalised and technologically mediated world? The purpose of this contribution is to examine these questions by delving into three main issues: the new conceptions of architecture that could emerge from the contemporary materialisms, the new understandings of the material outcome of architectural creative work and the influence of the above conceptions and understandings on the development of the creative process.

The Return of Gaia

By personifying planet Earth while attributing to it divine substance and power, Hesiod in his *Theogony* implicitly attributed to Gaia intelligence, a trait that could guarantee its survival. Gaia was not just the passive support of all living organisms, but was conceived as the veritably alive, a self-regulating entity that could think, contemplate and be conscious of itself through the alive entities – primarily the humans – who were its thinking brain. Even though humans were always an integral part of nature as its dispersed fragments or agents were increasingly interconnected[11] in the sciences and techniques of the Anthropocene, they were conceived and developed as artefacts hostile to nature. Over a span of less than twenty years we have increasingly appreciated humanity as the global intelligence of nature, as its highest level of consciousness is permanently self-enriched. Gaia reappears in its original conception since one of its components, humanity, after creating augmented interconnection mechanisms (social and communication networks, sophisticated technological innovations and the World-Wide Web) developed global intelligence, knowledge and experiences that could now speculate in order to guarantee its protection, adaptation and survival. It is true that we are not as yet a truly collective species, confined and tamed, part of the biosphere, as we are individual creatures. However, we are increasingly becoming conscious of our need to be alienated from the anthropocentric experience of the Anthropocene and to redefine ourselves on the basis of a new relationship with Gaia, in a new conception of politics for its global survival; what we would call G(aia)eopolitics.

Architecture as a discipline has developed, by and large,[12] in the lineage of anthropocentricism and has defined itself on the basis of an understanding of the human as the departure point and the destination of its contemplation and practices. Consistent with this understanding, architecture is primarily conceived as being about ideas: architectural axiomatic ideas, abstractions and their materialisation. Architecture constructs, fabricates architectural ideas, its proper ideas: ideas about space in time, hosting, assuring or generating actions and activities. Architectural ideas are virtualities engaged in a certain way for architectural expression and are inseparable from this expression and the related technical means and materialities involved. Architectural ideas form a normative framework through the definition of a number of *arches;* in other words, principles that govern creative thinking and drive the design process. Architecture is the construction-texturing of *arche*, it is ARCHI-tecture.[13] What is architecture becoming in a world view where the human is decentralised and all the polarities emerging from its conceived dominance are now being reconsidered?

Architecture has always been nourished by a fascination for the human as reference point, inspiration, departure and legitimising argument. Despite its apparent difficulty in being disengaged from its anthropocentric understanding, architecture is affected by the revised human figure conceived as being an inseparable part of the biosphere, its materiality, assembled by human and nonhuman agents,[14] entangled with the inorganic, the inanimate, and, more recently, by *in silico* processes. It actually reflects upon the human and seeks, as it has always done, for the legitimisation of its architectural ideas, for the support of other disciplines, different in each period of its history, but always relevant to its priorities, problematics and questionings. Architectural discourses are proudly plugged into arguments borrowed from other disciplines, where with a lot of amateurism and arbitrage, but also with highly creative enthusiasm, they dig for arguments, positions and axioms capable of being transcribed into architectural principles (*arches*), and to reconstruct the creative process and means towards discovery.

Since the human is no longer conceived as an isolated, auto-referential subject, but is always dependent upon, affected and formatted by its symbiotic ecologies, which are both human and nonhuman, it becomes imperative for architecture to be redefined as the product of a certain co-authorship of human and nonhuman agent constructs, a new 'user' who can be both human and nonhuman, or not necessarily human at all.[15] We can recognise three common and concomitant pillars in the way that contemporary architectural thinking and experimentation organise conceptions of the entanglement of the material and immaterial human with the material and immaterial nonhuman.

The first is time. As this entanglement has an evolutionary duration, the notion of time becomes a constant reference in architectural contemplation. Architecture abandons its timeless auto-referentiality to open itself up to a time-dependent ontology, beyond the past–future time polarity, so as to expose itself to the effects and affects of real time. The accelerated performance of planetary computation rendered time a decisive agent of architectural contemplation and design, not as simulated processes of time-based design but as empowering speculations towards bold and relevant innovation. That conception of time-based design had a strong impact on the understanding of the outcome of architectural work as an object that should incorporate capacities that would enable it to deal with time.

The second pillar is based upon a biological, ecosystemic-ecological understanding of the human and its continuous or permanent dependence on and interaction with any kind of social, material and socio-cultural environments. Biology suggests that there is no living being identical to another, a conviction that brings to the foreground notions such as variation, adaptability, agility, interaction, capacities and potentials that are presented as values that legitimise the principles (*arches*) driving the design process, and form the criteria upon which architectural proposals are judged.

The third pillar is based upon a cybernetic and computational investigation of the relationship between human and nonhuman and the impact this relationship can have on the generation and materialisation of architectural forms. Computation appears as an apparatus that produces phenomena that can enhance the forming power of subjects. However, this machine-mediated power can be activated only if there is a system of relationships through which the subject can be affected and recognise itself.[16] Computation through experimentation, primarily on materiality, can contribute to the creation of new systems of relationships, driving architectural contemplation and making new formations, abstractions and understandings. This attitude is enhanced and legitimised through references to the so-called 'affective turn', which divulges ways of understanding spheres of encounters, interactions and experiences that fall outside the dominant paradigm of representation on which the history of architecture is grounded. Moreover, this trans-disciplinary engagement with the non-verbally represented and non-conscious emotions and affectivity found a fertile ground, prepared by architectural contemplation and design, in the 1990s, when the individualisation of architectural creations and the glorification of the subjective in architectural discourses highlighted the importance of the emotional as a driving force of the creative act.

None of the three pillars has ever appeared in isolation. They have always been intertwined with different priorities, emphases and gravities, allowing for a rich variety of understandings of the basis of the entanglement between human and nonhuman to emerge. An overview of recent examples of architectural experimentation, following the posthuman turn, allows for the recognition of two different conceptions of the human. These conceptions have a direct impact on the reformulation of the social project of architecture, which constitutes the profound, emotional, ideological and cognitive foundation of architecture as discipline and praxis.

On the one hand, this entanglement between human and nonhuman is conceived as an opportunity to develop the natural potential of human capacities and to assure humans a more efficient control of their individual destiny. This conception stems from the latent belief that planetary computation, including the World-Wide Web, big data, artificial intelligence, 3D printing, robotics and nanotechnologies, will act as prosthetics to a deficient human conceived as the Promethean rescued species. Algorithmic governance via planetary computational platforms can augment the human's infinite virtual perfectibility and sovereignty. Hence, the mission of architecture is to contribute to this perfectibility both by the creating subject, the architect, and the appropriating subject, the user.

On the other hand, this entanglement is approached as a new possibility for a new species to be generated based on a machine–human hybridisation plugged into the accidental mega-structure of planetary computation, which can open itself up to new forms of innovation, performativity and non-preconceived ideas. Primarily inspired by the development of artificial intelligence and robotics, this approach does not expect to have the consciousness, memory, intelligence and emotions of the alive, situated in the biological substrate of the human body, but, on the contrary, to open it up to the material realm of the world. We are not moving towards the enhancement or the augmentation of the existing human, but rather towards a radical revision of the human at both the intellectual and biological level.[17] In this case the mission of architecture is to contribute to the innovative alienation of both the creating subject, the architect, and the reciprocal impact on the intellect and bodily experience of the appropriating subject, the user.

In both the aforementioned cases, architecture is mobilised as a creative act neither as the requested answer-solution to a well-defined problem, nor as expectation or inspiration presented in a brief. Rather, it states itself primarily as a speculative question about what architecture can do for a certain trans-disciplinary geopolitical issue related to a broader consideration of its social, political, cultural, ecological and material aspects. In other words, the question is, what can architecture do for the returning Gaia?

Building the *syn*

In ancient and modern Greek, the word *syn* or *sym* means 'with', 'accompanied by' or 'with the contribution of', just as in the Latin *cum* or *con* or *com*. What if we considered architecture to be about the creation of a *syn*? To be about bringing together different distinctive elements?[18] Each period of its history defines its own distinctive elements (constructive, structural, functional, meaningful. . .) in order to create a whole, *holon* (όλον), a *synolon*. This 'togetherness' constitutes an integral part of the way buildings and spaces have been conceived and designed in time. This *syn* is the deep essence of the idea of the designed space that not only epitomises the spirit of the assemblage but also its true purpose, that is, the creation of the *holon*.[19] This is why designed buildings and spaces were always manifestations of the conceptions of the *holon*, and as such distinct captures of world views. They were always conceived as wholes, assembled by parts such that their materialised form and organisational structures could host and affect bodies, objects and conditions, as well as affect minds experiencing them.

The way the outcome of architecture is conceived, nowadays, is profoundly affected by contemporary conceptions of the human and architecture. What could a building be without a nonhuman understanding of the world? What are the references and attributes of the *syn* in the nonhuman era?

The first characteristic of this understanding is the continuum (Greek: συν-έχεια, συν = *con* = plus and έχει from έχω = to have) between the substance of the building and its alterity. The building is no longer considered as something tangible, perceived or presented to the senses (*objectum*) thrown before us (*ob*- 'on the way of' + *jicere* 'to throw'), that is to say, an object on the wayside. It is no longer understood as finite *holon* exposed to our experience as indisputable material, completed, factual or objective and present to function and serve regardless of whether it is liked or not. On the contrary, it is conceived as part of a bigger *holon*, a broader assemblage of other entities, human and nonhuman, infused in an alterity.[20] This alterity, though immanent, is imminent within the building when it becomes open to establishing multiple, unstable, unpredictable and emergent relations with the other entities of this complex and dynamic environment. The building as an assemblage is conceived as a larval subject[21] whose evolution not only depends on the 'genetic' information it carries, but is formed through the broader economic, political, ethical and aesthetic context in which it grows. As part of such an assemblage, the building is no longer constrained by its own materiality. It becomes an interface in a dynamic system of relationships depended upon and defined by a flux of information and data, a point in a point cloud. Thus, between its proper substance and its alterity there has to be a continuum: a *syn+eheia*.

This continuum is assured through a second characteristic of the contemporary understanding of the building, which is the *sym+biosis* established between buildings and the human. Buildings are conceived not only as material substances, but as alive through their dynamic folding and unfolding in their surrounding continuum. Architects attribute life to them by seeing them as objects beyond sheltering us or beyond having material expression, for not only do they develop an affective relationship with us, but they 'underwrite as well as undermine social arrangements'. Buildings and the things in and around them are understood not only as promoting human life, 'earning the name Architecture when doing so justly and beautifully, but also as having lives of their own. These lives require bringing-into-being as well as care and regard thereafter, out of respect, in return for their services.'[22] Buildings are conceived as alive either as a material embodiment to the human, as an efficient and inseparable extension of its body, augmenting its capacities and performativity, or as auto-regulating systems that can absorb intelligence and cognition from humans to create new and, to a certain extent, unpredictable symbiotic relationships with their human and nonhuman environments. In such a symbiotic condition, buildings play an important role in the (auto-)regulatory dynamics of the evolution of Gaia and constitute an important agent of geopolitics.

The third characteristic of the conception of the building, aligned with the human–nonhuman continuum, is the sym-pathetic and synergetic relationships it establishes with its human, natural and material environments. As an assemblage in a dynamic continuum, the building has to act or react so that it can be synergetic. At the same time, it will have to endure the effects of the actions of others so that the assemblage will affect and be affected. In this perpetual dynamic process the building is no longer conceived as an artificial and mute object, an artefact or inanimate object. It becomes an intelligent, alive and affective system and environment. It is so neither in the metaphorical sense that all other architectural paradigms have followed as a reference point for their design proposals, nor in animistic terms such that the building has been attributed a kind of anima; but in biogenetic terms it has a protosubjectivity that carries, uses and (trans)forms information as it evolves and develops.

The fourth characteristic of the new conception of the building is that it emerges from the praxis of multiple agents, parameters and relationships. It is the result of a syn-praxis. By shifting the essence from its internal elements and relationships into other complex, dynamic and fluid assemblages, the building is understood as the temporary result of a continuous praxis, emerging from the information flux, affecting the relationships with other agents, a *pragma* (the Greek word for thing) in the making or becoming. It needs energy and information to interact, self-engage and get self-organised in an affective, sympathetic and symbiotic relation with its inhabitants, inasmuch as with all other agents involved from its design to its fabrication, to its inhabitation, to its survival, mutation or even death. It is attached to a series of transformable interfaces that form its own ecosystem. The building, as carrier of information, ceases to have any presence unless it is in symbiosis with the flow of this information in its body and its broader ecosystem. To exist, a building will have to be able to establish dynamic relationships with other agents of this ecosystem, towards forming a specific assemblage of agents, a machinic assemblage, a *synpraxis*.

To think before or after the myth? The building of the nonhuman era reflects a new conception of time. It does not merely constitute foresight or hindsight, not focusing simply on anticipating the future or contemplating the past. The building is bound up to its temporality and futurity, these two seemingly opposing and polemic binary understandings of human contemplation that have nourished cultural creation for time immemorial. In this way the building opens up its 'doors' and gives 'space' to both Prometheus and Epimetheus[23] to anticipate, contemplate and inhabit it as part of a broader ecosystem. Material + immaterial, natural + artificial, techne + chronos,[24] past + present + future will be syn+chronic.

Creative Matter

Conceptions about architecture define the 'why' of the creative act, and conceptualisations of the building define the 'what'. Further elaboration is required for the 'how', the process – the third structural element of the creative act. The 'who', the fourth element, in the anthropocentric paradigm was the architect-human and as such was almost always beyond any specific consideration.[25] The 'how', the process, was the expertise of the 'who', the regulated and regulating action of a subject, the arranging activity or assemblage process followed by the architect.

In a non-historical unfolding of the genealogies of architectural materiality, an ongoing juxtaposition lies between Alberti's dispassionate statement that one can think of a form without thinking of its material expression and Brunelleschi's hands-on or experimental, emergent explorations with material properties and capacities towards form-determination, thus triggering discussion on the distinction between designer and master builder, thinker and maker,[26] royal and nomadic science, noble scientist and metallurgist,[27] discursive and affective, sapient and sentient,[28] top-down and bottom-up, epistemology and ontology. Almost six centuries after Brunelleschi, Mies van der Rohe reconnected form and material by defining architecture as the art of organising two bricks together, while half a century later Karl Chu defined it as the art of arranging two bits, or quibits (quantum bits) together.[29] We are following a progressive shift in the definition of the nature of 'why' (the art of) entangled with the 'what' to be created, arranged or assembled, moving from the dominance of the formal to the dominance of the material, be it brick or quibit. This shift has a strong impact on the 'how'.

For centuries, architecture took shape in the formulation of the project: projects about buildings, spaces and spatial arrangements. The project was always an operational, individual or collective anticipation of a desired future. As Benjamin Bratton indicates, 'the word "a project" is a projection of a potential intervention into a situation defined by a certain spatial and temporal range'.[30] Its etymology reveals the action of throwing ahead, from the Latin *projicere,* which has the same meaning as the Greek πρόβλημα (*provlima*, problem) or πρό(σ)θεσις (pro(s)thesis, pro-position).[31] It means that the project has an anticipatory logic of projecting into the future, hence, a speculation. An anticipation is an idea, an expectation that drives the design process and defines the criteria for the evaluation of the project's outcomes. This was the foundation of the design activity in the anthropocentric paradigm: the human thinks, expects and transcribes anticipations into architectural ideas or concepts that are translated into operational and meaningful forms. The materiality of the form would be defined after the completion of the formal elaboration.[32]

Is this structure of 'how' valid for a 'what' as conceived in the nonhuman era and as presented above? Since the 'what' is conceived as live, evolving, emerging and generated in a dynamic, sympathetic and symbiotic continuum, its development can no longer be dependent upon a deterministic concept or an ideation of its formal and material substance. The contemporary 'what' is conceived as generated through the dynamics of intra-actions, as Karen Barad suggests,[33] between human and nonhuman agencies. The main issue that the 'how' copes with, in this case, is how materiality will become an active agent in the creative process and how it will undertake morphogenetic responsibilities. In other words, how will matter become creative? This understanding drives architecture to move from a concept-based design process to the design of a system of relations that will organise the different parameters affecting the constitution of the 'what', a machine that will mobilise the, more or less, unpredictable interaction of agents and will undertake the 'genetic' process of becoming from which the 'what' will be formalised. We are heading towards a new situation, from the 'what is arranged' to the 'what is arranging'.

Over the last ten years we have been experiencing the progressive predominance of the idea that matter (including that part of matter that is human embodiment) is intelligent and self-organising, destabilising the established sovereignty of the human over the nonhuman. In this way, matter is neither dialectically opposed to culture, nor to technological mediation, but is continuous with them.[34] However, it does not distinguish the dominance of one species – be it human or nonhuman – over the dominance of another. Matter is no longer conceived as just the substance of the 'what' but as an agent in the 'arranging' process.

This position shifts away from the anthropocentric understanding according to which form is imposed on inanimate matter through the exertion of anthropogenic power. This position is accompanied by certain ethics, politics and economies of post-colonialist and advanced capitalist contexts, promoting aesthetics that follow different typologies that obey laws from which architectural values emerge, such as sameness, regularity, repetition, perfection, rationality, meaning, clarity, continuity. These values come from the difference in understanding the 'why' and are top-down, Newtonian and deterministic. We can trace the origins of this anthropocentric conception of matter in Aristotle's hylomorphic doctrine, in which matter was conceived as the passive and indeterminate substance that underwent change, while form was the constant, actualising principle. Architecture responds to this position through the hegemony of the architect to impose form by telling a material what to do, according to the prevailing values. This object-based design of disciplinary societies[35] uses materials as means to express and fulfil this role through the exploitation of their linear properties. In order to facilitate the efficient materialisation of values, tools and machines were invented and introduced to control and harness the arbitrary and recalcitrant emergence of nature. The machine's role was destined to produce an aesthetics of speed, repetition, accuracy and perfection by obeying the architect-ruler.

According to contemporary thought, matter is self-organising, active, morphogenetic and inhabited by singularities.[36] Self-organising matter is emergent and follows no laws, which allows for variation and enriches its expressivity. Manuel DeLanda strengthens Aristotle's accidental nature of form as a contingent entity, an entity as an effect of processes in time.[37] He proposes the replacement of Aristostle's hylomorphic doctrine by morphogenesis, as well as the replacement of standardised and controlled performance by the pursuit of active and changeable performance or even performativity. The emerging question is how such problematics have fostered the materiality of architecture. Architecture is now oriented towards variation and the non-standard, conceived as a condition coming from programmable differences of significance. Scripting is an antidote against standardisation in materiality.[38] Design does not refer to the design of form in a top-down trajectory, but the design of a system, of a set of rules. Materials have immanent properties and can be the driving force as vibrant, with morphogenetic capacities and resistant behaviours to their recalcitrant extremes.[39] What is the materiality of an architecture that emerges from the shift from an object-based to a process-based design?

In the previous section we examined the 'what' as a *holon*, a 'togetherness', a *synolon* or an assemblage. Whether assembling has to do with the brick as a standardised form of materiality ordered from above, the architect, or with the quibit – the immaterial nature of a quantum – it is about the definition of rules, hierarchies and logics through which a *synolon* is assembled, syn-thesised/com-posed or syn-taxed; it is constructed. However, there are fundamental differences in the way the 'how' is structured in the two different natures and conceptions of the 'what' to be arranged that are described above. Moreover, although the brick and the quibit share the same epistemological uncertainty, it is only the latter that conveys its ontological indeterminacy.

Mute bricks and live bits or quibits open up the discussion between human and nonhuman perceptions of the materiality of architecture, reintroducing a dispute regarding the epistemological brick versus the ontological quibit, while omitting what preceded the brick, that is, clay and water, its primordial ingredients, or the experimentation with materiality that produces affects. It is a way of understanding, a way of cutting the world up into smaller pieces in order to gain a richer and different insight. Recent philosophical debate focuses on issues related to machine mediation, transversal cuttings and readings of the world as part of the non-anthropocentric shift. This debate turns the Kantian human away from its centralised self by enabling it to see with eyes that are mediated by machines, materials and other species at different spatio-temporal scales. The Kantian human, who would statically stand to overlook in order to understand the stationary landscape, could now see it in time and motion through a vehicular – mediated – trajectory in which time, accelerated, acquires motion for both the landscape and the human. Machine mediation offers viewings at different scales and resolutions[40] and effectuates variable cuts of the world whereby new knowledge is constructed.

Two drawbacks can be observed in the way machines are mediated in architectural design. The first is that the high speed of machine mediation accentuates the time lapse in which architecture follows a world view shift, a characteristic handicap of architecture that is more acute due to the inherent speed of information flow in the information society. Despite its efforts to change the receptive apparatuses with which the world would be seen and understood through the mediation of different machines, materials and other species at various spatio-temporal scales, architecture has not succeeded in radically repositioning the human away from the centre. Contemporary technological development and computation have augmented acceleration erratically, hindering the necessary time for elaboration, maturation and development of the cognitive, conceptual or refractive dimensions of experience.[41]

The second drawback of machine mediation in experiments with materials is the defeat of reasoning by the dominant and abundant affects driving the production of infinite alternatives. A non-anthropocentric view, in this case, is substituted by a superfluous anti-humanism.[42] The inherent speed of contemporary technological development and computation and their capacity to generate infinite and overwhelming alternatives with little or no evidence of speculation renders them false.[43] Designers have a naive optimism that new techniques will change everything. This abundance of affects not only does not relocate and reposition the human, but shortens its long circuits and disables its potential to update reason away from the banality of the here and now.[44] Moreover, the hypertrophy of sensation accentuates the corporeal against its cognitive counterpart, which is quickly consumed and becomes addictive to further demand that, due to its immediacy, retreats from judgement.

Materialism can be useful due to materiality's capacity to act as a force for inventing new modes of reasoning. If the posthuman were a force beyond the human as a rational entity, our project would now be how to find a new, updated rationality. Neomaterialism has been criticised for an overemphasis on the singularities of the here and now and for lacking the capacity to create abstract schemes through which we can aspire to a collective agency; a reason why the posthuman might be considered dead. The project, our project, should be about redefining the human by combining its affective and cognitive aspects. If we think about the affective in terms of Deleuze and Massumi,[45] we then have an opening up of future alternatives that force us to think. The misconception of the Deleuzian scheme is that many thinkers trapped Deleuze's thinking in the virtual. Deleuze, on the contrary, argued for the value of the actual, stating that the virtual is the domain through which we can construct myths with their speculative capacity. To remain in the virtual and to be optimistic is a fatalistic error since it creates the abundance of alternatives. The 'art of dosage' is this experimentation with the 'what if'. The radical deterritorialisation is to create a new myth, a new earth and 'the people yet to come'.[46] This urges further clarification of another misconception dear to digital architects: the difference between the 'becoming of continuity' and the 'continuity of becoming'[47] or 'the becoming of a myth' versus 'the myth of the continuous becoming'. These notions lead us not to think that it is the same to argue that what becomes is a continuous world and what is continuous is the becoming of that world.

Xeno-materiality

The impact of anthropocentrism on architecture and the different myths, abstractions, axioms or protocols architecture has been affiliated with, have shaped its history as a discipline in a perpetual effort to construct social narratives of various world views in time. Architecture has always been engaged, inspired and directed by its own mythologies, which organise and concretise arguments for its own social and cultural projects. It is now challenged to get away from the commitment to represent its pre-existing mythologies and to move towards the construction of new ones yet to come, and to virtually emerge from new speculations on the ontology of material beyond the human as a cognitive and sensing entity. Architecture is looking towards updating its axiomatics in a materiality through which it should be considered as an ethico-aesthetic praxis. It is looking for the creative abilities of the new conceptions of matter. How can materiality's mental and abstract pole affect its course so that it will be further folded and become abstract thinking and reason without losing its close affinity to trouble and complexity?[48] Should we not be delaying decisions on linearity or the so-called affective turn, even the question of what is it that we are discussing: the materiality of construction or the construction of materiality?[49]

The new project of architecture is to allow the sensing of the world differently through machine-mediated experimentation in order to generate new temporary and circumstantial axioms and updated abstractions that operate as speculative spatio-temporal organisations. Contemporary architectural experiments, taking place in different research and educational environments and practices, are now following two different directions. There are experiments either with materiality or within materiality. In the first case, experiments focus on new materials, new fabrication methods, new techniques, thus predicating the emergence of new design methods and processes. In this way they tend to reduce architecture to a technical process, strongly related to engineering, and implicitly allied and aligned with the positivist myth that technological development can save the world and can resolve problems and contemporary questions related to the built environment. In the second case, experiments within materiality start from the critique of the top-down logic of the previous case and are oriented towards the creation of possibilities for emergent spatio-temporal material constructs. This approach, a panacea, is very close to being trapped in a misleading optimism that everything that emerges from bottom up is efficient and for this reason appropriate.

For any experimentation on the materiality of architecture to be valid and relevant to the new project of architecture, it might have to combine top-down and bottom-up trajectories, 'an abductive inference that synthetically manipulates parameters'.[50] This experimentation is about materials, but also about speculation. It is about the ways in which qualities can be embedded in this experimentation, but also about the ways in which new qualities of crafting can be discovered by working with machines. Furthermore, it is about the exploitation of the granularity (dustism) that large data sets can provide. Inhuman affects revise reasoning and reposition culture as a speculative force that parts away from the banality of presentism.[51]

Architecture might have to cross-infect human and nonhuman for a symbiotic creativity that would yield new materials whose potential to self-organise would create flows of heterogeneous spatio-temporalities and variations. This heterogeneity, a pursued abstraction related to the 'other', could be achieved by fading in and out material trajectories. New materials, or what Robin Mackay (following Lyotard) would call *les immatériaux*, 'have nothing to do with the dematerialisation or the disappearance of materials into the spiritual or the virtual',[52] but with materials whose properties we can invent even if they do not exist. Mackay carries on proposing speculations on anonymous materials, employing high throughput computation to embed desired properties at the quantum level. However, to embed certain characteristics and qualities of matter to computation we need a passage through the abstract. With this statement he forces an update and urges for a bridge between the affective (empirical) and the rational (abstract):

> the immaterial materials suffer from their invisibility but it is here that a culture is fashioned through images, sounds and words. Legitimisation of these materials allows them a proper place. But this already entails a kind of destabilisation of the human and an admission to inhabit a culture that is no longer ours, it's no longer human.[53]

Materiality could be thought of at a micro-scale, such as dust that can 'powder' and granulate geometries, producing random otherness thereafter. Algorithms are like managing and manipulating matter in its dust existence. Dust geometries are a cognitive construct; they are abstractions. The big data idea and its relationship with materiality allow us to consider thousands of particles at the same moment, in a way that ordinary, limited and small data sets could not achieve. Particles not only change under observation (particle waves) but also in the way they observe and interact with other entities. In a sense 'intra-action' is prior to interaction.[54] Think of intra-action as the analogue, the event, the matter prior to the digital, the objects and their relations, the material. By moving down scales we start to observe an unprecedented reality of matter that redistributes and reconstructs materiality, a new aesthetic vocabulary as Parikka[55] would suggest; hence, a new architecture altogether, an architecture away from the tyranny of the grand geometers. The ontological indeterminacy is coupling with our epistemological uncertainty, and this forces us to invent new orientations in construction and fabrication.

Computation and fabrication were long associated with the aesthetics of the continuum. Philosophical virtual continuity was represented in artefacts, as actual curvilinear constructions of a continuously deposited paste. As a consequence, actual entities lost their discreteness and buildings became landscapes. Conversely, a discrete approach to the actual never betrays its virtual continuity. Discrete fabrication, in this sense, can yield individual or separate unit production in either low volumes with very high complexity, or in high volumes of low complexity that require extremely flexible manufacturing systems that can improve quality and time-to-market speed while cutting costs and limiting waste. Fabrication is discrete either in its printed voxels or in its aggregates of modular elements. Agent-based, cellular and 3D-printed voxels are cases of a discrete conception of design that suggests sympathy as a mode of continuity.

Robotics could acquire an added value in the exploration of unprecedented fabrication techniques and unimaginable scales of construction. A world can be constructed and approached at a scale radically different from the human scale. A domain for the construction of new conceptual resources is now wide open. It would be a fatal error to use and apply the same concepts interscalarly. Negarestani is right about the inadequacy of both top-down and bottom-up models, precisely because they descend or ascend scales with the same conceptual armature.[56] By pulverising, we aim to revise our concepts, in other words, to re-cut the world and to allow for the constitution of new events, new materials, new construction methods, new scales. Machines provide us with a new sensibility.[57] As Bratton states, 'new technologies do not allow for new forms, but new technologies allow for new models about what is to be made'.[58]

New speculative, but not dogmatic, axioms and mythologies are expressed with the machinic parrhesia; the world, and therefore architecture, becomes a challenging project. Digitising the analogue, once again, but this time with aspirations towards a new earth, the returning Gaia, by experimenting with its dust we can construct new perspectives on matter. It is experimentation with the 'other', the 'xenon' that aims at proposing a new way of forming an innovative view of earth by redefining its geopolitics and territorial disputes, from polluted waters that travel through nations to micro particles in the air. Architecture is working on 'xenomateriality' to define new polities, new spatio-temporal assemblages with specific demands.

Architecture is working for the construction of a new world view, a new mythology with universal appeal, welcoming the returning Gaia. A return that reunites and reconciles Prometheus and Epimetheus together with all the myths they have created: the myths of nature, the myths of the alive, the myths of the machine, the myths of technologies, the myths of culture, the myths of the human, the myths of matter and the myths of the environment. The new project of architecture is to criss-cross transversally all these mythologies; to construct transmythologies.

Notes

1. Luc Ferry, *Mythologie et philosophie n°5: Prométhée et la boite de Pandore* Vol. 5 – *Prométhée et la boîte de Pandore – La naissance de l'humanité, Le Figaro* (Paris: Plon, 2014).
2. Rosi Braidotti, *The Posthuman* (Cambridge: Polity, 2013), p. 13.
3. Ibid., pp. 2–3.
4. Ibid., p. 15.
5. '[I]t is this common and collective process to which "social construction" refers, not to the various materials from which things are made'; Bruno Latour, paper prepared for a chapter in Don Idhe (ed.), *Chasing Technology: Matrix of Materiality*, Indiana Series for the Philosophy of Science (Indiana University Press, 2003), pp. 27–46, http://www.bruno-latour.

fr/sites/default/files/87-CONSTRUCTIVISM-GB.pdf, position p. 3 (last accessed 15 March 2017).

6. Brian Massumi, *What Politics Can Learn from Animals* (Durham, NC: Duke University Press, 2014), p. 51: 'The logic of mutual inclusion dodges the infernal alternative between the solitude of generic differences and the gogo of undifferentiation upon which these accusations of anthropomorphism are implicitly based.'
7. Bernard Stiegler, *Technics and Time, 1: The Fault of Epimetheus*, trans. Richard Beardsworth and George Collins (Stanford: Stanford University Press, 1998).
8. Ibid., p. 17.
9. Braidotti, *The Posthuman*, p. 3.
10. Stiegler, *The Fault of Epimetheus*, p. 186.
11. Luc Ferry, *La révolution transhumaniste* (Paris: Plon, 2016).
12. Peter Eisenmann, 'Post-Functionalism', *Oppositions*, 6 (1976), reprinted in M. Hays (ed.), *Architecture Theory since 1968* (Cambridge, MA: MIT Press, 1998), pp. 234–9: 'In the present essay, he historicizes such concerns as part of a new episteme, a posthumanistic paradigm heralded by James Joyce, Arnold Schoenberg, Hans Richter, and others, and theorized in the antihumanism of Michel Foucault and Claude Levi-Strauss', https://mitpress.mit.edu/books/architecture-theory-1968 (last accessed 15 March 2017).
13. Daniel Payot, *Le Philosophe et l'architecte: Sur quelques déterminations philosophiques de l'idée d'architecture* (Paris: Aubier Montaigne, 1982). '*Arche* (ancient Greek: *ἀρχή*) is a Greek word with the primary senses of "beginning", "origin" or "source of action" (*εξ' ἀρχής:* from the beginning, or *εξ' ἀρχής λόγος:* the original argument), and later first principle or element, first so used by Anaximander (Simplicius in *Ph.* 150.23), principles of knowledge (*ἀρχαί*) (Aristot., *Metaph.* 995b8). By extension, it may mean "first place, power", "method of government", "empire, realm", "authorities" (in plural: *ἀρχαί*), "command". The first principle or element corresponds to the "ultimate underlying substance" and "ultimate undemonstrable principle". In the philosophical language of the archaic period (8th–6th century BC), *arche* (or *archai*) designates the source, origin or root of things that exist. In ancient Greek philosophy, Aristotle foregrounded the meaning of *arche* as the element or principle of a thing, which although undemonstrable and intangible in itself, provides the conditions of the possibility of that thing'; https://en.wikipedia.org/wiki/Arche (last accessed 15 March 2017).
14. All these distinctions could be understood through the ways in which humanity is provisionally redefined to effectuate a cut through which we see architecture.
15. Benjamin Bratton, 'On Speculative Design', *Dis Magazine*, February 2016, http://dismagazine.com/discussion/81971/on-speculative-design-benjamin-h-bratton/ (last accessed 15 March 2017).

16. Claire Colebrook, in the preface of her book *Blake, Deleuzian Aesthetics, and the Digital* (London: Continuum, 2012), p. x, considers as a condition of subjectivity with Platonic references that 'a subject can only speak, conceptualize or act if there is already, in advance, some system of relations through which he can affect himself, return to himself and recognize himself'.
17. Ibid.
18. Maria Voyatzaki, 'Building ++', in Kas Oosterhuis (ed.), *New Generation Building* (Delft: Baltzer Science Publishers, 2014), pp. 61–4.
19. Here *holon* is conceived not in its holistic sense but as an assemblage of multiplicities capable of expressing themselves in univocity, as determined by Deleuze.
20. Félix Guattari, 'On Machines', ed. A. Benjamin, *Complexity, Journal of Philosophy and the Visual Arts*, 6 (1995), pp. 8–12.
21. Gilles Deleuze, *Difference and Repetition* (New York: Columbia University Press, 1994).
22. All this was stated on the symposium call website 'The Secret Life of Buildings', 17–22 October 2016 at the University of Texas at Austin, School of Architecture: 'We meet buildings only at their surfaces: feet to floor, eyes to walls, hands to handles. We breathe their air; we hear their echoes. But buildings are also objects, busy in ways that do not occur to us: protecting, quivering, heating, decaying, storing, piping, embracing, rejecting, organizing and flattering . . . these among many actions on our behalf, and more on their own. Buildings are real, not just special effects. They have attitudes; they exemplify as well as underwrite as well as undermine social arrangements. We do not completely understand them and they do not completely understand us, in part because history fades and in part because patience is unevenly distributed. [. . .] "Speculative Realism" and within that, "Object Oriented Ontology", name trends in recent philosophy that seem especially suited to thinking of architecture in this non- anthropocentric way'; http://soa.utexas.edu/events/secret-life-buildings (last accessed 15 March 2017).
23. Les Amis, *Commemorating Epimetheus*, ed. Eric Ramsey (West Lafayette: Purdue University Press, 2009).
24. Stiegler, *The Fault of Epimetheus*.
25. Architectural discourses, from their appearance in the Renaissance with Alberti's ten books, have primarily dealt with the 'why', the 'what' and the 'how'. The discourse on the 'who' is mainly centred either on the education of the architect or on the structure of creative thinking, both aimed at the improvement of the 'how'.
26. Mario Carpo, *The Alphabet and the Algorithm* (Cambridge, MA: MIT Press, 2011).
27. Gilles Deleuze and Félix Guattari, *A Thousand Plateaus, Nomadology: The War Machine*, trans. Brian Massumi (Minneapolis: University of Minnesota Press, 1981).

28. Reza Negarestani, 'The Labor of the Inhuman', in R. Mackay and A. Avanessian (eds), *Accelerate: The Accelerationist Reader* (London: Urbanomic, 2014).
29. Karl Chu once said: 'no longer is architecture the art of putting two bricks together, as Mies van der Rohe once suggested, instead, it has become the art of arranging two bits, or quibits, together', http://www.presidents-medals.com/Entry-9891 (last accessed 15 March 2017).
30. Bratton, 'On Speculative Design'.
31. Cf. Stiegler, *The Fault of Epimetheus*, p. 152.
32. Cf. Voyatzaki, 'Building ++'.
33. Cf. Karen Barad, 'Intra-actions', *Mousse Magazine 34*, ed. Adam Kleinman, summer 2012, http://moussemagazine.it (last accessed 15 March 2017).
34. For example, in her book *The Posthuman*, p. 35, Braidotti introduces this statement in her monistic philosophy of becoming.
35. Michel Foucault, *Discipline and Punish* (New York: Vintage, 1975).
36. Deleuze and Guattari, in their book *A Thousand Plateaus*, reacted to the Romanesque rigidity and aesthetics that derived from typologies. They refer to the Gothic as a method and not a style.
37. Manuel DeLanda, 'Material Expressivity' (2009), https://lebbeuswoods.wordpress.com/2009/01/05/manuel-delanda-matters-4/ (last accessed 15 March 2017)
38. Mark Burry, *Scripting Cultures* (Chichester: John Wiley and Sons, 2011).
39. Jane Bennett, *Vibrant Matter: A Political Ecology of Things* (Durham, NC: Duke University Press, 2010).
40. Contemplation, as an issue in contemporary architecture, more than ever before relates to the content of Lewis Carroll's book *Alice in Wonderland*.
41. Having said that, is it not this acceleration that provides a certain alienation that defies the reflective practice of the human? My argument is more about a refractive practice than a reflective one, and the acceleration of computation can help in this. It is true though that the decision-making capacities of machines return concepts and ideas that suit the regimes of power that mobilise those technologies, such as Google, the stock market or drone warfare.
42. For further elaboration on the effects of anti-humanism on the intellectual world, see Rosi Braidotti's book *The Posthuman*.
43. Such is the case of the continuity of the white paste of the closed systems of parametricism, where systems are linearly translated into forms.
44. Claire Colebrook, *Death of the Posthuman, Essays on Extinction, Vol. 1* (Ann Arbor: Open Humanities Press, 2014).
45. Both Deleuze and Massumi take Spinoza's affect a step towards the abstraction of Samuel Butler's term, Erewhon.
46. Gilles Deleuze and Félix Guattari, *A Thousand Plateaus: Capitalism and Schizophrenia*, trans. Brian Massumi (Minneapolis: University of Minnesota Press, 1987).

47. Luciana Parisi, *Contagious Architecture: Computation, Aesthetics and Space* (Cambridge, MA: MIT Press, 2013).
48. Donna Haraway, 'Staying with the Trouble: Anthropocene, Capitalocene, Chthulucene', in Jason W. Moore (ed.), *Anthropocene or Capitalocene? Nature, History and the Crisis of Capitalism* (Oakland: Kairos PM Publishers, 2016).
49. Emmanouil Zaroukas, 'The Myths of the Human: The Human as Political Being; The Political Substance of Architecture', lecture given at Aristotle University of Thessaloniki, 23 March 2016.
50. Negarestani, 'The Labor of the Inhuman', p. 436. The crucial part is that this discourse takes place within the abstract mode of thinking, that is, logic. We can find here both Whitehead and Peirce arguing for the abductive premises of logic. Whitehead argues about the ingress of eternal objects within the actual occasion that forces that occasion to be speculative about its future.
51. Emmanouil Zaroukas, 'Architecture at the Age of Ant(i(que))-humanism', lecture given at Aristotle University of Thessaloniki, 21 December 2015.
52. *Les immatériaux* is a term borrowed from the exhibition 'Les Immatériaux' organised by Jean-François Lyotard and Thierry Chaput, director of the Centre de Création Industrielle de Paris, at Centre Pompidou, March 1985, thirty-five years after its inauguration.
53. Robin Mackay, 'Matter, Material, Immaterial: Art, Philosophy and Curating Thirty Years after Lyotard', lecture, https://www.artandeducation.net/classroom/video/66062/matter-material-immaterial-art-philosophy-and-curating-thirty-years-after-lyotard-by-robin-mackay (last accessed 15 March 2017).
54. Barad, 'Intra-actions'.
55. Jussi Parikka, 'Earth Forces, Contemporary Land Arts, Technology and New Materialist Aesthetics', *Cultural Studies Review*, 21.2 (2015), pp. 47–75, http://epress.lib.uts.edu.au/journals/index.php/csrj/index (last accessed 15 March 2017).
56. Negarestani, 'The Labor of the Inhuman'.
57. Emmanouil Zaroukas, 'From Hacking to the Incomputable', lecture given at Aristotle University of Thessaloniki, 23 December 2015.
58. Bratton, 'On Speculative Design'.

Notes on Contributors

Jen Archer-Martin is Subject Coordinator of Spatial Design, Te Kunenga ki Pūrehuroa Massey University, Aotearoa, New Zealand. Recent creative works include *taking note(s)_performing care*, durational documentation performance at the symposium *Performing, Writing*, Wellington, NZ (2017), www.takingnotes.performingwriting.com, and *Make/Use* (2015), www.makeuse.nz.

Levi R. Bryant is Professor of Philosophy at Collin College. He is the author of *The Democracy of Objects* (Open Humanities Press, 2011) and *Onto-Cartography: An Ontology of Machines and Media* (Edinburgh University Press, 2014). He has written widely on speculative realism, object-oriented ontology, Deleuze, Lacan and Badiou.

Vera Bühlmann is Professor of Architecture Theory at Vienna Technical University, and head of the Department of Architecture Theory and Philosophy of Technics (ATTP) (www.attp.tuwien.ac.at) at the Institute for Architectural Sciences, Faculty of Architecture and Spatial Planning. Between 2003 and 2007 she co-edited three books and co-curated several events and symposia on design research as well as scenography. In 2006 she received the Edward Bruns Essay Prize from the Society of Literature, Sciences and the Arts for her essay 'Intelligent skin – real virtual', awarded by N. Katherine Hayles.

Mark Burry has been Founding Director of the Smart Cities Research Institute, located at the Swinburne University of Technology, since May 2017, after his post at the University of Melbourne, in 2014, as Professor of Urban Futures at the Faculty of Architecture, Building and Planning. He is a practising architect who has published internationally on two main themes: putting theory into practice with regard to procuring 'challenging' architecture, and the life, work and theories of the architect Antoni Gaudí. He has been Senior Architect to the Sagrada Família Basilica Foundation.

Marcos Cruz is Professor of Innovative Environments and director of the BiotA Lab at the Bartlett, where he also leads the newly created MArch/MSc in Biointegrated Design. His most recent publications include the authored book *Unit 20 / Hyper-articulated Morphologies* (List Lab, 2016) and 'Bioreceptive Design', *Architectural Research Quarterly* (2016).

Manuel DeLanda is an artist, philosopher, film-maker, computer programmer and independent researcher in cognitive and computer science. He is the author of *War in the Age of Intelligent Machines* (Swerve, 1991), *A Thousand Years of Nonlinear History* (Swerve, 1997), *Intensive Science and Virtual Philosophy* (Bloomsbury, 2002), *A New Philosophy of Society* (Continuum, 2006), *Deleuze: History and Science* (Atropos, 2010), *Philosophy and Simulation* (Continuum, 2011) and *Philosophical Chemistry* (Bloomsbury, 2015). He currently teaches in the architecture departments of Princeton University, University of Pennsylvania and the Pratt Institute.

Pia Ednie-Brown is an Associate Professor in the School of Architecture and Design at RMIT University in Melbourne, Australia. She has edited two books: *Plastic Green: Designing for Environmental Transformation* (RMIT Press, 2009) and an issue of *Architectural Design, AD: The Innovation Imperative: Architectures of Vitality* (Wiley, 2013).

Kas Oosterhuis is a Professor at Qatar University in Doha, further expanding the Hyperbody brand into a global network of advanced research groups. He is a practising architect, having realised ground-breaking and award-winning projects in the Netherlands, Hungary and the United Arab Emirates. His most recent book is entitled *Towards a New Kind of Building, a Designer's Guide to Nonstandard Architecture* (NAi Publishers, 2011). The LIWA tower, Capital Centre District, Abu Dhabi, 2014, a 20,000 sq m office building, is his most recent award-winning project.

Jussi Parikka is a Professor at the Winchester School of Art, University of Southampton. His recent books include *A Geology of Media* (University of Minnesota Press, 2015) and, with Joasia Krysa, the co-edited volume *Writing and Unwriting (Media) Art History: Erkki Kurenniemi in 2048* (MIT Press, 2015).

Luciana Parisi is Reader in Cultural Theory, chair of the PhD Programme in Cultural Theory and co-director of the Digital Culture Unit at Goldsmiths, London. She is the author of *Abstract Sex: Philosophy, Biotechnology and the Mutations of Desire* (Continuum, 2004) and *Contagious Architecture. Computation, Aesthetics and Space* (MIT Press, 2013). She is currently researching the philosophical consequences of logical thinking in machines.

Julieanna Preston is Professor of Spatial Practice at Te Kunenga ki Pūrehuroa Massey University, Aotearoa, NZ. Recent works include 'murmur' [performance] (2017), Old Town Wall, Newcastle-Upon-Tyne, UK, and, with H. Frichot and K. Grillner, 'Feminist Practices Around the Kitchen Table', in *Feminist Futures of Spatial Practice: Materialisms, Activisms, Dialogues, Pedagogies, Projections* (Förlag År Tryckeri, 2017).

Lars Spuybroek is Professor of Architecture at the Georgia Institute of Technology in Atlanta. He is the author of *The Architecture of Continuity*, *Research and Design: Textile Tectonics* (2011) and *The Sympathy of Things: Ruskin and the Ecology of Design* (2016).

Maria Voyatzaki (Vogiatzaki) is Professor of Architecture at Anglia Ruskin University, UK and Professor of Architectural Design and Technology, School of Architecture, Aristotle University of Thessaloniki, Greece. She is chief editor of *e-archidoct Journal*. Recent publications include 'Building ++' (NGB Baltzer Science Publishers, 2014), 'Breaking the Mould', in *Future Concrete: A Material in the Making* (SKIRA, 2016), 'Technology in vivo', *Techne 13, Journal of Technology for Architecture and the Environment* (2017) and (co-authored with D. Gourdoukis) 'From Morphology to Morphogenesis: On Speculative Architectural Design Pedagogy', in *Analyzing Form and Morphogenesis in Modern Architectural Contexts* (IGI Global, 2017).

Fernando Zalamea is Professor of Mathematics at Universidad Nacional de Colombia. He is the author of twenty books, including *Synthetic Philosophy of Contemporary Mathematics* (2012) and *Peirce's Logic of Continuity* (2012). He was named in 2015 in the book *100 Global Minds; The Most Daring Cross-Disciplinary Thinkers in the World* (Dublin: Roads Publishing, 2015).

Index

CPSIA information can be obtained
at www.ICGtesting.com
Printed in the USA
JSHW020453280920
8208JS00001B/3

9 781474 474542